CANADIAN
HIGH DIVIDEND
INVESTING

CANADIAN HIGH DIVIDEND INVESTING

(215 Stocks Scored & Analyzed)

2023

IAN DUNCAN MACDONALD

Informus Inc
Toronto

Copyright © 2023 by Ian Duncan MacDonald

Paperback edition published 2023

Library and Archives Canada Cataloguing in Publication

MacDonald, Ian D., author

Canadian High Dividend Investing
Ian Duncan MacDonald

Issued in print and electronic formats

ISBN 9798858595885

1.Stocks. 2. Dividends.0 I. Title. Canadian High Dividend Investing

Published by
Informus Inc, Publishing Division,
2 Vista Humber Drive, Toronto, Ontario, Canada, M9P 3R7

www.informus.ca
tel. 929-800-2397
tel. 416-245-4994

Publisher: Informus Inc   **Cover Design**: Ian D. MacDonald

Dedicated to the thousands around the world
who have read my investment books
and
listened to my podcasts.

CONTENTS

(*Throughout this book you will come across phrases that are highlighted like (*"retirement study (1ch 1)" *They are duplicated in an alpha index at the end of the book. The* **"(1ch1)"** *indicates that this is the* **first index item** *appearing in* **Chapter 1**. *These are words and phrases repeated in the INDEX for your quick reference to select items throughout the book.)*

OTHER BOOKS BY IAN MACDONALD   page 316

CHAPTER 1
STRONG STOCKS

Recent studies have shown that 60% of the working population have become far less confident about their finances and being able to ever retire. They doubt they will be able to maintain their pre-retirement lifestyle. Women who live longer than men worry most about out living their savings. A recent retirement study (1ch 1) (available at https://cpplc.ca) explores retirement concerns and how they have grown. This book will remove many of these retirement fears.

Many years ago, in my early fifties, I too had great concerns about retirement. I had just lost $300,000 of my life savings by naively allowing an investment advisor to have his way with my money. I really had not understood nor paid attention to where he was investing my money. All I knew was that it was in mutual funds. My then limited understanding of mutual funds was that they were a "safer" investment because they spread your money among hundreds of stocks.

The financial advisor assured me that when I retired, I would liquidate 4% of my mutual funds each year and live comfortably on this income. By limiting it to 4%, I was assured that this income would last until I was ninety. Ninety seemed, at that time, to be a very long way off. It does not seem to be that far off now that I am retired.

It is easy for advisors to sell wonderful investment theories and solutions when they are investing someone else's money. Their own money is not at risk.

For many investment advisors, the temptation seems to be too to sell investments that maximize the advisors' income rather than the wealth of their naïve, trusting client's. After losing that $300,000, I recognized that the investment advisor's retirement plan seemed flawed, if by the time I retired all my savings were gone.

That loss motivated me to become a self-directed investor. I did not think that I could do any worse with my remaining life savings than this investment advisor had done, with his decades of experience.

In retrospect, there seems to be something almost ridiculous about entrusting your money to an "experienced professional" who is paid by a financial institution to transfer as much money as they can from your pocket to the institution's pocket. Although the financial industry advertises that the industry will work in the client's best interests, the investment industry predominately uses commission salespeople to convince investors to buy their financial products. These "financial advisors" are motivated by a system of rewards and incentives to push products that maximize commissions. The Small Investment Protection Association (SIPA reported that ninety-six percent of financial advisors in Canada are registered as commission salespeople.

My last twenty years of successful self-directed investing has confirmed that I was right in trusting in my own judgment and stock research. I will be sharing with you in this book what I have learned. You will be provided with the tools I used to easily build an ever-growing portfolio. It can provide you with a dependable, generous, ever-rising income for the rest of your life. This is done without withdrawing from your portfolio 4% of its value each year.

The primary secret to investment success is being very selective. I invest in twenty, (not five, not 100, but twenty) carefully chosen financially strong stocks with long histories of paying high dividends (Dividend stocks are the shares of companies who distribute a portion of their profits to shareholders in the form of regular payments either monthly or quarterly).

There are pluses and minuses to investing in dividend stocks. If your objective is safety and reliability, I have found the pluses of dividend stocks easily outweigh the minuses.

Advantages of Investing in Dividend Stocks (2ch1)

1. **Income Generation**: Dividend stocks can provide a steady income stream, especially for investors who rely on the regular cash flow from their investments to pay their living expenses. Dividends can be particularly attractive for retirees and those seeking a passive lifetime income.

2. **Potential for Total Return**: Dividend stocks can offer the potential for not only dividend income but capital appreciation from the rising share prices of financially strong companies. Prior to retirement, reinvesting your dividends can compound your returns and greatly maximize the growth in your portfolio.

3. **Stability and Defensive Qualities**: Dividend-paying companies are almost always well-established and financially stable. They usually operate in mature industries and have a long history of generating consistent profits. Your dividends are paid out of these profits. This stability can provide a level of income protection during market downturns because dividends are isolated from falling share prices.

4. **Dividend Growth Potential**: Many companies have a long track record of increasing their dividend payouts to keep their dividend yield percentages consistent with the rise in their share price. By investing in such companies, investors can benefit from a growing dividend income, which offsets the impact of inflation.

Disadvantages of Investing in Dividend Stocks (3ch1)

1. **Limited Growth Potential**: Companies that distribute a significant portion of their earnings as dividends could be seen as limiting the money, they have available for reinvestment in corporate growth opportunities. Consequently, their share price growth could be slower than some non-dividend-paying companies. This is primarily of concern to speculators whose objective is not income but being able to buy a stock at a low price and sell it as soon as the share price has grown significantly. Unfortunately, accurately determining when a stock price is at its lowest price and when it is at its highest price is not possible. Not being able to get the timing right, speculators almost always lose money over time.

2. **Interest Rate Sensitivity**: Dividend stocks can be sensitive to changes in interest rates. When interest rates are high, dividend yields can become less attractive relative to fixed-income investments like bonds. This can lead to a decrease in the stock price even though stock's high dividend payments would remain consistent as it is tied into a company's profits, not its share price. Fixed income interest rates are tied to constantly changing volatile economic conditions. If you intend to hold a profitable, high dividend paying stock for the rest of life, speculating on whether to commit or not commit to fixed income rates becomes almost irrelevant.

3. **Market Volatility**: Although dividend stocks are generally considered less volatile than non-dividend-paying stocks, they can still experience price fluctuations and be subject to market risks. Stock price volatility is primarily of interest to speculators. Those investing for dividend income would not be impacted by share price volatility. Looking at share prices after each market crash over the last twenty-four years, shows how long it would normally take for a dividend stock price to recover and reach new share price records highs. Share price volatility is just of passing interest when you are living off your dividend income. (24 years of share prices for the 215 stocks are detailed in this book.)

There are other important considerations, for example, the number of stocks in your portfolio. The old saying, "Don't put all your eggs in one basket", can be applied to investing in stocks. My recommendation is that your portfolio consist of 20 financially strong, high dividend stocks (4ch1)

To invest in more than twenty makes keeping track of all 20 a chore. Each quarter you may want to analyze the stocks in your portfolio. While this may take a few hours with 20 stocks, you do not want to spend days trying to do it with 100 stocks. If monitoring gets tedious and boring, you will start making excuses for neglecting regular oversights.

The other reality is that there are only a limited number of financially strong high dividend paying stocks available. Every stock you add to your portfolio is always a compromise between safety and income(5ch1) You do not want to dilute the strength of your portfolio by watering down its strength.

Monitoring your portfolio becomes especially important during a recession when share prices will decline. During the 2020 recession (6ch1), I neither bought nor sold any stocks. When I scored all my portfolio's stocks, I could see that the scores had barely changed despite a significant drop in share prices. They all remained financially strong companies.

The drop in the share price did impact on the dividend yield percent. A lower share price increased the dividend yield percent even though the dividend dollar payout remained the same. Calculated as a percentage of the share price, the dividend yield percent had to mathematically rise.

A recession is a good time to buy more shares of financially strong companies with good scores – if you have the cash to do so. Recessions usually last about one year and occur about every four years. When they do descend on you, it is important to remind yourself that this is a natural occurrence, and that the world is not coming to an end.

Market crashes are part of investing. I was asked if I had a cash reserve during the 2020 recession. Yes, I always have a significant emergency cash reserve. It grew during the recession because there was so little to spend money on. As prices regained that reserve cash was allowed to shrink.

While I may only do a detailed rescoring of my stocks a few times a year, I do a daily check of the total value of my portfolio at the end of the previous day and how much new cash (if any) is now appearing in my trading account. Usually, this cash would be regular dividend payments paid on either the first or the fifteenth of each month. However, sometimes cash unexpectedly appears. It could be a payout from a company being bought out where shareholders are receiving their portion of the sale. I then check further to see why this cash is appearing. I am rarely surprised because during the day I read and listen to financial news and am aware of what is reported happening in the stock market.

Investing in fewer than 20 dividend stocks does reduce the safety of your portfolio. If one of the 20 stocks should lose 100% its value, you would only lose 5% of what you had invested equally in each of the 20 stocks. The chances of a strong stock ever losing all its value is almost impossible, but if it did happen your normal dividend income from your total portfolio, would be greater than 5%, and would easily offset the 5% loss of that one stock. For added security, the annual share price growth of all 20 stocks, most years, can be12% or more. This gain in the value of total portfolio makes the loss of a stock almost inconsequential.

Since you are not buying stocks to sell them the first time, they increase 10% or drop 10%, years can go by without you having to make a change to your safe portfolio. It almost manages itself. You are removed from the emotional roller coaster ride that speculators experience as they live through the gyrations of share prices fluctuating up and down. Fortunately, speculators have no control over the profits from which dividends are paid. It is the skilled, experienced executives who make the revenue and expense decisions that create the company's profits from which you receive your dividends.

When you buy financially strong, high dividend stocks, you are buying income. My portfolio's value and its payouts have grown steadily despite my taking a 6-digit dividend income out of it each year. That dividend income flowed in steadily through the 2000, 2008 and 2020 market crashes. You can see the impact of those market crashes in the following 24-year history of the Bank of Montreal dividend payouts. The market crash years of 2020, 2008 and 2000 (7ch1) have been highlighted. (I have owned shares in the Bank of Montreal for a very long time).

Compare the following page for the **Bank of Montreal** (8ch1) with the adjacent page for **Real Estate Split Corporation**. Although you do not yet understand the stock scoring system that is used throughout this book, you can easily grasp why the Bank of Montreal was the highest scoring stock on the Toronto Stock Exchange and why Real Estate Split Corporation was the lowest scoring high dividend stock. Pages, like these two, are provided for all 215 stocks paying a dividend yield of 3.5% or more listed on the Toronto Stock Exchange.

In picking stocks, it is all a matter of comparing one stock's data with another and then choosing the "best" one. Ask yourself the following five questions as you look at these following two pages. You do not have to be an accountant or a stock market guru to recognize which of these two stocks is stronger and safer.

(1) What do these two stocks have in common?

(2) Which is paying the higher dividend?

(3) Which is the financially strongest?

(4) Which would be most reliable?

(5) Which one is more desirable than the other?

BANK OF MONTREAL

(BMO)

Updated April 2023

IDM STOCK SCORING CALCULATION

(1) Stock Price $ 123.94   Score 10   *(7)* Analysts Strong Buys #0   Score 0

(2) Price 4 Years Ago $ 98.92   Score 9   *(8)* Dividend Yield % 4.62   Score 8

(3) Current to Four Year Price   Score 9   *(9)* Operating Margin % 45.08   Score 6

(4) Book Value $ 104.94   Score 10   *(10)* Trading Volume 1,515,668 Score 9

(5) Price to Book Comparison   Score 1   *(11)* Price to Earnings 7.8x   Score 9

(6) Analyst Buys # 7   Score 5

Total of All 11 Scores = 76

This stock's total score in 2021 was **74**, in 2020 it was **66** , in 2019 it was **74** .

HISTORICAL STOCK PRICES & DIVIDEND PAYOUTS

Year	Stock	Dividend	Year	Stock	Dividend
2022	$ 136.21	$ 1.33	2010	$ 63.09	$ 0.70
2021	$ 107.46	$ 1.06	2009	$ 49.02	$ 0.70
2020	$ 70.77	$ 1.06	2008	$ 48.77	$ 0.70
2019	$ 105.82	$ 1.00	2007	$ 69.46	$ 0.68
2018	$ 97.51	$ 0.93	2006	$ 69.67	$ 0.53
2017	$ 90.67	$ 0.88	2005	$ 56.65	$ 0.46
2016	$ 82.30	$ 0.84	2004	$ 51.90	$ 0.40
2015	$ 78.82	$ 0.80	2003	$ 40.10	$ 0.33
2014	$ 76.28	$ 0.76	2002	$ 38.62	$ 0.30
2013	$ 61.37	$ 0.74	2001	$ 35.20	$ 0.28
2012	$ 58.67	$ 0.70	2000	$ 30.25	$ 0.25
2011	$ 62.14	$ 0.70	1999	$ 30.40	$ 0.23

NOTES: BMO provides a range of personal and commercial banking, wealth management, global markets and investment banking products and services.

REAL ESTATE SPLIT CORPORATION

(RS)

Updated July 2023

IDM STOCK SCORING CALCULATION

(1) Stock Price $ 13.90   Score 5

(2) Price 4 Years Ago $ 0   Score 1

(3) Current to Four Year Price Score 0

(4) Book Value $ 0   Score 0

(5) Price to Book Comparison Score 0

(6) Analyst Buys # 0   Score 0

(7) Analysts Strong Buys # 0 Score 0

(8) Dividend Yield % 11.22   Score 2

(9) Operating Margin % 0   Score 0

(10) Trading Volume 15,633   Score 1

(11) Price to Earnings 0.0x   Score 0

Total of All 11 Scores = 10

This stock's total score in 2021 was **16**, in 2020 it was **NA**, in 2019 it was **NA**.

HISTORICAL STOCK PRICES & DIVIDEND PAYOUTS

Year	Stock	Dividend	Year	Stock	Dividend
2022	$ 17.04	$ 0.13	2010	$ NA	$ NA
2021	$ 17.85	$ 0.10	2009	$ NA	$ NA
2020	$ 14.50	$ 0.10	2008	$ NA	$ NA
2019	$ NA	$ NA	2007	$ NA	$ NA
2018	$ NA	$ NA	2006	$ NA	$ NA
2017	$ NA	$ NA	2005	$ NA	$ NA
2016	$ NA	$ NA	2004	$ NA	$ NA
2015	$ NA	$ NA	2003	$ NA	$ NA
2014	$ NA	$ NA	2002	$ NA	$ NA
2013	$ NA	$ NA	2001	$ NA	$ NA
2012	$ NA	$ NA	2000	$ NA	$ NA
2011	$ NA	$ NA	1999	$ NA	$ NA

NOTES: **RS** is a Canadian based mutual fund company managed by Middlefield Limited.

(1) What do these two stocks have in common?

Both stocks are Canadian stocks paying high dividends traded on the Toronto Stock Exchange. Their current stock prices are lower than they were in 2022.

(2) Which is paying the higher dividend?

Real Estate Split's dividend yield percent of 11.23%. This is almost three times greater than the dividend yield percent of 4.62% the Bank of Montreal is paying.

(3) Which one is financially strongest and most reliable?

Real Estate Split has a Book Value of zero, an Operating Margin of zero and has no Price-to-Earnings ratio. It is reported to be a mutual fund. Mutual funds are marketed by the fund companies to make money for the fund company. They sell the sizzle not the steak. The sizzle, in this case, is an 11.23% dividend which would attract some investor.

With the information provided we have no idea what this mutual fund is invested in. Even if we did know what it was invested in, the fund managers can change the investments at any time. To buy a mutual fund is to put your blind faith in a fund manager.

The situation with the Bank of Montreal is quite different. it has an Operating Margin 45.08%, a Book Value of $104.94 and Price-to-Earnings ratio of 7.8x.

The higher an operating margin, the stronger, more profitable the company. The closer the Book Value to the current share price, or exceeding the share price, the financially stronger the company. The lower the Price-to-Earnings ratio the financially stronger the company.

While Real Estate Split has been listed on the stock exchange for only three years. The historical record on the Bank of Montreal page going back to 1999. However, its history goes back two centuries. The Bank of Montreal was Canada's first chartered bank in 1821.

Looking at the trend information on this page you can see in 1999 that the Bank's dividend payout was $0.23, and the share price was $30.40. These figures rose steadily year -after -year. The dividend payout by 2022 was $1.33and the share price was $136.21.

Supposedly greed and fear are what motivates most investors. They want to make as much money as quickly possible while avoiding as much loss as possible. If you had $100,000 to invest in only one of these two stocks which one, would you invest in?

If you are a speculator by nature, you might choose Real Estate Split. All you would see is that over the next year you might receive is the $11, 220 in dividend income on that $100,000. The $4,620 realized from the $100,000 invested in the Bank of Montreal would hold little attraction for you.

It is important to remember that unlike fixed income investments, like bonds, the periodic payments of dividends by companies are the result of decisions made by a company based on the company's circumstances at a set time.

This book was not written for speculators even though speculators represent most investors(9ch1). Speculators choose stocks to invest in whose share price they believe is currently underpriced. They are convinced every share they buy is going to increase to a magnificent amount, at which point they will sell their shares and reap a huge profit on the trade.

Unfortunately, predicting the best time to sell a stock is easier said than done. Often at the first sign of a share price decline, nervous speculators believe they must sell their shares to realize either a small gain or a small loss. Speculators are notorious for buying a stock at its highest price and selling at its lowest price. I am told 97% of speculators lose on their stock investments.

If you are a risk adverse investor, not a speculator, you would understand that dividends are paid out of profits. For the three years that Real Estate Split has been listed on the stock market, you can see no indication that it has ever realized a profit. You really have no understanding of where the dividend money is coming from or whether they will ever again pay a dividend. Unlike bond interest payments there is no requirement for the board of directors of a company to decide to pay a dividend. Until you have more information to justify investing in such a stock you should search for a safer place to invest your money.

Some speculators might choose to make a compromise with their $100,000. They might choose to invest $50,000 in the Bank of Montreal and $50,000. Real Estate Split. While they might not realize an 11.23% dividend income, they could realize a dividend income of 7.93% when the two dividend payouts were averaged.

Fortunately, you are not forced to invest in either of these two stocks. The reason the Bank of Montreal has a high score, and Real Estate Split has a low score is due to the amount of information available on each of these stocks. In this book, you have the records of 215 high dividend stocks to choose from. Is it possible that there are stocks within the 215 that pay a higher dividend than Real Estate Split's 11.23% and have much better scores?

There are several stronger stocks paying more than 11.23% dividends. To easily find them go to Chapter 7. It provides a one-line summary of all 215 stocks sorted by dividend yield percent. (Three other chapters provide for quick reference similar summaries, sorting the 215 stocks alphabetically, by score and by share price).

Here are just 10 stocks extracted from Chapter 7 whose dividend percent yield exceeds the 11.23% of Real Estate Split. As you can see, avoiding stocks that you are not confident in is not difficult.

Score	Stock	Symbol	Price	Dividend %	Operating Margin
51	Northwest Healthcare Properties REIT	NWH.UN	$6.28	12.74%	26.22%
23	Fiera Capital Corporation	FSZ	$6.83	12.59%	10.28%
38	Gear Energy Ltd	GXE	$0.97	12.37%	39.96%
28	Inovalis Real Estate Investment Trust	INO.UN	$3.34	12.35%	-136.97%
23	Sustainable Power & Infrastructure Split Corp	PWI	$6.50	12.31%	0%
18	Global Dividend Growth Split Corporation	GDV	$9.91	12.11%	0%
58	Peyto Exploration & Development Corporation	PEY	$10.96	12.04%	61.37%
37	True North Commercial Real Estate invest Trust	TNT.UN	$2.52	11.79%	6.11%
17	Dividend Select 15 Corporation	DS	$6.81	11.56%	0%

When I set out to become a successful investor, I thought that investing in the shares of companies looked like it was just another form of commercial risk. I had spent decades as a senior executive building commercial risk systems for Dun Bradstreet, Creditel and Equifax.

Before I was an executive at Dun & Bradstreet, I was initially trained by them as a commercial credit reporter. As such, I interviewed thousands of business owners and applied D&B risk ratings to their businesses. Later as a senior executive with the two other commercial risk data companies, Creditel and Equifax, I was responsible for designing powerful commercial risk scoring systems which had to be able to score and sort millions of businesses from highest to lowest risk within seconds. Banks, insurance companies, wholesalers, and manufacturers depended on my scoring systems to make crucial risk decisions involving millions of dollars.

When faced with the $300,000 loss in my portfolio it dawned on me that stocks were companies. I should be able to score the stocks of these companies the same as any commercial risk.

I immediately set out to build stock scoring software to guide me in my selection of the best, high dividend stocks. (*It is the same* **stock scoring software**(10ch1) *used throughout this book, and is* **emailed, when requested**, *to those who purchase my books. To receive it all you need do is send a request to* imacd@informus.ca *telling me which book you purchased and where you are located*).

In building the scoring matrix, I quickly saw that the stock market is an auction vehicle(11ch1) not a supermarket with stocks ready to be picked off the shelf at a set price. Speculators sell stocks that they expect are going to decline in value. However, to sell a stock they must find a speculator who thinks the stock is going to increase in value to buy it. One of them is going to be wrong about the immediate direction of that share's price.

When millions of shares are being exchanged, it means millions of speculators are placing bets on which direction the stock price is heading. These millions of decisions are all just guesses, no one knows what impact their bid will have upon the share price or whether their bid will just cancel out the bids of other investors who are guessing that the share is moving in the opposite direction.

Sometimes, speculators get "lucky". Their shares rose as they hoped. Some who win big are convinced that they are stock picking geniuses. This encourages them to speculate again and again until all their money is lost. Others come to their senses and realize that no one can accurately predict future share prices. The vast majority who lose will shrug and say that the "market" was against them. This implies that there is some super power that makes decisions as to who is going to win or lose. The reality is there is no "superpower". There is just this auction vehicle that allows buyers and sellers to bid against each other to acquire a stock.

Why do speculators keep on speculating if they keep on losing? Most get a thrill from buying a stock that they are sure will make them rich. While their certainty of the stock's potential is often based only on rumor and media hype, this does not matter to them.

It is the same thrill of anticipated riches (12ch1) that motivates the masses to buy lottery tickets. A six-dollar lottery ticket provides them with the possibility that on Saturday night that they could be $70,000,000 richer. When Saturday comes and goes and the lottery ticket buyers are no richer, they shrug it off. All they have lost is the six dollars they paid for the lottery ticket. Hooked on the anticipated thrill, they are ready to risk another six dollars on the next lottery draw.

Investing in stocks involves much more than six dollars. Thousands of dollars, even millions, can be in play. The amazing thing is that speculators seem unable to accept that the stock market is not a lottery. With just a little effort and thought it becomes hard not to make money on the stock market. If you have bought this book, thinking it was going to help you get rich overnight, like winning the lottery, you will be disappointed.

What you will learn is that a disciplined, wise investor who carefully selects stocks can double a portfolio's value within five years in the following ways:

(1) Using the stock scoring method in this book, you will be able to identify the 20 best, safest, financially strong dividend paying stocks for your portfolio. Your objective is to buy those stocks with the intention of never selling them, no matter how high or low their share prices become.

(2) To grow your portfolio quickly, you will initially reinvest your dividend (13ch1) income until you "retire ". This re-investment of dividends creates a compounding effect as you add more stocks to your portfolio whose share prices keep increasing and paying ever rising dividends.

(3) The share prices of financially strong companies grow steadily. They increase their dividend payouts to keep them close to or higher than their competitors' share prices. Thus, while a stock may now be paying a monthly dividend of $1.00 a share, if you go back 20 years (this can be easily viewed in historical price and dividend data in this book) you may see that in 2001 the stock was paying $0.10 a share. Every year since

then the dividend payouts may have increased in unison with the company's increasing share price as the company grew and prospered.

In retirement, when you begin to live off the dividends, instead of re-investing them, your portfolio may be sufficiently large that the dividend payments remove the need to ever sell stocks to cover your living expenses. That portfolio will keep growing as share prices increase. Retirement is achieving financial independence (14ch1). Since you would no longer need to work (unless you choose to) you can retire at any time as soon as your dividend income comfortably exceeds your living expenses.

Why do companies increase their dividend payouts? Some companies want to reward shareholders for not selling their stock. Others want to keep their dividend payouts a percent higher than their competitors' dividend payouts to keep their share prices higher. More importantly, the managers of most companies own shares in their company. They will do what they can to ensure that both the share price and dividends go up. They want to grow their own wealth.

One big incentive is that Canadians in most provinces are exempt from paying income tax on the first $55,00 of dividend income (15ch1) from stocks traded on Canadian stock exchanges. With income splitting, allowed by Revenue Canada, a couple can realize a $110,000 in such exemptions (there are some exceptions, such as Real Estate Investment Trusts. Their "dividends" are classified as distributions, not dividends. However, some of the money distributed by REIT's can be tax free if it is classified as a return of the original capital that had been invested). This $55,000 break on personal income tax is to prevent double taxation. Income tax was paid on the company's profits by the corporation before they distributed it via dividends to their shareholders.

If your investment income is significant, it can be wise to have a certified accountant do your income tax return to make sure you are not paying more tax than necessary. Although my income is equivalent to the salary I earned as an executive, the amount of income tax I pay on it is less than half of what I used to pay. This has implications for how large your portfolio should be.

How much money should you have in your portfolio? Only you can answer that question. While a million-dollar portfolio may seem like a great deal of money. You soon recognize that a million dollars translates into a reliable annual dividend income of between $60,000 and $100,000.

Can you live on $60,000 a year? That would depend upon not only on your ability to generate income but also on your ability to manage expenses (Chapter 10 gives pointers on managing expenses). If you need more than $60,000 to live comfortably then it is important that you start to build a large dividend portfolio as early in life as possible. By reinvesting your dividend income, that you do not need now to live on, you can quickly grow your portfolio. The compounding effect of re-investing dividend income is a powerful investment tool. It can double the value of your portfolio within 5 years.

In Chapter 2, I walk you through the essential research tools that are easily accessible. I do not recommend using the self-directed investment research services of one financial institution over another (I certainly have not seen all that are available). I happen to use the *"Easy Web On-Line Banking"* service of the TD Bank, only because they have provided me with banking services since I was a teenager. There are non-financial institutions that also provide useful stock research data e.g., Yahoo Finance, Google, Globe & Mail, and many more. I found it is important to stick to one source of stock assessment data to ensure that your stock scores are consistent. While you would think the same data on a stock would be the same from all sources, it isn't.

If you have never owned or used a personal computer (16ch1) it is going to be almost impossible for you to function as a self-directed investor. The only option you would have to acquire stocks would probably be to become a "full-service client" of a financial institution. If that is your only option, then this book will have at least prepared you in how to instruct an investment advisor as to what stocks you want in your portfolio. (Thus, your first investment challenge may be in becoming comfortable using a computer and the internet. It is not difficult).

The first step, in your investment journey, is to open a self-directed stock trading account (17ch1) with an institution online. If you now have money on deposit in a chequing account with a bank, then you are already an "established customer". It can take only a few minutes to open a self-directed investment account online. You will be transferring money from your chequing account to your stock trading account to pay for your anticipated stock purchases. Later you will either be transferring dividend payments back to your chequing account to pay your living expenses or reinvesting that dividend income in new share purchases.

It is wise to avoid physically going into the financial institution's place of business to open your self-directed trading account. If you do go in, expect them to try to pressure you into becoming a full-service client (18ch1). Paying an institution for full-service will hinder your objective of achieving financial independence.

Why do financial institutions try so hard to convert self-directed investors to full-service investors? Because their employees' mandate is to separate you from as much of your wealth as they can with their fees and commissions. An investment advisor will be taking about 2% to 4% of your portfolio's value every year for his "services" for the rest of your life. On a million-dollar portfolio that could be $20,000 a year. In ten years, they would have realized $200,000 of your money. This is money that could have been invested making money for you not them. They take this money whether your portfolio grows or shrinks.

Once your trading account is established you can buy and sell thousands of shares of a stock (no matter its value) for a one-time transaction fee of zero or less than $10. The charge depends on the institution. If you hold that stock for the next 50 years, the most the institution would receive from the purchase would be that initial $10. Thus, choosing an institution only because they charge no transaction fee may not be a wise decision if the research services and other services they offer are limited.

There are some financial institutions who charge nothing for their service of you ordering stocks through their computer system. How do they make money for providing a free service? They can make money by lending out your idle cash - basically making money off the uninvested funds in your account. Setting up margin accounts is another money maker, where for a fee, they will lend the financial institution's money to you to trade with. Another source is the kickbacks from large volume traders who are allowed to use your share orders to their advantage in making trades.

I expect these money-making strategies are also being followed at those institutions who charge a fee for handling each trade. That does not bother me because the reason I choose to pay my $9.00 fee to TD Bank for each trade is that I get great benefit out of having daily access to their research data. I doubt if they feel cheated by my lack of trades in any year.

When you are dealing with a financial advisor never forget that you are viewed by them as a source of revenue to be maximized. In my first investment book, *"Income and Wealth from Self-Directed Investing"*, I described how the 80-year-old Miss Innocence chose to receive an annual income of $35,000 from her million-dollar portfolio. The bank that was providing her with full-service-investing was (much to her surprise when it was shown to her) taking $25,000 in charges from her portfolio every year. Which was 2.5% of her portfolio, not the 1% she thought they were supposed to be taking. The "safe investments" her advisor put in her portfolio, lost $300,000 in 4 years.

After I reviewed her monthly statements with her, it came as a surprise to Miss Innocence that the $35,000 annual income she was receiving was coming from the selling pieces of her portfolio every month. It was not from the monthly dividends or interest she thought the portfolio was earning. The bank had assured her that her million-dollar portfolio would last her lifetime. At the rate it was losing money it would have lasted only a few more years.

Financial institutions promote full-service investing as removing all the stresses from your life, saving you the time of managing your investments, and most importantly acting like a "speed bump" to stop you from making impulsive foolish investment decisions. They avoid detailing their charges and what time they will be spending with you. They want you to put blind faith in the choices they will make with your money. They do not want you to ask too many questions or put demands on their time.

Even when your self-directed trading account is established, investment advisers will try to switch you to full-service investing. Few investment advisors, if any, have spent any time closely studying dividend stocks. They want to sell you vague mutual funds, index funds and ETFS. These are packages that only require a general knowledge of stocks and require no research effort on their part. Not wanting to deplete your life saving by investing in a fund that must be slowly liquidated is something that investment advisers do not want to hear.

Your purpose in life is not to provide an investment adviser with a steady income for decades as they nibble away on your portfolio.

CHAPTER 2

FINDING YOUR TWENTY STOCKS (1ch2)

Where do you find the 20 financially strongest, high dividend paying stocks that you would want in your portfolio?

First step, using your password, go to your self-directed investor account. (Your institution's investment system will probably be like that of the TD Bank that I am using. (As per the example following).

The **"Home"** screen will display the total amount of cash you have transferred for investing from your chequing account to your trading account. As you add stocks to your portfolio it will start recording the value of the stocks you have purchased and added to your portfolio.

To begin the search for a stock to add to your portfolio, you select **"RESEARCH"** from the menu (3ch2) on that home screen. This selection will take you to the research screen. Note this RESEARCH screen provides 24 options. The only options needed to find investible stocks are the **"Overview"**(4ch2) and **"Screeners"**(5ch2) option.

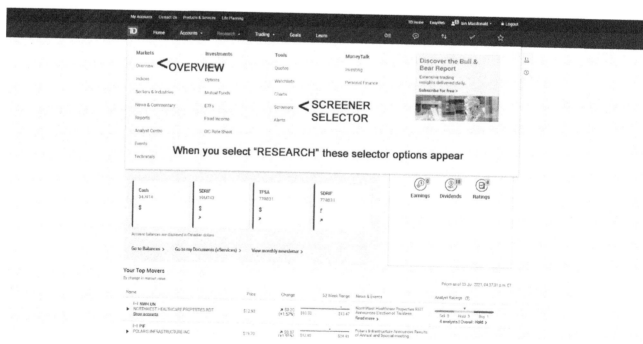

You start your search for stocks you wish to buy with the **"SCREENERS"** option.

There are **16,001** North American stocks available for purchase. Thanks to the tax breaks available to Canadians who invest in dividend stocks traded on Canadian stock exchanges, the first selector we are going to use is the **"EXCHANGE"** selector (6ch2) for "Canadian Stocks". This selector immediately separates the Canadian stocks from the US stocks. The Screener software brings the stock possibilities down to **3,688** Canadian stocks. This is too many to work with. We need another selector.

Since this book is only concerned about stocks paying a dividend of 3.5% dividend you can use the **"DIVIDEND YIELD"** selector.(7ch2). It first identifies that there are **785** companies in Canada paying dividends. We do not want all dividend payers. We just want the highest dividend payers. This raises the question of what is the minimum dividend yield percent you would need to give you enough income to live on? Although the inflation rate for the last decade has been running around 1.8%, the average over the last century would be 3.5%. To be safe, the minimum dividend income percent can be set at 3.5%.

Dividend percentages of stocks are not set in stone. They fluctuate. For example, in September of 2020 several of the Canadian banks were displaying dividend percentages between 6% and 7%. In 2019 the dividend percentage for these same companies had been between 3% to 5%.

What accounts for such a fluctuation?

The 2020 market crash caused some share prices to drop significantly. For example, the Canadian Imperial Bank of Commerce (8ch2) went from **$113.00** a share in May of **2019** to **$91.12** a share in May of **2020**. In 2019 its dividend percent was **5.00%** but in 2020 with share prices now lower, its dividend percent rose to **6.41%.** This had nothing to do with their profitability or operating margin. Dividend payments are not directly related to a share's price. What happened to CIBC bank shares during and after the market crash in 2020 is an illustration of factors that can impact share prices.

The CIBC made a dividend payment of $1.40 per share in June of 2019 and in June of 2020, just three months after the market crash, they paid a slightly higher dividend of $1.46 in June of 2020. At this point their quarterly dividend payments were frozen at the $1.46 by the federal government. The Government was concerned that the Covid 19 Pandemic would lead to record loan defaults and bankruptcies that could seriously weaken the financial strength of Canadian banks. The government did not want to have the responsibility of having to bail the banks out of serious financial difficulty.

After the 2020 market crash, in June of 2021, the share price of the CIBC had soared to $141.47, greatly exceeding the 2019 price. This higher price caused the dividend percent to mathematically shrink to 4.13%. The CIBC and all the other banks continued to pay the same dividends and were financially stronger than they had ever been. They were sitting on mountains of cash waiting for the government to allow them to increase dividend payments.

25

This anticipated increased payout made their stocks attractive to investors. They had bid up its price.

When selecting stocks by dividend percent you must also consider the financial strength of the company and its potential for capital gain (9ch2). As share prices increase in financially strong companies so usually does the amount of money you will receive in dividends. Temporary fluctuations in price and dividend percentages should be carefully investigated.

A financially strong Real Estate Investment Trust (REIT) (10ch2) paying a dividend of 8% is attractive. You may want it in your portfolio for the reliable income it will deliver to your portfolio. However, by looking at dividend payouts and share prices over the last twenty years, you may see a minimal change in share price and dividend payout. You might choose to search for stocks with greater potential for frequent increases in dividend payout and share price increases.

To illustrate this, in twenty years, the share price of the Canadian Imperial Bank of Commerce grew from $47.83 to $141.47 (an increase of 295%). During this same period, their quarterly dividend payments went from $0.37 to $1.46 (an even greater increase of 394%).

If a **3.5% dividend yield** (11ch2) were used as a selector to reduce the number of stocks you needed to consider for your portfolio, it would drop the number for consideration from 785 down to **514**. This is too many to work with. I know this 514 contains many preferred shares. Preferred shares have almost zero potential for a share price increase, so we need a selector to eliminate them. To bring the possibilities down you could use the criteria of **OPERATING MARGIN** (12ch2) which would eliminate any preferred shares.

The following is an illustration of four selectors I often use to bring any number of shares down to a workable number.

Four summary sorts of the 215 stocks selected for this book appear in this book (the sorts are alphabetical, by score, by price and by dividend yield percent). Five key facts for each stock are included on one line for each of the stocks (e.g. score, company name, stock symbol, share price, dividend yield percent and operating margin percent). These four summaries allow you to easily identify which stocks you want to look at more closely in your quest to narrow your choice down to the 20 best stock from the 215 for your portfolio.

You are creating your own unique portfolio. The 215 listed stocks contain penny stocks that can be purchased for under one dollar and other stocks that cost over $100. While every stock is paying a dividend of 3.5% or more some are financially weaker than others. They are all included in the 214 stocks because it is important that you be able to recognize the differences between strong and weak stocks. You are the one who must understand why you chose the 20 stocks for your portfolio. When you understand your chosen stocks and their history you will be disinclined to make impulsive selling and buying decisions. In the next chapter you learn where all the information in the scoring matrix comes from. Investing is a lifetime activity. You will encounter opportunities to buy stocks that are not included in this book, perhaps a foreign stock or one that you have heard or read about. To compare them to the stocks in this book you need to understand the IDM scoring system.

CHAPTER 3

SCORE DATA SOURCES (1ch3)

This chapter shows where each of the eleven information elements for calculating a stock's IDM total score originates. In the previous chapter you learned the importance of the "SCREENER" programs to narrow down to a few stocks those you might consider scoring in your quest for the best 20 stocks for your portfolio. Now you will explore the "**OVERVIEW**" screen to learn where the data to be entered into the IDM stock scoring software comes from.

In the next chapter you will see how the data is used in calculating a stock's score. While software can instantly calculate a score, you will see that it is possible to manually calculate the score. It takes more time but I learned a long time ago that if you want people to have faith in a score, they must understand exactly how it is created.

Following is a typical stock overview screen. In this example, I have used **Enbridge Inc.** (2ch3) This is a picture of the top half of Enbridge's Overview screen. The first item, the name, confirms that you have received the stock you requested. You would have entered the stock's name or its stock symbol in the small box in the top right corner, identified as "**Enter Name or Symbol**".

Do not be intimidated by all the information displayed on this screen. There are only three items that you need from this top half of the overview screen. They are "**Stock Price**", "**Analyst Buys**" and "**Volume**".

When you click on "**Analysts**" it will take you to a new screen where stock analyst recommendations are displayed. They could be recommending "sell" the stock," hold" it, "buy" it. This will be accompanied by the analyst's projection for the share price. Do not be concerned if the stock you are reviewing has no recommendations. Most stocks are of little interest to analysts and will not have analyst stock recommendations.

You will also click on "**Charts**" to bring you to the screen where historical share prices and dividend payouts are displayed on a graph.

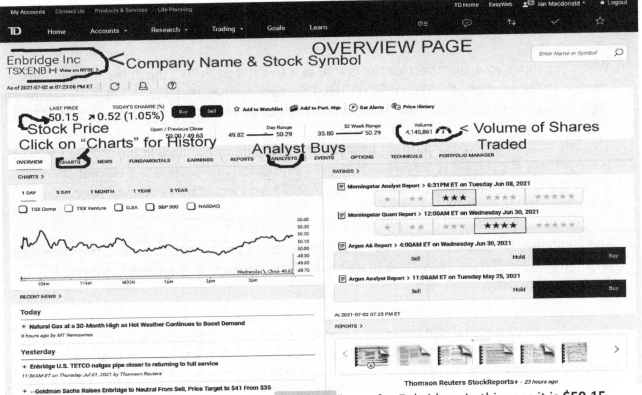

The most important item you need is the **"Last Price"** (3ch3) for Enbridge. In this case it is **$50.15**. It will be entered into the stock scoring software.

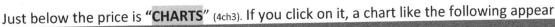

Just below the price is **"CHARTS"** (4ch3). If you click on it, a chart like the following appear

Run your cursor across the historical graph. A **"D"** inside a circle on the chart indicates that a dividend was paid on a certain date. If you place your cursor on the D, the **date** the dividend

(5ch3) was paid, the price that stock **opened** (6ch3) at on that day, its highest price, lowest price and **closing** price will appear.

When you move your cursor across the graph, as it touches each "D", the dates and amounts change. In the example, the Date is 6/3/2019. The stock opened that day at $49.86. It reached a high share price of $50.05. It reached a low share price of $47.13 and a closing price of $47.14.

This information becomes important because one of the items required in the scoring software is the **_price of the stock 4 years ago_** (7ch3) It gives a historical perspective to a current share price. If you were compiling the score on July 7, 2023, you would move your cursor on the graph back to July 7, 2019.

The graph may not display the exact day four years ago. If you cannot go back to the same day and month, then choose a day close to that date. That will be close enough to give you a historical perspective.

Where this chart is useful is in confirming that this company has been steadily increasing its dividend and share prices every year for 20 years or more. While it is unusual to see a continuous string of dividend payment increases when you do see it, it is sign that you can expect the dividend payments and share price to increase steadily in the future.

In building a commercial risk database of 2,200,000 businesses I learned that financially strong companies who have found the formula for a strong, profitable operation, do not lose their success formula (8ch3) overnight. Large business that fail - fail slowly, like a tire with a slow leak, not like a tire blow out.

In the example of this Enbridge graph, you can see the following dividend and share price increases.

Month	Day	Year	Dividend Paid $	Stock Price $
May	13	2021	$0.83	$49.86
May	12	2016	$0.53	$52.09
May	11	2011	$0.24	$31.36
May	16	2001	$0.09	$10.30

You will often see dividend payouts increasing through recessions and market crashes. A stock like Enbridge can not only continually increase your wealth but is also expected to increase your income, keeping it well ahead of inflation. Over the 20 years in the graph, the value of the

Enbridge shares are about 5 times greater than they were in 2001 and the dividend payouts are more than 9 times greater. Such growth continuity is rare, but it does exist as you will see when you review the data for all stocks later in the book.

Also, from the top half of the Overview page you need to click on the "ANALYSTS" (9ch3) selector. It brings up a chart like the one that follows. Most stocks are not being followed by analysts so often no recommendations will appear. However, when a "BUY" (10ch3) or a "STRONG BUY" (11ch3) recommendation appears it can be an indicator that the share price will increase. Why? because the number of buy recommendations do influence some investors. Thus, the buy recommendations are important enough of a consideration to be included as an element in the stock scoring software.

How "Buy" and "Strong Buy" recommendations are reported can vary from one data supplier to another. For consistent comparison purposes it is recommended that you settle on one data provider for the information you load into the scoring software.

I had to create a definition of a "strong buy" after TD direct investing changed how it reported strong buys. Thus, if an analyst recommends a buy and gives a projected share price 50% higher than the current share price, this became my definition of a "strong buy". You will rarely see recommendations high enough to be "strong buys", but they need to be noted when you do see them. Some analyst is risking his reputation by giving such a high recommendation. Previously, you were never giving reasons as to how and why an analyst decided a stock was a "strong buy". You were expected to blindly accept them. Now there is some logic behind a "strong buy" recommendation.

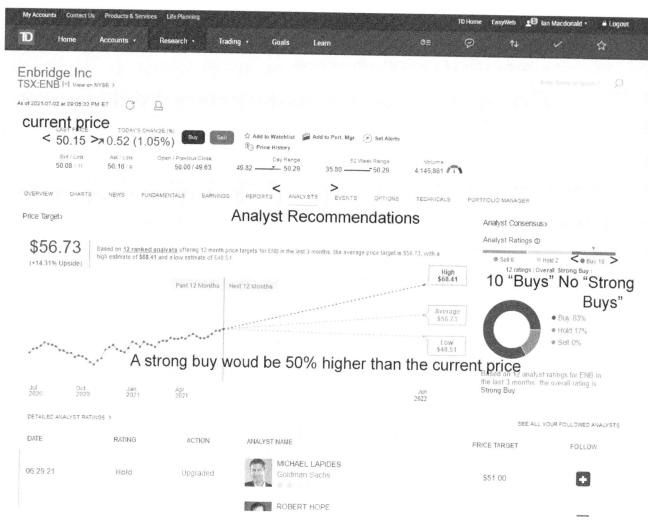

In addition to Buy recommendations, you can also see "hold" and "sell" recommendations. It is rare to see a sell recommendation especially for a high dividend paying stock. Thus," sells" and "holds" were ignored in the stock scoring because the software was designed to identify stocks you wanted to buy because their share prices were going to climb, not shrink.

How accurate are these "buy" recommendations by analysts? Their accuracy is questionable. I am more interested in how they motivate investors to buy a stock because Increased buying often translates into an increasing share price. There are two objectives in buying financially strong, high dividend stocks. Income is one and the second is capital gain from increased share prices. You want to realize both when the opportunity presents itself.

The final item from the top half of the Overview page is the **VOLUME** (12ch3). This is the average number of daily shares being traded. The more shares traded, the more attractive, stable, and established the company.

A company with fewer than five thousand shares being traded daily will see rapid fluctuations up and down in their share price. Few investors are interested in their shares. Buyers must keep raising their bid prices for the stocks until finally the few owners of the stock are enticed to sell. Sellers are faced with the same problem in reverse. They must keep dropping the price until a buyer is enticed to buy.

On stocks trading a million or more shares (13ch3) in a day you will see the share price usually fluctuating by only a few cents in a day. Large numbers of buyers and sellers offset each other's bid prices. Usually, the greater the trading volume the more stable and stronger the stock.

Occasionally remarkable positive news or negative news can cause sudden high volumes of stock trades. You can avoid being surprised by such dramatic occurrences by keeping abreast of business news every day. Once you are heavily invested in the stock market you will find that business news becomes very captivating.

In a market crash (14ch3) it is amazing how quickly stocks can decline as speculators, especially those who have bought stocks on margin, quickly liquidate their holdings. This is the ideal time for dividend investors to buy, at bargain prices, financially strong, high dividend paying companies who have paid ever increasing high dividends for decades.

A crash is not the time for you to sell your financially strong, high paying, high dividend stocks. A crash is when you live off your dividend income and patiently wait for your portfolio's share value to again reach new heights as it inevitably will.

The next area to turn to is the bottom half of the OVERVIEW page, as displayed below. This is where the remaining information for the stock scoring software is located.

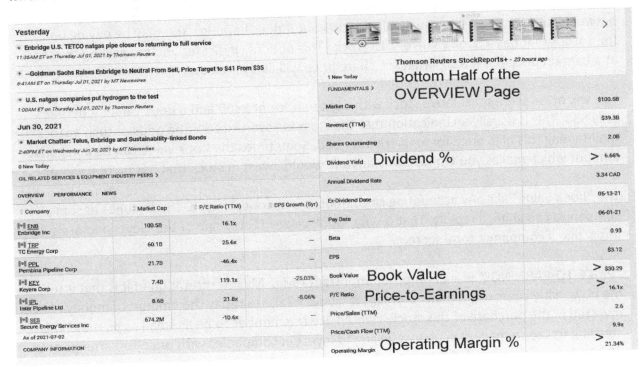

Most of the information in the bottom half of this screen is not used in the score calculation. Only four data items are extracted. They are dividend yield, book value, operating margin and price-to earnings ratio.

......

The **DIVIDEND YIELD** (15ch3) number is obviously important to dividend investors. A 3.5% dividend yield was the selector used to extract the stocks for your consideration in this book. Later in the book, you will see charts that show stocks paying very high dividends usually score poorly. The "sweet spot" to look for are stocks paying dividend yields between 5% and 9.5%. These are usually companies with high enough profits that they can not only pay generous dividends but have enough excess capital to invest in strengthening their companies. An investment in growth provides for constantly rising sales, profits, and dividend payments. Many strong dividend paying companies invest 60% of their profits in growth and 40% in dividend payments.

Dividends are paid to attract new investors and to encourage existing investors not to sell their shares. It allows Stockholders to share in the success of the company they invested in. Dividends send a message that we are a strong company who can afford to pay dividends and intend to be here for decades to come.

A stock's **BOOK VALUE** (16ch3) is an accounting calculation. It has little to do with the market value of the company if it were to be sold or its liquidation value if it were to go bankrupt. Certified accountants calculate asset values and subtract liability values to come up with this the company's book value.

Ideally, as an investor, you like to see a share price close to the book value. A close relationship between share price and book value is unusual but it does happen. You may be paying only $8 for a stock that has a book value of $10 stock. This not only indicates you are getting the share at a bargain price but is a sign that the share price will likely increase.

You will often see a speculative stock with a share price of $300 and a book value of perhaps only $30. This is usually an indication that the stock is "overpriced". The odds of such a stock maintaining this high price for long are not good. Sometimes the book value can be a negative amount which makes you wonder why anyone would invest in stock that has no real value?

The "book value" like any accounting calculation is a historical figure. The fortunes of some companies can change rapidly. That is why "book value" is only one of the eleven factors impacting a company's total score.

"PRICE-TO-EARNINGS" (17ch3) is another important ratio. My interpretation of it is that it tells me how many years of company earnings it would it take to repay the amount of money I have invested in the purchase of this stock. I would like the number to be as small as possible. It is startling to see so many speculators willing to invest in companies with price-to-earnings of 300.1x or in some cases 3000.1x.

An attractive Price-to Earnings ratio would be in the 5.1x to the 25.x range. If the company has no earnings, then a zero will appear or even a negative figure. I have seen stocks with negative P/E ratios in the thousands which makes you wonder about who would consider buying such a stock.

The "**OPERATING MARGIN**" (18ch3) is probably the most important figure used to calculate a stocks score. It represents sales less the expense to generate those sales taken as a percentage of the revenues. Dividends are paid out of the operating margin.

I have seen Real Estate Investment Trusts with operating margins exceeding 80%. Such high margins allow them to pay high dividends. I have also seen companies who were losing money with negative operating margins, who would not only not be paying dividends, but would be an indicator that the company has a serious problem.

Ideally, you would want to add stocks to your portfolio stocks with operating margins exceeding 20%. However, there are exceptions. A few industries traditionally operate successfully with operating margins of less than 20%. Therefore, when considering stocks with lower operation margins check the operating margins of other companies in the same industry to see if the operating margin of the stock you are considering is an exception. You also always want the operating margin to be accompanied by a long history of increasing share prices and dividend payouts. Things are neither great nor small except by comparison. It is important to compare the operating margins of prospective companies in the same industry to find the best ones.

The next chapter shows you how all the selected information from the Overview screen is used to calculate a score. The scoring system allows you to sort any. collection of stocks, from most to least desirable for your portfolio.

CHAPTER 4

HOW STOCKS ARE SCORED (1ch4)

The IDM stock scoring system I developed is based on the premise that if the ideal investment stock (2ch4) existed, it would have the following characteristics.

(1) The stock price would be greater than $100.
(2) It had a stock price that was greater than $100 four years ago.
(3) The stock price now is 99.50% greater than it was 4 years ago.
(4) It would have a book value greater than $100.
(5) The current stock price would be greater than 49.50% of the book value.
(6) Five or more analysts are rating the stock a "buy".
(7) Five or more analysts are rating the stock a "strong buy".
(8) It would have a dividend yield percent between 7.50% and 10.49%.
(9) The operating margin would be greater than 79.50%.
(10) The average daily volume of shares traded would be greater than 2,000,000.
(11) The stock's price-to-earnings ratio would be between 0.1x to 5.49x.

Unfortunately, the prefect dividend stock that would score 100 out of 100 does not exist. The highest score, out of the thousands that I have calculated has been a 78. There are few stocks scoring over 70. Thus, in choosing the 20 stocks for your portfolio, you will be making compromises between dividend yield percentage, potential for share price growth and financial strength. There are 11 facts that are scored. Together the eleven sub scores make up the total grand score for a stock.

You are advised to always re-score a stock just before purchasing it to confirm that no significant changes have occurred that could have altered the score since it was last scored.

You can use the eleven-item written matrix, that follows, to manually calculate a score. **However, it is much faster to use the software that is supplied, on request without charge, to those who buy my investment books. Send your request for the stock scoring software by email to imacd@informus.ca. Sometimes an email can get lost, if you do not receive a return email with the software attached within 24 hours phone 1-929-800-2397 or 416-245-4994.**

Following is a photograph of the data entry screen for the IDM stock scoring software (3ch4). Let us start with the first item, at the top of the stock scoring software's entry screen:

(1) **"CURRENT PRICE OF STOCK"** (4ch4). You will notice on the screen that there is an "O" beside this listing. This indicates where to find this data to be entered. The "O" stands for the **Overview page** that was reviewed in the previous Chapter Three.

The **A, B,** and **C** in the chart, show where the data for input can be found.
(A = This figure, does not exist, it is automatically calculated by the IDM software)
(B = These two numbers are extracted from Analysts Recommendation Charts
(C) This figure is extracted from the Historical Chart showing historical Share Prices and Dividend Payouts).

We also reviewed all these sources in the previous chapter. Although there are eleven calculations of sub scores to arrive at the **"OVERALL RATING SCORE"** (5ch4), you only need to enter nine data items. The software automatically calculates two of the sub-scores, #3 and #5.

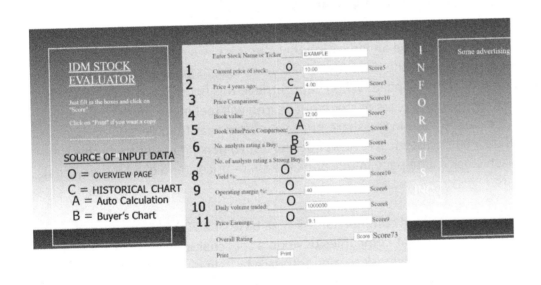

1

CURRENT PRICE OF STOCK

Supply and demand determine the price that speculators bid on a stock. The stock market is an auction vehicle that each day processes the bids from millions of stock buyers and sellers. A high price for a stock reflects the desire of thousands of optimistic investors to own that specific stock. Thus, the higher the price, the higher the score. The scoring software applies the following numerical values to a stock based on its trading price the day the score was calculated:

1. 0 to 99 cents scores =   1
2. $1 t0 $1.99 scores =   2
3. $2 to $4.99 scores =   3
4. 5 to $9,99 scores =   4
5. $10 to $14.99 scores = 5
6. $15 to $19.99 scores = 6
7. $20 to $29.99 scores = 7
8. $30 to $49.99 scores = 8
9. $50 to $99.99 scores = 9
10. Over $100 scores =   10

2

HISTORICAL PRICE (6ch4)

A stock that increases over time can be an indication that the stock will continue to grow. Since the score only considers the stock at the price it was at 4 years ago, as you are retrieving this price from the chart on the Overview page. When your retrieve this figure, take a few seconds to run your cursor back over twenty years of share prices. You will feel much more confident with the stock if you see steady gains in the share price year-after-year for a decade or more. Every investor should do a quick historical review, but few do. To make it easier to do this I have now added to each stock's data page in this book the share prices (and dividend payouts) going back for 24 years.

In 1991 I created a large computerized commercial risk data base of 2,200,000 risk-scored businesses. This task proved to me that companies develop a set "character" just like humans. It allowed me to develop very predictive risk scoring software to help banks, insurance companies, wholesalers and manufacturers make safe sales. I used a similar methodology when I built the IDM stock scoring software, for my personal use in 2017. I was not surprised to see the reliable scores for public companies traded on a stock exchange.

I have recognized that managers of strong public companies are obsessed with seeing their share prices go up each year. From experience I have seen that 95% of these financially strong companies will not deviate from their characteristic successful path. The managers of such companies are the kind you can have confidence in. I have rarely need to make changes in my portfolio because strong companies with consistent high scores rarely deviated from their traditional paths.

If you see a stock price that was climbing for many years and that has then shrunk back to a lower value, it may just be a passing aberration and the stock may again continue its climb.

Especially if the other 10 factors in the score are strong. When you see a constant erratic pace of one year the price is up and next year it is down or a downward spiral that goes on for years, you may want to look for a stock with a more positive pattern.

The historical price factor only measures the dollar amount of the stock four years ago. The next factor compares the current price with that price four years ago.

1. $0 to 99 cents scores = 1
2. $1 to $1.99 scores... = 2
3. $2 to $4.99 scores... = 3
4. $5 to $9.99 scores ...= 4
5. $10 to $14.99 scores = 5
6. $15 to $19.99 scores = 6
7. $20 to $29.99 scores = 7
8. $30 to $49.99 scores = 8
9. *$50 to $99.99 scores = 9*
10. *over $100 scores ...= 10*

3

PRICE TREND (7ch4)

When a stock is much higher than it was four years ago, it may give you confidence that the share price may continue to grow. If it is less than what the stock was four years ago you might have some concerns about its potential for growth. With this scoring factor nothing needs to be entered. The program automatically compares the two years of stock pricing and calculates the score. If the share price is less than the current one the stock earns a zero. It goes up from there.

In each stock's unique data page further on in this book, you can see the share price of the stock for each of the last 24 years going back to 1999. This gives you more insight into where the share price may be heading. The stock market crash years of 2000, 2008 and 2020 are highlighted in the page for each stock so you can see what happened to share prices in those years and how long it took for the share price to recover and reach new highs, which they often did.

1. The Stock has been sold for less than 4 years   = 0
2. The Current Price is less than the price 4 years ago, by more than 50.50% = 1

3. The Current Price is less than the price 4 years ago, by 11.50% to 50.49% = 2
4. The Current Price is less than the price 4 years by .50% to 10.49% = 5
5. Current Price is within .51% to 1.49% of the price it was at 4 years ago = 6
6. Current Price is 1.50% to 10.49% more than the price 4 years ago ... = 7
7. Current Price is 10.50% to 99.4% more than the price 4 years ago = 9
8. Current Price is more than 99.50% greater than the price of 4 years ago = 10

4

BOOK VALUE (8ch4)

The Book Value of a stock is calculated by the company's accountants who total the assets of the company then subtract depreciation and liabilities. That calculated figure is then divided by the number of shares outstanding.

If the "Book Value" is higher than the current share price, (which is a rare occurrence) then the stock is often considered to be a bargain. It is like being able to buy a Mercedes for the price of a Honda. This does not mean that a book's value is the same as the market value. It isn't until a company is put up for sale that you get a more realistic view of its market value. That value could be much higher or lower in such a sale. Something is only worth what someone will pay for it at any given time. Few co

Value is usually all about supply and demand. You should be concerned when you see a company whose Book Value is a minus figure, some examples of this appear among 215 stocks listed in this book. You will also find that certain industries traditionally have high or low average book values. To get an understanding of a stock's low book value, compare it with the book value of several competitive compares.

The following shows that the score is only measuring dollar amount of the book value. In the next factor it compares the book value to the current share price.

1. $0 to 99 cents scores = 1
2. $1 to $1.99 scores = 2
3. $2 to $4.99 scores = 3
4. $5 to $9.99 scores = 4
5. $10 to $14.99 scores = 5
6. $15 to $19.99 scores = 6
7. $20 to $29.99 scores = 7
8. $30 to $49.99 scores = 8

9. $50 to $99.99 scores = 9
10. over $100 scores = 10

5

BOOK VALUE TO PRICE (9ch4)

This comparison between book value and current share price is another calculation automatically done by the stock scoring software. A book value close to or higher than the current stock price is a positive sign that the share price has the potential to rise.

1. Current Price is less than the Book Value by more than 49.49% = 10
2. Current Price is less than the Book Value by 10.50% to 49.50% = 8
3. Current Price is less than the Book Value by 0.50% to 10.49% = 6
4. Current Price is between 0.51% and 1.49% of the Book Value = 4
5. Current Price is 1.50% to 9.49% greater than the Book Value = 2
6. Current Price is 9.50% to 49.49% greater than the Book Value = 1
7. Current Price is 49.50% greater than the Book Value = 0

6

ANALYST BUY RATINGS (10ch4)

A few stocks will capture the attention of analysts from the major banks and brokerage companies. They will usually be the larger more actively traded speculative stocks. For these stocks they will make projections as to where they think a share price is headed. They will summarize their projections with one of the following four tags: **BUY, STRONG BUY, HOLD** and **SELL**. No one, including analysts, can accurately predict future share prices. These recommendations are calculated guesses. Some databases keep track of how accurate they are. It seems they are about 50% accurate in their projected share prices. Their recommendations can be enough to influence some investors to buy a stock.

What the IDM score is tracking is how much influence an analyst's recommendations might have on the share price. Most of the sub scores are measured out of ten however the BUY sub score is only measured out of five. This lower limit is partly out of my concern about rumors that some analysts could be manipulated by their employers to rate a company a buy, if it is in the bank's best interest that a customer's stock increase in price. If shares were being used as collateral by the bank, would it ever be possible for a bank's analyst to make a buy recommendation instead of a sell recommendation? I have never seen detailed written explanations supporting analysts ratings. It seems you are just supposed to blindly accept them.

I have also noticed that while buy recommendations are not uncommon, you rarely see an analyst give a company a "sell" recommendation. It appears the company must almost be bankrupt before the stock gets a sell recommendation. "Sell" and "Hold" recommendations were ignored in building the score matrix because they have no more influence on buying a stock than the absence of a "buy" recommendation. Most stocks are not analyzed and have no analyst recommendations.

1. 0 analyst   = 0
2. 1 analyst   = 2
3. 2 to 3 analysts   = 3
4. 4 to 5 analysts   .   = 4
5. 5 or more analysts = 5

7

STRONG BUY RATINGS (11ch4)

I had to come up with the definition of what a strong buy recommendation is when the TD Bank stopped reporting "strong buys" and only reported "buys". TD is my primary stock data research source. Prior to this I accepted their analyst's classification of a "strong buy".

Now, I define a "strong buy" as being when an analyst applies a buy rating to a share whose future price, they predict, will be at least 50% higher than the current share price. Strong buy recommendations are rare, but they do occur. Their ratings do encourage some investors to buy a stock and cannot be ignored. Like the "buy" ratings, the most points a "strong buy" rating can register is 5.

Any analyst going out on a limb by predicting a 50% share price increase has his credibility on the line. This is worth considering in your scoring for the few extra points the stock may earn. Fewer strong buys recommendations are required to increase a score.

This "Strong Buy" definition does require that you look at all the buy recommendations and add up how many are 50% higher than the current share price. Since few stocks have buy recommendations, this is not a burden.

1. 0 analysts   = 0
2. 1 analyst   = 3
3. 2 to 4 analysts = 4
4. 5 or more analysts = 5

8

DIVIDEND YIELD PERCENT (12ch4)

What a company pays out in dividends has nothing to do with its share price. The two are only remotely connected. Share prices are determined by speculators bidding on stocks. Dividends are derived from profits which are not controlled by speculators. Dividends are controlled by the skilled, experienced managers of a company making revenue and expense decisions that result in the profit from which dividends are paid.

You will see a $50 stock that was paying a dividend of $2.50 (or 5%) drop down to $20 a share. The $2.50 dividend does not automatically decline in unison with this decline in share price. The only thing that changes is the dividend yield percent. The $2.50 dividend's yield percent would now mathematically increase to 12.5% on the new $20 share price.

Such a drop in share price is the result of pessimistic speculators selling their shares below a market price. The pessimists sold because they feared that if they did not sell that they the shares would lose even more value. Interestingly to sell the stock they must lower the share price enough to attract optimistic speculators who think the stock is going to increase in value. Due to this constant interplay between pessimists and optimists, no one can ever accurately predict what price in the future a share price will be.

When a company pays a dividend, it is an indication that it has the surplus funds to weather a downturn in the economy. However, the dividend is just one factor in determining a company's IDM score.

You will see in the charts in this book several companies paying dividends of 20% or more who score poorly. When you investigate these companies closely, you may find that the high dividend yield percent was a one-time thing. It may have been a way for the major shareholders to get their money out of a company teetering on the edge of insolvency. In such cases check to see if the operating margins and book values of the companies are close to zero.

When you see dividends that appear to be too high you must also consider if the management see little benefit in reinvesting any of their profits back into the company. Thus, be wary of a too high a dividend combined with low operating margins, low book values and other weaknesses. Be especially wary if you detect that the company with a low operating margin is borrowing money to maintain their dividend payouts. Some companies do this to stop pessimistic speculators from easily detecting their problems and reducing their share price bids.

The sweet spot in "high" dividend investing seems to be a stock consistently paying a dividend yield between 6% and 9%.

I have found it interesting the comments I get from investors in blue chip stocks. They claim that a company cannot possibly be financially strong and pay a 6% dividend. The blue-chip stocks they invest in often have share prices exceeding $100 and often pay a dividend no higher than 1.5%. By necessity this turns blue-chip investors into buy low/sell high speculators. They cannot weather a recession by living off the income of a 1.5% dividend when inflation has averaged 3.5% annually over the last 100 years.

As you will see in the data pages for the 215 stocks in this book there are many financially strong, stocks paying a dividend yield of 6% or more.

You will notice in this matrix that once the stock exceeds a 10.50% dividend it only receives a score of 2. This reflects the potential risk of stocks with very high dividend yield percents.

1. No Dividend Paid = 0
2. 0.001% to 1.49% Dividend = 1
3. 1.50% to 2.49% Dividend = 4
4. 2.50% to 4.49% Dividend = 6
5. 4.50% to 7.49% Dividend = 8
6. 7.50% to 10.49% Dividend = 10
7. Over 10.50% Dividend = 2

9

OPERATING MARGIN (13ch4)

When all the expenses that were used to achieve corporate revenues are subtracted from the corporation's revenue figure, whatever is left is your operating margin. The chief executive can then request the company's board of directors to approve investing this remaining money in new equipment or acquisitions to make the corporation more profitable. It could also be kept in reserve to protect the company from any downturns in the economy. The other option is to pay a portion of it in dividends to the company's shareholders. Many financially strong companies consistently pay out about 40% of their operating margins in dividends. They do this to reward those who have supported the company by investing in it. The remaining 60% usually is invested back into the company growth.

Several REITS (Real Estate Investment Trusts) and other companies set up to collect royalties can often have operating margins of more than 80%. They often have the highest dividends available to dividend investors. Their only drawback is that their share prices do not normally rise significantly from one year to the next. However, since our objective is both income and capital gain, it pays to have some high, steady dividend producers in your portfolio. There are exceptions where the share prices of some REITS can increase rapidly by several multiples.

You will also run across companies who have negative operating margins. They are not making a profit. They are not generating enough revenue to cover what was spent to generate the revenue.

A company exists to make profits. One that cannot make profits may have a limited future as it depletes its assets in a bid to survive.

I like to own companies with an operating margin of at least 20% while recognizing that in some industries few companies have an operating margin above 10%. There are some industries I hesitate to invest in, especially those in natural resources. Their fortunes rise and fall on the whims of world markets. The availability of their product seems to range between a shortage of supply driving prices up for a short time or an oversupply that drives prices down for extended periods. This decline weeds out the weak companies, causes a shortage of supply which then causes prices to rise again. There is nothing perceived unique about a commodity that protects it from price competition. I like strong stocks in stable industries that develop unique products.

1. A margin less than 1.49% = 0
2. 1.50% to 4.49%   = 1
3. 4.50% to 9.49%   = 2
4. 9.50% to 14.49%   = 3
5. 14.50% to 19.49%   = 4
6. 19.50% to 29.49%   = 5
7. 29.50% to 49.49%   = 6
8. 49.50% to 69.49%   = 8
9. 69.50% to 79.49%   = 9

10

TRADING VOLUMES (14ch4)

It can be difficult to both buy and sell a stock that trades only a few thousand shares a day. Such stocks are ignored by analysts because few investors are interested in them. Investors see little potential for their share prices to increase in such stocks. Often the few interested in buying low volume traded shares must keep increasing their bid prices to get the price offer high enough for those few holding the stocks to sell them.

 Some stocks can have zero trades in a day or only a few hundred. Preferred shares were excluded from this book because most preferred shares trade at such low volumes.

 After scoring hundreds of preferred shares, I found that one in one hundred might show a small share price gain. Almost all preferred shares are well below the $25 price they were issued at. While you may make some money on their higher dividend, you can lose more on their declining share value. They are stocks in name only. Like bonds, preferred shares are a form of loan. Since they do not have financial statements, the ones I reviewed lacked operating margins, analyst recommendations and other data that can be used in calculating a meaningful score.

Stocks that trade in millions of shares in a day rarely show dramatic price fluctuations. They are established, high profile companies who are considered to have potential for much higher share prices or they would not have been bid up to their present level.

1. Fewer than 10,000 shares..... = 0
2. 10,001 to 30,000 shares........ = 1
3. 30,001 to 50,000 shares........ = 2
4. 50,001 to 100,000 shares...... = 3
5. 100,001 to 250,000 shares.... = 4
6. 250,001 to 500,000 shares.... = 5
7. 500,001 to 750,000 shares..... =6
8. 750,001 to 1,000,000 shares. = 8
9. 1,000,001 to 2,000,000 shares. =9
10. Over 2,000,001 shares ...... = 10

11
PRICE-TO-EARNINGS (15ch4)

To me the price-to-earnings ratio indicates how many years it would take to recover from a company's earnings the price that I paid for their stock. The lower the price-to-earning's number, the less time it would take to recover my investment.

Of course, the company must have profitable earnings otherwise it would have an unattractive zero price-to-earnings ratio or a minus ratio figure. As such, they are not the financially strong stocks you would normally want in a portfolio.

Usually a price-to-earnings ratio below 20x is considered "good". However, it is not unusual to see a "hot" in demand speculative stock with a price-to-earnings ratios in the hundreds, even thousands. In such cases the concern is that these prices cannot be maintained. The frenzy that drove the stock price up so high could reverse and bring the share price crashing down the first time its potential looks questionable. Such very high ratios are difficult to maintain and are usually the result of speculators who irrationally think the gravy train is going to chug on forever.

1. 0 or a minus figure = 0
2. 01x to 5.49x   = 10
3. 5.50x to 15.49x   = 9
4. 15.50x to 20.49x   = 8

47

5. 20.50x to 25.49x   = 7
6. 25.50x to 30.49x   = 6
7. 30.50x to 35.49x   = 5
8. 35.50x to 40.49x   = 4
9. 40.50x to 99.99x   = 2
10. 100x or more   =1

STOCK BALANCING (1CH5)

The following is a chart that may help you balance your portfolio of 20 stocks. The objective is for all 20 stocks, when bundled together, to average an annual dividend yield of 6% (2ch5). The understanding is that you will be investing approximately the same amount in each of the 20 stocks.

This method of investing only works for self-directed investors because if you involve a financial advisor, their fees, charges, and commissions eat up too much of the dividend income and it will be unlikely for you to realize an annual 6% average dividend income.

To achieve this average dividend yield of 6%, you might, for example, add a strong stock scoring 65 that is only paying a dividend yield of 4%. You then need to add a stock that is paying a dividend yield of 8% to offset the 4%. Together, the two will give you an average for the two stocks of 6%. You are unlikely to find a stock paying 6% or more whose score is over 60. Thus, you will probably be selecting a lower scoring stock with a higher dividend.

You should always aim at adding the highest IDM scores possible. I would advise that your bottom risk limit for an IDM risk score should be 45. Between 45 and 59 would be an acceptable risk. Stocks with scores of 60 and higher would be a good risk. While a score over 75 is great, you will rarely see one that high.

In the following chart, the 2 blocks on the left are for listing the stocks scoring under 60. The first column is for entering the Stock Symbol, the second is for the Dividend Yield Percent and the third is for the Stock's IDM Score.).

The columns to its right are for entering the same 3 data elements but for stocks with higher dividend yields to offset the lower dividend yields on the left.

The middle gray column is for entering in the average dividend yield you have realized by twining the stock records on the right with the stock records on the left. At the bottom of the charts is a box where you can enter the average for all 20 stocks. You add up the 10 averages in the middle column and divide them by 10.

While the dividend yield percentages for 20 stocks will change over time. This chart will show how the average dividend yield of your portfolio looked when you created it. I have found this composite average can remain steady for a long time.

Under *"Stock"* you would enter in the Stock's symbol. Under *"Div%"* you would enter in the reported dividend yield for that stock. Under *"Score"* you would enter the IDM score that you have calculated for the stock or extracted from one of my books.

REMINDER: All investment book buyers can request the free stock scoring software (3ch5) to be emailed to them by sending a message to imacd@informus.ca. You can also request this stock averaging Excel spread sheet (4ch5) at the same time.

IDM SCORES 45 TO 59   Dividend   IDM SCORES OVER 60

	Stock	Div %	Score	**Average**	Stock	Div %	Score
1							
2							
3							
4							
5							

	Stock	Div %	Score		Stock	Div %	Score
6							
7							
8							
9							
10							

Average Score of all 20 = [   ]

As the share price of a stock increases, you will often find that the dividend payouts are increased by the company to maintain a steady dividend yield percent. These increases can keep your income ahead of inflation. Dividend payouts usually rise faster than share prices and are far more predictable.

CHAPTER 6

SORTED BY SCORES (1ch6)

This is the first of four chapters that summarize the data on these 215 high dividend Canadian stocks. These four summaries are sorted by (1) stock score, (2) alphabetically by company name, (3) by the stock's dividend percent and (4) by the stock's operating margin.

You might use these four summaries as a preliminary quick review of all 215 stocks to pick out those stocks you wish to investigate further on each stock's full data page. Each stock's full data pages are in an alphabetical sequence starting in Chapter 10.

The stocks in this chapter are sorted in descending order by their IDM scores. You might consider such things as:

(1) The highest scoring stocks are often the most expensive stocks to buy. You are far more likely to see a stock below $10 in price double its share price in the next year than a $100 stock.

(2) The lowest scoring stores have zero percent operating margins. If they are not making a profit where is the money to pay their dividends coming from. Are they borrowing money to pay dividends?

(3) There are a few stocks with operating margins exceeding 100. They have higher scores.

(4) Within the same score group, stocks are then sorted alphabetically by company name.

All these are Canadian stocks traded on the Toronto Stock Exchange (TSX).

SCORE..	COMPANY	SYMBOL..	PRICE	DIVIDEND	OP. MARGIN
10	Real Estate Split Corporation	RS	$13.90	11.22%	0%
12	DRI Healthcare Trust	DHT.U	$7.15	4.20%	0%
12	TDB Split Corporation	XTD	$4.03	14.89%	0%

15	Big Banc Split Corporation	BNK	$11.46	6.93%	0%
16	C-Com Satellite Systems Inc	CMI	$0.90	5.32%	1.72%
17	Dividend Select 15 Corporation	DS	$6.81	11.56%	0%
18	Automotive Finco Corporation	AFCC	$1.05	19.45%	0%
18	Global Dividend Growth Split Corporation	GDV	$9.91	12.11%	0%
19	Dividend Growth Split Corporation	DGS	$5.21	23.03%	0%
19	Top 10 Split Trust	TXT.UN	$2.09	6.76%	0%
20	Nergenrx Inc	NXG	$0.30	6.67%	0.37%
20	Newport Exploration Limited	NWX	$0.25	15.69%	0%
20	RE Royalties Ltd	RE	$0.72	5.56%	35.06%
21	Pine Trail Real Estate Investment Trust	PINE>UN	$0.06	6.00%	-34.9%

22 to 25

22	Alpine Summit Energy Partners Inc	ALPS.U	$0.81	46.67%	22.89%
22	Brompton Lifeco Split Corporation	LCS	$6.05	14.88%	0%
23	Fiera Capital Corporation	FSZ	$6.83	12.59%	10.28%
23	Sustainable Power & Infrastructure Split Corp	PWI	$6.50	12.31%	0%
23	Tier One Capital LP	TLP.UN	$3.00	16.67%	0%
24	Brompton Split Bank Corporation	SBC	$10.70	11.21%	0%
25	Canadian Banc Corp	BK	$13.18	15.46%	0%
25	Sailfish Royalty Corporation	FISH	$0.81	8.18%	77.10%

26 to 30

26	Elysee Development Corporation	ELC	$0.44	4.49%	0%
26	Extendicare Inc	EXE	$7.16	6.70%	1.66%
26	High Artic Energy Services Inc	HWO	$1.19	4.92%	-41.92%
26	International Clean Power Dividend Fund	CLP.UN	7.01	7.13%	0%
26	SSC Security Services Corporation	SECU	$2.79	4.30%	0.09%
27	Canadian High Income Equity Fund	CIQ.UN	$7.13	6.73%	0%
27	Life & Banc Split Corporation	LBS	$8.58	13.99%	0%
27	Mackenzie Master LP	MKZ.UN	$0.45	18.60%	85.87%
27	Stingray Group Inc	RAY.B	$5.36	5.60%	20.34%
28	Inovalis Real Estate Investment Trust	INO.UN	$3.34	12.35%	-136.97%
30	American Hotel Income Properties REIT Ltd	HOT.U	$1.85	9.73%	-1.07%
30	Amerigo Resources Ltd	ARG	$1.75	6.86%	7.97%
30	Corby Spirit and Wine Limited	CSW.B	$13.65	6.15%	19.71%
30	Prime Dividend Corporation	PDV	$5.60	10.24%	0%
30	Slate Grocery Real Estate Investment Trust	SGR.UN	$13.15	8.71%	0%
30	Source Rock Royalties Ltd	SRR	$0.78	8.46%	41.31%
30	Tidewater Midstream and Infrastructure Ltd	TWM	$0.96	4.17%	1.00%
26	Titan Mining Corporation	TI	$0.43	9.30%	-7.09%

31 to 35

31	Big Pharma Split Corporation	PRM	$15.15	8.17%	0%
31	Dexterra Croup Inc	DXT	$5.40	6.48%	1.61%

31	E Split Corporation	ENS	$15.15	10.30%	0%
31	Zoomermedia Ltd	ZUM	$0.04	6.67%	4.07%
32	Blue Ribbon Inc	RBN.UN	$7.62	6.30%	0%
33	Australian Real Estate Investment Trus	HRR.UN	$8.22	8.03%	0%
33	Wall Financial Corporation	WFC	$19.35	15.50%	31.72%
34	BTB Real Estate Investment Trust	BTB.UN	$3.32	9.04%	0%
34	Rogers Sugar Inc	RSI	$5.77	6.24%	1.76%
34	Western Forest Products Inc	WEF	$1.05	4.76%	0.70%
35	Chartwell Retirement Residences	CSH.UN	$9.23	6.63%	4.92%
35	Dividend 15 Split Corporation	DFN	$7.43	16.15%	77.95%
35	Dream Residential Real Estate Investment Trust	DRR.U	$7.85	5.35%	34.18%
35	Financial 15 Split Corporation	FTN	$8.72	17.30%	0%
35	Sagicor Financial Company Limited	SFC	$4.40	6.91%	-9.26%
35	Slate Office Real Estate Investment Trust	SOT.UN	$1.97	6.09%	36.63%

36 to 40

36	Brookfield Global Infrastructure Securities IF	BGI	$4.46	13.49%	66.02%
36	Caribbean Utilities Company Limited	CUP.U	$13.75	5.09%	12.00%
36	Precious Metal and Mining Trust	MMP.UN	$2.04	5.88%	0%
36	Sienna Senior Living Inc	SIA	$11.20	8.36%	1.73%
36	Superior Plus Corporation	SPB	$9.35	7.70%	-2.98%
37	Aecon Group Inc	ARE	$13.10	5.65%	2.07%
37	AirBoss of America Corporation	BOS	$7.15	5.59%	7.27%
37	Dynacor Group Inc	DNG	$3.00	4.00%	8.86%
37	Gamehost Inc	GH	$9.53	3.78%	30.03%
37	K-Bro Linen Inc	KBL	$31.15	3.85%	4.86%
37	Medical Facilities Corporation	DR	$8.05	4.00%	7.80%
37	Premium Income Corporation	PIC.A	$4.95	16.42%	70.34%
37	Propel Holdings Inc	PRL	$7.50	5.33%	16.13%
37	True North Commercial Real Estate invest Trust	TNT.UN	$2.52	11.79%	6.11%
38	Accord Financial Corporation	ACD	$7.14	4.20%	39.61%
39	A&W Revenue Royalties Income Fund	AW.UN	$36.25	5.30%	0%
38	Gear Energy Ltd	GXE	$0.97	12.37%	39.96%
38	McChip Resources Inc	MCS	$0.89	6.74%	0%
39	Andrew Peller Limited	ADW.A	$4.75	5.18%	0.05%
39	Builders Capital Mortgage Corporation	BCF	$8.50	9.28%	-77.42%
40	Decisive Dividend Corporation	DE	$6.65	9.32%	6.02%
40	Hemisphere Energy Corporation	HME	$1.24	8.06%	41.32%

41 to 45

41	Alphamin Resources Corporation	AFM	$1.04	5.77%	40.6%
41	Brookfield Infrastructure Partners LP	BIP.UN	$47.47	4.30%	0%
41	Findev Inc	FDI	$0.41	7.23%	72.30%
41	KP Tissue Inc	KPT	$10.48	6.87%	0%
41	Neo Performance Materials Inc	NEO	$8.20	4.88%	4.25%
41	Topaz Energy Corporation	TPZ	$20.92	5.74%	35.60%

#	Company	Ticker	Price	Yield	%
42	Bridgemarq Real Estate Services Inc	BRE	$14.91	9.05%	34.85%
42	Canadian Net Real Estate Income Trust	NET.UN	$5.48	6.30%	69.32%
42	Chemtrade Logistcs Income Fund	CHE.UN	$8.63	6.95%	12.80%
....42	Corus Entertainment Inc	CJR.B	$1.39	8.63%	-19.38%
42	Evertz Technologies Limited	ET	$12.50	6.08%	20.83%
42	Secure Energy Services Inc	SES	$6.49	6.16%	4.30%
42	TransAlta Renewables Inc	RNW	$13.24	7.10%	16.98%
43	Algonquin Power & Utilities Corporation	AQN	$11.60	5.06%	11.16%
43	Bird Construction Inc	BDT	$8.69	4.94%	2.80%
43	Ecora Resources PLC	ECOR	$2.03	6.05%	79.88%
43	Morguard Real Estate Investment Trust	MRT.UN	$5.40	4.44%	27.31
44	Canaccord Genuit Group Inc	CF	$8.31	4.09%	1.16%
44	Cascades Inc	CAS	$10.90	4.40%	0.74%
44	Chesswood Group Ltd	CHW	$8.14	7.37%	14.73%
44	Corby Spirit and Wine Limited	CSW.A	$15.01	5.60%	19.71%
44	Exco Technologies Ltd	XTC	$7.82	5.37%	6.12%
44	Innergex Renewable Energy **Inc**	INE	$13.39	5.38%	22.34%
45	Brookfield Renewable Corporation	BEPC	$46.90	3.85%	81.07%
45	Urbanfund Corporation	UFC	$1.03	4.85%	42.48%
45	Yellow Pages Limited	Y	$12.30	6.50%	28.34%

46 to 50

#	Company	Ticker	Price	Yield	%
46	Canadian Utilities Limited	CU.X	$38.59	4.65%	28.87%
46	Crombie Real Estate Investment Trust	CRR.UN	$15.08	5.90%	59.57%
46	Firm Capital Property Trust	FCD.UN	$5.30	9.81%	68.44%
46	First National Financial Corporation	FN	$38.50	6.23%	14.77%
47	Artis Real Estate Investment Trust	AX.UN	$7.44	8.06%	2.43%
47	Brookfield Asset Management Limited	BAM	$44.01	4.01%	62.20%
47	PHX Energy Services Corporation	PHX	$6.06	9.90%	13.81%
47	Pine Cliff Energy Limited	PNE	$1.43	9.09%	40.69%
47	Polaris Renewable Energy Inc	PIF	$14.25	5.71%	24.70%
48	Alvopetro Energy Ltd	ALV	$7.94	9.54%	61.69%
48	CT Real Estate Investment Trust	CRT.UN	$15.55	5.58%	56.11%
48	Dominion Lending Centres Inc	DLCG	$2.42	6.61%	0%
48	Dream Impact Trust	MPCT.UN	$2.42	6.61%	0%
48	Energy Income Fund	ENI.UN	$1.77	6.78%	69.72%
48	Information Services Corporation	ISV	$20.97	4.39%	23.64%
48	Parkland Corporation	PKI	$33.00	4.12%	2.29%
48	Timbercreek Financial Corporation	TF	$7.51	9.19%	59.21%
48	Trican Well Service Ltd	TCW	$3.67	4.36%	16.26%
49	Diversified Royalty Corporation	DIV	$2.85	8.42%	73.68%
49	Orca Energy Group Inc	ORC.B	$5.24	10.12%	44.90%
49	Pizza Pizza Royalty Corporation	PZA	$14.81	6.08	98.24%
49	Plaza Retail Real Estate Investment Trust	PLZ.UN	$3.97	7.05%	59.81%
49	Transcontinental Inc	TCL.B	$13.58	6.63%	6.53%
50	The North West Company Inc	NWC	$31.90	4.76%	7.21%

51	Atco Limited	ACO.Y	$46.21	4.12%	26.36%
51	Atrium Mortgage Investment Corporation	AI	$12.20	7.38%	84.28%
51	Dream Office Real Estate Investment Trust	D.UN	$14.45	6.92%	6.71%
51	European Residential Real Estate Investment Trust	ERE.UN	$2.97	5.92%	58.07%
51	Melcor Real Estate Investment Trust	MR.UN	$4.70	10.21%	53.12%
51	Melcor Real Estate Investment Trust	MR.UN	$4.70	10.21%	53.12%
51	Northwest Healthcare Properties REIT	NWH.UN	$6.28	12.74%	26.22%
51	Olympia Financal Group Inc	OLY	$71.75	7.59%	27.79%
51	Transcontinental Inc	TCL.A	$13.45	6.69%	6.53%
52	Capital Power Corporation	CPX	$43.77	5.30%	9.05%
52	Choice Properties Real Estates Investment Trust	CHP.UN	$13.93	5.38%	49.79%
52	Inplay Oil Corporation	IPO	$2.45	7.35%	42.65%
52	Keyera Corporation	KEY	$30.48	6.30%	6.45%
52	Mint Income Fund	MID.UN	$6.48	7.41%	82.75%
52	Surge Energy Inc	SGY	$7.99	6.01%	32.62%
52	Westshore Terminals	WTE	$32.05	4.37	36.44%
53	Acadian Timber Corporation	ADN	$15.64	7.42%	19.75%
53	B2 Gold Corporation	BTO	$5.55	4.03%	29.00%
55	Becker Milk Company Limited	BEK.B	$13.00	6.15%	31.05%
53	Boston Pizza Royalties Income Fund	BPF.UN	$15.48	8.29%	96.94%
53	CanWel Building Materials Group Ltd	DBM	$6.09	9.20	4.48%
53	Firm Capital Mortgage Investment Corporation	FC	$10.70	8.75%	49.72%
53	Lundin Mining Corporation	LUN	$10.32	3.49%	15.05%
53	Mullen Group Limited	MTL	$15.29	4.71%	11.29%
54	CI Financial Corporation	CIX	$12.53	5.75%	24.91%
54	Headwater Exploration Inc	HWX	$6.42	6.23%	53.16%
54	H&R Real Estate Investment Trust	HR.UN	$10.36	5.79%	15.54%
54	McCan Mortgage Corporation	MKP	$15.95	9.03%	33.37%
54	Pro Real Estate Investment Trust	PRV.UN	$5.32	8.45%	51.98%
55	Killam Apartment Real Estate Investment Trust	KMP...	$17.50	4.00%	38.93%
55	Pipestone Energy Corporation	PIPE	$2.27	5.29%	48.59%
55	Wajax Corporation	WJX	$27.28	4.84%	5.69%

56 to 60

56	Algoma Central Corp	ALC	$15.70	4.59%	15.09%
56	Automotive Properties REIT	APR.UN	$11.56	6.96%	102.86%
56	BSR Real Estate Investment Trust	HOM.U	$13.20	3.94%	39.61%
56	Canacol Energy Ltd	CNE	$10.05	10.35%	33.21%
56	Cardinal Energy Ltd	CJ	$7.18	10.03%	50.09%
56	Enbridge Inc	ENB	$50.26	7.06%	12.92%
56	Goodfellow Inc	GDL	$12.35	8.10%	6.40%
56	Melcor Developments Limited	MRD	$11.13	5.75%	57.20%
56	Russel Metals Inc	RUS	$36.13	4.43%	9.67%
57	Freehold Royalties Limited	FRU	$13.48	8.01%	64.06%
57	Riocan Real Estate Investment Trust	REI.UN	$19.20	5.83%	15.21%

#	Company	Ticker	Price		
58	AGF Management	AGF.B	$8.14	5.41%	16.97%
58	Cogeco Communications Inc	CCA	$66.27	4.68%	25.73%
58	Peyto Exploration & Development Corporation	PEY	$10.96	12.04%	61.37%
59	Exchange Income Corporation	EIF	$53.65	4.70%	11.21%
59	Labrador Iron Ore Royalty Corporation	LIF	$30.88	8.44%	75.90%
59	Telus Corporation	T	$24.32	5.98%	14.90%
60	Canadian Utilities Limited	CU	$39.14	4.58%	29.87%
60	Smart Centres Real Estate Investment Trust	SRU.UN	$23.71	7.80%	46.60%

61 to 65

#	Company	Ticker	Price		
61	Atco Limited	ACO.X	$45.95	4.28%	26.36%
61	Northland Power Inc	NPI	$26.72	4.48%	40.48%
62	Alaris Equity Partners	AD.UN	$16.36	8.31%	85.00%
62	Cogeco Inc	CGO	$55.29	5.29%	25.24%
62	Paramount Resources Limited	POU	$28.80	5.21%	48.39%
62	Suncor Energy Inc	SU	$39.09	5.33%	21.60%
62	Sun Life Financial Inc	SLF	$67.40	4.45%	34.16%
62	TC Energy Corporation	TRP	$51.67	7.20%	22.61%
62	Whitecap Resources Inc	WCP	$9.59	6.04%	42.89%
63	BCE Inc	BCE	$64.44	6.01	21.04%
63	Canoe EIT Income Fund	EIT.UN	$12.93	9.28%	85.75%
63	Nexus Industrial Real Estate Investment Trust	NXR.UN	$8.42	7.60%	105.25%
64	Crescent Point Energy Corporation	CPG	$9.10	4.40%	19.12%
64	IGM Financial Inc	IGM	$40.73	5.52%	29.95%
64	Power Corporation	POW	$35.66	5.89%	4.19%
65	Great-West Lifeco Inc	GWO	$38.07	5.46%	8.94%
65	Laurentian Bank Of Canada	LB	$42.88	4.38%	24.22%
65	Parex Resources Inc	PXT	$26.56	5.65%	58.11%

66 to 76

#	Company	Ticker	Price		
66	Canadian Western Bank	CWB	$24.22	5.28%	42.21%
66	GoEasy Ltd	GSY	$109.12	3.52%	32.99%
66	National Bank of Canada	NA	$98.71	4.13%	41.35%
67	Dream Industrial Real Estate Investment Trust	DIR.UN	$13.79	5.08%	64.39%
68	Bank of Nova Scotia	BNS	$68.19	6.04%	38.84%
68	Canadian Natural Resources Limited	CNQ	$80.89	4.45%	34.90%
68	Royal Bank of Canada	RY	$125.52	4.30%	35.97%
69	AltaGas Ltd	ALA	$22.90	4.87%	6.62%
69	Birchcliff Energy Ltd	BIR	$7.89	10.14%	55.18%
69	Emera Inc	EMA	$56.55	4.88%	24.28%
69	Pembina Pipeline Corporation	PPL	$41.65	6.41%	32.60%
72	Allied Properties REIT	AP.UN	$23.03	7.82%	41.24%
72	Canadian Imperial Bank of Commerce	CM	$56.66	6.00%	30.29%
72	Manulife Financial Corporation	MFC	$24.16	6.0%	38.44%
73	Granite Real Estate Investment Trust	GRT.UN	$82.87	3.86%	64.14%
73	The Toronto-Dominion Bank	TD	$83.88	4.58%	34.35%

76   Bank of Montreal   BMO $123.94   4.62%   45.08%

CHAPTER 7

SORTED ALPHABETICALLY (1ch7)

In this chapter, the same summarized information on each stock is sorted alphabetically by company name. This can be useful in quickly finding four important information facts on a stock that you may have heard about. For even more detailed and historical information on that stock you can then go to the stock's unique full data page in Chapter 11.

SCORE..	COMPANY	SYMBOL..	PRICE	DIVIDEND	OP. MARGIN

A

SCORE..	COMPANY	SYMBOL..	PRICE	DIVIDEND	OP. MARGIN
39	A&W Revenue Royalties Income Fund	AW.UN	$36.25	5.30%	0%
53	Acadian Timber Corporation	ADN	$15.64	7.42%	19.75%
38	Accord Financial Corporation	ACD	$7.14	4.20%	39.61%
37	Aecon Group Inc	ARE	$13.10	5.65%	2.07%
58	AGF Management	AGF.B	$8.14	5.41%	16.97%
37	AirBoss of America Corporation	BOS	$7.15	5.59%	7.27%
62	Alaris Equity Partners	AD.UN	$16.36	8.31%	85.00%
56	Algoma Central Corp	ALC	$15.70	4.59%	15.09%
43	Algonquin Power & Utilities Corporation	AQN	$11.60	5.06%	11.16%
72	Allied Properties REIT	AP.UN	$23.03	7.82%	41.24%
41	Alphamin Resources Corporation	AFM	$1.04	5.77%	40.6%
22	Alpine Summit Energy Partners Inc	ALPS.U	$0.81	46.67%	22.89%
69	AltaGas Ltd	ALA	$22.90	4.87%	6.62%
48	Alvopetro Energy Ltd	ALV	$7.94	9.54%	61.69%
30	American Hotel Income Properties REIT Ltd	HOT.U	$1.85	9.73%	-1.07%
30	Amerigo Resources Ltd	ARG	$1.75	6.86%	7.97%
39	Andrew Peller Limited	ADW.A	$4.75	5.18%	0.05%
47	Artis Real Estate Investment Trust	AX.UN	$7.44	8.06%	2.43%
61	Atco Limited	ACO.X	$45.95	4.28%	26.36%
51	Atco Limited	ACO.Y	$46.21	4.12%	26.36%
ci 51	Atrium Mortgage Investment Corporation	AI	$12.20	7.38%	84.28%
33	Australian Real Estate Investment Trust	HRR.UN	$8.22	8.03%	0%
18	Automotive Finco Corporation	AFCC	$1.05	19.45%	0%
ci 56	Automotive Properties REIT	APR.UN	$11.56	6.96%	102.86%

B

	53	B2 Gold Corporation	BTO	$5.55	4.03%	29.00%
i	76	Bank of Montreal	BMO	$123.94	4.62%	45.08%
ci	68	Bank of Nova Scotia	BNS	$68.19	6.04%	38.84%
ci	63	BCE Inc	BCE	$64.44	6.01	21.04%
	55	Becker Milk Company Limited	BEK.B	$13.00	6.15%	31.05%
	15	Big Banc Split Corporation	BNK	$11.46	6.93%	0%
	31	Big Pharma Split Corporation	PRM	$15.15	8.17%	0%
	69	Birchcliff Energy Ltd	BIR	$7.89	10.14%	55.18%
	43	Bird Construction Inc	BDT	$8.69	4.94%	2.80%
	32	Blue Ribbon Inc	RBN.UN	$7.62	6.30%	0%
c	53	Boston Pizza Royalties Income Fund	BPF.UN	$15.48	8.29%	96.94%
	42	Bridgemarq Real Estate Services Inc	BRE	$14.91	9.05%	34.85%
	22	Brompton Lifeco Split Corporation	LCS	$6.05	14.88%	0%
	24	Brompton Split Bank Corporation	SBC	$10.70	11.21%	0%
	47	Brookfield Asset Management Limited	BAM	$44.01	4.01%	62.20%
	45	Brookfield Renewable Corporation	BEPC	$46.90	3.85%	81.07%
	36	Brookfield Global Infrastructure Securities IF	BGI	$4.46	13.49%	66.02%
	41	Brookfield Infrastructure Partners LP	BIP.UN	$47.47	4.30%	0%
	56	BSR Real Estate Investment Trust	HOM.U	$13.20	3.94%	39.61%
ci	34	BTB Real Estate Investment Trust	BTB.UN	$3.32	9.04%	0%
	39	Builders Capital Mortgage Corporation	BCF	$8.50	9.28%	-77.42%

C

	44	Canaccord Genuit Group Inc	CF	$8.31	4.09%	1.16%
	56	Canacol Energy Ltd	CNE	$10.05	10.35%	33.21%
	27	Canadian High Income Equity Fund	CIQ.UN	$7.13	6.73%	0%
	25	Canadian Banc Corp	BK	$13.18	15.46%	0%
i	72	Canadian Imperial Bank of Commerce	CM	$56.66	6.00%	30.29%
	68	Canadian Natural Resources Limited	CNQ	$80.89	4.45%	34.90%
	42	Canadian Net Real Estate Income Trust	NET.UN	$5.48	6.30%	69.32%
	46	Canadian Utilities Limited	CU.X	$38.59	4.65%	28.87%
	60	Canadian Utilities Limited	CU	$39.14	4.58%	29.87%
	66	Canadian Western Bank	CWB	$24.22	5.28%	42.21%
i	63	Canoe EIT Income Fund	EIT.UN	$12.93	9.28%	85.75%
	53	CanWel Building Materials Group Ltd	DBM	$6.09	9.20	4.48%
ci	52	Capital Power Corporation	CPX	$43.77	5.30%	9.05%
	56	Cardinal Energy Ltd	CJ	$7.18	10.03%	50.09%
	36	Caribbean Utilities Company Limited	CUP.U	$13.75	5.09%	12.00%
	44	Cascades Inc	CAS	$10.90	4.40%	0.74%
	16	C-Com Satellite Systems Inc	CMI	$0.90	5.32%	1.72%
	35	Chartwell Retirement Residences	CSH.UN	$9.23	6.63%	4.92%
	42	Chemtrade Logistcs Income Fund	CHE.UN	$8.63	6.95%	12.80%
	44	Chesswood Group Ltd	CHW	$8.14	7.37%	14.73%
	52	Choice Properties Real Estates Investment Trust	CHP.UN	$13.93	5.38%	49.79%
	54	CI Financial Corporation	CIX	$12.53	5.75%	24.91%
	58	Cogeco Communications Inc	CCA	$66.27	4.68%	25.73%

62	Cogeco Inc	CGO	$55.29	5.29%	25.24%
30	Corby Spirit and Wine Limited	CSW.B	$13.65	6.15%	19.71%
44	Corby Spirit and Wine Limited	CSW.A	$15.01	5.60%	19.71%
....42	Corus Entertainment Inc	CJR.B	$1.39	8.63%	-19.38%
46	Crombie Real Estate Investment Trust	CRR.UN	$15.08	5.90%	59.57%
48	CT Real Estate Investment Trust	CRT.UN	$15.55	5.58%	56.11%
64	Crescent Point Energy Corporation	CPG	$9.10	4.40%	19.12%

D

40	Decisive Dividend Corporation	DE	$6.65	9.32%	6.02%
31	Dexterra Croup Inc	DXT	$5.40	6.48%	1.61%
c 49	Diversified Royalty Corporation	DIV	$2.85	8.42%	73.68%
35	Dividend 15 Split Corporation	DFN	$7.43	16.15%	77.95%
19	Dividend Growth Split Corporation	DGS	$5.21	23.03%	0%
17	Dividend Select 15 Corporation	DS	$6.81	11.56%	0%
48	Dominion Lending Centres Inc	DLCG	$2.42	6.61%	0%
35	Dream Residential Real Estate Investment Trust	DRR.U	$7.85	5.35%	34.18%
48	Dream Impact Trust	MPCT.UN	$2.42	6.61%	0%
67	Dream Industrial Real Estate Investment Trust	DIR.UN	$13.79	5.08%	64.39%
51	Dream Office Real Estate Investment Trust	D.UN	$14.45	6.92%	6.71%
12	DRI Healthcare Trust	DHT.U	$7.15	4.20%	0%
37	Dynacor Group Inc	DNG	$3.00	4.00%	8.86%

E

43	Ecora Resources PLC	ECOR	$2.03	6.05%	79.88%
31	E Split Corporation	ENS	$15.15	10.30%	0%
26	Elysee Development Corporation	ELC	$0.44	4.49%	0%
69	Emera Inc	EMA	$56.55	4.88%	24.28%
c 56	Enbridge Inc	ENB	$50.26	7.06%	12.92%
48	Energy Income Fund	ENI.UN	$1.77	6.78%	69.72%
51	European Residential Real Estate Investment Trust	ERE.UN	$2.97	5.92%	58.07%
42	Evertz Technologies Limited	ET	$12.50	6.08%	20.83%
59	Exchange Income Corporation	EIF	$53.65	4.70%	11.21%
44	Exco Technologies Ltd	XTC	$7.82	5.37%	6.12%
26	Extendicare Inc	EXE	$7.16	6.70%	1.66%

F

23	Fiera Capital Corporation	FSZ	$6.83	12.59%	10.28%
35	Financial 15 Split Corporation	FTN	$8.72	17.30%	0%
41	Findev Inc	FDI	$0.41	7.23%	72.30%
ci 53	Firm Capital Mortgage Investment Corporation	FC	$10.70	8.75%	49.72%
46	Firm Capital Property Trust	FCD.UN	$5.30	9.81%	68.44%
46	First National Financial Corporation	FN	$38.50	6.23%	14.77%
57	Freehold Royalties Limited	FRU	$13.48	8.01%	64.06%

G

37	Gamehost Inc	GH	$9.53	3.78%	30.03%
38	Gear Energy Ltd	GXE	$0.97	12.37%	39.96%
52	Gibson Energy Inc	GEI	$21.90	7.12%	3.79%
18	Global Dividend Growth Split Corporation	GDV	$9.91	12.11%	0%
66	GoEasy Ltd	GSY	$109.12	3.52%	32.99%
56	Goodfellow Inc	GDL	$12.35	8.10%	6.40%
73	Granite Real Estate Investment Trust	GRT.UN	$82.87	3.86%	64.14%
i 65	Great-West Lifeco Inc	GWO	$38.07	5.46%	8.94%

H

54	Headwater Exploration Inc	HWX	$6.42	6.23%	53.16%
40	Hemisphere Energy Corporation	HME	$1.24	8.06%	41.32%
54	H&R Real Estate Investment Trust	HR.UN	$10.36	5.79%	15.54%
26	High Artic Energy Services Inc	HWO	$1.19	4.92%	-41.92%

I

64	IGM Financial Inc	IGM	$40.73	5.52%	29.95%
48	Information Services Corporation	ISV	$20.97	4.39%	23.64%
44	Innergex Renewable Energy Inc	INE	$13.39	5.38%	22.34%
52	Inplay Oil Corporation	IPO	$2.45	7.35%	42.65%
28	Inovalis Real Estate Investment Trust	INO.UN	$3.34	12.35%	-136.97%
26	International Clean Power Dividend Fund	CLP.UN	$7.01	7.13%	0%

J/K

37	K-Bro Linen Inc	KBL	$31.15	3.85%	4.86%
52	Keyera Corporation	KEY	$30.48	6.30%	6.45%
55	Killam Apartment Real Estate Investment Trust	KMP	$17.50	4.00%	38.93%
41	KP Tissue Inc	KPT	$10.48	6.87%	0%

L

59	Labrador Iron Ore Royalty Corporation	LIF	$30.88	8.44%	75.90%
ci 65	Laurentian Bank Of Canada	LB	$42.88	4.38%	24.22%
27	Life & Banc Split Corporation	LBS	$8.58	13.99%	0%
53	Lundin Mining Corporation	LUN	$10.32	3.49%	15.05%

M

27	Mackenzie Master LP	MKZ.UN	$0.45	18.60%	85.87%
c 72	Manulife Financial Corporation	MFC	$24.16	6.0%	38.44%
i 54	McCan Mortgage Corporation	MKP	$15.95	9.03%	33.37%

38	McChip Resources Inc	MCS	$0.89	6.74%	0%
37	Medical Facilities Corporation	DR	$8.05	4.00%	7.80%
56	Melcor Developments Limited	MRD	$11.13	5.75%	57.20%
51	Melcor Real Estate Investment Trust	MR.UN	$4.70	10.21%	53.12%
52	Mint Income Fund	MID.UN	$6.48	7.41%	82.75%
43	Morguard Real Estate Investment Trust	MRT.UN	$5.40	4.44%	27.31
53	Mullen Group Limited	MTL	$15.29	4.71%	11.29%

N

i	66	National Bank of Canada	NA	$98.71	4.13%	41.35%
	20	Nergenrx Inc	NXG	$0.30	6.67%	-0.37%
	41	Neo Performance Materials Inc	NEO	$8.20	4.88%	4.25%
	20	Newport Exploration Limited	NWX	$0.25	15.69%	0%
ci	63	Nexus Industrial Real Estate Investment Tst	NXR.UN	$8.42	7.60%	105.25%
c	61	Northland Power Inc	NPI	$26.72	4.48%	40.42%
ci	51	Northwest Healthcare Properties REIT	NWH.UN	$6.28	12.74%	26.22%

O

51	Olympia Financial Group Inc	OLY	$71.75	7.59%	27.79%
49	Orca Energy Group Inc	ORC.B	$5.24	10.12%	44.90%

P

	62	Paramount Resources Limited	POU	$28.80	5.21%	48.39%
	65	Parex Resources Inc	PXT	$26.56	5.65%	58.11%
	48	Parkland Corporation	PKI	$33.00	4.12%	2.29%
i	69	Pembina Pipeline Corporation	PPL	$41.65	6.41%	32.60%
	58	Peyto Exploration & Development Corporation	PEY	$10.96	12.04%	61.37%
	47	PHX Energy Services Corporation	PHX	$6.06	9.90%	13.81%
	47	Pine Cliff Energy Limited	PNE	$1.43	9.09%	40.69%
	21	Pine Trail Real Estate Investment Trust	PINE>UN	$0.06	6.00%	-34.9%
	55	Pipestone Energy Corporation	PIPE	$2.27	5.29%	48.59%
ci	49	Pizza Pizza Royalty Corporation	PZA	$14.81	6.08	98.24%
c	49	Plaza Retail Real Estate Investment Trust	PLZ.UN	$3.97	7.05%	59.81%
i	47	Polaris Renewable Energy Inc	PIF	$14.25	5.71%	24.70%
ci	64	Power Corporation	POW	$35.66	5.89%	4.19%
	36	Precious Metal and Mining Trust	MMP.UN	$2.04	5.88%	0%
	37	Premium Income Corporation	PIC.A	$4.95	16.42%	70.34%
	30	Prime Dividend Corporation	PDV	$5.60	10.24%	0%
	37	Propel Holdings Inc	PRL	$7.50	5.33%	16.13%
ci	54	Pro Real Estate Investment Trust	PRV.UN	$5.32	8.45%	51.98%

Q/R

10	Real Estate Split Corporation	RS	$13.90	11.22%	0%
20	RE Royalties Ltd	RE	$0.72	5.56%	35.06%
ci 57	Riocan Real Estate Investment Trust	REI.UN	$19.20	5.83%	15.21%
34	Rogers Sugar Inc	RSI	$5.77	6.24%	1.76%
68	Royal Bank of Canada	RY	$125.52	4.30%	35.97%
56	Russel Metals Inc	RUS	$36.13	4.43%	9.67%

S

35	Sagicor Financial Company Limited	SFC	$4.40	6.91%	-9.26%
25	Sailfish Royalty Corporation	FISH	$0.81	8.18%	77.10%
42	Secure Energy Services Inc	SES	$6.49	6.16%	4.30%
36	Sienna Senior Living Inc	SIA	$11.20	8.36%	1.73%
30	Slate Grocery Real Estate Investment Trust	SGR.UN	$13.15	8.71%	0%
35	Slate Office Real Estate Investment Trust	SOT.UN	$1.97	6.09%	36.63%
i 60	Smart Centres Real Estate Investment Trust	SRU.UN	$23.71	7.80%	46.60%
30	Source Rock Royalties Ltd	SRR	$0.78	8.46%	41.31%
26	SSC Security Services Corporation	SECU	$2.79	4.30%	0.09%
27	Stingray Group Inc	RAY.B	$5.36	5.60%	20.34%
62	Suncor Energy Inc	SU	$39.09	5.33%	21.60%
ci 62	Sun Life Financial Inc	SLF	$67.40	4.45%	34.16%
36	Superior Plus Corporation	SPB	$9.35	7.70%	-2.98%
52	Surge Energy Inc	SGY	$7.99	6.01%	32.62%
23	Sustainable Power & Infrastructure Split Corp	PWI	$6.50	12.31%	0%

T

c 62	TC Energy Corporation	TRP	$51.67	7.20%	22.61%
12	TDB Split Corporation	XTD	$4.03	14.89%	0%
59	Telus Corporation	T	$24.32	5.98%	14.90%
50	The North West Company Inc	NWC	$31.90	4.76%	7.21%
73	The Toronto-Dominion Bank	TD	$83.88	4.58%	34.35%
30	Tidewater Midstream and Infrastructure Ltd	TWM	$0.96	4.17%	1.00%
23	Tier One Capital LP	TLP.UN	$3.00	16.67%	0%
ci 48	Timbercreek Financial Corporation	TF	$7.51	9.19%	59.21%
26	Titan Mining Corporation	TI	$0.43	9.30%	-7.09%
19	Top 10 Split Trust	TXT.UN	$2.09	6.76%	0%
41	Topaz Energy Corporation	TPZ	$20.92	5.74%	35.60%
42	TransAlta Renewables Inc	RNW	$13.24	7.10%	16.98%
51	Transcontinental Inc	TCL.A	$13.45	6.69%	6.53%
49	Transcontinental Inc	TCL.B	$13.58	6.63%	6.53%
48	Trican Well Service Ltd	TCW	$3.67	4.36%	16.26%
37	True North Commercial Real Estate invest Trust	TNT.UN	$2.52	11.79%	6.11%

U/V/W

45	Urbanfund Corporation	UFC	$1.03	4.85%	42.48%

55	**Wajax Corporation**	WJX	$27.28	4.84%	5.69%
33	**Wall Financial Corporation**	WFC	$19.35	15.50%	31.72%
34	**Western Forest Products Inc**	WEF	$1.05	4.76%	0.70%
52	**Westshore Terminals**	WTE	$32.05	4.37	36.44%
62	**Whitecap Resources Inc**	WCP	$9.59	6.04%	42.89%

X/Y/Z

ci 45	**Yellow Pages Limited**	Y	$12.30	6.50%	28.34%
31	**Zoomermedia Ltd**	ZUM	$0.04	6.67%	4.07%

CHAPTER 8

SORTED BY DIVIDEND (1ch8)

In Chapter Eight the high dividend stocks are sorted in descending order by dividend percent. This is useful when trying to find a safe stock paying a higher dividend yield percent. You may want to offset a lower dividend paying stock that you previously added to your portfolio (as explained in Chapter 5. Several high scoring stocks are paying a dividend under 5%).

Because of the way the score is constructed, it is entirely possible for a company paying a dividend of less than 3% to have a score in the sixties, even in the seventies. Many companies can be financially strong but not paying a high enough dividend to interest an investor seeking high, safe dividend yields for their portfolio.

The attractive income tax advantages given to Canadians receiving dividends only applies to stocks listed on Canadian stock exchanges. If you choose to invest in foreign stocks, it is recommended that you investigate what tax hold backs you will encounter on your dividend earnings. Also be aware that that currency exchange transfer charges will be encountered.

Some experts advise that you should diversify your portfolio by including stocks from several countries. You may want to look at stocks listed my book **New York Stock Exchange's 108 Best High Dividend Stocks,** which lists 24 high dividend foreign stocks traded on that exchange.

You can also achieve similar foreign diversification (2ch8) by investing in Canadian companies who do a high percentage of their business in foreign countries. Some of the Canadian banks and insurance companies are realizing more than 30% of their revenues from foreign sources. Several REITs own properties in the United States and Europe.

Six large Canadian banks dominate Canada's blue chips. They not only operate coast-to-coast through a network of thousands of branches but also internationally. The TD Bank has almost as many branches in the USA as they have in Canada. Some of these banks have been paying ever increasing dividends without interruptions for almost 200 years.

SCORE..	COMPANY	SYMBOL..	PRICE	DIVIDEND	OP. MARGIN
	Dividend Yield %				
	46% to 11%				
22	Alpine Summit Energy Partners Inc	ALPS.U	$0.81	**46.67%**	22.89%
19	Dividend Growth Split Corporation	DGS	$5.21	**23.03%**	0%
18	Automotive Finco Corporation	AFCC	$1.05	**19.45%**	0%
27	Mackenzie Master LP	MKZ.UN	$0.45	**18.60%**	85.87%
35	Financial 15 Split Corporation	FTN	$8.72	**17.30%**	0%
23	Tier One Capital LP	TLP.UN	$3.00	**16.67%**	0%
37	Premium Income Corporation	PIC.A	$4.95	**16.42%**	70.34%
35	Dividend 15 Split Corporation	DFN	$7.43	**16.15%**	77.95%
20	Newport Exploration Limited	NWX	$0.25	**15.69%**	0%
33	Wall Financial Corporation	WFC	$19.35	**15.50%**	31.72%
25	Canadian Banc Corp	BK	$13.18	**15.46%**	0%
12	TDB Split Corporation	XTD	$4.03	**14.89%**	0%
22	Brompton Lifeco Split Corporation	LCS	$6.05	**14.88%**	0%
27	Life & Banc Split Corporation	LBS	$8.58	**13.99%**	0%
36	Brookfield Global Infrastructure Securities IF	BGI	$4.46	**13.49%**	66.02%
51	Northwest Healthcare Properties REIT	NWH.UN	$6.28	**12.74%**	26.22%
23	Fiera Capital Corporation	FSZ	$6.83	**12.59%**	10.28%
38	Gear Energy Ltd	GXE	$0.97	**12.37%**	39.96%
28	Inovalis Real Estate Investment Trust	INO.UN	$3.34	**12.35%**	-136.97%
23	Sustainable Power & Infrastructure Split Corp	PWI	$6.50	**12.31%**	0%
18	Global Dividend Growth Split Corporation	GDV	$9.91	**12.11%**	0%
58	Peyto Exploration & Development Corporation	PEY	$10.96	**12.04%**	61.37%
37	True North Commercial Real Estate invest Trust	TNT.UN	$2.52	**11.79%**	6.11%
17	Dividend Select 15 Corporation	DS	$6.81	**11.56%**	0%
10	Real Estate Split Corporation	RS	$13.90	**11.22%**	0%
24	Brompton Split Bank Corporation	SBC	$10.70	**11.21%**	0%
	Dividend Yield				
	10% to 8%				
56	Canacol Energy Ltd	CNE	$10.05	**10.35%**	33.21%
31	E Split Corporation	ENS	$15.15	**10.30%**	0%
30	Prime Dividend Corporation	PDV	$5.60	**10.24%**	0%
51	Melcor Real Estate Investment Trust	MR.UN	$4.70	**10.21%**	53.12%
69	Birchcliff Energy Ltd	BIR	$7.89	**10.14%**	55.18%
49	Orca Energy Group Inc	ORC.B	$5.24	**10.12%**	44.90%
56	Cardinal Energy Ltd	CJ	$7.18	**10.03%**	50.09%

47	PHX Energy Services Corporation	PHX	$6.06	**9.90%**	13.81%
46	Firm Capital Property Trust	FCD.UN	$5.30	**9.81%**	68.44%
30	American Hotel Income Properties REIT Ltd	HOT.U	$1.85	**9.73%**	-1.07%
48	Alvopetro Energy Ltd	ALV	$7.94	**9.54%**	61.69%
40	Decisive Dividend Corporation	DE	$6.65	**9.32%**	6.02%
26	Titan Mining Corporation	TI	$0.43	**9.30%**	-7.09%
39	Builders Capital Mortgage Corporation	BCF	$8.50	**9.28%**	-77.42%
63	Canoe EIT Income Fund	EIT.UN	$12.93	**9.28%**	85.75%
53	CanWel Building Materials Group Ltd	DBM	$6.09	**9.20**	4.48%
48	Timbercreek Financial Corporation	TF	$7.51	**9.19%**	59.21%
47	Pine Cliff Energy Limited	PNE	$1.43	**9.09%**	40.69%
42	Bridgemarq Real Estate Services Inc	BRE	$14.91	**9.05%**	34.85%
34	BTB Real Estate Investment Trust	BTB.UN	$3.32	**9.04%**	0%
54	McCan Mortgage Corporation	MKP	$15.95	**9.03%**	33.37%
53	Firm Capital Mortgage Investment Corporation	FC	$10.70	**8.75%**	49.72%
30	Slate Grocery Real Estate Investment Trust	SGR.UN	$13.15	**8.71%**	0%
....42	Corus Entertainment Inc	CJR.B	$1.39	**8.63%**	-19.38%
30	Source Rock Royalties Ltd	SRR	$0.78	**8.46%**	41.31%
54	Pro Real Estate Investment Trust	PRV.UN	$5.32	**8.45%**	51.98%
59	Labrador Iron Ore Royalty Corporation	LIF	$30.88	**8.44%**	75.90%
49	Diversified Royalty Corporation	DIV	$2.85	**8.42%**	73.68%
36	Sienna Senior Living Inc	SIA	$11.20	**8.36%**	1.73%
62	Alaris Equity Partners	AD.UN	$16.36	**8.31%**	85.00%
53	Boston Pizza Royalties Income Fund	BPF.UN	$15.48	**8.29%**	96.94%
25	Sailfish Royalty Corporation	FISH	$0.81	**8.18%**	77.10%
31	Big Pharma Split Corporation	PRM	$15.15	**8.17%**	0%
56	Goodfellow Inc	GDL	$12.35	**8.10%**	6.40%
47	Artis Real Estate Investment Trust	AX.UN	$7.44	**8.06%**	2.43%
40	Hemisphere Energy Corporation	HME	$1.24	**8.06%**	41.32%
33	Australian Real Estate Investment Trus	HRR.UN	$8.22	**8.03%**	0%
57	Freehold Royalties Limited	FRU	$13.48	**8.01%**	64.06%

Dividend Yield
7% to 6%

72	Allied Properties REIT	AP.UN	$23.03	**7.82%**	41.24%
60	Smart Centres Real Estate Investment Trust	SRU.UN	$23.71	**7.80%**	46.60%
36	Superior Plus Corporation	SPB	$9.35	**7.70%**	-2.98%
51	Olympia Financal Group Inc	OLY	$71.75	**7.59%**	27.79%
53	Acadian Timber Corporation	ADN	$15.64	**7.42%**	19.75%
52	Mint Income Fund	MID.UN	$6.48	**7.41%**	82.75%
51	Atrium Mortgage Investment Corporation	AI	$12.20	**7.38%**	84.28%
44	Chesswood Group Ltd	CHW	$8.14	**7.37%**	14.73%
52	Inplay Oil Corporation	IPO	$2.45	**7.35%**	42.65%
41	Findev Inc	FDI	$0.41	**7.23%**	72.30%
62	TC Energy Corporation	TRP	$51.67	**7.20%**	22.61%
26	International Clean Power Dividend Fund	CLP.UN	7.01	**7.13%**	0%
42	TransAlta Renewables Inc	RNW	$13.24	**7.10%**	16.98%

56	Enbridge Inc	ENB	$50.26	**7.06%**	12.92%
49	Plaza Retail Real Estate Investment Trust	PLZ.UN	$3.97	**7.05%**	59.81%
56	Automotive Properties REIT	APR.UN	$11.56	**6.96%**	102.86%
42	Chemtrade Logistcs Income Fund	CHE.UN	$8.63	**6.95%**	12.80%
15	Big Banc Split Corporation	BNK	$11.46	**6.93%**	0%
51	Dream Office Real Estate Investment Trust	D.UN	$14.45	**6.92%**	6.71%
35	Sagicor Financial Company Limited	SFC	$4.40	**6.91%**	-9.26%
30	Amerigo Resources Ltd	ARG	$1.75	**6.86%**	7.97%
41	KP Tissue Inc	KPT	$10.48	**6.87%**	0%
48	Energy Income Fund	ENI.UN	$1.77	**6.78%**	69.72%
19	Top 10 Split Trust	TXT.UN	$2.09	**6.76%**	0%
38	McChip Resources Inc	MCS	$0.89	**6.74%**	0%
27	Canadian High Income Equity Fund	CIQ.UN	$7.13	**6.73%**	0%
26	Extendicare Inc	EXE	$7.16	**6.70%**	1.66%
51	Transcontinental Inc	TCL.A	$13.45	**6.69%**	6.53%
20	Nergenrx Inc	NXG	$0.30	**6.67%**	-0.37%
31	Zoomermedia Ltd	ZUM	$0.04	**6.67%**	4.07%
35	Chartwell Retirement Residences	CSH.UN	$9.23	**6.63%**	4.92%
49	Transcontinental Inc	TCL.B	$13.58	**6.63%**	6.53%
48	Dominion Lending Centres Inc	DLCG	$2.42	**6.61%**	0%
48	Dream Impact Trust	MPCT.UN	$2.42	**6.61%**	0%
45	Yellow Pages Limited	Y	$12.30	**6.50%**	28.34%
31	Dexterra Croup Inc	DXT	$5.40	**6.48%**	1.61%
69	Pembina Pipeline Corporation	PPL	$41.65	**6.41%**	32.60%
32	Blue Ribbon Inc	RBN.UN	$7.62	**6.30%**	0%
42	Canadian Net Real Estate Income Trust	NET.UN	$5.48	**6.30%**	69.32%
52	Keyera Corporation	KEY	$30.48	**6.30%**	6.45%
34	Rogers Sugar Inc	RSI	$5.77	**6.24%**	1.76%
54	Headwater Exploration Inc	HWX	$6.42	**6.23%**	53.16%
46	First National Financial Corporation	FN	$38.50	**6.23%**	14.77%
42	Secure Energy Services Inc	SES	$6.49	**6.16%**	4.30%
30	Corby Spirit and Wine Limited	CSW.B	$13.65	**6.15%**	19.71%
55	Becker Milk Company Limited	BEK.B	$13.00	**6.15%**	31.05%
35	Slate Office Real Estate Investment Trust	SOT.UN	$1.97	**6.09%**	36.63%
42	Evertz Technologies Limited	ET	$12.50	**6.08%**	20.83%
49	Pizza Pizza Royalty Corporation	PZA	$14.81	**6.08%**	98.24%
43	Ecora Resources PLC	ECOR	$2.03	**6.05%**	79.88%
68	Bank of Nova Scotia	BNS	$68.19	**6.04%**	38.84%
62	Whitecap Resources Inc	WCP	$9.59	**6.04%**	42.89%
72	Manulife Financial Corporation	MFC	$24.16	**6.04%**	38.44%
63	BCE Inc	BCE	$64.44	**6.01%**	21.04%
52	Surge Energy Inc	SGY	$7.99	**6.01%**	32.62%
72	Canadian Imperial Bank of Commerce	CM	$56.66	**6.00%**	30.29%
21	Pine Trail Real Estate Investment Trust	PINE>UN	$0.06	**6.00%**	-34.9%

Dividend Yield
5%

59	Telus Corporation	T	$24.32	**5.98%**	14.90%
51	European Residential Real Estate Investment Trust	ERE.UN	$2.97	**5.92%**	58.07%
46	Crombie Real Estate Investment Trust	CRR.UN	$15.08	**5.90%**	59.57%
64	Power Corporation	POW	$35.66	**5.89%**	4.19%
36	Precious Metal and Mining Trust	MMP.UN	$2.04	**5.88%**	0%
57	Riocan Real Estate Investment Trust	REI.UN	$19.20	**5.83%**	15.21%
54	H&R Real Estate Investment Trust	HR.UN	$10.36	**5.79%**	15.54%
41	Alphamin Resources Corporation	AFM	$1.04	**5.77%**	40.6%
54	CI Financial Corporation	CIX	$12.53	**5.75%**	24.91%
56	Melcor Developments Limited	MRD	$11.13	**5.75%**	57.20%
41	Topaz Energy Corporation	TPZ	$20.92	**5.74%**	35.60%
47	Polaris Renewable Energy Inc	PIF	$14.25	**5.71%**	24.70%
37	Aecon Group Inc	ARE	$13.10	**5.65%**	2.07%
65	Parex Resources Inc	PXT	$26.56	**5.65%**	58.11%
44	Corby Spirit and Wine Limited	CSW.A	$15.01	**5.60%**	19.71%
27	Stingray Group Inc	RAY.B	$5.36	**5.60%**	20.34%
37	AirBoss of America Corporation	BOS	$7.15	**5.59%**	7.27%
48	CT Real Estate Investment Trust	CRT.UN	$15.55	**5.58%**	56.11%
20	RE Royalties Ltd	RE	$0.72	**5.56%**	35.06%
64	IGM Financial Inc	IGM	$40.73	**5.52%**	29.95%
65	Great-West Lifeco Inc	GWO	$38.07	**5.46%**	8.94%
58	AGF Management	AGF.B	$8.14	**5.41%**	16.97%
52	Choice Properties Real Estates Investment Trust	CHP.UN	$13.93	**5.38%**	49.79%
44	Innergex Renewable Energy **Inc**	INE	$13.39	**5.38%**	22.34%
44	Exco Technologies Ltd	XTC	$7.82	**5.37%**	6.12%
35	Dream Residential Real Estate Investment Trust	DRR.U	$7.85	**5.35%**	34.18%
62	Suncor Energy Inc	SU	$39.09	**5.33%**	21.60%
37	Propel Holdings Inc	PRL	$7.50	**5.33%**	16.13%
16	C-Com Satellite Systems Inc	CMI	$0.90	**5.32%**	1.72%
39	A&W Revenue Royalties Income Fund	AW.UN	$36.25	**5.30%**	0%
52	Capital Power Corporation	CPX	$43.77	**5.30%**	9.05%
62	Cogeco Inc	CGO	$55.29	**5.29%**	25.24%
55	Pipestone Energy Corporation	PIPE	$2.27	**5.29%**	48.59%
66	Canadian Western Bank	CWB	$24.22	**5.28%**	42.21%
62	Paramount Resources Limited	POU	$28.80	**5.21%**	48.39%
39	Andrew Peller Limited	ADW.A	$4.75	**5.18%**	0.05%
36	Caribbean Utilities Company Limited	CUP.U	$13.75	**5.09%**	12.00%
67	Dream Industrial Real Estate Investment Trust	DIR.UN	$13.79	**5.08%**	64.39%
43	Algonquin Power & Utilities Corporation	AQN	$11.60	**5.06%**	11.16%

Dividend Yield
4% to 3%

76	Bank of Montreal	BMO	$123.94	**4.62%**	45.08%
43	Bird Construction Inc	BDT	$8.69	**4.94%**	2.80%
26	High Artic Energy Services Inc	HWO	$1.19	**4.92%**	41.92%
69	Emera Inc	EMA	$56.55	**4.88%**	24.28%
41	Neo Performance Materials Inc	NEO	$8.20	**4.88%**	4.25%

69	AltaGas Ltd	ALA	$22.90	**4.87%**	6.62%
45	Urbanfund Corporation	UFC	$1.03	**4.85%**	42.48%
55	Wajax Corporation	WJX	$27.28	**4.84%**	5.69%
50	The North West Company Inc	NWC	$31.90	**4.76%**	7.21%
34	Western Forest Products Inc	WEF	$1.05	**4.76%**	0.70%
53	Mullen Group Limited	MTL	$15.29	**4.71%**	11.29%
59	Exchange Income Corporation	EIF	$53.65	**4.70%**	11.21%
58	Cogeco Communications Inc	CCA	$66.27	**4.68%**	25.73%
46	Canadian Utilities Limited	CU.X	$38.59	**4.65%**	28.87%
76	Bank of Montreal	BMO	$123.94	**4.62%**	45.08%
56	Algoma Central Corp	ALC	$15.70	**4.59%**	15.09%
60	Canadian Utilities Limited	CU	$39.14	**4.58%**	29.87%
73	The Toronto-Dominion Bank	TD	$83.88	**4.58%**	34.35%
26	Elysee Development Corporation	ELC	$0.44	**4.49%**	0%
68	Canadian Natural Resources Limited	CNQ	$80.89	**4.45%**	34.90%
62	Sun Life Financial Inc	SLF	$67.40	**4.45%**	34.16%
43	Morguard Real Estate Investment Trust	MRT.UN	$5.40	**4.44%**	27.31
56	Russel Metals Inc	RUS	$36.13	**4.43%**	9.67%
44	Cascades Inc	CAS	$10.90	**4.40%**	0.74%
64	Crescent Point Energy Corporation	CPG	$9.10	**4.40%**	19.12%
48	Information Services Corporation	ISV	$20.97	**4.39%**	23.64%
52	Westshore Terminals	WTE	$32.05	**4.37**	36.44%
65	Laurentian Bank Of Canada	LB	$42.88	**4.38%**	24.22%
48	Trican Well Service Ltd	TCW	$3.67	**4.36%**	16.26%
41	Brookfield Infrastructure Partners LP	BIP.UN	$47.47	**4.30%**	0%
26	SSC Security Services Corporation	SECU	$2.79	**4.30%**	0.09%
44	Canaccord Genuit Group Inc	CF	$8.31	**4.09%**	1.16%
68	Royal Bank of Canada	RY	$125.52	**4.30%**	35.97%
61	Atco Limited	ACO.X	$45.95	**4.28%**	26.36%
38	Accord Financial Corporation	ACD	$7.14	**4.20%**	39.61%
12	DRI Healthcare Trust	DHT.U	$7.15	**4.20%**	0%
30	Tidewater Midstream and Infrastructure Ltd	TWM	$0.96	**4.17%**	1.00%
66	National Bank of Canada	NA	$98.71	**4.13%**	41.35%
51	Atco Limited	ACO.Y	$46.21	**4.12%**	26.36%
48	Parkland Corporation	PKI	$33.00	**4.12%**	2.29%
53	B2 Gold Corporation	BTO	$5.55	**4.03%**	29.00%
47	Brookfield Asset Management Limited	BAM	$44.01	**4.01%**	62.20%
37	Dynacor Group Inc	DNG	$3.00	**4.00%**	8.86%
55	Killam Apartment Real Estate Investment Trust	KMP...$17.50		**4.00%**	38.93%
37	Medical Facilities Corporation	DR	$8.05	**4.00%**	7.80%
56	BSR Real Estate Investment Trust	HOM.U	$13.20	**3.94%**	39.61%
73	Granite Real Estate Investment Trust	GRT.UN	$82.87	**3.86%**	64.14%
45	Brookfield Renewable Corporation	BEPC	$46.90	**3.85%**	81.07%
37	K-Bro Linen Inc	KBL	$31.15	**3.85%**	4.86%
37	Gamehost Inc	GH	$9.53	**3.78%**	30.03%
66	GoEasy Ltd	GSY	$109.12	**3.52%**	32.99%
53	Lundin Mining Corporation	LUN	$10.32	**3.49%**	15.05%

CHAPTER 9
SORTED BY STOCK PRICE (1CH9)

Chapter Eight is sorted in descending order by stock price.

It is unusual for high priced stock (over $50) to show a quick rapid gain in share price. However, it is not unusual for low-priced stocks (under $10) to double within a year. For most high-priced stocks, you will often see hundreds of thousands, even millions of shares, being traded daily. The stock price may only move a few cents up or down each day. The price bids of buyers and sellers often cancel out each other which keeps the share price steady.

What many investors hope to find is a low-priced stock with a high score. Your chances of seeing a $5 stock double are far greater than if the stock were $100. Since you are investing equally in different stocks, if you were investing $100,000, you would be able to buy 20,000 of the $5 stocks. If the price went up $5 to $10 you have doubled your money. That stock is now worth $200,000.

If the same $100,000 was invested in a $100 stock, you would have 1,000 Shares. If that stock went up $5, you would now have $105,000. A 5% return on an investment is not bad but if both the $5 stock and the $100 stock had good scores of 50, would you not prefer doubling their money? Thus, price must always be taken in consideration with the stock score. For a safe, balanced portfolio with potential to grow and provide a good dividend income, you need both high-and-low-priced stocks, as explained in Chapter five.

It is not too surprising that those stocks that are the highest price in this list usually score over 50. However, the highest priced stocks are not necessarily the ones that are paying the highest dividends, nor do they have the best potential for share price growth. In Chapter 10, you will find a page for each of the 215 stocks listed in this book. The pages are sorted in alphabetical order by company name. Here you will find historical share prices and dividend payments going back 24 years if they have been around that long. These historical trends give you a good idea as to how much of a growth in share price and dividend payout you might expect in the future.

In 1991 I proved in the commercial risk scores I was calculating for 2,200,000 business that like human beings, companies also have consistent characters. If the management of the company is focused on profits and growth you will see this behavior repeating itself for decades. Like DNA, profitable behavior is instilled in each generation of executive by the executives that preceded them.

This does not mean that companies can not become unprofitable and fail, but it reduces the risk of this happening. Running a business is a constant job of adapting the business to new technologies, new competitors, and new challenges. Companies are not blocks of wood. They are constantly adjusting and readjusting to the changing needs of their existing customers while trying to attract new customers. Most companies experience a loss of at least 20% of their customers each year through normal attrition. A financially strong company has learned over many decades how to constantly reinvent itself and replenish that normal attrition.

In the following chart there are 4 stocks that cost less than $5 a share who score over 50. Such low-priced stocks with good scores could indicate a bargain with the potential for good capital gain and a significant dividend yield percent.

Before buying a share always re-score the stock and do a Google search (2ch9) to see if any serious negatives have been reported since the scores in the book were calculated. (*enter in the Google search window the company name and stock symbol along with words "complaints" and "legals".*) Most stocks are stable but doing this final re-scoring check is still recommended.

SCORE..	COMPANY	SYMBOL..	PRICE	DIVIDEND	OP. MARGIN
		$125.52 to $40.73			
68	Royal Bank of Canada	RY	$125.52	4.30%	35.97%
76	Bank of Montreal	BMO	$123.94	4.62%	45.08%
66	GoEasy Ltd	GSY	$109.12	3.52%	32.99%
66	National Bank of Canada	NA	$98.71	4.13%	41.35%
73	The Toronto-Dominion Bank	TD	$83.88	4.58%	34.35%
73	Granite Real Estate Investment Trust	GRT.UN	$82.87	3.86%	64.14%
68	Canadian Natural Resources Limited	CNQ	$80.89	4.45%	34.90%

51	Olympia Financal Group Inc	OLY	**$71.75**	7.59%	27.79%
68	Bank of Nova Scotia	BNS	**$68.19**	6.04%	38.84%
62	Sun Life Financial Inc	SLF	**$67.40**	4.45%	34.16%
58	Cogeco Communications Inc	CCA	**$66.27**	4.68%	25.73%
63	BCE Inc	BCE	**$64.44**	6.01	21.04%
72	Canadian Imperial Bank of Commerce	CM	**$56.66**	6.00%	30.29%
69	Emera Inc	EMA	**$56.55**	4.88%	24.28%
62	Cogeco Inc	CGO	**$55.29**	5.29%	25.24%
59	Exchange Income Corporation	EIF	**$53.65**	4.70%	11.21%
62	TC Energy Corporation	TRP	**$51.67**	7.20%	22.61%
56	Enbridge Inc	ENB	**$50.26**	7.06%	12.92%
41	Brookfield Infrastructure Partners LP	BIP.UN	**$47.47**	4.30%	0%
45	Brookfield Renewable Corporation	BEPC	**$46.90**	3.85%	81.07%
51	Atco Limited	ACO.Y	**$46.21**	4.12%	26.36%
61	Atco Limited	ACO.X	**$45.95**	4.28%	26.36%
47	Brookfield Asset Management Limited	BAM	**$44.01**	4.01%	62.20%
52	Capital Power Corporation	CPX	**$43.77**	5.30%	9.05%
65	Laurentian Bank Of Canada	LB	**$42.88**	4.38%	24.22%
69	Pembina Pipeline Corporation	PPL	**$41.65**	6.41%	32.60%
64	IGM Financial Inc	IGM	**$40.73**	5.52%	29.95%

$39.14 to $20.92

60	Canadian Utilities Limited	CU	**$39.14**	4.58%	29.87%
62	Suncor Energy Inc	SU	**$39.09**	5.33%	21.60%
46	Canadian Utilities Limited	CU.X	**$38.59**	4.65%	28.87%
46	First National Financial Corporation	FN	**$38.50**	6.23%	14.77%
65	Great-West Lifeco Inc	GWO	**$38.07**	5.46%	8.94%
39	A&W Revenue Royalties Income Fund	AW.UN	**$36.25**	5.30%	0%
56	Russel Metals Inc	RUS	**$36.13**	4.43%	9.67%
64	Power Corporation	POW	**$35.66**	5.89%	4.19%
48	Parkland Corporation	PKI	**$33.00**	4.12%	2.29%
52	Westshore Terminals	WTE	**$32.05**	4.37	36.44%
50	The North West Company Inc	NWC	**$31.90**	4.76%	7.21%
37	K-Bro Linen Inc	KBL	**$31.15**	3.85%	4.86%
59	Labrador Iron Ore Royalty Corporation	LIF	**$30.88**	8.44%	75.90%
52	Keyera Corporation	KEY	**$30.48**	6.30%	6.45%
62	Paramount Resources Limited	POU	**$28.80**	5.21%	48.39%
55	Wajax Corporation	WJX	**$27.28**	4.84%	5.69%
61	Northland Power Inc	NPI	**$26.72**	4.48%	40.42%
65	Parex Resources Inc	PXT	**$26.56**	5.65%	58.11%
59	Telus Corporation	T	**$24.32**	5.98%	14.90%
66	Canadian Western Bank	CWB	**$24.22**	5.28%	42.21%
72	Manulife Financial Corporation	MFC	**$24.16**	6.0%	38.44%
60	Smart Centres Real Estate Investment Trust	SRU.UN	**$23.71**	7.80%	46.60%
72	Allied Properties REIT	AP.UN	**$23.03**	7.82%	41.24%
69	AltaGas Ltd	ALA	**$22.90**	4.87%	6.62%
48	Information Services Corporation	ISV	**$20.97**	4.39%	23.64%

41	Topaz Energy Corporation	TPZ	**$20.92**	5.74%	35.60%

$19.35 to $11.13

33	Wall Financial Corporation	WFC	**$19.35**	15.50%	31.72%
57	Riocan Real Estate Investment Trust	REI.UN	**$19.20**	5.83%	15.21%
55	Killam Apartment Real Estate Investment Trust	KMP...	**$17.50**	4.00%	38.93%
62	Alaris Equity Partners	AD.UN	**$16.36**	8.31%	85.00%
54	McCan Mortgage Corporation	MKP	**$15.95**	9.03%	33.37%
56	Algoma Central Corp	ALC	**$15.70**	4.59%	15.09%
53	Acadian Timber Corporation	ADN	**$15.64**	7.42%	19.75%
48	CT Real Estate Investment Trust	CRT.UN	**$15.55**	5.58%	56.11%
53	Boston Pizza Royalties Income Fund	BPF.UN	**$15.48**	8.29%	96.94%
53	Mullen Group Limited	MTL	**$15.29**	4.71%	11.29%
31	Big Pharma Split Corporation	PRM	**$15.15**	8.17%	0%
31	E Split Corporation	ENS	**$15.15**	10.30%	0%
46	Crombie Real Estate Investment Trust	CRR.UN	**$15.08**	5.90%	59.57%
44	Corby Spirit and Wine Limited	CSW.A	**$15.01**	5.60%	19.71%
42	Bridgemarq Real Estate Services Inc	BRE	**$14.91**	9.05%	34.85%
49	Pizza Pizza Royalty Corporation	PZA	**$14.81**	6.08	98.24%
51	Dream Office Real Estate Investment Trust	D.UN	**$14.45**	6.92%	6.71%
47	Polaris Renewable Energy Inc	PIF	**$14.25**	5.71%	24.70%
52	Choice Properties Real Estates Investment Trust	CHP.UN	**$13.93**	5.38%	49.79%
10	Real Estate Split Corporation	RS	**$13.90**	11.22%	0%
67	Dream Industrial Real Estate Investment Trust	DIR.UN	**$13.79**	5.08%	64.39%
36	Caribbean Utilities Company Limited	CUP.U	**$13.75**	5.09%	12.00%
30	Corby Spirit and Wine Limited	CSW.B	**$13.65**	6.15%	19.71%
49	Transcontinental Inc	TCL.B	**$13.58**	6.63%	6.53%
57	Freehold Royalties Limited	FRU	**$13.48**	8.01%	64.06%
51	Transcontinental Inc	TCL.A	**$13.45**	6.69%	6.53%
44	Innergex Renewable Energy Inc	INE	**$13.39**	5.38%	22.34%
42	TransAlta Renewables Inc	RNW	**$13.24**	7.10%	16.98%
56	BSR Real Estate Investment Trust	HOM.U	**$13.20**	3.94%	39.61%
25	Canadian Banc Corp	BK	**$13.18**	15.46%	0%
30	Slate Grocery Real Estate Investment Trust	SGR.UN	**$13.15**	8.71%	0%
37	Aecon Group Inc	ARE	**$13.10**	5.65%	2.07%
55	Becker Milk Company Limited	BEK.B	**$13.00**	6.15%	31.05%
63	Canoe EIT Income Fund	EIT.UN	**$12.93**	9.28%	85.75%
54	CI Financial Corporation	CIX	**$12.53**	5.75%	24.91%
42	Evertz Technologies Limited	ET	**$12.50**	6.08%	20.83%
56	Goodfellow Inc	GDL	**$12.35**	8.10%	6.40%
45	Yellow Pages Limited	Y	**$12.30**	6.50%	28.34%
51	Atrium Mortgage Investment Corporation	AI	**$12.20**	7.38%	84.28%
43	Algonquin Power & Utilities Corporation	AQN	**$11.60**	5.06%	11.16%
56	Automotive Properties REIT	APR.UN	**$11.56**	6.96%	102.86%
15	Big Banc Split Corporation	BNK	**$11.46**	6.93%	0%
36	Sienna Senior Living Inc	SIA	**$11.20**	8.36%	1.73%
56	Melcor Developments Limited	MRD	**$11.13**	5.75%	57.20%

$10.96 to $7.01

58	Peyto Exploration & Development Corporation	PEY	$10.96	12.04%	61.37%
44	Cascades Inc	CAS	$10.90	4.40%	0.74%
24	Brompton Split Bank Corporation	SBC	$10.70	11.21%	0%
53	Firm Capital Mortgage Investment Corporation	FC	$10.70	8.75%	49.72%
41	KP Tissue Inc	KPT	$10.48	6.87%	0%
54	H&R Real Estate Investment Trust	HR.UN	$10.36	5.79%	15.54%
53	Lundin Mining Corporation	LUN	$10.32	3.49%	15.05%
56	Canacol Energy Ltd	CNE	$10.05	10.35%	33.21%
18	Global Dividend Growth Split Corporation	GDV	$9.91	12.11% 0%	
62	Whitecap Resources Inc	WCP	$9.59	6.04%	42.89%
37	Gamehost Inc	GH	$9.53	3.78%	30.03%
36	Superior Plus Corporation	SPB	$9.35	7.70%	-2.98%
35	Chartwell Retirement Residences	CSH.UN	$9.23	6.63%	4.92%
64	Crescent Point Energy Corporation	CPG	$9.10	4.40%	19.12%
35	Financial 15 Split Corporation	FTN	$8.72	17.30%	0%
43	Bird Construction Inc	BDT	$8.69	4.94%	2.80%
42	Chemtrade Logistcs Income Fund	CHE.UN	$8.63	6.95%	12.80%
27	Life & Banc Split Corporation	LBS	$8.58	13.99%	0%
39	Builders Capital Mortgage Corporation	BCF	$8.50	9.28%	-77.42%
63	Nexus Industrial Real Estate Investment Trust	NXR>UN	$8.42	7.60%	105.25%
44	Canaccord Genuit Group Inc	CF	$8.31	4.09%	1.16%
33	Australian Real Estate Investment Trus	HRR.UN	$8.22	8.03%	0%
41	Neo Performance Materials Inc	NEO	$8.20	4.88%	4.25%
58	AGF Management	AGF.B	$8.14	5.41%	16.97%
44	Chesswood Group Ltd	CHW	$8.14	7.37%	14.73%
37	Medical Facilities Corporation	DR	$8.05	4.00%	7.80%
52	Surge Energy Inc	SGY	$7.99	6.01%	32.62%
48	Alvopetro Energy Ltd	ALV	$7.94	9.54%	61.69%
69	Birchcliff Energy Ltd	BIR	$7.89	10.14%	55.18%
35	Dream Residential Real Estate Investment Trust	DRR.U	$7.85	5.35%	34.18%
44	Exco Technologies Ltd	XTC	$7.82	5.37%	6.12%
32	Blue Ribbon Inc	RBN.UN	$7.62	6.30%	0%
48	Timbercreek Financial Corporation	TF	$7.51	9.19%	59.21%
37	Propel Holdings Inc	PRL	$7.50	5.33%	16.13%
47	Artis Real Estate Investment Trust	AX.UN	$7.44	8.06%	2.43%
35	Dividend 15 Split Corporation	DFN	$7.43	16.15%	77.95%
56	Cardinal Energy Ltd	CJ	$7.18	10.03%	50.09%
37	AirBoss of America Corporation	BOS	$7.15	5.59%	7.27%
12	DRI Healthcare Trust	DHT.U	$7.15	4.20%	0%
38	Accord Financial Corporation	ACD	$7.14	4.20%	39.61%
27	Canadian High Income Equity Fund	CIQ.UN	$7.13	6.73%	0%
26	International Clean Power Dividend Fund	CLP.UN	$7.01	7.13%	0%

$6.83 to $4.03

23	Fiera Capital Corporation	FSZ	$6.83	12.59%	10.28%
17	Dividend Select 15 Corporation	DS	$6.81	11.56%	0%
40	Decisive Dividend Corporation	DE	$6.65	9.32%	6.02%
23	Sustainable Power & Infrastructure Split Corp	PWI	$6.50	12.31%	0%
42	Secure Energy Services Inc	SES	$6.49	6.16%	4.30%
52	Mint Income Fund	MID.UN	$6.48	7.41%	82.75%
54	Headwater Exploration Inc	HWX	$6.42	6.23%	53.16%
51	Northwest Healthcare Properties REIT	NWH.UN	$6.28	12.74%	26.22%
53	CanWel Building Materials Group Ltd	DBM	$6.09	9.20	4.48%
47	PHX Energy Services Corporation	PHX	$6.06	9.90%	13.81%
22	Brompton Lifeco Split Corporation	LCS	$6.05	14.88%	0%
34	Rogers Sugar Inc	RSI	$5.77	6.24%	1.76%
30	Prime Dividend Corporation	PDV	$5.60	10.24%	0%
53	B2 Gold Corporation	BTO	$5.55	4.03%	29.00%
42	Canadian Net Real Estate Income Trust	NET.UN	$5.48	6.30%	69.32%
31	Dexterra Group Inc	DXT	$5.40	6.48%	1.61%
43	Morguard Real Estate Investment Trust	MRT.UN	$5.40	4.44%	27.31
27	Stingray Group Inc	RAY.B	$5.36	5.60%	20.34%
54	Pro Real Estate Investment Trust	PRV.UN	$5.32	8.45%	51.98%
46	Firm Capital Property Trust	FCD.UN	$5.30	9.81%	68.44%
49	Orca Energy Group Inc	ORC.B	$5.24	10.12%	44.90%
19	Dividend Growth Split Corporation	DGS	$5.21	23.03%	0%
37	Premium Income Corporation	PIC.A	$4.95	16.42%	70.34%
39	Andrew Peller Limited	ADW.A	$4.75	5.18%	0.05%
51	Melcor Real Estate Investment Trust	MR.UN	$4.70	10.21%	53.12%
36	Brookfield Global Infrastructure Securities IF	BGI	$4.46	13.49%	66.02%
35	Sagicor Financial Company Limited	SFC	$4.40	6.91%	-9.26%
12	TDB Split Corporation	XTD	$4.03	14.89%	0%

$3.97 to $0.25

49	Plaza Retail Real Estate Investment Trust	PLZ.UN	$3.97	7.05%	59.81%
48	Trican Well Service Ltd	TCW	$3.67	4.36%	16.26%
28	Inovalis Real Estate Investment Trust	INO.UN	$3.34	12.35%	-136.97%
34	BTB Real Estate Investment Trust	BTB.UN	$3.32	9.04%	0%
37	Dynacor Group Inc	DNG	$3.00	4.00%	8.86%
23	Tier One Capital LP	TLP.UN	$3.00	16.67%	0%
51	European Residential Real Estate Investment Trust	ERE.UN	$2.97	5.92%	58.07%
26	SSC Security Services Corporation	SECU	$2.79	4.30%	0.09%
37	True North Commercial Real Estate invest Trust	TNT.UN	$2.52	11.79%	6.11%
49	Diversified Royalty Corporation	DIV	$2.85	8.42%	73.68%
52	Inplay Oil Corporation	IPO	$2.45	7.35%	42.65%
48	Dominion Lending Centres Inc	DLCG	$2.42	6.61%	0%
48	Dream Impact Trust	MPCT.UN	$2.42	6.61%	0%
55	Pipestone Energy Corporation	PIPE	$2.27	5.29%	48.59%
19	Top 10 Split Trust	TXT.UN	$2.09	6.76%	0%
36	Precious Metal and Mining Trust	MMP.UN	$2.04	5.88%	0%
43	Ecora Resources PLC	ECOR	$2.03	6.05%	79.88%

35	Slate Office Real Estate Investment Trust	SOT.UN	$1.97	6.09%	36.63%
30	American Hotel Income Properties REIT Ltd	HOT.U	$1.85	9.73%	-1.07%
48	Energy Income Fund	ENI.UN	$1.77	6.78%	69.72%
30	Amerigo Resources Ltd	ARG	$1.75	6.86%	7.97%
47	Pine Cliff Energy Limited	PNE	$1.43	9.09%	40.69%
....42	Corus Entertainment Inc	CJR.B	$1.39	8.63%	-19.38%
40	Hemisphere Energy Corporation	HME	$1.24	8.06%	41.32%
26	High Artic Energy Services Inc	HWO	$1.19	4.92%	41.92%
18	Automotive Finco Corporation	AFCC	$1.05	19.45%	0%
34	Western Forest Products Inc	WEF	$1.05	4.76%	0.70
41	Alphamin Resources Corporation	AFM	$1.04	5.77%	40.6%
45	Urbanfund Corporation	UFC	$1.03	4.85%	42.48%
38	Gear Energy Ltd	GXE	$0.97	12.37%	39.96%
30	Tidewater Midstream and Infrastructure Ltd	TWM	$0.96	4.17%	1.00%
16	C-Com Satellite Systems Inc	CMI	$0.90	5.32%	1.72%
38	McChip Resources Inc	MCS	$0.89	6.74%	0%
22	Alpine Summit Energy Partners Inc	ALPS.U	$0.81	46.67%	22.89%
25	Sailfish Royalty Corporation	FISH	$0.81	8.18%	77.10%
30	Source Rock Royalties Ltd	SRR	$0.78	8.46%	41.31%
20	RE Royalties Ltd	RE	$0.72	5.56%	35.06%
27	Mackenzie Master LP	MKZ.UN	$0.45	18.60%	85.87%
26	Elysee Development Corporation	ELC	$0.44	4.49%	0%
26	Titan Mining Corporation	TI	$0.43	9.30%	-7.09%
41	Findev Inc	FDI	$0.41	7.23%	72.30%
20	Nergenrx Inc	NXG	$0.30	6.67%	-0.37%
20	Newport Exploration Limited	NWX	$0.25	15.69%	0%
21	Pine Trail Real Estate Investment Trust	PINE>UN	$0.06	6.00%	-34.9%
31	Zoomermedia Ltd	ZUM	$0.04	6.67%	4.07%

CHAPTER 10

215 DATA PAGES FOR 215 STOCKS (1ch10)

In Chapter 10 you will find a data page, for every Canadian common stock paying a dividend of 3.5% or more. Eleven data elements are measured in calculating a stock's IDM score. The current share price and the dividend yield are highlighted. A score Immediately allows you to compare the strengths of any group of stocks you are considering.

As much as we may search for it, the perfect stock does not exist. In building a strong portfolio of 20 stocks you must recognize that it is the strength of all 20 stocks, not any one stock that will provide you with a good income and grow your wealth.

No one can accurately predict future stock performance. Only you by studying the current and historical signs of corporate financial strength are making the decision of which h 20 stocks to add to your portfolio.

On each stock's data page is a snapshot of the stock's share price and dividend payout for each year from 2022 to 1999. You will notice that many of the stocks did not exist 20 years ago (whenever an "NA" appears this indicates the information did not exist that year, perhaps because the stock had not yet been listed on the Toronto Stock Exchange). Few stocks have consistently increased share prices and dividend payouts.

The years 2000, 2008 and 2020 have been high-lighted so that you can see what impact the market crashes in those years had upon the trend of share prices and dividend payouts. Many stocks quickly recovered which is to be remembered as we face future market crashes and recessions that occur about every five years. In calculating these annual historical share prices and dividend payouts I tried (wherever possible for a truer comparison) to choose those figures appearing closest to the same date each year.

When available, a stock's scores for 3 previous years are also displayed. A short summary of the company's operation is described.

What you are looking for in each stock's data are signs of good management, reliability, and steady growth. Things are neither good nor bad except by comparison. By comparing data pages, you can quickly build a strong portfolio of 20 stocks. It is very much a process of elimination.

Scoring the stock and the historical trend data removes much of the risk. To have faith in the stocks (2ch10) you have chosen, it is critical that you make your own choice so that you know exactly why your 20 stocks were the best that could be found for your unique portfolio.

A AND W REVENUE ROYALTIES INCOME FUND
(AW.UN)
New Addition April 2023

IDM STOCK SCORING CALCULATION

(1) Stock Price $ 36.25 — Score 8
(2) Price 4 Years Ago $ 41.41 — Score 8
(3) Current to Four Year Price Score 2
(4) Book Value $ 13.73 — Score 5
(5) Price to Book Comparison Score 0
(6) Analyst Buys #0 — Score 0

(7) Analysts Strong Buys #0 Score 0
(8) Dividend Yield % 5.30 — Score 8
(9) Operating Margin % 0 — Score 0
(10) Trading Volume 8988 — Score 0
(11) Price to Earnings 17.3 — Score 8

Total of All 11 Scores = 39

This stock's total score in 2021 was **51**, in 2020 it was **53**, in 2019 it was **53**

HISTORICAL STOCK PRICES & DIVIDEND PAYOUTS

Year	Stock	Dividend	Year	Stock	Dividend
2022	$ 41.00	$ 0.15	2010	$ 16.17	$ 0.11
2021	$ 35.52	$ 0.14	2009	$ 12.50	$ 0.11
2020	$ 27.7	$ 0.00	2008	$ 13.74	$ 0.11
2019	$ 38.53	$ 0.15	2007	$ 14.30	$ 0.10
2018	$ 32.66	$ 0.13	2006	$ 15.49	$ 0.09
2017	$ 40.19	$ 0.13	2005	$ 13.00	$0.09
2016	$29.00	$ 0.13	2004	$ 12.18	$ 0.09
2015	$28.61	$ 0.12	2003	$ 10.27	$ 0.09
2014	$ 22.24	$ 0.12	2002	$ 11.59	$ 0.04
2013	$ 21.95	$ 0.12	2001	$ NA	$ NA
2012	$ 21.51	$ 0.12	2000	$ NA	$ NA
2011	$ 21.77	$ 0.12	1999	$ NA	$ NA

NOTES: AW.UN is a limited purpose fund established to pay unit holders. It is headquartered in North Vancouver, British Columbia.

ACADIAN TIMBER CORPORATION
(ADN)
Updated April 2023

IDM STOCK SCORING CALCULATION

(1) Stock Price $ 15.64   Score 6

(2) Price 4 Years Ago $16.57 Score 6

(3) Current to Four Year Price Score 5

(4) Book Value $ 17.99   Score 6

(5) Price to Book Comparison Score 8

(6) Analyst Buys #0   Score 0

(7) Analysts Strong Buys #0   Score 0

(8) Dividend Yield % 7.42   Score 8

(9) Operating Margin % 19.75 Score 5

(10) Trading Volume   4024   Score 0

(11) Price to Earnings 7.4x   Score 9

Total of All 11 Scores = 53

This stock's total score in 2021 was **52** , in 2020 it was **51**, in 2019 it was **51**.

HISTORICAL STOCK PRICES & DIVIDEND PAYOUTS

Year	Stock	Dividend	Year	Stock	Dividend
2022	$ 19.65	$ 0.29	2010	$ 7.28	$0.05
2021	$ 18.56	$ 0.29	2009	$ 5.99	$ 0.07
2020	$ 13.09	$ 0.29	2008	$ 10.05	$ 0.07
2019	$ 15.75	$ 0.29	2007	$ 11.75	$ 0.07
2018	$19.40	$ 0.28	2006	$ 10.00	$ 0.07
2017	$18.35	$ 0.28	2005	$ NA	$ NA
2016	$ 19.50	$ 0.25	2004	$ NA	$ NA
2015	$ 17.97	$ 0.23	2003	$ NA	$ NA
2014	$13.60	$ 0.21	2002	$ NA	$ NA
2013	$15.20	$ 0.21	2001	$ NA	$ NA
2012	$ 11.11	$ 0.21	2000	$ NA	$ NA
2011	$ 11.85	$ 0.21	1999	$ NA	$ NA

NOTES: ADN is a Canada-based supplier of primary forest products. It is headquartered in Edmundston, New Brunswick.

ACCORD FINANCIAL CORPORATION

(ACD)

Updated April 2023

IDM STOCK SCORING CALCULATION

(1) Stock Price $ 7.14   Score *4*   *(7)* Analysts Strong Buys # *0* Score *0*
(2) Price 4 Years Ago $ 10.   Score *5*   *(8)* Dividend Yield %   4.20   Score *6*
(3) Current to Four Year Price Score *2*   *(9)* Operating Margin % 39.61 Score *6*
(4) Book Value $ 11.80   Score *5*   *(10)* Trading Volume 100   Score *0*
(5) Price to Book Comparison Score *8*   *(11)* Price to Earnings   47.0x   Score *2*
(6) Analyst Buys #0   Score *0*

Total of all 11 Scores = 38

This stock's score in 2021 was **NA**, in 2020 it was **NA**, in 2019 it was **43**.

HISTORICAL STOCK PRICES & DIVIDEND PAYOUTS

Year	Stock	Dividend	Year	Stock	Dividend
2022	$ 8.65	$0.07	2010	$ 5.45	$0.07
2021	$6.94	$0.05	2009	$ 6.15	$0.07
2020	$4.41	$0.05	2008	$7.50	$0.07
2019	$10.05	$0.09	2007	$8.75	$0.06
2018	$8.60	$0.09	2006	$7.70	$0.06
2017	$8.99	$0.09	2005	$8.15	$0.04
2016	$9.45	$0.09	2004	$8.35	$0.04
2015	$9.75	$0.09	2003	$5.40	$0.04
2014	$9.85	$0.08	2002	$5.50	$0.04
2013	$8.17	$0.08	2001	$6.25	$0.04
2012	$6.85	$0.07	2000	$5.20	$0.04
2011	$7.75	$0.07	1999	$4.45	$0.03

NOTES: ACD is a Canada based commercial finance company headquartered in Toronto, Ontario.

AECON GROUP INC
(ARE)

Updated April 2023

IDM STOCK SCORING CALCULATION

(1) Stock Price $ 13.10   Score 5
(2) Price 4 Years Ago $ 17.95   Score 6
(3) Current to Four Year Price Score 2
(4) Book Value $15.50   Score 1
(5) Price to Book Comparison Score 0
(6) Analyst Buys # 2   Score 3

(7) Analysts Strong Buys # 0 Score 0
(8) Dividend Yield % 5.65   Score 8
(9) Operating Margin % 2.07   Score 1
(10) Trading Volume 507159   Score 6
(11) Price to Earnings 30.8x   Score 5

Total of All 11 Scores = 37

This stock's total score in 2021 was **47** , in 2020 it was **44** , in 2019 it was **NA** .

HISTORICAL STOCK PRICES & DIVIDEND PAYOUTS

Year	Stock	Dividend	Year	Stock	Dividend
2022	$ 16.34	$ 0.18	2010	$13.71	$ 0.05
2021	$ 19.91	$ 0.17	2009	$ 9.06	$ 0.05
2020	$ 17.44	$ 0.14	2008	$ 16.79	$ 0.05
2019	$ 18.21	$ 0.14	2007	$6.11	$ 0.07
2018	$ 18.04	$ 0.13	2006	$ 6.12	$ NA
2017	$ 17.08	$ 0.13	2005	$ 6.40	$ NA
2016	$ 15.80	$ 0.12	2004	$ 5.10	$ NA
2015	$10.88	$ 0.10	2003	$ 4.75	$ 0.03
2014	$ 16.70	$ 0.09	2002	$ 5.50	$ 0.12
2013	$ 12.55	$0.08	2001	$ 3.50	$ NA
2012	$ 13.75	$ 0.07	2000	$ 3.00	$ NA
2011	$ 9.74	$ 0.05	1999	$ 2.56	$ NA

NOTES: ARE is a Canada-based construction and infrastructure development company. It is headquartered in Etobicoke, Ontario.

AGF MANAGEMENT LTD

(AGF.B)

Updated April 2023

IDM STOCK SCORING CALCULATION

(1) Stock Price $ 8.14   Score 4
(2) Price 4 Years Ago $ 5.95   Score 4
(3) Current to Four Year Price Score 9
(4) Book Value $ 15.99   Score 6
(5) Price to Book Comparison Score 8
(6) Analyst Buys # 1   Score 2

(7) Analysts Strong Buys # 0 Score 0
(8) Dividend Yield % 5.41   Score 8
(9) Operating Margin %16.97   Score 4
(10) Trading Volume 225510   Score 4
(11) Price to Earnings   7.9x   Score 9

Total of All 11 Scores = 58

This stock's total score in 2021 was **57**, in 2020 it was **54**, in 2019 it was **47**.

HISTORICAL STOCK PRICES & DIVIDEND PAYOUTS

Year	Stock	Dividend	Year	Stock	Dividend
2022	$ 7.84	$ 0.10	2010	$17.92	$ 0.26
2021	$ 7.49	$ 0.08	2009	$ 10.63	$ 0.25
2020	$ 3.83	$ 0.08	2008	$ 23.28	$ 0.25
2019	$ 5.41	$ 0.08	2007	$ 34.35	$ 0.20
2018	$ 6.70	$ 0.08	2006	$ 24.70	$ 0.18
2017	$ 6.16	$ 0.08	2005	$ 17.50	$ 0.15
2016	$ 5.18	$ 0.08	2004	$ 18.50	$ 0.11
2015	$ 8.20	$ 0.08	2003	$ 12.20	$ 0.07
2014	$13.25	$ 0.27	2002	$23.25	$ 0.07
2013	$ 10.92	$ 0.27	2001	$ 23.70	$ 0.05
2012	$ 15.58	$ 0.27	2000	$ 17.90	$ 0.04
2011	$ 19.30	$ 0.26	1999	$ 11.60	$ 0.04

NOTES: AGF.B is a diversified global asset management company with retail, institutional, alternative, and high-net-worth businesses. It is headquartered in Toronto, Ontario.

AIR BOSS OF AMERICA CORPORATION

(BOS)

New Addition April 2023

IDM STOCK SCORING CALCULATION

(1) Stock Price $ 7.15   *Score 4*   *(7) Analysts Strong Buys #2*   *Score 4*
(2) Price 4 Years Ago $ 8.10   *Score 4*   *(8) Dividend Yield % 5.59*   *Score 8*
(3) Current to Four Year Price Score 2   *(9) Operating Margin % 7.27*   *Score 0*
(4) Book Value $ 9.82   *Score 4*   *(10) Trading Volume 26583*   *Score 1*
(5) Price to Book Comparison Score 8   *(11) Price to Earnings -4.4x*   *Score 0*
(6) Analyst Buys # 1   *Score 2*

Total of All 11 Scores = 37

This stock's total score in 2021 was **NA**, in 2020 it was **NA** , in 2019 it was **NA** .

HISTORICAL STOCK PRICES & DIVIDEND PAYOUTS

Year	Stock	Dividend	Year	Stock	Dividend
2022	$ 35.82	$ 0.10	2010	$ 4.90	$ 0.02
2021	$ 37.93	$ 0.07	2009	$ 2.70	$ 0.03
2020	$ 11.50	$ 0.07	2008	$ 2.70	$ 0.03
2019	$ 8.18	$ 0.07	2007	$ 4.65	$ 0.03
2018	$ 12.39	$ 0.07	2006	$ 4.85	$ NA
2017	$ 11.96	$ 0.07	2005	$ 1.85	$ NA
2016	$ 16.06	$ 0.06	2004	$ 1.94	$ NA
2015	$ 15.35	$ 0.06	2003	$ 2.55	$ NA
2014	$ 8.30	$ 0.05	2002	$ 2.25	$ NA
2013	$ 5.34	$ 0.05	2001	$ 1.08	$ NA
2012	$ 4.97	$ 0.04	2000	$ 3.45	$ NA
2011	$ 7.40	$ 0.03	1999	$ 3.50	$ NA

NOTES: BOS manufacturers and markets rubber-based products. It is headquartered in Newmarket, Ontario.

ALARIS EQUITY PARTNERS INCOME TRUST
(AD.UN)
Updated
April 2023

IDM STOCK SCORING CALCULATION

(1) Stock Price $ 16.36   Score 6
(2) Price 4 Years Ago $ 18.22 Score 6
(3) Current to Four Year Price Score 5
(4) Book Value $ 19.84   Score 6
(5) Price to Book Comparison Score 8
(6) Analyst Buys # 0   Score 0

(7) Analysts Strong Buys # 0 Score 0
(8) Dividend Yield % 8.31   Score 10
(9) Operating Margin % 85.0 Score 10
(10) Trading Volume 44478   Score 2
(11) Price to Earnings 6.1   Score 9

Total of All 11 Scores = 62

This stock's total score in 2021 was **56** , in 2020 it was **44**, in 2019 it was **58**.

HISTORICAL STOCK PRICES & DIVIDEND PAYOUTS

Year	Stock	Dividend	Year	Stock	Dividend
2022	$ 20.30	$ 0.33	2010	$ 9.60	$ 0.08
2021	$ 16.08	$ 0.31	2009	$ 4.80	$ 0.07
2020	$ 7.52	$ 0.14	2008	$ 0	$ NA
2019	$ 20.69	$ 0.14	2007	$ 0	$ NA
2018	$ 17.36	$ 0.14	2006	$ 0	$ NA
2017	$ 22.48	$ 0.14	2005	$ 0	$ NA
2016	$ 28.90	$ 0.14	2004	$ 0	$ NA
2015	$ 33.89	$ 0.13	2003	$ 0	$ NA
2014	$ 29.53	$ 0.12	2002	$ 0	$ NA
2013	$ 30.33	$ 0.10	2001	$ 0	$ NA
2012	$ 18.57	$ 0.10	2000	$ 0	$ NA
2011	$ 13.30	$ 0.09	1999	$ 0	$ NA

NOTES: **AD.UN** is a private equity company providing financing to private companies.
It is headquartered in Calgary, Alberta.

ALGOMA CENTRAL CORPORATION

(ALC)

Updated April 2023

IDM STOCK SCORING CALCULATION

(1) Stock Price $ 15.70   *Score* 6

(2) Price 4 Years Ago $ 13.68 *Score* 5

(3) Current to Four Year Price *Score* 9

(4) Book Value $ 19.10   *Score* 6

(5) Price to Book Comparison *Score* 8

(6) Analyst Buys # 0   *Score* 0

(7) Analysts Strong Buys # 0 *Score* 0

(8) Dividend Yield % 4.59   *Score* 8

(9) Operating Margin % 15.09 *Score* 4

(10) Trading Volume 20327 *Score* 1

(11) Price to Earnings 5.7x *Score* 9

Total of All 11 Scores = 56

This stock's total score in 2021 was **43**, in 2020 it was **51**, in 2019 it was **NA**.

HISTORICAL STOCK PRICES & DIVIDEND PAYOUTS

Year	Stock	Dividend	Year	Stock	Dividend
2022	$ 17.23	$0.17	2010	$ 7.25	$ 0.04
2021	$ 13.49	$0.17	2009	$ 6.00	$ 0.04
2020	$ 13.20	$ 0.12	2008	$ 11.90	$ 0.04
2019	$13.25	$ 0.10	2007	$ 12.55	$ 0.04
2018	$ 14.67	$ 0.09	2006	$ 8.85	$ 0.03
2017	$ 12.63	$ 0.07	2005	$ 7.97	$ 0.03
2016	$ 13.43	$ 0.07	2004	$ 6.00	$ 0.03
2015	$ 16.52	$ 0.07	2003	$ 4.15	$ 0.03
2014	$ 15.39	$ 0.07	2002	$ 3.15	$ 0.03
2013	$ 14.72	$ 0.07	2001	$ 2.29	$ 0.03
2012	$ 11.71	$ 0.05	2000	$ 2.45	$ 0.03
2011	$ 9.43	$ 0.04	1999	$ 5.07	$ 0.03

NOTES: ALC is Canada based marine shipping company that operates a fleet of dry and liquid bulk carriers on the Great Lakes and St Lawrence Seaway. It is headquartered in St. Catherines, Ontario.

Algonquin Power & Utilities Corporation

(AQN)

Updated April 2023

IDM STOCK SCORING CALCULATION

(1) Stock Price $ 11.60   Score   5
(2) Price 4 Years Ago $ 15.30 Score 6
(3) Current to Four Year Price Score 2
(4) Book Value $ 10.31   Score 5
(5) Price to Book Comparison Score 1
(6) Analyst Buys # 3   Score 3

(7) Analysts Strong Buys # 0   Score 0
(8) Dividend Yield % 5.06   Score 8
(9) Operating Margin % 11.16 Score 3
(10) Trading Volume 6633093 Score 10
(11) Price to Earnings -25.6x   Score 0

Total of All 11 Scores = 43

This stock's total score in 2021 was **57**, in 2020 it was **57**, in 2019 it was **59**.

HISTORICAL STOCK PRICES & DIVIDEND PAYOUTS

Year	Stock	Dividend	Year	Stock	Dividend
2022	$ 19.38	$0.18	2010	$ 4.45	$ 0.06
2021	$ 20.16	$ 0.17	2009	$ 2.81	$ 0.02
2020	$ 19.81	$ 0.15	2008	$7.89	$ 0.07
2019	$ 15.30	$ 0.14	2007	$ 9.25	$ 0.07
2018	$ 12.24	$ 0.12	2006	$ 10.40	$ 0.07
2017	$ 12.83	$ 0.11	2005	$ 9.52	$ 0.07
2016	$ 10.67	$ 0.10	2004	$ 9.37	$ 0.23
2015	$ 9.64	$ 0.09	2003	$ 8.70	$ 0.23
2014	$ 7.62	$ 0.08	2002	$ 9.65	$ 0.23
2013	$7.52	$ 0.08	2001	$ 10.19	$ 0.23
2012	$ 6.15	$ 0.07	2000	$ 7.50	$ 0.24
2011	$ 5.37	$ 0.06	1999	$ 10.60	$ 0.24

NOTES: ALQ is a Canada based diversified international electrical generation, transmission, and distribution company. It is headquartered in Oakville, Ontario.

Allied Properties Real Estate Investment Trust (AP.UN)

Updated 13 April 2023

IDM STOCK SCORING CALCULATION

(1) Stock Price $ 23.03   Score 7
(2) Price 4 Years Ago $ 49.30   Score 8
(3) Current to Four Year Price   Score 1
(4) Book Value $ 51.43   Score 9
(5) Price to Book Comparison Score 10
(6) Analyst Buys #1   Score 2

(7) Analysts Strong Buys # 5   Score 5
(8) Dividend Yield %   7.82   Score 10
(9) Operating Margin % 41.24 Score 6
(10) Trading Volume 637451   Score 6
(11) Price to Earnings 17.4x   Score 8

Total of All 11 Scores = 72

This stock's total score in 2021 was **67**, in 2020 it was **73** , in 2019 it was **NA**

HISTORICAL STOCK PRICES & DIVIDEND PAYOUTS

Year	Stock	Dividend	Year	Stock	Dividend
2022	$ 41.73	$ 0.14	2010	$ 21.00	$ 0.11
2021	$ 42.65	$ 0.14	2009	$ 12.94	$ 0.11
2020	$ 44.56	$ 0.13	2008	$ 20.53	$ 0.11
2019	$ 47.43	$ 0.13	2007	$ 21.10	$ 0.11
2018	$ 40.45	$ 0.13	2006	$ 19.21	$ 0.10
2017	$ 36.63	$ 0.12	2005	$ 14.01	$ NA
2016	$ 35.35	$ 0.12	2004	$ 12.65	$ NA
2015	$ 40.00	$ 0.12	2003	$ 9.20	$ NA
2014	$ 34.21	$ 0.11	2002	$ NA	$ NA
2013	$ 34.49	$ 0.11	2001	$ NA	$ NA
2012	$ 27.42	$ 0.11	2000	$ NA	$ NA
2011	$ 23.15	$0.11	1999	$ NA	$ NA

NOTES: **AP.UN** is a closed-end real estate investment trust providing offices in Canada's major cities. It is headquartered in Toronto.

ALPHAMIN RESOURCES CORPORATION
(AFM)
Updated July 2023

IDM STOCK SCORING CALCULATION

(1) Stock Price $ 1.04   Score 2
(2) Price 4 Years Ago $ 0.22   Score 1
(3) Current to Four Year Price Score 10
(4) Book Value $ 0.33   Score 1
(5) Price to Book Comparison Score 0
(6) Analyst Buys # 0   Score 0

(7) Analysts Strong Buys # 0 Score 0
(8) Dividend Yield % 5.77   Score 8
(9) Operating Margin % 40.6   Score 6
(10) Trading Volume 116,611   Score 4
(11) Price to Earnings 13.5   Score 9

Total of All 11 Scores = 41

This stock's total score in 2021 was **NA**, in 2020 it was **NA**, in 2019 it was **NA**.

HISTORICAL STOCK PRICES & DIVIDEND PAYOUTS

Year	Stock	Dividend	Year	Stock	Dividend
2022	$ 0.75	$ 0.03	2010	$ 0.17	$ NA
2021	$ 0.84	$ NA	2009	$ 0.12	$ NA
2020	$ 0.19	$ NA	2008	$ 0.17	$ NA
2019	$ 0.23	$ NA	2007	$ 0.46	$ NA
2018	$ 0.27	$ NA	2006	$ 0.95	$ NA
2017	$ 0.33	$ NA	2005	$ 1.50	$ NA
2016	$ 0.27	$ NA	2004	$ 1.75	$ NA
2015	$ 0.18	$ NA	2003	$ 1.45	$ NA
2014	$ 0.22	$ NA	2002	$ 0.90	$ NA
2013	$ 0.12	$ NA	2001	$ 1.01	$ NA
2012	$ 0.50	$ NA	2000	$ 1.00	$ NA
2011	$ 0.71	$ NA	1999	$ 1.90	$ NA

NOTES: **AFM** is a Mauritius-based company, which is engaged in the production and sale of tin concentrate from the Bisie Tin mine in the Democratic Republic of the Congo (DRC).

ALPINE SUMMIT ENERGY PARTNERS INC

(ALPS.U)

Updated April 2023

IDM STOCK SCORING CALCULATION

(1) Stock Price $ 0.81   Score 1   *(7)* Analysts Strong Buys # 0   Score 0

(2) Price 4 Years Ago $0.00   Score 1   *(8)* Dividend Yield % 46.67   Score 2

(3) Current to Four Year Price   Score 0   *(9)* Operating Margin % 22.89   Score 5

(4) Book Value $ 0.26   Score 1   *(10)* Trading Volume 53986   Score 3

(5) Price to Book Comparison   Score 0   *(11)* Price to Earnings 5.8x   Score 9

(6) Analyst Buys # 0   Score 0

Total of All 11 Scores = 22

This stock's total score in 2021 was **NA**, in 2020 it was **NA**, in 2019 it was **NA**

HISTORICAL STOCK PRICES & DIVIDEND PAYOUTS

Year	Stock	Dividend	Year	Stock	Dividend
2022	$ 6.32	$ 0.03	2010	$ NA	$ NA
2021	$ NA	$ NA	2009	$ NA	$ NA
2020	$ NA	$ NA	2008	$ NA	$ NA
2019	$ NA	$ NA	2007	$ NA	$ NA
2018	$ NA	$ NA	2006	$ NA	$ NA
2017	$ NA	$ NA	2005	$ NA	$ NA
2016	$ NA	$ NA	2004	$ NA	$ NA
2015	$ NA	$ NA	2003	$ NA	$ NA
2014	$ NA	$ NA	2002	$ NA	$ NA
2013	$ NA	$ NA	2001	$ NA	$ NA
2012	$ NA	$ NA	2000	$ NA	$ NA
2011	$ NA	$ NA	1999	$ NA	$ NA

NOTES: ALPS.U is an energy developer and financial company. It is headquartered in Vancouver, British Columbia.

ALTAGAS LTD
(ALA)
Updated April 2023

IDM STOCK SCORING CALCULATION

(1) Stock Price $ 22.90   Score 7   *(7)* Analysts Strong Buys # 0   Score 0

(2) Price 4 Years Ago $ 18.65   Score 6   *(8)* Dividend Yield % 4.87   Score 8

(3) Current to Four Year Price Score 9   *(9)* Operating Margin % 6.62   Score 2

(4) Book Value $ 26.48   Score 7   *(10)* Trading Volume 1319412   Score 9

(5) Price to Book Comparison   Score 8   *(11)* Price to Earnings 16.4x   Score 8

(6) Analyst Buys # 7   Score 5

Total of All 11 Scores = 69

This stock's total score in 2021 was **58** , in 2020 it was **68** , in 2019 it was **58**

HISTORICAL STOCK PRICES & DIVIDEND PAYOUTS

Year	Stock	Dividend	Year	Stock	Dividend
2022	$ 27.78	$ 0.27	2010	$ 18.43	$ 0.18
2021	$ 22.97	$ 0.08	2009	$ 15.44	$ 0.18
2020	$ 14.90	$ 0.08	2008	$ 25.00	$ 0.17
2019	$ 17.91	$ 0.08	2007	$ 26.22	$ 0.17
2018	$ 24.78	$ 0.018	2006	$29.10	$ 0.16
2017	$ 31.31	$ 0.17	2005	$ 23.36	$ 0.15
2016	$ 30.32	$ 0.17	2004	$ 19.52	$ 0.11
2015	$ 41.92	$0.15	2003	$ NA	$ 0.08
2014	$ 45.97	$ 0.13	2002	$ NA	$ 0.06
2013	$ 35.30	$ 0.12	2001	$ NA	$ 0.03
2012	$ 30.35	$ 0.12	2000	$ NA	$ NA
2011	$ 25.06	$ 0.11	1999	$ NA	$ NA

NOTES: **ALA** an energy infrastructure company that links natural gas and gas liquids to domestic and foreign markets. It is headquartered in Calgary, Alberta.

ALVOPETRO ENERGY LTD
(ALV)
Updated April 2023

IDM STOCK SCORING CALCULATION

(1) Stock Price $ 7.94   Score 4   *(7)* Analysts Strong Buys #0   Score 0
(2) Price 4 Years Ago $ 2.85   Score 3   *(8)* Dividend Yield % 9.54   Score 10
(3) Current to Four Year Price Score 10   *(9)* Operating Margin % 61.99   Score 8
(4) Book Value $ 2.81   Score 3   *(10)* Trading Volume 24949   Score 1
(5) Price to Book Comparison   Score 0   *(11)* Price to Earnings 6.9x   Score 9
(6) Analyst Buys #0   Score 0

Total of All 11 Scores = 48

This stock's total score in 2021 was **NA** , in 2020 it was **NA**, in 2019 it was **NA** .

HISTORICAL STOCK PRICES & DIVIDEND PAYOUTS

Year	Stock	Dividend	Year	Stock	Dividend
2022	$ 4.98	$ 0.10	2010	$ NA	$ NA
2021	$ 2.67	$ NA	2009	$ NA	$ NA
2020	$ 1.80	$ NA	2008	$ NA	$ NA
2019	$ 1.43	$ NA	2007	$ NA	$ NA
2018	$ 0.44	$ NA	2006	$ NA	$ NA
2017	$ 0.57	$ NA	2005	$ NA	$ NA
2016	$ 0.87ALV	$ NA	2004	$ NA	$ NA
2015	$ 1.71	$ NA	2003	$ NA	$ NA
2014	$ 2.85	$ NA	2002	$ NA	$ NA
2013	$ NA	$ NA	2001	$ NA	$ NA
2012	$ NA	$ NA	2000	$ NA	$ NA
2011	$ NA	$ NA	1999	$ NA	$ NA

NOTES: ALV is Canada-based company, independent upstream and midstream operator in Brazil, exploring onshore natural gas potential in the state of Bahia in Brazil. The company is headquartered in Calgary, Alberta.

AMERICAN HOTEL INCOME PROPERTIES REIT LTD

(HOT.U)

Updated April 2023

IDM STOCK SCORING CALCULATION

(1) Stock Price $ 1.85   Score 2
(2) Price 4 Years Ago $ 3.29   Score 3
(3) Current to Four Year Price Score 2
(4) Book Value $ 4.72   Score 3
(5) Price to Book Comparison Score 10
(6) Analyst Buys # 0   Score 0

(7) Analysts Strong Buys # 0 Score 0
(8) Dividend Yield % 9.73   Score 10
(9) Operating Margin %-1.07 Score 0
(10) Trading Volume 2029   Score 0
(11) Price to Earnings 0.0x Score 0

Total of All 11 Scores = 30

This stock's total score in 2021 was **NA** , in 2020 it was **NA** , in 2019 it was **28**.

HISTORICAL STOCK PRICES & DIVIDEND PAYOUTS

Year	Stock	Dividend	Year	Stock	Dividend
2022	$ 3.05	$ 0.01	2010	$ NA	$ NA
2021	$ 2.98	$ NA	2009	$ NA	$ NA
2020	$ 1.81	$ 0.04	2008	$ NA	$ NA
2019	$ 5.33	$ 0.05	2007	$ NA	$ NA
2018	$ 6.23	$ 0.05	2006	$ NA	$ NA
2017	$ NA	$ NA	2005	$ NA	$ NA
2016	$ NA	$ NA	2004	$ NA	$ NA
2015	$ NA	$ NA	2003	$ NA	$ NA
2014	$ NA	$ NA	2002	$ NA	$ NA
2013	$ NA	$ NA	2001	$ NA	$ NA
2012	$ NA	$ NA	2000	$ NA	$ NA
2011	$ NA	$ NA	1999	$ NA	$ NA

NOTES: HOT.U is a Canada-based limited partnership company that invests in hotel real estate properties across the United States. Company is headquartered in Vancouver, British Columbia.

AMERIGO RESOURCES LTD

(ARG)

Updated April 2023

IDM STOCK SCORING CALCULATION

(1) Stock Price $ 1.75   *Score* 2   *(7)* Analysts Strong Buys #0   *Score* 0
(2) Price 4 Years Ago $ 1.10   *Score* 2   *(8)* Dividend Yield % 6.86   *Score* 8
(3) Current to Four Year Price *Score* 9   *(9)* Operating Margin % 7.97   *Score* 2
(4) Book Value $ 0.96   *Score* 1   *(10)* Trading Volume 232,196 *Score* 4
(5) Price to Book Comparison   *Score* 0   *(11)* Price to Earnings   62.5x *Score* 2
(6) Analyst Buys #0   *Score* 0

Total of All 11 Scores = 30

This stock's total score in 2021 was **NA** , in 2020 it was **NA** , in 2019 it was **NA**
.

HISTORICAL STOCK PRICES & DIVIDEND PAYOUTS

Year	Stock	Dividend	Year	Stock	Dividend
2022	$ 1.59	$ 0.03	2010	$ 0.89	$ NA
2021	$ 1.24	$ 0.02	2009	$ 0.32	$ NA
2020	$ 0.27	$ NA	2008	$ 2.16	$ 0.07
2019	$ 0.83	$ NA	2007	$ 3.08	$ 0.07
2018	$ 1.02	$ NA	2006	$ 2.44	$ 0.04
2017	$ 1.02	$ NA	2005	$ 2.01	$ 0.04
2016	$ 0.16	$ NA	2004	$ 1.45	$ NA
2015	$ 0.42	$ NA	2003	$ 0.67	$ NA
2014	$ 0.49	$ NA	2002	$ 0.19	$ NA
2013	$ 0.60	$ NA	2001	$ 0.28	$ NA
2012	$ 0.80	$ 0.02	2000	$ 1.04	$ NA
2011	$ 1.14	$ 0.02	1999	$ 0.84	$ NA

NOTES: ARG is a Canada-based company, producing copper concentrate and molybdenum concentrate in Chile. Company is headquartered in Vancouver, British Columbia.

ANDREW PELLER LTD

(ADW.A)

Updated April 2023

IDM STOCK SCORING CALCULATION

(1) Stock Price $ 4.75   Score 3
(2) Price 4 Years Ago $ 13.12   Score 5
(3) Current to Four Year Price Score 1
(4) Book Value $ 6.15   Score 4
(5) Price to Book Comparison Score 8
(6) Analyst Buys # 0   Score 0

(7) Analysts Strong Buys # 0 Score 0
(8) Dividend Yield % 5.18   Score 8
(9) Operating Margin % 0.05   Score 0
(10) Trading Volume 2,471   Score 0
(11) Price to Earnings 2.92x Score 10

Total of All 11 Scores = 39

This stock's total score in 2021 was **NA** , in 2020 it was **NA** , in 2019 it was **NA**.

HISTORICAL STOCK PRICES & DIVIDEND PAYOUTS

Year	Stock	Dividend	Year	Stock	Dividend
2022	$ 5.85	$ 0.06	2010	$ 2.67	$ 0.03
2021	$ 10.81	$ 0.06	2009	$ 2.50	$ 0.03
2020	$ 9.24	$ 0.05	2008	$ 3.21	$ 0.03
2019	$ 13.69	$ 0.05	2007	$ 3.74	$ 0.02
2018	$ 18.03	$ 0.05	2006	$ 2.87	$ 0.02
2017	$ 11.05	$ 0.04	2005	$ 3.16	$ 0.02
2016	$ 9.81	$ 0.04	2004	$ 2.46	$ 0.02
2015	$ 5.04	$ 0.04	2003	$ 1.83	$ 0.02
2014	$ 4.75	$ 0.03	2002	$ 1.95	$ 0.02
2013	$ 4.03	$ 0.03	2001	$ 1.25	$ 0.02
2012	$ 3.35	$ 0.03	2000	$ 1.36	$ 0.02
2011	$ 3.08	$ 0.03	1999	$ 1.54	$ 0.02

NOTES: ADW.A is a Canada-based company producing and marketing wines and craft beverage alcohol products. Company is headquartered in Grimsby, Ontario.

ARTIS REAL ESTATE INVESTMENT TRUST
(AX.UN)

Updated April 2023

IDM STOCK SCORING CALCULATION

(1) Stock Price $ 7.44   Score 4
(2) Price 4 Years Ago $7.25   Score 4
(3) Current to Four Year Price Score 7
(4) Book Value $ 19.32   Score 6
(5) Price to Book Comparison Score 10
(6) Analyst Buys # 0   Score 0

(7) Analysts Strong Buys # 0 Score 0
(8) Dividend Yield %8.06   Score 10
(9) Operating Margin % 2.43 Score 1
(10) Trading Volume 424005 Score 5
(11) Price to Earnings -26.1   Score 0

Total of All 11 Scores = 47

This stock's total score in 2021 was **57**, in 2020 it was **47**, in 2019 it was **55**.

HISTORICAL STOCK PRICES & DIVIDEND PAYOUTS

Year	Stock	Dividend	Year	Stock	Dividend
2022	$13.17	$ 0.05	2010	$ 11.35	$ 0.09
2021	$11.13	$ 0.05	2009	$ 8.23	$ 0.09
2020	$ 7.25	$ 0.04	2008	$ 16.74	$ 0.09
2019	$ 11.78	$ 0.09	2007	$ 17.24	$ 0.09
2018	$ 13.47	$ 0.09	2006	$ 14.80	$ 0.09
2017	$ 13.11	$ 0.09	2005	$ 6.30	$ 0.05
2016	$ 13.40	$ 0.09	2004	$ 4.05	$ NA
2015	$ 14.07	$ 0.09	2003	$ NA	$ NA
2014	$ 15.73	$ 0.09	2002	$ NA	$ NA
2013	$ 17.03	$ 0.09	2001	$ NA	$ NA
2012	$ 16.84	$ 0.09	2000	$ NA	$ NA
2011	$ 13.70	$ 0.09	1999	$ NA	$ NA

NOTES: AX.UN closed-end real estate investment trust that manages, leases and develops primarily industrial, office and retail properties in Canada and the United State. The Company is headquartered in Winnipeg, Manitoba.

ATCO LIMITED

(ACO.X)
Updated April 2023

IDM STOCK SCORING CALCULATION

(2) Price 4 Years Ago $ 45.95 Score 8

(3) Current to Four Year Price Score 5

(4) Book Value $ 38.42 Score 8

(5) Price to Book Comparison Score 1

(6) Analyst Buys # 4 Score 4

(8) Dividend Yield % 4.28 Score 6

(9) Operating Margin % 26.36 Score 5

(10) Trading Volume 101696 Score 4

(11) Price to Earnings 13.7 Score 9

Total of All 11 Scores = 61

This stock's total score in 2021 was **57**, in 2020 it was **59**, in 2019 it was **62** .

HISTORICAL STOCK PRICES & DIVIDEND PAYOUTS

Year	Stock	Dividend	Year	Stock	Dividend
2022	$ 45.77	$ 0.46	2010	$ 24.39	$ 0.13
2021	$ 42.19	$ 0.45	2009	$ 17.17	$ 0.13
2020	$ 38.97	$ 0.44	2008	$ 23.81	$ 0.12
2019	$ 45.00	$ 0.40	2007	$ 23.50	$ 0.11
2018	$ 41.38	$ 0.38	2006	$ 17.56	$ 0.10
2017	$ 51.71	$ 0.33	2005	$ 15.60	$ 0.10
2016	$ 39.28	$ 0.28	2004	$ 12.20	$ 0.09
2015	$ 45.12	$ 0.25	2003	$ 10.52	$ 0.08
2014	$ 53.11	$ 0.21	2002	$ 12.37	$ 0.07
2013	$ 45.96	$ 0.19	2001	$ 13.12	$ 0.07
2012	$ 34.97	$ 0.16	2000	$ 8.37	$ 0.06
2011	$ 29.35	$ 0.14	1999	$ 9.50	$ 0.05

NOTES: **ACO.X** is a Canada-based diversified company. offers workforce, residential housing, utilities, and energy Infrastructure. Its Utilities business includes Electricity and Natural Gas transmission. The company is headquartered in Calgary, Alberta.

ATCO LIMITED

(ACO.Y)

Updated May 2023

IDM STOCK SCORING CALCULATION

(1) Stock Price $ 46.21   Score 8   *(7)* Analysts Strong Buys #0   Score 0
(2) Price 4 Years Ago $ 10.83   Score 5   *(8)* Dividend Yield % 4.12   Score 6
(3) Current to Four Year Price   Score 10   *(9)* Operating Margin % 26.36 Score 5
(4) Book Value $ 38.42   Score 8   *(10)* Trading Volume 70   Score 0
(5) Price to Book Comparison   Score 1   *(11)* Price to Earnings 0.0   Score 0
(6) Analyst Buys # 5   Score 4

Total of All 11 Scores = 51

This stock's total score in 2021 was **49**, in 2020 it was **54**, in 2019 it was **55** .

HISTORICAL STOCK PRICES & DIVIDEND PAYOUTS

Year	Stock	Dividend	Year	Stock	Dividend
2022	$ 42.04	$ 0.46	2010	$ 25.74	$ 0.13
2021	$ 42.50	$ 0.45	2009	$ 18.25	$ 0.13
2020	$ 36.95	$ 0.44	2008	$ 23.50	$ 0.12
2019	$ 46.60	$ 0.40	2007	$ 23.25	$ 0.11
2018	$ 38.75	$ 0.38	2006	$ 17.74	$ 0.10
2017	$ 51.80	$ 0.33	2005	$ 15.95	$ 0.10
2016	$ 41.25	$ 0.28	2004	$ 13.17	$ 0.09
2015	$ 45.30	$ 0.25	2003	$ 10.56	$ 0.08
2014	$ 52.99	$ 0.21	2002	$ 12.81	$ 0.07
2013	$ 42.50	$ 0.19	2001	$ 12.00	$ 0.07
2012	$ 34.96	$ 0.16	2000	$ 8.25	$ 0.06
2011	$29.37	$ 0.14	1999	$ 9.92	$ 0.05

NOTES: AC0.X is a Canada-based diversified company. offers workforce, residential housing, utilities, and energy Infrastructure. Its Utilities business includes Electricity and Natural Gas transmission. The Company is headquartered in Calgary, Alberta.

ATRIUM MORTGAGE INVESTMENT CORPORATION
(AI)
Updated April 2023

(1) Stock Price $ 12.20   Score 5   *(7)* Analysts Strong Buys #0   Score 0

(2) Price 4 Years Ago $ 13.43   Score 5   *(8)* Dividend Yield % 7.38   Score 8

(3) Current to Four Year Price   Score 5   *(9)* Operating Margin % 84.28 Score 10

(4) Book Value $ 10.97   Score 5   *(10)* Trading Volume 23,857   Score 1

(5) Price to Book Comparison   Score 1   *(11)* Price to Earnings 11.5x   Score 9

(6) Analyst Buys # 1   Score 2

Total of All 11 Scores = 51

This stock's total score in 2021 was **57**, in 2020 it was **61** , in 2019 it was **55**.

HISTORICAL STOCK PRICES & DIVIDEND PAYOUTS

Year	Stock	Dividend	Year	Stock	Dividend
2022	$ 13.28	$ 0.07	2010	$ NA	$ NA
2021	$ 14.54	$ 0.07	2009	$ NA	$ NA
2020	$ 11.19	$ 0.07	2008	$ NA	$ NA
2019	$ 13.35	$ 0.07	2007	$ NA	$ NA
2018	$ 12.59	$ 0.07	2006	$ NA	$ NA
2017	$ 12.23	$ 0.07	2005	$ NA	$ NA
2016	$ 12.50	$ 0.07	2004	$ NA	$ NA
2015	$ 12.14	$ 0.07	2003	$ NA	$ NA
2014	$ 11.25	$ 0.07	2002	$ NA	$ NA
2013	$ 10.90	$ 0.07	2001	$ NA	$ NA
2012	$ 11.99	$ 0.20	2000	$ NA	$ NA
2011	$ NA	$ NA	1999	$ NA	$ NA

NOTES: AI is a non-bank lender that provides mortgages that in Canada for all types of residential, multi-residential and commercial real property. The company is headquartered in Toronto, Ontario.

AUSTRALIAN REAL ESTATE INVESTMENT TRUST (HRR.UN)

Updated April 2023

IDM STOCK SCORING CALCULATION

(1) Stock Price $ 8.22   Score 4
(2) Price 4 Years Ago $ 11.77 Score 5
(3) Current to Four Year Price Score 2
(4) Book Value $ 9.25   Score 4
(5) Price to Book Comparison Score 8
(6) Analyst Buys # 0   Score 0

(7) Analysts Strong Buys # 0 Score 0
(8) Dividend Yield % 8.03   Score 10
(9) Operating Margin % 0   Score 0
(10) Trading Volume 0   Score 0
(11) Price to Earnings -2.4x   Score 0

Total of All 11 Scores = 33

This stock's total score in 2021 was **34**, in 2020 it was **52**, in 2019 it was **33**.

HISTORICAL STOCK PRICES & DIVIDEND PAYOUTS

Year	Stock	Dividend	Year	Stock	Dividend
2022	$ 10.80	$ 0.06	2010	$ NA	$ NA
2021	$ 10.80	$ 0.06	2009	$ NA	$ NA
2020	$ 9.44	$ 0.06	2008	$ NA	$ NA
2019	$ 11.77	$ 0.06	2007	$ NA	$ NA
2018	$ 11.00	$ 0.06	2006	$ NA	$ NA
2017	$ 10.42	$ 0.06	2005	$ NA	$ NA
2016	$ 11.12	$ 0.06	2004	$ NA	$ NA
2015	$ 9.82	$ 0.06	2003	$ NA	$ NA
2014	$ 9.01	$ 0.06	2002	$ NA	$ NA
2013	$ 8.45	$ 0.06	2001	$ NA	$ NA
2012	$ NA	$ NA	2000	$ NA	$ NA
2011	$ NA	$ NA	1999	$ NA	$ NA

NOTES: HRR.UN is a Canada-based investment fund that provides unitholders with stable monthly cash distributions and the opportunity for capital appreciation. It invests in equity securities listed on the Australian Securities Exchange (ASX) issued by Australian real estate investment trusts. It is headquartered in Oakville, Ontario.

AUTOMOTIVE FINCO CORPORATION

(AFCC)

Updated April 2023

IDM STOCK SCORING CALCULATION

(1) Stock Price $ 1.05   Score 2
(2) Price 4 Years Ago $ 1.38   Score 2
(3) Current to Four Year Price Score 2
(4) Book Value $1.38   Score 2
(5) Price to Book Comparison Score 8
(6) Analyst Buys #0   Score 0

(7) Analysts Strong Buys #0 Score 0
(8) Dividend Yield % 19.54   Score 2
(9) Operating Margin % 0   Score 0
(10) Trading Volume 1,873   Score 0
(11) Price to Earnings -22.2x   Score 0

Total of All 11 Scores =18

This stock's total score in 2021 was **13**, in 2020 it was **38**, in 2019 it was **38**.

HISTORICAL STOCK PRICES & DIVIDEND PAYOUTS

Year	Stock	Dividend	Year	Stock	Dividend
2022	$ 1.70	$ 0.02	2010	$ 4.42	$ NA
2021	$ 2.00	$ 0.02	2009	$ 0.97	$ NA
2020	$ 1.42	$ 0.02	2008	$ 4.50	$ NA
2019	$ 1.35	$ 0.02	2007	$ 7.65	$ NA
2018	$ 2.20	$ 0.02	2006	$ 9.15	$ NA
2017	$ 2.93	$ 0.01	2005	$ 1.95	$ NA
2016	$ 1.42	$ NA	2004	$ 0.75	$ NA
2015	$ 1.80	$ NA	2003	$ 1.80	$ NA
2014	$ 1.65	$ NA	2002	$ 0.30	$ NA
2013	$ 1.12	$ NA	2001	$ 0.45	$ NA
2012	$ 2.70	$ NA	2000	$ 0.90	$ NA
2011	$ 10.65	$ NA	1999	$ 0.67	$ NA

NOTES: AFCC is a finance company providing debt financing and making other investments in the auto retail sector. It is headquartered in Toronto, Ontario.

AUTOMOTIVE PROPERTIES REAL ESTATE INVESTMENT TRUST

(APR.UN)

Updated April 2023

IDM STOCK SCORING CALCULATION

(1) Stock Price $ 11.56   Score 5
(2) Price 4 Years Ago $ 10.43 Score 5
(3) Current to Four Year Price Score 9
(4) Book Value $ 10.62   Score 5
(5) Price to Book Comparison Score 2
(6) Analyst Buys # 1   Score 2

(7) Analysts Strong Buys # 0   Score 0
(8) Dividend Yield % 6.96   Score 8
(9) Operating Margin % 102.86 Score 10
(10) Trading Volume 16,128   Score 1
(11) Price to Earnings 6.8x   Score 9

Total of All 11 Scores = 56

This stock's total score in 2021 was **55** , in 2020 it was **38**, in 2019 it was **59** .

HISTORICAL STOCK PRICES & DIVIDEND PAYOUTS

Year	Stock	Dividend	Year	Stock	Dividend
2022	$ 14.15	$ 0.07	2010	$ NA	$ NA
2021	$ 12.68	$ 0.07	2009	$ NA	$ NA
2020	$ 9.26	$ 0.07	2008	$ NA	$ NA
2019	$ 10.43	$ 0.07	2007	$ NA	$ NA
2018	$ 10.43	$ 0.07	2006	$ NA	$ NA
2017	$ 11.19	$ 0.07	2005	$ NA	$ NA
2016	$ 10.01	$ 0.07	2004	$ NA	$ NA
2015	$ 9.73	$ 0.09	2003	$ NA	$ NA
2014	$ NA	$ NA	2002	$ NA	$ NA
2013	$ NA	$ NA	2001	$ NA	$ NA
2012	$ NA	$ NA	2000	$ NA	$ NA
2011	$ NA	$ NA	1999	$ NA	$ NA

NOTES: APR.UN is a Canada-based open-ended real estate investment trust focused on owning and acquiring primarily income-producing automotive dealership properties. It is headquartered in Toronto, Ontario.

B2B GOLD CORP
(BTO)
Updated April 2023

IDM STOCK SCORING CALCULATION

(1) Stock Price $ 5.55   Score *4*
(2) Price 4 Years Ago $ 3.64   Score *3*
(3) Current to Four Year Price Score *9*
(4) Book Value $ 3.77   Score *3*
(5) Price to Book Comparison Score *1*
(6) Analyst Buys # 4   Score *4*

(7) Analysts Strong Buys #0   Score *0*
(8) Dividend Yield % 4.03   Score *6*
(9) Operating Margin % 29.00   Score *5*
(10) Trading Volume 3,901,102 Score *10*
(11) Price to Earnings 17.5x   Score *8*

Total of All 11 Scores =53

This stock's total score in 2021 was **NA** , in 2020 it was **NA**, in 2019 it was **NA** .

HISTORICAL STOCK PRICES & DIVIDEND PAYOUTS

Year	Stock	Dividend	Year	Stock	Dividend
2022	$ 5.45	$ 0.05	2010	$ 1.53	$ NA
2021	$ 5.92	$ 0.05	2009	$ 0.68	$ NA
2020	$ 7.04	$ 0.01	2008	$ 1.36	$ NA
2019	$ 3.69	$ NA	2007	$ NA	$ NA
2018	$ 3.69	$ NA	2006	$ NA	$ NA
2017	$ 3.43	$ NA	2005	$ NA	$ NA
2016	$ 2.79	$ NA	2004	$ NA	$ NA
2015	$ 1.89	$ NA	2003	$ NA	$ NA
2014	$ 3.15	$ NA	2002	$ NA	$ NA
2013	$ 2.53	$ NA	2001	$ NA	$ NA
2012	$ 3.73	$ NA	2000	$ NA	$ NA
2011	$ 3.22	$ NA	1999	$ NA	$ NA

NOTES: **BTO** is a Canada-based gold producer with three operating mines in Mali, the Philippines and in Namibia. It is headquartered in Vancouver, British Columbia.

BANK OF MONTREAL

(BMO)

Updated April 2023

IDM STOCK SCORING CALCULATION

(1) Stock Price $ 123.94   Score 10
(2) Price 4 Years Ago $ 98.92 Score 9
(3) Current to Four Year Price Score 9
(4) Book Value $ 104.94   Score 10
(5) Price to Book Comparison   Score 1
(6) Analyst Buys # 7   Score 5

(7) Analysts Strong Buys #0   Score 0
(8) Dividend Yield % 4.62   Score 8
(9) Operating Margin % 45.08   Score 6
(10) Trading Volume 1,515,668 Score 9
(11) Price to Earnings 7.8x   Score 9

Total of All 11 Scores = 76

This stock's total score in 2021 was **74**, in 2020 it was **66**, in 2019 it was **74**.

HISTORICAL STOCK PRICES & DIVIDEND PAYOUTS

Year	Stock	Dividend	Year	Stock	Dividend
2022	$ 136.21	$ 1.33	2010	$ 63.09	$ 0.70
2021	$ 107.46	$ 1.06	2009	$ 49.02	$ 0.70
2020	$ 70.77	$ 1.06	2008	$ 48.77	$ 0.70
2019	$ 105.82	$ 1.00	2007	$ 69.46	$ 0.68
2018	$ 97.51	$ 0.93	2006	$ 69.67	$ 0.53
2017	$ 90.67	$ 0.88	2005	$ 56.65	$ 0.46
2016	$ 82.30	$ 0.84	2004	$ 51.90	$ 0.40
2015	$ 78.82	$ 0.80	2003	$ 40.10	$ 0.33
2014	$ 76.28	$ 0.76	2002	$ 38.62	$ 0.30
2013	$ 61.37	$ 0.74	2001	$ 35.20	$ 0.28
2012	$ 58.67	$ 0.70	2000	$ 30.25	$ 0.25
2011	$ 62.14	$ 0.70	1999	$ 30.40	$ 0.23

NOTES: BMO provides a range of personal and commercial banking, wealth management, global markets and investment banking products and services.

BANK OF NOVA SCOTIA

(BNS)

Updated April 2023

IDM STOCK SCORING CALCULATION

(1) Stock Price $ 68.19   Score 9   *(7)* Analysts Strong Buys #0   Score 0
(2) Price 4 Years Ago $ 73.78   Score 9   *(8)* Dividend Yield % 6.04   Score 8
(3) Current to Four Year Price Score 5   *(9)* Operating Margin % 38.94   Score 6
(4) Book Value $ 61.46   Score 9   *(10)* Trading Volume 4,270,480   Score 10
(5) Price to Book Comparison   Score 1   *(11)* Price to Earnings 9.5   Score 9
(6) Analyst Buys # 1   Score 2

Total of All 11 Scores = 68

This stock's total score in 2021 was **72**, in 2020 it was **66**, in 2019 it was **74**.

HISTORICAL STOCK PRICES & DIVIDEND PAYOUTS

Year	Stock	Dividend	Year	Stock	Dividend
2022	$ 81.35	$ 1.00	2010	$ 51.78	$ 0.49
2021	$ 78.62	$ 0.90	2009	$ 38.18	$ 0.49
2020	$ 55.17	$ 0.90	2008	$ 46.55	$ 0.47
2019	$ 73.78	$ 0.87	2007	$ 53.39	$ 042
2018	$ 78.92	$ 0.82	2006	$ 46.52	$ 0.36
2017	$ 77.80	$ 0.76	2005	$ 39.75	$ 0.32
2016	$ 65.80	$ 0.72	2004	$ 35.40	$ 0.50
2015	$ 65.40	$ 0.68	2003	$ 29.27	$ 0.20
2014	$ 64.03	$ 0.64	2002	$ 26.97	$ 0.18
2013	$ 58.09	$ 0.60	2001	$ 22.17	$ 0.15
2012	$ 55.88	$ 0.55	2000	$ 18.62	$ 0.12
2011	$57.69	$0.52	1999	$ 16.20	$ 0.10

NOTES: BNS is an international bank and a financial services provider in Latin America, the Caribbean and Central America, and Asia. It is headquartered in Toronto, Ontario.

BCE INC
(BCE)

Updated April 2023

IDM STOCK SCORING CALCULATION

(1) Stock Price $ 64.44   Score 9
(2) Price 4 Years Ago $ 59.94 Score 9
(3) Current to Four Year Price Score 7
(4) Book Value $ 24.32   Score 7
(5) Price to Book Comparison Score 0
(6) Analyst Buys # 1   Score 2

(7) Analysts Strong Buys #0   Score 0
(8) Dividend Yield % 6.01   Score 8
(9) Operating Margin % 21.04   Score 5
(10) Trading Volume 1,470,365 Score 9
(11) Price to Earnings 21.6x   Score 7

Total of All 11 Scores =63

This stock's total score in 2021 was **64**, in 2020 it was **59,** in 2019 it was **69**.

HISTORICAL STOCK PRICES & DIVIDEND PAYOUTS

Year	Stock	Dividend	Year	Stock	Dividend
2022	$ 68.30	$ 0.92	2010	$ 30.52	$ 0.43
2021	$ 56.73	$ 0.88	2009	$ 25.13	$ 0.39
2020	$ 56.29	$ 0.83	2008	$ 36.80	$ 0.36
2019	$ 59.94	$ 0.79	2007	$ 37.39	$ 0.36
2018	$ 55.44	$ 0.76	2006	$ 27.41	$ 0.33
2017	$ 58.88	$ 0.72	2005	$ 30.04	$ 0.33
2016	$ 59.19	$ 0.68	2004	$ 27.45	$ 0.30
2015	$ 53.62	$ 0.65	2003	$ 26.86	$ 0.30
2014	$48.80	$ 0.62	2002	$ 27.84	$ 0.30
2013	$ 47.19	$ 0.58	2001	$ 35.26	$ 0.30
2012	$ 39.94	$ 0.52	2000	$42.68	$ 0.08
2011	$ 35.46	$ 0.49	1999	$ 15.74	$ 0.08

NOTES: BCE is a Canada-based communications company that provides broadband wireless, Internet, television (TV), media and business communications services. It is headquartered in Verdun, Quebec.

BECKER MILK COMPANY LIMITED
(BEK.B)
Updated April 2023

IDM STOCK SCORING CALCULATION

(1) Stock Price $ 13.00	*Score 5*	
(2) Price 4 Years Ago $ 12.41	*Score 5*	
(3) Current to Four Year Price	*Score 7*	
(4) Book Value $ 20.35	*Score 7*	
(5) Price to Book Comparison	*Score 8*	
(6) Analyst Buys # 0	*Score 0*	

(7) Analysts Strong Buys #0	*Score 0*
(8) Dividend Yield % 6.15	*Score 8*
(9) Operating Margin % 31.05	*Score 6*
(10) Trading Volume 0	*Score 0*
(11) Price to Earnings 7.2x	*Score 9*

Total of All 11 Scores = 55

This stock's total score in 2021 was **48**, in 2020 it was **51**, in 2019 it was **52**.

HISTORICAL STOCK PRICES & DIVIDEND PAYOUTS

Year	Stock	Dividend	Year	Stock	Dividend
2022	$ 14.10	$ 0.40	2010	$ 9.28	$ 0.26
2021	$ 13.45	$ 0.40	2009	$ 6.85	$ 0.26
2020	$ 11.40	$ 0.40	2008	$ 10.51	$ 0.26
2019	$ 12.41	$ 0.35	2007	$ 11.37	$ 0.26
2018	$ 13.00	$ 0.35	2006	$ 8.65	$ 0.26
2017	$ 13.74	$ 0.35	2005	$ 10.85	$ 0.26
2016	$ 13.13	$ 0.35	2004	$ 10.72	$ 0.26
2015	$ 15.76	$ 0.35	2003	$ 7.18	$ 0.26
2014	$ 17.51	$ 0.35	2002	$ 6.56	$ 0.26
2013	$ 13.04	$ 0.35	2001	$ 4.37	$ 0.26
2012	$ 10.94	$ 0.31	2000	$ 4.59	$ 0.13
2011	$ 9.19	$ 0.26	1999	$ 8.53	$ 0.13

NOTES: BEK.B is a Canada is engaged in the ownership and management of retail commercial properties in Ontario, Canada. The Company primarily leases retail stores. Its headquarters is in Toronto, Ontario.

BIG BANC SPLIT CORPORATION
(BNK)
Updated April 2023

IDM STOCK SCORING CALCULATION

(1) Stock Price $ 11.46   Score 5

(2) Price 4 Years Ago $ 0   Score 1

(3) Current to Four Year Price Score 0

(4) Book Value $ 0   Score 0

(5) Price to Book Comparison Score 1

(6) Analyst Buys #0   Score 0

(7) Analysts Strong Buys #0   Score 0

(8) Dividend Yield % 6.93   Score 8

(9) Operating Margin % 0   Score 0

(10) Trading Volume 600   Score 0

(11) Price to Earnings 0.0x   Score 0

Total of All 11 Scores =15

This stock's total score in 2021 was **15** , in 2020 it was **NA** , in 2019 it was **NA**
.

HISTORICAL STOCK PRICES & DIVIDEND PAYOUTS

Year	Stock	Dividend	Year	Stock	Dividend
2022	$ 11.46	$ 0.07	2010	$ NA	$ NA
2021	$ 13.66	$ 0.07	2009	$ NA	$ NA
2020	$ 9.20	$ 0.22	2008	$ NA	$ NA
2019	$ NA	$ NA	2007	$ NA	$ NA
2018	$ NA	$ NA	2006	$ NA	$ NA
2017	$ NA	$ NA	2005	$ NA	$ NA
2016	$ NA	$ NA	2004	$ NA	$ NA
2015	$ NA	$ NA	2003	$ NA	$ NA
2014	$ NA	$ NA	2002	$ NA	$ NA
2013	$ NA	$ NA	2001	$ NA	$ NA
2012	$ NA	$ NA	2000	$ NA	$ NA
2011	$ NA	$ NA	1999	$ NA	$ NA

NOTES: BNK is a mutual fund company. It provides preferred shares holders with fixed cumulative preferential monthly cash distributions and to return the original issue price to holders on the maturity date, and to provide holders of Class A shares with regular monthly non-cumulative cash distributions. It invests equity securities of Canadian banks.

BIG PHARMA SPLIT CORPORATION
(PRM)
Updated April 2023

IDM STOCK SCORING CALCULATION

(1) Stock Price $ 15.15   Score 6   **(7)** Analysts Strong Buys # 0   Score 0
(2) Price 4 Years Ago $ 11.60   Score 5   **(8)** Dividend Yield % 8.17   Score 10
(3) Current to Four Year Price   Score 9   **(9)** Operating Margin % 0   Score 0
(4) Book Value $ 0   Score 1   **(10)** Trading Volume 0   Score 0
(5) Price to Book Comparison Score 0   **(11)** Price to Earnings 0.00x   Score 0
(6) Analyst Buys # 0   Score 0

Total of All 11 Scores = 31

This stock's total score in 2021 was **18**, in 2020 it was **17**, in 2019 it was **17**.

HISTORICAL STOCK PRICES & DIVIDEND PAYOUTS

Year	Stock	Dividend	Year	Stock	Dividend
2022	$ 15.00	$ 0.10	2010	$ NA	$ NA
2021	$ 13.75	$ 0.10	2009	$ NA	$ NA
2020	$ 12.69	$ 0.10	2008	$ NA	$ NA
2019	$ 11.22	$ 0.10	2007	$ NA	$ NA
2018	$ 11.41	$ 0.10	2006	$ NA	$ NA
2017	$ NA	$ NA	2005	$ NA	$ NA
2016	$ NA	$ NA	2004	$ NA	$ NA
2015	$ NA	$ NA	2003	$ NA	$ NA
2014	$ NA	$ NA	2002	$ NA	$ NA
2013	$ NA	$ NA	2001	$ NA	$ NA
2012	$ NA	$ NA	2000	$ NA	$ NA
2011	$ NA	$ NA	1999	$ NA	$ NA

NOTES: PRM is a Canada-based mutual fund company investing in preferred shares to provide their holders with a fixed cumulative preferential quarterly cash distribution. The investments are comprised of the equity securities of the largest pharmaceutical companies. Its headquarters is in Oakville, Ontario.

BIRCHCLIFF ENERGY LTD

(BIR)

Updated May 2023

IDM STOCK SCORING CALCULATION

(1) Stock Price $ 7.89   Score 4
(2) Price 4 Years Ago $ 3.12   Score 3
(3) Current to Four Year Price Score 10
(4) Book Value $ 9.07   Score 4
(5) Price to Book Comparison Score 8
(6) Analyst Buys #4   Score 4

(7) Analysts Strong Buys #0 Score 0
(8) Dividend Yield % 10.14   Score 10
(9) Operating Margin % 55.18 Score 8
(10) Trading Volume 886,001   Score 8
(11) Price to Earnings 3.3x   Score10

Total of All 11 Scores = 69

This stock's total score in 2021 was **NA** , in 2020 it was **NA** , in 2019 it was NA
.

HISTORICAL STOCK PRICES & DIVIDEND PAYOUTS

Year	Stock	Dividend	Year	Stock	Dividend
2022	$ 6.96	$ 0.01	2010	$ 8.65	$ NA
2021	$ 3.08	$ 0.01	2009	$ 7.12	$ NA
2020	$ 1.31	$ 0.03	2008	$ 9.91	$ NA
2019	$ 3.48	$ 0.03	2007	$ 3.73	$ NA
2018	$ 3.15	$ 0.03	2006	$ 6.90	$ NA
2017	$ 7.00	$ 0.03	2005	$ NA	$ NA
2016	$ 5.59	$ NA	2004	$ NA	$ NA
2015	$ 6.86	$ NA	2003	$ NA	$ NA
2014	$ 10.31	$ NA	2002	$ NA	$ NA
2013	$ 8.21	$ NA	2001	$ NA	$ NA
2012	$ 9.28	$ NA	2000	$ NA	$ NA
2011	$ 11.39	$ NA	1999	$ NA	$ NA

NOTES: BIR. is a Canada-based intermediate oil and gas company. The Company is engaged in exploring for, developing, and producing natural gas, light oil, condensate and other natural gas Liquids (NGLs)

BIRD CONSTRUCTION INC
(BDT)
Updated May 2023

IDM STOCK SCORING CALCULATION

(1) Stock Price $ 8.69   *Score 4*

(2) Price 4 Years Ago $ 5.63   *Score 4*

(3) Current to Four Year Price *Score 9*

(4) Book Value $ 5.08   *Score 4*

(5) Price to Book Comparison *Score 0*

(6) Analyst Buys # 3   *Score 3*

(7) Analysts Strong Buys # 0   *Score 0*

(8) Dividend Yield % 4.94   *Score 8*

(9) Operating Margin % 2.80   *Score 1*

10) Trading Volume 13,572   *Score 1*

(11) Price to Earnings 9.4x   *Score 9*

Total of All 11 Scores = 43

This stock's total score in 2021 was **18**, in 2020 it was **37**, in 2019 it was **27**.

HISTORICAL STOCK PRICES & DIVIDEND PAYOUTS

Year	Stock	Dividend	Year	Stock	Dividend
2022	$ 9.01	$ 0.03	2010	$ 11.08	$ 0.05
2021	$ 9.07	$ 0.03	2009	$ 8.17	$ 0.04
2020	$ 4.84	$ 0.03	2008	$ 10.63	$ 0.04
2019	$ 7.85	$ 0.03	2007	$ 5.33	$ 0.03
2018	$ 8.45	$ 0.03	2006	$ 5.56	$ 0.03
2017	$ 10.01	$ 0.03	2005	$ 2.63	$ 0.08
2016	$ 11.83	$ 0.06	2004	$ 2.11	$ 0.07
2015	$10.02	$ 0.06	2003	$ 1.50	$ NA
2014	$ 14.05	$ 0.06	2002	$ 1.85	$ NA
2013	$ 13.35	$ 0.06	2001	$ 1.38	$ 0.11
2012	$ 14.63	$ 0.06	2000	$ 0.69	$ 0.07
2011	$ 12.25	$ 0.17	1999	$ 0.29	$ NA

NOTES: **BDT** operates as a general contractor in the Canadian construction market. The Company focuses on projects in the industrial, commercial, and institutional sectors of the general contracting industry.

BLUE RIBBON INC
(RBN.UN)
Updated May 2023

IDM STOCK SCORING CALCULATION

(1) Stock Price $ 7.62   Score 4
(2) Price 4 Years Ago $ 8.09   Score 4
(3) Current to Four Year Price Score 5
(4) Book Value $ 7.63   Score 4
(5) Price to Book Comparison Score 6
(6) Analyst Buys #0   Score 0

(7) Analysts Strong Buys # 0   Score 0
(8) Dividend Yield % 6.30   Score 8
(9) Operating Margin % 0   Score 0
10) Trading Volume 15,300   Score1
(11) Price to Earnings 12.9x   Score 0

Total of All 11 Scores = 32

This stock's total score in 2021 was **23**, in 2020 it was **52** , in 2019 it was **25**.

HISTORICAL STOCK PRICES & DIVIDEND PAYOUTS

Year	Stock	Dividend	Year	Stock	Dividend
2022	$ 8.57	$ 0.04	2010	$ 9.60	$ 0.07
2021	$ 8.33	$ 0.04	2009	$ 5.58	$ 0.06
2020	$ 5.86	$ 0.05	2008	$ 9.55	$ 0.09
2019	$ 8.15	$ 0.05	2007	$ 10.06	$ 0.09
2018	$ 8.91	$ 0.05	2006	$ 10.88	$ 0.09
2017	$ 9.72	$ 0.05	2005	$ 11.11	$ 0.08
2016	$ 8.35	$ 0.07	2004	$ 10.73	$ 0.08
2015	$ 10.17	$ 0.07	2003	$ 9.01	$ 0.08
2014	$ 11.60	$ 0.07	2002	$ 10.20	$ 0.05
2013	$ 11.50	$ 0.07	2001	$ 8.89	$ 0.07
2012	$ 11.40	$ 0.06	2000	$ 6.90	$ 0.07
2011	$ 10.71	$ 0.06	1999	$ 6.95	$ 0.05

NOTES: RBN.UN is a Canada-based closed-end investment trust.

BOSTON PIZZA ROYALTIES INCOME FUND
(BPF.UN)
Updated May 2023

IDM STOCK SCORING CALCULATION

(1) Stock Price $ 15.48   Score 6

(2) Price 4 Years Ago $ 16.86 Score 6

(3) Current to Four Year Price Score 5

(4) Book Value $ 13.04   Score 5

(5) Price to Book Comparison Score 1

(6) Analyst Buys # 0   Score 0

(7) Analysts Strong Buys # 0 Score 0

(8) Dividend Yield % 8.29   Score 10

(9) Operating Margin % 96.94 Score 10

(10) Trading Volume 13,664   Score 1

(11) Price to Earnings 12.5x   Score 9

Total of All 11 Scores = 53

This stock's total score in 2021 was **49**, in 2020 it was **38**, in 2019 it was **48**.

HISTORICAL STOCK PRICES & DIVIDEND PAYOUTS

Year	Stock	Dividend	Year	Stock	Dividend
2022	$ 17.30	$ 0.09	2010	$11.90	$ 0.12
2021	$ 13.05	$ 0.07	2009	$ 8.81	$ 0.12
2020	$ 12.85	$ 0.10	2008	$ 12.45	$ 0.12
2019	$ 17.19	$ 0.12	2007	$ 15.20	$ 0.11
2018	$ 19.73	$ 0.12	2006	$ 16.70	$ 0.10
2017	$ 23.00	$0.12	2005	$ 14.75	$ 0.10
2016	$ 18.50	$ 0.12	2004	$ 12.46	$ 0.09
2015	$ 22.89	$ 0.10	2003	$ 9.60	$ 0.08
2014	$ 19.75	$ 0.10	2002	$ 10.12	$ 0.04
2013	$ 20.34	$ 0.10	2001	$ NA	$ NA
2012	$ 16.25	$ 0.10	2000	$ NA	$ NA
2011	$ 14.39	$0.08	1999	$ NA	$ NA

NOTES: BPF is a limited purpose open-ended mutual fund trust.

BRIDGMARQ REAL ESTATE SERVICES INC
(BRE)
Updated May 2023

IDM STOCK SCORING CALCULATION

(1) Stock Price $ 14.91   Score 5   *(7)* Analysts Strong Buys # 0 Score 0

(2) Price 4 Years Ago $ 14.9   Score 5   *(8)* Dividend Yield % 9.05   Score 10

(3) Current to Four Year Price Score 6   *(9)* Operating Margin % 34.85 Score 6

(4) Book Value $ 5.09   Score 1   *(10)* Trading Volume 4,589   Score 0

(5) Price to Book Comparison Score 0   *(11)* Price to Earnings 11.3x   Score 9

(6) Analyst Buys # 0   Score 0

Total of All 11 Scores = 42

This stock's total score in 2021 was **37** , in 2020 it was **34** , in 2019 it was **NA**
.

HISTORICAL STOCK PRICES & DIVIDEND PAYOUTS

Year	Stock	Dividend	Year	Stock	Dividend
2022	$ 15.78	$ 0.11	2010	$ 13.00	$ 0.12
2021	$ 16.69	$ 0.11	2009	$ 7.70	$ 0.12
2020	$ 8.43	$ 0.11	2008	$ 11.01	$ 0.10
2019	$ 16.61	$ 0.11	2007	$ 12.49	$ 0.10
2018	$ 7.89	$ 0.11	2006	$ 13.66	$ 0.10
2017	$ 16.14	$ 0.11	2005	$ 13.75	$ 0.09
2016	$ 14.59	$ 0.11	2004	$ 11.65	$ 0.09
2015	$ 14.07	$ 0.10	2003	$ 10.38	$ 0.08
2014	$ 14.62	$ 0.10	2002	$ NA	$ NA
2013	$ 12.86	$ 0.09	2001	$ NA	$ NA
2012	$ 14.15	$0.09	2000	$ NA	$ NA
2011	$ 15.16	$ 0.09	1999	$ NA	$ NA

NOTES: BRE is a closed-end investment fund.

BROMPTON LIFECO SPLIT CORP
(LCS)
Updated May 2023

IDM STOCK SCORING CALCULATION

(1) Stock Price $ 6.05   Score 4
(2) Price 4 Years Ago $ 4.13   Score 3
(3) Current to Four Year Price   Score 9
(4) Book Value $ 0   Score 1
(5) Price to Book Comparison   Score 0
(6) Analyst Buys # 0   Score 0

(7) Analysts Strong Buys # 0   Score 0
(8) Dividend Yield % 14.88   Score 2
(9) Operating Margin % 0   Score 0
(10) Trading Volume 58,499   Score 3
(11) Price to Earnings 0.0x   Score 0

Total of All 11 Scores =22

This stock's total score in 2021 was **19** , in 2020 it was **NA**, in 2019 it was **12**.

HISTORICAL STOCK PRICES & DIVIDEND PAYOUTS

Year	Stock	Dividend	Year	Stock	Dividend
2022	$ 6.50	$ 0.07	2010	$ 5.97	$0.07
2021	$ 6.33	$ 0.07	2009	$ 2.51	$ NA
2020	$ 6.28	$ 0.07	2008	$ 10.24	$ 0.07
2019	$ 5.11	$ 0.07	2007	$ 13.25	$ 0.11
2018	$ 6.55	$ 0.07	2006	$ NA	$ NA
2017	$ 7.25	$ 0.07	2005	$ NA	$ NA
2016	$ 3.92	$ NA	2004	$ NA	$ NA
2015	$ 6.39	$ 0.07	2003	$ NA	$ NA
2014	$ 7.65	$ 0.07	2002	$ NA	$ NA
2013	$ 5.72	$ 0.07	2001	$ NA	$ NA
2012	$ 3.00	$ NA	2000	$ NA	$ NA
2011	$ 5.86	$ 0.07	1999	$ NA	$ NA

NOTES: **LCS** is Canada-based mutual fund corporation.

BROMPTON SPLIT BANC CORP

(SBC)

Updated May 2023

IDM STOCK SCORING CALCULATION

(1) Stock Price $ 10.70   Score 5
(2) Price 4 Years Ago $ 9.76   Score 4
(3) Current to Four Year Price Score 7
(4) Book Value $ 8.89   Score 4
(5) Price to Book Comparison Score 1
(6) Analyst Buys # 0   Score 0

(7) Analysts Strong Buys #0   Score 0
(8) Dividend Yield % 11.21   Score 2
(9) Operating Margin % 0   Score 0
(10) Trading Volume 19,100   Score 1
(11) Price to Earnings -3.2x   Score 0

Total of All 11 Scores = 24

This stock's total score in 2021 was **45**, in 2020 it was **34**, in 2019 it was **36** .

HISTORICAL STOCK PRICES & DIVIDEND PAYOUTS

Year	Stock	Dividend	Year	Stock	Dividend
2022	$ 13.22	$ 0.10	2010	$ 7.83	$ 0.07
2021	$ 10.51	$ 0.08	2009	$ 4.13	$ 0.07
2020	$ 6.17	$ 0.08	2008	$ 6.88	$ 0.07
2019	$ 10.12	$ 0.08	2007	$ 10.17	$ 0.07
2018	$ 10.88	$ 0.08	2006	$ 10.43	$ 0.07
2017	$ 9.97	$ 0.07	2005	$ 10.18	$ 0.03
2016	$ 8.39	$ 0.07	2004	$ NA	$ NA
2015	$ 8.78	$ 0.07	2003	$ NA	$ NA
2014	$ 9.58	$ 0.07	2002	$ NA	$ NA
2013	$ 7.31	$ 0.07	2001	$ NA	$ NA
2012	$ 6.87	$ 0.07	2000	$ NA	$ NA
2011	$8.19	$ 0.07	1999	$ NA	$ NA

NOTES: SBC is a Canada-based mutual fund company

118

BROOKFIELD ASSET MANAGEMENT LTD

(BAM)

Updated May 2023

IDM STOCK SCORING CALCULATION

(1) Stock Price $ 44.01   Score 8
(2) Price 4 Years Ago $0.00   Score 1
(3) Current to Four Year Price Score 0
(4) Book Value $ 36.71   Score 9
(5) Price to Book Comparison   Score 1
(6) Analyst Buys # 3   Score 3

7) Analysts Strong Buys # 0   Score 0
(8) Dividend Yield % 4.01   Score 6
(9) Operating Margin % 62.20   Score 8
(10) Trading Volume   96,888   Score 3
(11) Price to Earnings   7.2   Score 9

Total of All 11 Scores = 47

This stock's total score in 2021 was **NA** , in 2020 it was **NA** , in 2019 it was **NA**
.

HISTORICAL STOCK PRICES & DIVIDEND PAYOUTS

Year	Stock	Dividend	Year	Stock	Dividend

New Listing, No History Available

Year	Stock	Dividend	Year	Stock	Dividend
2022	$ NA	$ NA	2010	$ NA	$ NA
2021	$ NA	$ NA	2009	$ NA	$ NA
2020	$ NA	$ NA	2008	$ NA	$ NA
2019	$ NA	$ NA	2007	$ NA	$ NA
2018	$ NA	$ NA	2006	$ NA	$ NA
2017	$ NA	$ NA	2005	$ NA	$ NA
2016	$ NA	$ NA	2004	$ NA	$ NA
2015	$ NA	$ NA	2003	$ NA	$ NA
2014	$ NA	$ NA	2002	$ NA	$ NA
2013	$ NA	$ NA	2001	$ NA	$ NA
2012	$ NA	$ NA	2000	$ NA	$ NA
2011	$ NA	$ NA	1999	$ NA	$ NA

NOTES: BAM is primarily engaged in providing alternative asset management services.

BROOKFIELD RENEWABLE CORPORATION

(BEPC)

Updated May 2023

IDM STOCK SCORING CALCULATION

(1) Stock Price $ 46.90   Score 8

(2) Price 4 Years Ago $ 0   Score 1

(3) Current to Four Year Price Score 0

(4) Book Value $ 16.23   Score 6

(5) Price to Book Comparison Score 0

(6) Analyst Buys #1   Score 2

(7) Analysts Strong Buys # 0 Score 0

(8) Dividend Yield % 3.85   Score 6

(9) Operating Margin % 81.07 Score 10

(10) Trading Volume 70,205   Score 3

11) Price to Earnings 8.3x   Score 9

Total of All 11 Scores = 45

This stock's total score in 2021 was **NA**, in 2020 it was **NA**, in 2019 it was **NA**.

HISTORICAL STOCK PRICES & DIVIDEND PAYOUTS

Year	Stock	Dividend	Year	Stock	Dividend
2022	$ 47.05	$ NA	2010	$ NA	$ NA
2021	$ 49.04	$ NA	2009	$ NA	$ NA
2020	$ 38.66	$ NA	2008	$ NA	$ NA
2019	$ NA	$ NA	2007	$ NA	$ NA
2018	$ NA	$ NA	2006	$ NA	$ NA
2017	$ NA	$ NA	2005	$ NA	$ NA
2016	$ NA	$ NA	2004	$ NA	$ NA
2015	$ NA	$ NA	2003	$ NA	$ NA
2014	$ NA	$ NA	2002	$ NA	$ NA
2013	$ NA	$ NA	2001	$ NA	$ NA
2012	$ NA	$ NA	2000	$ NA	$ NA
2011	$ NA	$ NA	1999	$ NA	$ NA

NOTES: BEPC operates renewable power platforms. The Company's portfolio consists of hydroelectric, wind, solar and storage facilities in North America, South America, Europe and Asia.

BROOKFIELD GLOBAL INFASTRUCTURE SECURITIES INCOME FUND

(BGI)

Updated May 2023

IDM STOCK SCORING CALCULATION

(1) Stock Price $ 4.46   Score 3
(2) Price 4 Years Ago $ 6.73   Score 4
(3) Current to Four Year Price Score 2
(4) Book Value $ 4.49   Score 3
(5) Price to Book Comparison Score 6
(6) Analyst Buys # 0   Score 0

(7) Analysts Strong Buys # 0   Score 0
(8) Dividend Yield % 13.49   Score 2
(9) Operating Margin % 66.02 Score 8
(10) Trading Volume 14,700   Score 1
(11) Price to Earnings 21.9x   Score 7

Total of All 11 Scores = 36

This stock's total score in 2021 was **28**, in 2020 it was **34** , in 2019 it was **25** .

HISTORICAL STOCK PRICES & DIVIDEND PAYOUTS

Year	Stock	Dividend	Year	Stock	Dividend
2022	$ 7.27	$ 0.15	2010	$ NA	$ NA
2021	$ 7.21	$ 0.15	2009	$ NA	$ NA
2020	$ 5.79	$ 0.15	2008	$ NA	$ NA
2019	$ 6.89	$ 0.15	2007	$ NA	$ NA
2018	$ 5.94	$ 0.15	2006	$ NA	$ NA
2017	$ 7.08	$ 0.15	2005	$ NA	$ NA
2016	$ 5.62	$ 0.15	2004	$ NA	$ NA
2015	$9.31	$ 0.15	2003	$ NA	$ NA
2014	$ 9.79	$ 0.15	2002	$ NA	$ NA
2013	$ 9.30	$ 0.15	2001	$ NA	$ NA
2012	$ NA	$ NA	2000	$ NA	$ NA
2011	$ NA	$ NA	1999	$ NA	$ NA

NOTES: **BGI** is a closed-end investment fund.

BROOKFIELD INFASTRUCTURE PARTNERS LP

(BIP.UN)

Updated May 2023

IDM STOCK SCORING CALCULATION

(1) Stock Price $ 47.47   *Score* 8
(2) Price 4 Years Ago $ 52.3   *Score 9*
(3) Current to Four Year Price *Score 5*
(4) Book Value $ 177.23   *Score 6*
(5) Price to Book Comparison *Score 0*
(6) Analyst Buys # 4   *Score 4*

(7) Analysts Strong Buys # 0   *Score 0*
(8) Dividend Yield % 4.30   *Score* 6
(9) Operating Margin % 0   *Score 0*
(10) Trading Volume 44,388   *Score 2*
(11) Price to Earnings 273.4x   *Score 1*

Total of All 11 Scores = 41

This stock's total score in 2021 was **54**, in 2020 it was **59**, in 2019 it was **56**.

HISTORICAL STOCK PRICES & DIVIDEND PAYOUTS

Year	Stock	Dividend	Year	Stock	Dividend
2022	$ 52.59	$ NA	2010	$ 6.52	$ NA
2021	$ 43.23	$ NA	2009	$ 7.13	$ NA
2020	$ 36.01	$ NA	2008	$ NA	$ NA
2019	$ 33.59	$ NA	2007	$ NA	$ NA
2018	$ 29.45	$ NA	2006	$ NA	$ NA
2017	$ 31.83	$ NA	2005	$ NA	$ NA
2016	$ 22.19	$ NA	2004	$ NA	$ NA
2015	$ 21.86	$ NA	2003	$ NA	$ NA
2014	$ 17.43	$ NA	2002	$ NA	$ NA
2013	$ 15.65	$ NA	2001	$ NA	$ NA
2012	$ 12.32	$ NA	2000	$ NA	$ NA
2011	$ 9.45	$ NA	1999	$ NA	$ NA

NOTES:

NOTES: BIP.UN owns and operates utilities, transport, midstream and data businesses in North and South America, Europe, and the Asia Pacific region.

BSR REAL ESTATE INVESTMENT TRUST

(HOM.U)

Updated May 2023

IDM STOCK SCORING CALCULATION

(1) Stock Price $ 13.20   Score *5*
(2) Price 4 Years Ago $ 10.18 Score *5*
(3) Current to Four Year Price Score *9*
(4) Book Value $ 17.16   Score *6*
(5) Price to Book Comparison Score *8*
(6) Analyst Buys #   0   Score *0*

(7) Analysts Strong Buys # 0   Score *0*
(8) Dividend Yield % 3.94   Score *6*
(9) Operating Margin % 39.61   Score *6*
(10) Trading Volume 14,546   Score *1*
(11) Price to Earnings 3.3x   Score *10*

Total of All 11 Scores = 56

This stock's total score in 2021 was **16**, in 2020 it was **16**, in 2019 it was **24**.

HISTORICAL STOCK PRICES & DIVIDEND PAYOUTS

Year	Stock	Dividend	Year	Stock	Dividend
2022	$ 20.32	$ 0.04	2010	$ NA	$ NA
2021	$ 11.05	$ 0.04	2009	$ NA	$ NA
2020	$ 9.07	$ 0.04	2008	$ NA	$ NA
2019	$ 8.99	$ 0.04	2007	$ NA	$ NA
2018	$ 9.50	$ 0.06	2006	$ NA	$ NA
2017	$ NA	$ NA	2005	$ NA	$ NA
2016	$ NA	$ NA	2004	$ NA	$ NA
2015	$ NA	$ NA	2003	$ NA	$ NA
2014	$ NA	$ NA	2002	$ NA	$ NA
2013	$ NA	$ NA	2001	$ NA	$ NA
2012	$ NA	$ NA	2000	$ NA	$ NA
2011	$ NA	$ NA	1999	$ NA	$ NA

NOTES: HOM.U is an internally managed, unincorporated, open-ended real estate investment trust (REIT). The principal business of the Company is to acquire and operate multi-family residential rental properties across the United States.

BTB REAL ESTATE INVESTMENT TRUST

(BTB.UN)

Updated May 2023

IDM STOCK SCORING CALCULATION

(1) Stock Price $ 3.32   Score 3   *(7)* Analysts Strong Buys #0   Score 0
(2) Price 4 Years Ago $ 4.89   Score 3   *(8)* Dividend Yield % 9.04   Score 10
(3) Current to Four Year Price Score 2   *(9)* Operating Margin % 0   Score 0
(4) Book Value $ 0   Score 1   *(10)* Trading Volume 116,649   Score 4
(5) Price to Book Comparison Score 0   *(11)* Price to Earnings 7.3X   Score 9
(6) Analyst Buys #1   Score 2

Total of All 11 Scores = 34

This stock's total score in 2021 was **49**, in 2020 it was **50**, in 2019 it was **54**.

HISTORICAL STOCK PRICES & DIVIDEND PAYOUTS

Year	Stock	Dividend	Year	Stock	Dividend
2022	$ 4.23	$ 0.03	2010	$ 3.50	$ 0.03
2021	$ 4.08	$ 0.03	2009	$ 2.50	$ 0.03
2020	$ 3.73	$ 0.04	2008	$ 8.60	$ 0.12
2019	$ 4.81	$ 0.04	2007	$ 13.75	$ 0.12
2018	$ 4.57	$ 0.04	2006	$ 5.62	$ NA
2017	$ 4.75	$0.04	2005	$ NA	$ NA
2016	$ 4.65	$ 0.04	2004	$ NA	$ NA
2015	$ 4.86	$ 0.04	2003	$ NA	$ NA
2014	$ 4.60	$ 0.03	2002	$ NA	$ NA
2013	$ 4.65	$ 0.03	2001	$ NA	$ NA
2012	$ 4.50	$ 0.03	2000	$ NA	$ NA
2011	$ 4.55	$ 0.03	1999	$ NA	$ NA

NOTES: BTB.UN is a Canada-based real estate investment trust (REIT)

BUILDERS CAPITAL MORTGAGE CORPORATION
(BCF)
Updated May 2023

IDM STOCK SCORING CALCULATION

(1) Stock Price $ 8.50   Score 4
(2) Price 4 Years Ago $ 9.87   Score 4
(3) Current to Four Year Price Score 2
(4) Book Value $ 9.25   Score 4
(5) Price to Book Comparison Score 6
(6) Analyst Buys #0   Score 0

(7) Analysts Strong Buys # 0   Score 0
(8) Dividend Yield % 9.28   Score 10
(9) Operating Margin % -77.42 Score 0
(10) Trading Volume 1,850   Score 0
(11) Price to Earnings 9.2x   Score 9

Total of All 11 Scores =39

This stock's total score in 2021 was **33**, in 2020 it was **31**, in 2019 it was **40**.

HISTORICAL STOCK PRICES & DIVIDEND PAYOUTS

Year	Stock	Dividend	Year	Stock	Dividend
2022	$ 10.33	$ 0.20	2010	$ NA	$ NA
2021	$ 8.90	$ 0.20	2009	$ NA	$ NA
2020	$ 7.03	$ 0.20	2008	$ NA	$ NA
2019	$ 9.94	$ 0.20	2007	$ NA	$ NA
2018	$ 9.95	$ 0.20	2006	$ NA	$ NA
2017	$ 9.75	$ 0.20	2005	$ NA	$ NA
2016	$ 9.35	$ 0.20	2004	$ NA	$ NA
2015	$ 9.80	$ 0.20	2003	$ NA	$ NA
2014	$ 9.90	$ 0.20	2002	$ NA	$ NA
2013	$ NA	$ NA	2001	$ NA	$ NA
2012	$ NA	$ NA	2000	$ NA	$ NA
2011	$ NA	$ NA	1999	$ NA	$ NA

NOTES: BCF is a Canada-based mortgage investment corporation (MIC).

CANACOL ENERGY LTD

(CNE)

Updated May 2023

IDM STOCK SCORING CALCULATION

(1) Stock Price $ 10.05   *Score* 5
(2) Price 4 Years Ago $ 21.10 Score 7
(3) Current to Four Year Price Score 1
(4) Book Value $ 11.67   *Score* 5
(5) Price to Book Comparison Score 8
(6) Analyst Buys #0   *Score* 0

(7) Analysts Strong Buys # 1   *Score* 3
(8) Dividend Yield % 10.35   *Score* 10
(9) Operating Margin % 33.21   *Score* 6
(10) Trading Volume 1,581   *Score* 1
(11) Price to Earnings 1.7x   *Score* 10

Total of All 11 Scores = 56

This stock's total score in 2021 was **28** , in 2020 it was **33** , in 2019 it was **NA**

HISTORICAL STOCK PRICES & DIVIDEND PAYOUTS

Year	Stock	Dividend	Year	Stock	Dividend
2022	$ 15.60	$ 0.26	2010	$ NA	$ NA
2021	$ 18.10	$ 0.26	2009	$ NA	$ NA
2020	$ 18.00	$ 0.26	2008	$ NA	$ NA
2019	$ 22.65	$ NA	2007	$ NA	$ NA
2018	$ 21.75	$ NA	2006	$ NA	$ NA
2017	$19.55	$ NA	2005	$ NA	$ NA
2016	$ 16.35	$ NA	2004	$ NA	$ NA
2015	$ 13.00	$ NA	2003	$ NA	$ NA
2014	$ 35.65	$ NA	2002	$ NA	$ NA
2013	$ 15.50	$ NA	2001	$ NA	$ NA
2012	$ 50.50	$ NA	2000	$ NA	$ NA
2011	$ 76.00	$ NA	1999	$ NA	$ NA

NOTES: CNE is a Canada-based independent natural gas exploration and production company in Colombia

126

CANACCORD GENUITY GROUP INC
(CF)
Updated July 2023

IDM STOCK SCORING CALCULATION

(1) Stock Price $ 8.31   Score 4
(2) Price 4 Years Ago $ 5.36   Score 4
(3) Current to Four Year Price   Score 9
(4) Book Value $ 12.06   Score 5
(5) Price to Book Comparison   Score 8
(6) Analyst Buys # 4   Score 4

(7) Analysts Strong Buys # 0 Score 0
(8) Dividend Yield % 4.09   Score 6
(9) Operating Margin % 1.16   Score 0
(10) Trading Volume 134,873 Score 4
(11) Price to Earnings -7.2x   Score 0

Total of All 11 Scores = 44

This stock's total score in 2021 was **NA**, in 2020 it was **NA**, in 2019 it was **NA**.

HISTORICAL STOCK PRICES & DIVIDEND PAYOUTS

Year	Stock	Dividend	Year	Stock	Dividend
2022	$ 8.58	$ 0.09	2010	$ 10.05	$ 0.05
2021	$ 15.21	$ 0.07	2009	$ 10.41	$ 0.05
2020	$ 7.42	$ 0.06	2008	$ 8.05	$ 0.12
2019	$ 5.36	$ 0.05	2007	$ 17.11	$ 0.12
2018	$ 7.09	$ 0.01	2006	$ 16.69	$ 0.07
2017	$ 4.77	$ 0.01	2005	$ 9.00	$ 0.06
2016	$ 3.88	$ NA	2004	$ 8.08	$ 0.05
2015	$ 5.73	$ 0.05	2003	$ NA	$ NA
2014	$11.26	$ 0.05	2002	$ NA	$ NA
2013	$5.85	$ 0.05	2001	$ NA	$ NA
2012	$ 4.70	$ 0.05	2000	$ NA	$ NA
2011	$9.23	$0.09	1999	$ NA	$ NA

NOTES: CF is a Canada-based independent, full-service investment company that operates through two segments: capital markets and wealth management in North America, Europe, Asia, Australia, and the Middle East.

Canadian High Income Equity Fund
(CIQ.UN)

Updated May 2023

IDM STOCK SCORING CALCULATION

(1) Stock Price $ 7.13   *Score 4*
(2) Price 4 Years Ago $ 7.49   *Score 4*
(3) Current to Four Year Price Score 5
(4) Book Value $ 6.99   *Score 4*
(5) Price to Book Comparison Score 2
(6) Analyst Buys # 0   *Score 0*

(7) Analysts Strong Buys #0 Score 0
(8) Dividend Yield % 6.73   *Score 8*
(9) Operating Margin % 0   *Score 0*
(10) Trading Volume 0   *Score 0*
(11) Price to Earnings -13.3   *Score 0*

Total of All 11 Scores = 27

This stock's total score in 2021 was **19**, in 2020 it was **52**, in 2019 it was **21**.

HISTORICAL STOCK PRICES & DIVIDEND PAYOUTS

Year	Stock	Dividend	Year	Stock	Dividend
2022	$ 7.71	$ 0.04	2010	$ 111.73	$ 0.11
2021	$ 7.75	$ 0.04	2009	$ NA	$ NA
2020	$ 5.47	$ 0.05	2008	$ NA	$ NA
2019	$ 7.64	$ 0.05	2007	$ NA	$ NA
2018	$ 8.66	$ 0.05	2006	$ NA	$ NA
2017	$ 9.52	$ 0.05	2005	$ NA	$ NA
2016	$ 8.21	$ 0.07	2004	$ NA	$ NA
2015	$ 10.24	$ 0.07	2003	$ NA	$ NA
2014	$ 11.95	$ 0.07	2002	$ NA	$ NA
2013	$ 11.04	$ 0.07	2001	$ NA	$ NA
2012	$ 11.90	$ 0.07	2000	$ NA	$ NA
2011	$ 11.96	$ 0.07	1999	$ NA	$ NA

NOTES: CIQ.UN is a mutual fund trust.

CANADIAN BANC CORP

(BK)

Updated May 2023

IDM STOCK SCORING CALCULATION

(1) Stock Price $ 13.18   Score 5
(2) Price 4 Years Ago $ 11.35   Score 5
(3) Current to Four Year Price   Score 9
(4) Book Value $ 0   Score 1
(5) Price to Book Comparison   Score 0
(6) Analyst Buys #0   Score 0

(7) Analysts Strong Buys # 0   Score 0
(8) Dividend Yield % 15.46   Score 2
(9) Operating Margin % 0   Score 0
(10) Trading Volume 62,996   Score 3
(11) Price to Earnings 0   Score 0

Total of All 11 Scores = 25

This stock's total score in 2021 was **NA** , in 2020 it was **NA** , in 2019 it was **16.**

HISTORICAL STOCK PRICES & DIVIDEND PAYOUTS

Year	Stock	Dividend	Year	Stock	Dividend
2022	$ 14.72	$ NA	2010	$ 8.79	$ NA
2021	$ 11.15	$ NA	2009	$ 3.91	$ NA
2020	$ 5.60	$ NA	2008	$ 7.92	$ NA
2019	$ 11.40	$ NA	2007	$ 11.92	$ NA
2018	$ 14.05	$ NA	2006	$ 11.45	$ NA
2017	$ 12.28	$ NA	2005	$ NA	$ NA
2016	$ 9.52	$ NA	2004	$ NA	$ NA
2015	$ 13.33	$ NA	2003	$ NA	$ NA
2014	$ 12.10	$ NA	2002	$ NA	$ NA
2013	$ 8.76	$ NA	2001	$ NA	$ NA
2012	$ 9.17	$ NA	2000	$ NA	$ NA
2011	$ 10.33	$ NA	1999	$ NA	$ NA

NOTES: BK is a Canada-based mutual fund company.

CANADIAN IMPERIAL BANK OF COMMERCE

(CM)

Updated May 2023

IDM STOCK SCORING CALCULATION

(1) Stock Price $ 56.66   Score 9
(2) Price 4 Years Ago $ 53.60 Score 9
(3) Current to Four Year Price Score 7
(4) Book Value $ 55.38   Score 9
(5) Price to Book Comparison Score 2
(6) Analyst Buys # 2   Score 3

(7) Analysts Strong Buys # 0   Score 0
(8) Dividend Yield % 6.00   Score 8
(9) Operating Margin % 30.29   Score 6
(10) Trading Volume 2,636,413 Score 10
(11) Price to Earnings 11.2x   Score 9

Total of All 11 Scores = 72

This stock's total score in 2021 was **69**, in 2020 it was **67**, in 2019 it was **73**.

HISTORICAL STOCK PRICES & DIVIDEND PAYOUTS

Year	Stock	Dividend	Year	Stock	Dividend
2022	$ 75.68	$ 0.81	2010	$ 37.33	$ 0.43
2021	$ 61.95	$ 0.73	2009	$ 24.43	$ 0.43
2020	$ 38.33	$ 0.73	2008	$ 32.63	$ 0.43
2019	$ 52.80	$ 0.70	2007	$ 49.00	$ 0.39
2018	$ 57.03	$ 0.67	2006	$ 43.00	$ 0.34
2017	$ 58.02	$ 0.64	2005	$ 35.02	$ 0.33
2016	$ 47.91	$ 0.59	2004	$ 34.39	$ 0.25
2015	$ 46.60	$ 0.53	2003	$ 23.40	$ 0.20
2014	$ 47.41	$ 0.49	2002	$ 28.22	$ 0.20
2013	$ 39.84	$ 0.47	2001	$ 24.75	$ 0.18
2012	$ 38.12	$ 0.45	2000	$ 21.92	$ 0.17
2011	$ 41.87	$ 0.43	1999	$ 19.00	$ 0.15

NOTES: CM is a Canada-based financial institution offering advice, solutions, and services through its digital banking network across personal and business banking, commercial banking and wealth management, and capital markets businesses.

CANADIAN NATURAL RESOURCES LIMITED
(CNQ)
Updated May 2023

IDM STOCK SCORING CALCULATION

(1) Stock Price $ 80.89   Score 9
(2) Price 4 Years Ago $ 40.67 Score 8
(3) Current to Four Year Price Score 9
(4) Book Value $ 34.62   Score 8
(5) Price to Book Comparison Score 0
(6) Analyst Buys #3   Score 3

(7) Analysts Strong Buys #0   Score 0
(8) Dividend Yield % 4.45   Score 6
(9) Operating Margin % 34.90   Score 6
(10) Trading Volume 2,730,290 Score 10
(11) Price to Earnings 8.5x   Score 9

Total of All 11 Scores = 68

This stock's total score in 2021 was **59** , in 2020 it was **72** , in 2019 it was **70** .

HISTORICAL STOCK PRICES & DIVIDEND PAYOUTS

Year	Stock	Dividend	Year	Stock	Dividend
2022	$ 79.36	$ 0.75	2010	$ 36.13	$ 0.07
2021	$ 39.01	$ 0.47	2009	$ 23.55	$ 0.05
2020	$ 12.15	$ 0.42	2008	$ 35.88	$ 0.05
2019	$ 37.02	$ 0.33	2007	$ 29.33	$ 0.04
2018	$ 38.59	$ 0.34	2006	$ 33.34	$ 0.04
2017	$ 42.84	$ 0.28	2005	$ 16.59	$ 0.03
2016	$ 34.76	$ 0.23	2004	$ 8.99	$ 0.02
2015	$ 36.72	$ 0.23	2003	$ 6.39	$ 0.02
2014	$ 41.26	$ 0.22	2002	$ 6.03	$ 0.02
2013	$ 33.11	$ 0.12	2001	$ 5.65	$ 0.01
2012	$ 33.22	$ 0.10	2000	$ 4.41	$ NA
2011	$ 42.54	$ 0.09	1999	$ 3.35	$ NA

NOTES: CNQ is an independent crude oil and natural gas exploration, development, and production company.

CANADIAN NET REIT

(NET.UN)

Updated May 2023

IDM STOCK SCORING CALCULATION

(1) Stock Price $ 5.48   Score 4
(2) Price 4 Years Ago $ 5.70   Score 4
(3) Current to Four Year Price Score 5
(4) Book Value $ 5.76   Score 4
(5) Price to Book Comparison Score 6
(6) Analyst Buys # 2   Score 3

(7) Analysts Strong Buys #0   Score 0
(8) Dividend Yield % 6.30   Score 8
(9) Operating Margin % 69.32   Score 8
(10) Trading Volume 2,630   Score 0
(11) Price to Earnings -17.4x Score 0

Total of All 11 Scores = 42

This stock's total score in 2021 was **NA**, in 2020 it was **NA**, in 2019 it was **NA**.

HISTORICAL STOCK PRICES & DIVIDEND PAYOUTS

Year	Stock	Dividend	Year	Stock	Dividend
2022	$8.27	$ 0.03	2010	$ 1.80	$ NA
2021	$ 6.95	$ 0.03	2009	$ 1.20	$ NA
2020	$ 6.40	$ 0.02	2008	$ 2.00	$ NA
2019	$ 5.60	$ 0.02	2007	$ NA	$ NA
2018	$ 5.60	$ 0.02	2006	$ NA	$ NA
2017	$ 6.00	$ 0.04	2005	$ NA	$ NA
2016	$ 4.40	$ 0.04	2004	$ NA	$ NA
2015	$ 3.70	$ 0.04	2003	$ NA	$ NA
2014	$ 2.80	$ 0.04	2002	$ NA	$ NA
2013	$ 3.30	$ 0.07	2001	$ NA	$ NA
2012	$ 3.00	$ 0.06	2000	$ NA	$ NA
2011	$ 1.05	$ NA	1999	$ NA	$ NA

NOTES: NET.UN is a Canada-based open-ended real estate investment trust.

CANADIAN UTILITIES LIMITED

(CU.X)

Updated May 2023

IDM STOCK SCORING CALCULATION

(1) Stock Price $ 38.59   Score 8
(2) Price 4 Years Ago $ 37.35   Score 8
(3) Current to Four Year Price Score 7
(4) Book Value $ 25.49   Score 7
(5) Price to Book Comparison Score 0
(6) Analyst Buys # 1   Score 2

(7) Analysts Strong Buys # 0   Score 0
(8) Dividend Yield % 4.65   Score 8
(9) Operating Margin % 28.87   Score 6
(10) Trading Volume 4,085   Score 0
(11) Price to Earnings 0x   Score 0

Total of All 11 Scores = 46

This stock's total score in 2021 was **39**, in 2020 it was **55**, in 2019 it was **50**..

HISTORICAL STOCK PRICES & DIVIDEND PAYOUTS

Year	Stock	Dividend	Year	Stock	Dividend
2022	$ 36.00	$ 0.44	2010	$ 21.35	$ 0.19
2021	$31.50	$ 0.44	2009	$ 19.50	$ 0.18
2020	$ 30.41	$ 0.44	2008	$ 25.33	$ 0.17
2019	$ 33.60	$ 0.42	2007	$ 22.05	$ 0.15
2018	$ 35.00	$ 0.39	2006	$ 19.97	$ 0.14
2017	$ 36.15	$ 0.36	2005	$ 14.96	$ 0.14
2016	$ 35.50	$ 0.33	2004	$ 15.00	$ 0.13
2015	$ 42.25	$ 0.29	2003	$ 12.50	$ 0.13
2014	$ 38.44	$ 0.27	2002	$ 12.76	$ 0.12
2013	$ 37.62	$ 0.24	2001	$ 13.25	$ 0.12
2012	$ 31.15	$ 0.22	2000	$ 8.63	$ 0.11
2011	$ 26.66	$ 0.20	1999	$ 12.18	$ 0.11

NOTES: CU.X is a diversified global energy infrastructure corporation delivering essential services in Utilities (electricity and natural gas transmission and distribution, and international electricity operations) and Energy Infrastructure.

CANADIAN UTILITIES LIMITED

(CU)

Updated May 2023

IDM STOCK SCORING CALCULATION

(1) Stock Price $ 39.14   Score 8
(2) Price 4 Years Ago $ 36.89 Score 8
(3) Current to Four Year Price Score 7
(4) Book Value $25.49   Score 7
(5) Price to Book Comparison Score 0
(6) Analyst Buys #1   Score 2

(7) Analysts Strong Buys #0   Score 0
(8) Dividend Yield % 4.58   Score 8
(9) Operating Margin %29.87 Score 6
(10) Trading Volume 624,458 Score 6
(11) Price to Earnings 18.9x   Score 8

Total of All 11 Scores = 60

This stock's total score in 2021 was **49** , in 2020 it was **63**, in 2019 it was **57**.

HISTORICAL STOCK PRICES & DIVIDEND PAYOUTS

Year	Stock	Dividend	Year	Stock	Dividend
2022	$ 40.29	$ 0.44	2010	$ 21.56	$ 0.19
2021	$ 35.30	$ 0.44	2009	$ 17.82	$ 0.18
2020	$ 32.36	$ 0.44	2008	$ 23.00	$ 0.17
2019	$ 37.04	$ 0.42	2007	$ 23.50	$ 0.16
2018	$ 31.56	$ 0.39	2006	$ 19.33	$ 0.14
2017	$ 39.14	$ 0.36	2005	$ 15.46	$ 0.14
2016	$ 36.47	$ 0.33	2004	$14.47	$ 0.13
2015	$ 36.93	$ 0.29	2003	$ 11.55	$ 0.13
2014	$ 39.19	$ 0. 27	2002	$ 14.55	$ 0.12
2013	$ 39.72	$ 0.24	2001	$ 13.25	$ 0.12
2012	$ 33.96	$ 0.22	2000	$ 8.78	$ 0.11
2011	$ 28.66	$ 0.20	1999	$ 11.72	$ 0.11

NOTES: CU is a Canada-based diversified global energy infrastructure company. The Company is engaged in three business activities: Utilities, Energy Infrastructure and Retail Energy.

]

CANADIAN WESTERN BANK

(CWB)

Updated May 2023

IDM STOCK SCORING CALCULATION

(1) Stock Price $ 24.22   Score 7   *(7)* Analysts Strong Buys # 0   Score 0

(2) Price 4 Years Ago $ 30.02   Score 8   *(8)* Dividend Yield % 5.28   Score 8

(3) Current to Four Year Price   Score 2   *(9)* Operating Margin % 42.21   Score 6

(4) Book Value $ 39.58   Score 8   *(10)* Trading Volume 295,32   Score 5

(5) Price to Book Comparison   Score 8   *(11)* Price to Earnings 7.1x   Score 10

(6) Analyst Buys # 4   Score 4

Total of All 11 Scores = 66

This stock's total score in 2021 was **NA** , in 2020 it was **65**, in 2019 it was **NA**.

HISTORICAL STOCK PRICES & DIVIDEND PAYOUTS

Year	Dividend	Stock	Year	Dividend	Stock
2022	$ 36.34	$ 0.30	2010	$ 21.69	$ 0.11
2021	$ 34.08	$ 0.29	2009	$ 13.25	$ 0.11
2020	$ 18.19	$ 0.29	2008	$ 27.25	$ 0.10
2019	$ 29.30	$ 0.27	2007	$ 25.67	$ 0.08
2018	$ 33.88	$ 0.25	2006	$ 20.50	$ 0.06
2017	$ 25.88	$ 0.23	2005	$ 13.17	$ 0.04
2016	$ 20.89	$ 0.23	2004	$ 9.95	$ 0.04
2015	$ 31.37	$ 0.21	2003	$ 7.46	$ 0.06
2014	$ 36.17	$ 0.19	2002	$ 6.85	$ 0.05
2013	$ 28.35	$ 0.17	2001	$ 5.95	$ 0.04
2012	$ 26.25	$ 0.15	2000	$ 4.50	$ 0.04
2011	$ 30.19	$ 0.13	1999	$ 4.93	$ 0.04

NOTES: CWB is a Canada-based diversified financial services company that provides full-service business and personal banking, specialized financing, wealth management offerings, and trust services.

CANOE EIT INCOME FUND
(EIT.UN)
Updated May 2023

IDM STOCK SCORING CALCULATION

(1) Stock Price $ 12.93   Score   5
(2) Price 4 Years Ago $ 11.41 Score   5
(3) Current to Four Year Price Score 9
(4) Book Value $ 13.68   Score   5
(5) Price to Book Comparison Score 6
(6) Analyst Buys # 0   Score   0

(7) Analysts Strong Buys # 0   Score 0
(8) Dividend Yield % 9.28   Score   10
(9) Operating Margin % 85.75. Score 10
(10) Trading Volume 101,130   Score 4
(11) Price to Earnings 7.9x   Score 9

Total of All 11 Scores = 63

This stock's total score in 2021 was **52**, in 2020 it was **48**, in 2019 it was **25**.

HISTORICAL STOCK PRICES & DIVIDEND PAYOUTS

Year	Dividend	Stock	Year	Dividend	Stock
2022	$ 12.81	$ 0.10	2010	$ 13.14	$ 0.10
2021	$ 12.90	$ 0.10	2009	$ 9.33	$ 0.15
2020	$ 9.35	$ 0.10	2008	$ 13.56	$ 0.21
2019	$ 11.35	$ 0.10	2007	$ 18.42	$ 0.21
2018	$ 11.66	$ 0.10	2006	$ 18.36	$ 0.21
2017	$ 12.00	$ 0.10	2005	$ 26.21	$ 0.21
2016	$ 10.45	$ 0.10	2004	$ 21.84	$ 0.21
2015	$ 12.31	$ 0.10	2003	$ 19.29	$ 0.21
2014	$ 12.67	$ 0.10	2002	$ 19.95	$ 0.21
2013	$ 11.50	$ 0.10	2001	$ 20.21	$ 0.21
2012	$ 12.38	$ 0.10	2000	$ 18.75	$ 0.21
2011	$ 15.25	$ 0.10	1999	$ 16.20	$ 0.18

NOTES: EIT.UN is a closed-end investment trust.

Capital Power Corporation
(CPX)

Updated May 2023

IDM STOCK SCORING CALCULATION

(1) Stock Price $ 43.77   Score 8
(2) Price 4 Years Ago $ 30.20 Score 8
(3) Current to Four Year Price Score 9
(4) Book Value $ 20.99   Score 7
(5) Price to Book Comparison Score 0
(6) Analyst Buys # 3   Score 3

(7) Analysts Strong Buys # 0   Score 0
(8) Dividend Yield % 5.30   Score 8
(9) Operating Margin % 9.05   Score 2
(10) Trading Volume 322,986   Score 5
(11) Price to Earnings 51.8x   Score 2

Total of All 11 Scores =52

This stock's total score in 2021 was **59,** in 2020 it was **59,** in 2019 it was.**62**

HISTORICAL STOCK PRICES & DIVIDEND PAYOUTS

Year	Dividend	Stock	Year	Dividend	Stock
2022	$ 42.25	$ 0.55	2010	$ 22.12	$ 0.32
2021	$ 39.96	$ 0.51	2009	$ NA	$ NA
2020	$ 26.82	$ 0.48	2008	$ NA	$ NA
2019	$ 26.42	$ 0.45	2007	$ NA	$ NA
2018	$ 24.51	$ 0.42	2006	$ NA	$ NA
2017	$ 25.11	$ 0.39	2005	$ NA	$ NA
2016	$ 17.72	$ 0.36	2004	$ NA	$ NA
2015	$ 24.51	$ 0.34	2003	$ NA	$ NA
2014	$ 21.95	$ 0.32	2002	$ NA	$ NA
2013	$ 23.28	$ 0.32	2001	$ NA	$ NA
2012	$ 23.36	$ 0.32	2000	$ NA	$ NA
2011	$ 26.28	$ 0.32	1999	$ NA	$ NA

NOTES: CPX develops, acquires, owns, and operates renewable and thermal power generation facilities and manages its related electricity and natural gas portfolios by undertaking trading and marketing activities.

CARDINAL ENERGY LTD

(CJ)

Updated May 2023

IDM STOCK SCORING CALCULATION

(1) Stock Price $ 7.18   Score 4   *(7)* Analysts Strong Buys # 0   Score 0
(2) Price 4 Years Ago $ 2.94   Score 3   *(8)* Dividend Yield % 10.03   Score 10
(3) Current to Four Year Price Score 10   *(9)* Operating Margin % 50.09   Score 8
(4) Book Value $ 5.94   Score 4   *(10)* Trading Volume 534,946   Score 6
(5) Price to Book Comparison Score 1   *(11)* Price to Earnings 3.8x   Score 10
(6) Analyst Buys # 0   Score 0

Total of All 11 Scores = 56

This stock's total score in 2021 was **NA** , in 2020 it was **NA**, in 2019 it was **54**.

HISTORICAL STOCK PRICES & DIVIDEND PAYOUTS

Year	Dividend	Stock	Year	Dividend	Stock
2022	$ 8.94	$ 0.05	2010	$ NA	$ NA
2021	$ 3.45	$ NA	2009	$ NA	$ NA
2020	$ 0.67	$ NA	2008	$ NA	$ NA
2019	$ 2.40	$ 0.01	2007	$ NA	$ NA
2018	$ 5.22	$.0.04	2006	$ NA	$ NA
2017	$ 4.64	$.0.04	2005	$ NA	$ NA
2016	$ 9.56	$.0.04	2004	$ NA	$ NA
2015	$ 10.58	$ 0.07	2003	$ NA	$ NA
2014	$ 16.65	$ 0.05	2002	$ NA	$ NA
2013	$ NA	$ NA	2001	$ NA	$ NA
2012	$ NA	$ NA	2000	$ NA	$ NA
2011	$ NA	$ NA	1999	$ NA	$ NA

NOTES: CJ is a Canada-based oil and gas company.

CARIBBEAN UTILITIES COMPANY LIMITED

(CUP.U)

Updated May 2023

IDM STOCK SCORING CALCULATION

(1) Stock Price $ 13.75   Score 5
(2) Price 4 Years Ago $ 15.48 Score 6
(3) Current to Four Year Price Score 2
(4) Book Value $ 8.18   Score 4
(5) Price to Book Comparison Score 0
(6) Analyst Buys # 0   Score 0

(7) Analysts Strong Buys # 0   Score 0
(8) Dividend Yield % 5.09   Score 8
(9) Operating Margin % 12.00   Score 3
(10) Trading Volume 702   Score 0
(11) Price to Earnings 16.0x   Score 8

Total of All 11 Scores = 36

This stock's total score in 2021 was **41**, in 2020 it was **43**, in 2019 it was.**44**.

HISTORICAL STOCK PRICES & DIVIDEND PAYOUTS

Year	Dividend	Stock	Year	Dividend	Stock
2022	$ 15.00	$ 0.17	2010	$ 9.00	$ 0.17
2021	$ 15.10	$ 0.17	2009	$ 8.66	$ 0.17
2020	$ 15.01	$ 0.17	2008	$ 11.20	$ 0.17
2019	$ 16.01	$ 0.17	2007	$ 12.03	$ 0.17
2018	$ 12.99	$ 0.17	2006	$ 11.81	$.017
2017	$ 13.31	$ 0.17	2005	$ 11.69	$ 0.17
2016	$ 13.10	$ 0.17	2004	$ 12.59	$ 0.17
2015	$ 11.15	$ 0.17	2003	$ 13.05	$ 0.16
2014	$ 10.60	$ 0.17	2002	$ 11.00	$ 0.15
2013	$ 9.65	$ 0.17	2001	$ 12.32	$ 0.14
2012	$ 9.40	$ 0.17	2000	$ 10.50	$ 0.12
2011	$ 0.07	$ 0.17	1999	$ 10.50	$ NA

NOTES: CUP.U is engaged in generating, transmitting and distributing electricity in its license area of Grand Cayman, Cayman Islands.

CASCADES INC
(CAS)
Updated May 2023

IDM STOCK SCORING CALCULATION

(1) Stock Price $ 10.90   Score 5
(2) Price 4 Years Ago $ 7.84   Score 4
(3) Current to Four Year Price Score 9
(4) Book Value $ 18.64   Score 6
(5) Price to Book Comparison   Score 8
(6) Analyst Buys # 1   Score 2

(7) Analysts Strong Buys # 0   Score 0
(8) Dividend Yield % 4.40   Score 6
(9) Operating Margin % 0.74   Score 0
(10) Trading Volume 154,856   Score 4
(11) Price to Earnings -31.8x   Score 0

Total of All 11 Scores = 44

This stock's total score in 2021 was **NA**, in 2020 it was **NA,** in 2019 it was **NA**.

HISTORICAL STOCK PRICES & DIVIDEND PAYOUTS

Year	Dividend	Stock	Year	Dividend	Stock
2022	$ 8.35	$ 0.12	2010	$ 6.93	$ 0.04
2021	$ 14.84	$ 0.08	2009	$ 3.60	$ 0.04
2020	$ 14.13	$ 0.08	2008	$ 8.32	$ 0.04
2019	$ 12.13	$ 0.04	2007	$ 12.14	$ 0.04
2018	$ 12.30	$ 0.04	2006	$ 11.00	$ 0.04
2017	$ 15.65	$ 0.04	2005	$ 11.19	$ 0.04
2016	$ 9.27	$ 0.04	2004	$ 13.50	$ 0.04
2015	$ 7.59	$ 0.04	2003	$ 14.20	$ 0.04
2014	$ 7.25	$ 0.04	2002	$ 17.35	$ 0.04
2013	$ 5.16	$ 0.04	2001	$ 7.90	$ 0.12
2012	$ 4.02	$ 0.04	2000	$ 7.80	$ NA
2011	$ 7.15	$ 0.04	1999	$ 9.55	$ 0.10

NOTES: CAS is a Canada-based paper and packaging company.

C-COM SATELLITE SYSTEMS INC
(CMI)
Updated May 2023

IDM STOCK SCORING CALCULATION

(1) Stock Price $ 0.90   Score 1

(2) Price 4 Years Ago $ 1.76   Score 2

(3) Current to Four Year Price Score 2

(4) Book Value $ 0.60   Score 1

(5) Price to Book Comparison Score 0

(6) Analyst Buys # 0   Score 0

(7) Analysts Strong Buys # 0 Score 0

(8) Dividend Yield % 5.32   Score 8

(9) Operating Margin % 1.72   Score 1

(10) Trading Volume 505   Score 0

(11) Price to Earnings 107.6x   Score 1

Total of All 11 Scores =16

This stock's total score in 2021 was **NA**, in 2020 it was **NA**, in 2019 it was **NA**.

HISTORICAL STOCK PRICES & DIVIDEND PAYOUTS

Year	Stock	Dividend	Year	Stock	Dividend
2022	$ 1.45	$ 0.01	2010	$ 0.30	$ NA
2021	$3.02	$ 0.01	2009	$ 0.32	$ NA
2020	$ 1.87	$ 0.01	2008	$ 0.38	$ NA
2019	$ 1.75	$ 0.01	2007	$ 0.29	$ NA
2018	$ 1.15	$ 0.01	2006	$ 0.40	$ NA
2017	$ 0.97	$ 0.01	2005	$ 0.26	$ NA
2016	$ 1.11	$ 0.01	2004	$ 0.45	$ NA
2015	$ 1.12	$ 0.01	2003	$ 0.32	$ NA
2014	$ 1.49	$ 0.01	2002	$ 0.17	$ NA
2013	$ 1.10	$ 0.01	2001	$ 0.73	$ NA
2012	$ 0.79	$ 0.01	2000	$ 2.89	$ NA
2011	$ 0.39	$ NA	1999	$ NA	$ NA

NOTES: CMI is a Canada-based company, which is engaged in the development of satellite-based technology, which allows the delivery of high-speed Internet access for fixed, transportable and mobile end-users.

CHARTWELL RETIREMENT RESIDENCES

(CSH.UN)

Updated May 2023

IDM STOCK SCORING CALCULATION

(1) Stock Price $ 9.23   *Score* 4

(2) Price 4 Years Ago $ 14.50 *Score* 5

(3) Current to Four Year Price *Score* 2

(4) Book Value $ 3.26   *Score* 3

(5) Price to Book Comparison *Score* 0

(6) Analyst Buys # 4   *Score* 4

(7) Analysts Strong Buys # 0 *Score* 0

(8) Dividend Yield % 6.63   *Score* 8

(9) Operating Margin % 4.92 *Score* 2

(10) Trading Volume 381,231 *Score* 5

(11) Price to Earnings 82.6x   *Score* 2

Total of All 11 Scores = 35

This stock's total score in 2021 was **32** , in 2020 it was **38**, in 2019 it was **43**.

HISTORICAL STOCK PRICES & DIVIDEND PAYOUTS

Year	Stock	Dividend	Year	Stock	Dividend
2022	$ 11.15	$ 0.05	2010	$ 7.17	$ 0.04
2021	$ 13.25	$ 0.05	2009	$ 5.42	$ 0.06
2020	$ 9.87	$ 0.05	2008	$ 9.19	$ 0.06
2019	$ 14.50	$ 0.05	2007	$ 10.05	$ 0.06
2018	$ 15.30	$ 0.05	2006	$ 13.93	$ 0.09
2017	$ 16.08	$ 0.05	2005	$ 15.25	$ 0.09
2016	$ 15.86	$ 0.05	2004	$ 11.50	$ 0.09
2015	$ 11.96	$ 0.05	2003	$ NA	$ NA
2014	$ 10.80	$ 0.04	2002	$ NA	$ NA
2013	$ 9.77	$ 0.04	2001	$ NA	$ NA
2012	$ 10.04	$ 0.04	2000	$ NA	$ NA
2011	$ 8.65	$ 0.04	1999	$ NA	$ NA

NOTES: CSH.UN is a Canada-based open-ended real estate trust. The Company is engaged in the ownership, operations and management of retirement and long-term care communities in Canada.

CHEMTRADE LOGISTICS INCOME FUND

(CHE.UN)
Updated May 2023

IDM STOCK SCORING CALCULATION

(1) Stock Price $ 8.63   Score 4

(2) Price 4 Years Ago $ 10.10 Score 5

(3) Current to Four Year Price Score 2

(4) Book Value $ 4.90   Score 3

(5) Price to Book Comparison Score 0

(6) Analyst Buys # 3   Score 3

(7) Analysts Strong Buys # 0 Score 0

(8) Dividend Yield % 6.95   Score 8

(9) Operating Margin % 12.80 Score 3

(10) Trading Volume 483,003 Score 5

(11) Price to Earnings 11.1   Score 9

Total of All 11 Scores = 42

This stock's total score in 2021 was **35** , in 2020 it was **31**, in 2019 it was **36**.

HISTORICAL STOCK PRICES & DIVIDEND PAYOUTS

Year	Stock	Dividend	Year	Stock	Dividend
2022	$ 8.11	$ 0.05	2010	$ 11.46	$ 0.10
2021	$ 6.70	$ 0.05	2009	$ 7.42	$ 0.10
2020	$ 5.44	$ 0.05	2008	$ 13.74	$ 0.10
2019	$ 10.10	$ 0.10	2007	$ 9.75	$ 0.10
2018	$ 14.73	$ 0.10	2006	$ 7.90	$ 0.10
2017	$ 17.44	$ 0.10	2005	$ 15.75	$ 0.11
2016	$ 17.84	$ 0.10	2004	$ 17.85	$ 0.11
2015	$ 19.28	$ 0.10	2003	$ 15.15	$ 0.11
2014	$ 20.96	$ 0.10	2002	$ 14.50	$ 0.10
2013	$ 16.90	$ 0.10	2001	$ 10.86	$ 0.14
2012	$ 15.48	$ 0.10	2000	$ NA	$ NA
2011	$ 14.24	$ 0.10	1999	$ NA	$ NA

NOTES: CHE.UN provides industrial chemicals and services.

CHESSWOOD GROUP LTD

(CHW)

Updated May 2023

IDM STOCK SCORING CALCULATION

(1) Stock Price $ 8.14   Score 4

(2) Price 4 Years Ago $ 9.86   Score 4

(3) Current to Four Year Price Score 2

(4) Book Value $ 12.01   Score 5

(5) Price to Book Comparison   Score 8

(6) Analyst Buys # 0   Score 0

(7) Analysts Strong Buys # 0   Score 0

(8) Dividend Yield % 7.37   Score 8

(9) Operating Margin % 14.73   Score 4

(10) Trading Volume 1,697   Score 0

(11) Price to Earnings 5.7x   Score 9

Total of All 11 Scores = 44

This stock's total score in 2021 was **NA** , in 2020 it was **29**, in 2019 it was.**43**

HISTORICAL STOCK PRICES & DIVIDEND PAYOUTS

Year	Stock	Dividend	Year	Stock	Dividend
2022	$ 12.15	$ 0.04	2010	$ 4.39	$ 0.03
2021	$ 11.72	$ 0.03	2009	$ 2.09	$ 0.02
2020	$ 3.79	$ 0.04	2008	$ 1.52	$ 0.05
2019	$ 9.86	$ 0.07	2007	$ 6.66	$ .0.09
2018	$ 11.58	$ 0.07	2006	$ 8.23	$ 0.06
2017	$ 11.89	$ 0.07	2005	$ NA	$ NA
2016	$ 10.20	$ 0.07	2004	$ NA	$ NA
2015	$ 11.40	$ 0.06	2003	$ NA	$ NA
2014	$ 12.86	$ 0.06	2002	$ NA	$ NA
2013	$ 11.69	$ 0.06	2001	$ NA	$ NA
2012	$ 7.23	$ 0.05	2000	$ NA	$ NA
2011	$ 6.86	$ 0.05	1999	$ NA	$ NA

NOTES: CHW is engaged in various businesses through its five subsidiaries, Pawnee Leasing Corporation (Pawnee), Tandem Finance Inc. (Tandem), Blue Chip Leasing Corporation (Blue Chip), Vault Credit Corporation (Vault Credit) and Vault Home Credit Corporation (Vault Home).

CHOICE PROPERTIES REAL ESTATE INVESTMENT TRUST

(CHP.UN)

Updated May 2023

IDM STOCK SCORING CALCULATION

(1) Stock Price $ 13.93.   Score 5
(2) Price 4 Years Ago $13.68 Score 5
(3) Current to Four Year Price Score 7
(4) Book Value $ 5.29   Score 4
(5) Price to Book Comparison Score 0
(6) Analyst Buys # 3   Score 3

(7) Analysts Strong Buys # 0 Score 0
(8) Dividend Yield % 5.38   Score 8
(9) Operating Margin % 49.79 Score 8
(10) Trading Volume 191,388 Score 4
(11) Price to Earnings 16.1   Score 8

Total of All 11 Scores = 52

This stock's total score in 2021 was **36**, in 2020 it was **NA**, in 2019 it was **32**.

HISTORICAL STOCK PRICES & DIVIDEND PAYOUTS

Year	Stock	Dividend	Year	Stock	Dividend
2022	$ 15.08	$ 0.06	2010	$ NA	$ NA
2021	$ 14.29	$ 0.06	2009	$ NA	$ NA
2020	$ 12.74	$ 0.06	2008	$ NA	$ NA
2019	$ 13.68	$ 0.06	2007	$ NA	$ NA
2018	$ 12.11	$ 0.06	2006	$ NA	$ NA
2017	$ 13.84	$ 0.06	2005	$ NA	$ NA
2016	$ 14.20	$ 0.06	2004	$ NA	$ NA
2015	$ 10.80	$ 0.05	2003	$ NA	$ NA
2014	$ 10.59	$ 0.05	2002	$ NA	$ NA
2013	$ 10.39	$ 0.10	2001	$ NA	$ NA
2012	$ NA	$ NA	2000	$ NA	$ NA
2011	$.NA	$.NA	1999	$ NA	$ NA

NOTES: CHP.UN is an unincorporated, open-ended real estate investment trust.

CI FINANCIAL CORPORATION
(CIX)
Updated May 2023

IDM STOCK SCORING CALCULATION

(1) Stock Price $ 12.53   Score 5
(2) Price 4 Years Ago $ 20.46 Score 7
(3) Current to Four Year Price Score 2
(4) Book Value $ 8.72   Score 4
(5) Price to Book Comparison Score 1
(6) Analyst Buys # 2   Score 3

(7) Analysts Strong Buys # 0   Score 0
(8) Dividend Yield % 5.75   Score 8
(9) Operating Margin % 24.91 Score 5
(10) Trading Volume 2,672,741 Score 10
(11) Price to Earnings 12.5   Score 9

Total of All 11 Scores = 54

This stock's total score in 2021 was **53** , in 2020 it was **NA**, in 2019 it was **53**.

HISTORICAL STOCK PRICES & DIVIDEND PAYOUTS

Year	Stock	Dividend	Year	Stock	Dividend
2022	$ 13.67	$ 0.18	2010	$ 17.80	$ 0.07
2021	$ 22.75	$ 0.18	2009	$ 18.00	$ 0.10
2020	$ 17.27	$ 0.18	2008	$ 22.00	$ 0.17
2019	$ 20.46	$ 0.18	2007	$ 27.10	$ 0.18
2018	$ 22.73	$ 0.12	2006	$ 29.54	$ 0.06
2017	$ 27.16	$ 0.12	2005	$ 17.65	$ 0.05
2016	$ 26.69	$ 0.12	2004	$ 16.44	$ 0.13
2015	$ 35.11	$ 0.11	2003	$ 11.47	$ 0.08
2014	$ 35.30	$ 0.10	2002	$ 10.60	$ 0.05
2013	$ 31.03	$ 0.09	2001	$ 12.20	$ 0.01
2012	$ 22.18	$ 0.08	2000	$ 14.02	$ 0.01
2011	$ 23.41	$ 0.07	1999	$ 3.75	$ 0.01

NOTES: CIX. is a Canada-based diversified global asset and wealth management company.

COGECO COMMUNICATIONS INC

(CCA)

Updated May 2023

IDM STOCK SCORING CALCULATION

(1) Stock Price $ 66.27   Score 9

(2) Price 4 Years Ago $ 92.70 Score 9

(3) Current to Four Year Price Score 2

(4) Book Value $ 60.10   Score 9

(5) Price to Book Comparison Score 1

(6) Analyst Buys # 1   Score 2

(7) Analysts Strong Buys # 0 Score 0

(8) Dividend Yield % 4.68   Score 8

(9) Operating Margin % 25.73 Score 5

(10) Trading Volume 139,730 Score 4

(11) Price to Earnings 7.3x   Score 9

Total of All 11 Scores = 58

This stock's total score in 2021 was **NA**, in 2020 it was **NA**, in 2019 it was.**NA**

HISTORICAL STOCK PRICES & DIVIDEND PAYOUTS

Year	Stock	Dividend	Year	Stock	Dividend
2022	$ 80.41	$ 0.70	2010	$ 35.82	$ 0.14
2021	$ 118.13	$ 0.64	2009	$ 29.25	$ 0.12
2020	$ 102.10	$ 0.58	2008	$ 44.00	$ 0.10
2019	$ 104.23	$ 0.53	2007	$ 46.50	$ 0.08
2018	$ 70.60	$ 0.47	2006	$ 25.24	$ 0.04
2017	$ 87.10	$ 0.43	2005	$ 32.45	$ 0.04
2016	$ 63.45	$ 0.39	2004	$ 22.00	$ 0.02
2015	$ 66.41	$ 0.35	2003	$ 18.25	$ NA
2014	$ 62.70	$ 0.30	2002	$ 10.10	$ NA
2013	$ 48.36	$ 0.26	2001	$ 30.25	$ NA
2012	$ 36.18	$ 0.25	2000	$ 42.50	$ 0.06
2011	$ 48.08	$ 0.20	1999	$ 23.30	$ 0.06

NOTES: CCA is a diversified holding corporation, which operates in the communications and media

COGECO INC

(CGO)

Updated May 2023

IDM STOCK SCORING CALCULATION

(1) Stock Price $ 55.29   *Score 9*
(2) Price 4 Years Ago $ 83.56. Score 9
(3) Current to Four Year Price Score 2
(4) Book Value $ 58.30   *Score 9*
(5) Price to Book Comparison Score 6
(6) Analyst Buys # 0   *Score 0*

(7) Analysts Strong Buys # 1 Score 3
(8) Dividend Yield % 5.29   *Score 8*
(9) Operating Margin % 25.24 Score 5
(10) Trading Volume 30,848   *Score 2*
(11) Price to Earnings 5.8x   *Score 9*

Total of All 11 Scores = 62

This stock's total score in 2021 was **NA**, in 2020 it was **NA**, in 2019 it was **NA**.

HISTORICAL STOCK PRICES & DIVIDEND PAYOUTS

Year	Stock	Dividend	Year	Stock	Dividend
2022	$ 68.25	$ 0.63	2010	$ 30.00	$ 0.10
2021	$ 92.99	$ 0.55	2009	$ 22.51	$ 0.08
2020	$ 86.28	$ 0.47	2008	$ 31.00	$ 0.07
2019	$ 94.00	$ 0.43	2007	$ 38.36	$ 0.07
2018	$ 71.70	$ 0.39	2006	$ 22.25	$ 0.06
2017	$ 73.38	$ 0.34	2005	$ 24.36	$ 0.05
2016	$ 56.90	$0.29	2004	$ 18.00	$ 0.05
2015	$ 57.33	$ 0.26	2003	$ NA	$ 0.05
2014	$ 54.10	$ 0.22	2002	$ NA	$ 0.05
2013	$ 41.70	$ 0.19	2001	$ NA	$ 0.05
2012	$ 48.90	$ 0.18	2000	$ NA	$ 0.05
2011	$ 42.20	$ 0.12	1999	$ NA	$ 0.05

NOTES: CGO is a diversified holding corporation, which operates in the communications and media sectors

Corby Spirit and Wine Limited

(CSW.B)

Updated May 2023

IDM STOCK SCORING CALCULATION

(1) Stock Price $ 13.65   Score 5
(2) Price 4 Years Ago $ 16.50 Score 6
(3) Current to Four Year Price Score 2
(4) Book Value $ 6.44   Score 4
(5) Price to Book Comparison Score 0
(6) Analyst Buys # 0   Score 0

(7) Analysts Strong Buys # 0 Score 0
(8) Dividend Yield % 6.15   Score 8
(9) Operating Margin % 19.71 Score 5
(10) Trading Volume 830   Score 0
(11) Price to Earnings 0.0x   Score 0

Total of All 11 Scores = 30

This stock's total score in 2021 was **32** , in 2020 it was **NA**, in 2019 it was **39**.

HISTORICAL STOCK PRICES & DIVIDEND PAYOUTS

Year	Stock	Dividend	Year	Stock	Dividend
2022	$ 17.32	$ 0.24	2010	$ 14.55	$ 0.13
2021	$ 17.35	$ 0.21	2009	$ 13.04	$ 0.13
2020	$ 14.00	$ 0.20	2008	$ 15.47	$ 0.13
2019	$ 16.65	$ 0.22	2007	$ 20.56	$ 0.13
2018	$ 17.76	$ 0.21	2006	$ 19.89	$ 0.13
2017	$ 20.00	$ 0.20	2005	$ 16.70	$ 0.13
2016	$ 16.44	$ 0.19	2004	$ 14.42	$ 0.11
2015	$ 16.94	$ 0.18	2003	$ 12.81	$ 0.11
2014	$ 18.75	$ 0.16	2002	$ 13.61	$ 0.11
2013	$ 18.08	$ 0.16	2001	$ 12.13	$ 0.11
2012	$ 15.66	$ 0.14	2000	$ 11.10	$ 0.11
2011	$ 15.31	$ 0.13	1999	$ 14.19	$.011

NOTES: CSW.B is a Canada-based manufacturer, marketer and importer of spirits and wines.

CORBY SPRIRIT AND WINE LIMITED

(CSW.A)

Updated May 2023

IDM STOCK SCORING CALCULATION

(1) Stock Price $ 15.01   Score 6   *(7)* Analysts Strong Buys # 0 Score 0
(2) Price 4 Years Ago $ 15.78   Score 6   *(8)* Dividend Yield % 5.60   Score 8
(3) Current to Four Year Price   Score 5   *(9)* Operating Margin % 19.71 Score 5
(4) Book Value $ 6.44   Score 4   *(10)* Trading Volume 31,716   Score 2
(5) Price to Book Comparison   Score 0   *(11)* Price to Earnings 18.2x   Score 8
(6) Analyst Buys # 0   Score 0

Total of All 11 Scores = 44

This stock's total score in 2021 was **40,** in 2020 it was **NA**, in 2019 it was **40.**

HISTORICAL STOCK PRICES & DIVIDEND PAYOUTS

Year	Stock	Dividend	Year	Stock	Dividend
2022	$ 17.38	$ 0.24	2010	$ 13.97	$ 0.13
2021	$ 18.58	$ 0.21	2009	$ 13.80	$ 0.13
2020	$ 16.16	$ 0.20	2008	$ 17.01	$ 0.13
2019	$ 17.57	$ 0.22	2007	$ 23.27	$0.13
2018	$ 20.21	$ 0.22	2006	$ 21.06	$ 0.13
2017	$ 21.63	$ .0.21	2005	$ 16.74	$ 0.13
2016	$ 20.03	$ 0.19	2004	$ 15.20	$ 0.11
2015	$ 20.16	$ 0.18	2003	$ 12.00	$ 0.11
2014	$ 18.94	$ 0.17	2002	$ 14.65	$0.11
2013	$ 18.21	$ 0.16	2001	$ 14.31	$0.11
2012	$ 14.89	$ 0.14	2000	$ NA	$ 011
2011	$ 15.45	$ 0.13	1999	$ NA	$ 0.11

NOTES: CSW.A is a Canada-based manufacturer, marketer and importer of spirits and wines.

CORUS ENTERTAINMENT INC

(CJR.B)

Updated May 2023

IDM STOCK SCORING CALCULATION

(1) Stock Price $ 1.39   Score 2
(2) Price 4 Years Ago $ 6.14   Score 4
(3) Current to Four Year Price   Score 1
(4) Book Value $ 3.77   Score 3
(5) Price to Book Comparison   Score 10
(6) Analyst Buys # 0   Score 0

(7) Analysts Strong Buys # 1   Score 3
(8) Dividend Yield % 8.63   Score 10
(9) Operating Margin % -19.38   Score 4
(10) Trading Volume 441,756   Score 5
(11) Price to Earnings -0.9   Score 0

Total of All 11 Scores = 42

This stock's total score in 2021 was **31**, in 2020 it was **NA**, in 2019 it was **NA**.

HISTORICAL STOCK PRICES & DIVIDEND PAYOUTS

Year	Stock	Dividend	Year	Stock	Dividend
2022	$ 3.53	$ 0.06	2010	$ 19.91	$ 0.05
2021	$ 5.79	$ 0.06	2009	$ 14.97	$ 0.05
2020	$ 4.29	$ 0.06	2008	$ 18.14	$ 0.05
2019	$ 5.06	$ 0.06	2007	$ 19.50	$ 0.04
2018	$ 4.96	$ 0.10	2006	$ 19.51	$.0.05
2017	$ 13.78	$ 0.10	2005	$ 15.20	$ 0.03
2016	$ 12.90	$ 0.10	2004	$ 12.02	$ 0.01
2015	$ 12.47	$ 0.10	2003	$ NA	$ NA
2014	$ 24.50	$ 0.09	2002	$ NA	$ NA
2013	$ 25.25	$ 0.09	2001	$ NA	$ NA
2012	$ 24.75	0.08	2000	$ NA	$ NA
2011	$ 20.40	$ 0.06	1999	$ NA	$ NA

NOTES: CJR.B is a Canada-based diversified, integrated media and content company that develops and delivers brands and content across platforms. The Company operates in two segments: Television and Radio.

CROMBIE REAL ESTAT INVESTMENT TRUST

(CRR.UN)

Updated May 2023

IDM STOCK SCORING CALCULATION

(1) Stock Price $ 15.08   Score 6
(2) Price 4 Years Ago $ 15.64   Score 6
(3) Current to Four Year Price   Score 5
(4) Book Value $ 10.37   Score 5
(5) Price to Book Comparison   Score 1
(6) Analyst Buys # 2   Score 3

(7) Analysts Strong Buys # 0   Score 0
(8) Dividend Yield % 5.90   Score 8
(9) Operating Margin % 59.57   Score 8
(10) Trading Volume 68,669   Score 3
(11) Price to Earnings 223.7x   Score 1

Total of All 11 Scores = 46

This stock's total score in 2021 was **46**, in 2020 it was **NA**, in 2019 it was **59**.

HISTORICAL STOCK PRICES & DIVIDEND PAYOUTS

Year	Stock	Dividend	Year	Stock	Dividend
2022	$ 17.34	$ 0.07	2010	$ 11.28	$ 0.07
2021	$ 18.08	$ 0.07	2009	$ 9.18	$ 0.07
2020	$ 13.17	$ 0.07	2008	$ 11.10	$ 0.07
2019	$ 15.93	$ 0.07	2007	$ 13.85	$ 0.07
2018	$ 13.11	$ 0.07	2006	$ 10.90	$ 0.07
2017	$ 13.40	$ 0.07	2005	$ NA	$ 0.07
2016	$ 13.53	$ 0.07	2004	$ NA	$ NA
2015	$ 12.66	$ 0.07	2003	$ NA	$ NA
2014	$ 13.20	$ 0.07	2002	$ NA	$ NA
2013	$ 13.54	$ 0.07	2001	$ NA	$ NA
2012	$ 15.03	$ 0.07	2000	$ NA	$ NA
2011	$ 13.20	$ 0.07	1999	$ NA	$ NA

NOTES: CRR.UN is a Canada-based national real estate investment trusts.

CT REAL ESTATE INVESTMENT TRUST

(CRT.UN)

Updated May 2023CPG
IDM STOCK SCORING CALCULATION

(1) Stock Price $ 15.55   Score 6
(2) Price 4 Years Ago $ 15.03 Score 6
(3) Current to Four Year Price Score 7
(4) Book Value $ 7.24   Score 4
(5) Price to Book Comparison Score 0
(6) Analyst Buys # 1   Score 2

(7) Analysts Strong Buys # 0   Score 0
(8) Dividend Yield % 5.58   Score 8
(9) Operating Margin % 56.11 Score 8
(10) Trading Volume 59,508   Score 3
(11) Price to Earnings 36.9   Score 4

Total of All 11 Scores = 48

This stock's total score in 2021 was **46** , in 2020 it was **NA**, in 2019 it was **57**.

HISTORICAL STOCK PRICES & DIVIDEND PAYOUTS

Year	Stock	Dividend	Year	Stock	Dividend
2022	$ 15.50	$ 0.07	2010	$ NA	$ NA
2021	$ 17.08	$ 0.07	2009	$ NA	$ NA
2020	$ 13.79	$ 0.07	2008	$.NA	$ NA
2019	$ 14.22	$ 0.06	2007	$ NA	$ NA
2018	$ 12.90	$ 0.06	2006	$ NA	$ NA
2017	$ 13.97	$ 0.06	2005	$ NA	$ NA
2016	$ 14.80	$ 0.06	2004	$ NA	$ NA
2015	$ 12.73	$ 0.06	2003	$ NA	$ NA
2014	$ 11.74	$ 0.05	2002	$ NA	$ NA
2013	$ NA	$ NA	2001	$ NA	$ NA
2012	$ NA	$ NA	2000	$ NA	$ NA
2011	$ NA	$ NA	1999	$ NA	$ NA

NOTES:

Notes: **CRT.UN** is a Canada-based closed end real estate investment trust.

CRESCENT POINT ENERGY CORP

(CPG)

Updated May 2023

IDM STOCK SCORING CALCULATION

(1) Stock Price $ 9.10   *Score* 4   *(7)* Analysts Strong Buys # 0   *Score* 0
(2) Price 4 Years Ago $ 4.38   *Score*   *(8)* Dividend Yield % 4.40   *Score* 6
(3) Current to Four Year Price   *Score* 10   *(9)* Operating Margin % 19.12   *Score* 4
(4) Book Value $ 11.79   *Score* 5   *(10)* Trading Volume 2,176,770 *Score* 10
(5) Price to Book Comparison   *Score* 8   *(11)* Price to Earnings 10.2x *Score* 9
(6) Analyst Buys # 9   *Score* 5

Total of All 11 Scores = 64

This stock's total score in 2021 was **NA**, in 2020 it was **NA**, in 2019 it was **NA**.

HISTORICAL STOCK PRICES & DIVIDEND PAYOUTS

Year	Stock	Dividend	Year	Stock	Dividend
2022	$ 10.13	$ 0.07	2010	$ 38.92	$ 0.23
2021	$ 5.61	$ 0.00	2009	$ 34.32	$ 0.23
2020	$ 2.20	$ 0.00	2008	$ 36.13	$ 0.20
2019	$ 4.38	$ 0.01	2007	$ 19.63	$ 20
2018	$ 8.87	$ 0.03	2006	$ 21.83	$ 20
2017	$ 8.57	$ 0.03	2005	$ 20.44	$ 0.17
2016	$ 20.41	$ 0.03	2004	$ 14.95	$ 0.17
2015	$ 19.81	$ 0.23	2003	$ 11.95	$ 0.17
2014	$ 47.29	$ 0.23	2002	$ NA	$ NA
2013	$ 38.95	$ 0.23	2001	$ NA	$ NA
2012	$ 38.00	$ 0.23	2000	$ NA	$ NA
2011	$ 46.92	$ 0.23	1999	$ NA	$ NA

NOTES: CPG is a Canada-based oil and gas exploration company.

DECISIVE DIVIDEND CORPORATION

(DE)
Updated May 2023

IDM STOCK SCORING CALCULATION

(1) Stock Price $ 6.65   Score *4*
(2) Price 4 Years Ago $ 3.96   Score *3*
(3) Current to Four Year Price Score *9*
(4) Book Value $ 2.29   Score *3*
(5) Price to Book Comparison   Score *0*
(6) Analyst Buys # 0   Score *0*

(7) Analysts Strong Buys # 0   Score *0*
(8) Dividend Yield % 9.32   Score *10*
(9) Operating Margin % 6.02   Score *2*
(10) Trading Volume 16,865   Score *1*
(11) Price to Earnings 17.5x   Score *8*

Total of All 11 Scores = 40

This stock's total score in 2021 was **22**, in 2020 it was **NA**, in 2019 it was **30**.

HISTORICAL STOCK PRICES & DIVIDEND PAYOUTS

Year	Stock	Dividend	Year	Stock	Dividend
2022	$ 4.30	$ 0.03	2010	$ NA	$ NA
2021	$ 4.06	$ 0.02	2009	$ NA	$ NA
2020	$ 1.45	$ 0.03	2008	$ NA	$ N
2019	$ 3.96	$ 0.03	2007	$ NA	$ NA
2018	$ 4.16	$ 0.03	2006	$ NA	$ NA
2017	$ 4.23	$ 0.03	2005	$ NA	$ NA
2016	$ 3.33	$ 0.03	2004	$ NA	$ NA
2015	$ 2.55	$ 0.02	2003	$ NA	$ NA
2014	$ 1.00	$ NA	2002	$ NA	$ NA
2013	$ NA	$ NA	2001	$ NA	$ NA
2012	$ NA	$ NA	2000	$ NA	$ NA
2011	$ NA	$ NA	1999	$ NA	$ NA

NOTES: DE is a Canada-based acquisition-oriented company. The Company is focused on opportunities in manufacturing. Its segments include finished product and component manufacturing.

DEXTERRA GROUP INC

(DXT)

Updated May 2023

IDM STOCK SCORING CALCULATION

(1) Stock Price $ 5.40   Score 4

(2) Price 4 Years Ago $ 9.50   Score 4

(3) Current to Four Year Price Score 2

(4) Book Value $ 4.40   Score 3

(5) Price to Book Comparison Score 1

(6) Analyst Buys # 3   Score 3

(7) Analysts Strong Buys # 0 Score 0

(8) Dividend Yield % 6.48   Score 8

(9) Operating Margin % 1.61   Score 1

(10) Trading Volume 83,995   Score 3

(11) Price to Earnings 49.6x   Score 2

Total of All 11 Scores =31

This stock's total score in 2021 was **39** , in 2020 it was **NA**, in 2019 it was **NA**.

HISTORICAL STOCK PRICES & DIVIDEND PAYOUTS

Year	Stock	Dividend	Year	Stock	Dividend
2022	$ 5.53	$ 0.09	2010	$ 8.25	$ NA
2021	$ 6.85	$ 0.07	2009	$ 5.00	$ NA
2020	$ 4.79	$ 0.07	2008	$ 16.55	$ NA
2019	$ 9.30	$ 0.10	2007	$ 17.80	$ NA
2018	$ 12.50	$ 0.01	2006	$ NA	$ NA
2017	$ 6.50	$ 0.10	2005	$ NA	$ NA
2016	$ 9.50	$ 0 .10	2004	$ NA	$ NA
2015	$19.25	$ 0.40	2003	$ NA	$ NA
2014	$ 29.80	$ 0.40	2002	$ NA	$ NA
2013	$ 34.15	$ 0.31	2001	$ NA	$ NA
2012	$ 30.50	$ 0.25	2000	$ NA	$ NA
2011	$21..0	$ 0.20	1999	$ NA	$ NA

NOTES: DXT, formerly Horizon North Logistics Inc., is a Canada-based company that offers support services for the creation, management, and operation of infrastructure across Canada.

DIVERSIFIED ROYALTY CORPORATION

(DIV)

Updated May 2023

IDM STOCK SCORING CALCULATION

(1) Stock Price $ 2.85   Score 3
(2) Price 4 Years Ago $ 3.08   Score 3
(3) Current to Four Year Price Score 5
(4) Book Value $ 1.65   Score 2
(5) Price to Book Comparison Score 0
(6) Analyst Buys # 1   Score 2

(7) Analysts Strong Buys # 1   Score 3
(8) Dividend Yield % 8.42   Score 10
(9) Operating Margin % 73.68 Score 9
(10) Trading Volume 268,066   Score 5
(11) Price to Earnings 24.6x   Score 7

Total of All 11 Scores = 49

This stock's total score in 2021 was **40** , in 2020 it was **NA**, in 2019 it was **50**.

HISTORICAL STOCK PRICES & DIVIDEND PAYOUTS

Year	Stock	Dividend	Year	Stock	Dividend
2022	$ 2.71	$ 0.02	2010	$ 2.56	$ NA
2021	$ 2.67	$ 0.02	2009	$ 0.26	$ NA
2020	$ 1.86	$ 0.02	2008	$ 0.38	$ NA
2019	$ 3.08	$ 0.02	2007	$ 0.46	$ NA
2018	$ 3.07	$ 0.02	2006	$ 3.65	$ NA
2017	$ 2.59	$ 0.02	2005	$ 3.58	$ NA
2016	$ 2.28	$ 0.02	2004	$ 17.69	$ NA
2015	$ 2.95	$ 0.02	2003	$ 14.30	$ NA
2014	$ 2.77	$ 0.02	2002	$ 18.50	$ NA
2013	$ 1.70	$ NA	2001	$ 3.80	$ NA
2012	$1.71	$ NA	2000	$ 2.89	$ NA
2011	$ 2.23	$ NA	1999	$ 3.33	$ NA

NOTES: DIV, formerly BENEV Capital Inc., is a multi-royalty company. The Company is engaged in the business of acquiring royalties from multi-location businesses and franchisors in North America

DIVIDEND 15 SPLIT CORPORATION

(DFN)

Updated May 2023

IDM STOCK SCORING CALCULATION

(1) Stock Price $ 7.43   Score 4   *(7)* Analysts Strong Buys # 0   Score 0

(2) Price 4 Years Ago $ 8.24   Score 4   *(8)* Dividend Yield % 16.15   Score 2

(3) Current to Four Year Price   Score 5   *(9)* Operating Margin % 77.95   Score 9

(4) Book Value $ 6.23   Score 4   *(10)* Trading Volume 301,759   Score 5

(5) Price to Book Comparison   Score 1   *(11)* Price to Earnings 151.0x   Score 1

(6) Analyst Buys # 0   Score 0

Total of All 11 Scores = 35

This stock's total score in 2021 was **23** , in 2020 it was **NA**, in 2019 it was **21**.

HISTORICAL STOCK PRICES & DIVIDEND PAYOUTS

Year	Stock	Dividend	Year	Stock	Dividend
2022	$ 7.97	$ 0.10	2010	$ 11.38	$ 0.10
2021	$ 7.96	$ 0.10	2009	$ 10.22	$ 0.10
2020	$ 6.56	$ 0.10	2008	$ 13.85	$ 0.10
2019	$ 8.24	$ 0.10	2007	$ 17.32	$ 0.09
2018	$ 10.14	$ 0.10	2006	$ 15.42	$ 0.09
2017	$ 11.12	$ 0.10	2005	$ 13.07	$ 0.09
2016	$ 10.33	$ 0.10	2004	$ 12.82	0.09$
2015	$ 10.21	$ 0.10	2003	$ NA	$ NA
2014	$ 11.70	$ 0.10	2002	$ NA	$ NA
2013	$ 10.20	$ 0.10	2001	$ NA	$ NA
2012	$ 10.01	$ 0.10	2000	$ NA	$ NA
2011	$ 11.99	$ 0.10	1999	$ NA	$ NA

NOTES: DFN. is a Canada-based mutual fund that invests in a portfolio of dividend yielding common shares, including 15 Canadian companies.

DIVIDEND GROWTH SPLIT CORPORATION

(DGS)

Updated May 2023

IDM STOCK SCORING CALCULATION

(1) Stock Price $ 5.21   Score 4   *(7) Analysts Strong Buys # 0*   Score 0
(2) Price 4 Years Ago $ 4.82   Score 3   *(8) Dividend Yield % 23.03*   Score 2
(3) Current to Four Year Price Score 7   *(9) Operating Margin % 0*   Score 0
(4) Book Value $ 0   Score 1   *(10) Trading Volume 49,698*   Score 2
(5) Price to Book Comparison Score 0   *(11) Price to Earnings 0.0x*   Score 0
(6) Analyst Buys # 0   Score 0

Total of All 11 Scores = 19

This stock's total score in 2021 was **17**, in 2020 it was **NA**, in 2019 it was **16**.

HISTORICAL STOCK PRICES & DIVIDEND PAYOUTS

Year	Stock	Dividend	Year	Stock	Dividend
2022	$ 4.92	$ 0.10	2010	$ 9.06	$ 0.10
2021	$ 7.38	$ 0.10	2009	$ 6.75	$ 0.10
2020	$ 2.95	$ 0.10	2008	$ 11.75	$ 0.10
2019	$ 5.78	$ 0.10	2007	$ NA	$ NA
2018	$ 7.06	$ 0.10	2006	$ NA	$ NA
2017	$ 7.84	$ 0.10	2005	$ NA	$ NA
2016	$ 6.59	$ 0.10	2004	$ NA	$ NA
2015	$ 8.66	$ 0.10	2003	$ NA	$ NA
2014	$ 10.12	$ 0.10	2002	$ NA	$ NA
2013	$ 8.78	$ 0.10	2001	$ NA	$ N A
2012	$ 7.60	$ 0.10	2000	$ NA	$ NA
2011	$ 9.55	$ 0.10	1999	$ NA	$ NA

NOTES: DGS is a Canada-based mutual fund company

DIVIDEND SELECT 15 CORPORATION

(DS)

Updated May 2023

IDM STOCK SCORING CALCULATION

(1) *Stock Price $ 6.81*   *Score 4*

(2) *Price 4 Years Ago $ 7.28*   *Score 4*

(3) *Current to Four Year Price* *Score 5*

(4) *Book Value $ 0*   *Score 1*

(5) *Price to Book Comparison*   *Score 0*

(6) *Analyst Buys # 0*   *Score 0*

(7) *Analysts Strong Buys # 0* *Score 0*

(8) *Dividend Yield % 11.56*   *Score 2*

(9) *Operating Margin % 0*   *Score 0*

(10) *Trading Volume 10,230*   *Score 1*

(11) *Price to Earnings 0.0x*   *Score 0*

Total of All 11 Scores = 17

This stock's total score in 2021 was **22** , in 2020 it was **NA**, in 2019 it was.**23**

HISTORICAL STOCK PRICES & DIVIDEND PAYOUTS

Year	Stock	Dividend	Year	Stock	Dividend
2022	$ 8.10	$ 0.07	2010	$ NAA	$.NA
2021	$ 8.60	$ 0.06	2009	$ NA	$ NA
2020	$ 6.10	$ 0.05	2008	$ NA	$ NA
2019	$ 7.28	$ 0.06	2007	$ NA	$ NA
2018	$ 8.10	$ 0.07	2006	$ NA	$ NA
2017	$ 8.35	$ 0.07	2005	$ NA	$ NA
2016	$ 8.00	$ 0.07	2004	$ NA	$ NA
2015	$ 8.85	$ 0.08	2003	$.NA	$ NA
2014	$ 9.93	$ 0.06	2002	$ NAA	$ NA
2013	$ 9.17	$ 0.06	2001	$ NA	$ NA
2012	$ 8.80	$ 0.06	2000	$ NA	$ NA
2011	$ 9.23	$ 0.06	1999	$ NA	$ NA

NOTES: No data available.

DOMAN BUILDING MATERIALS GROUP LTD

(DBM)

Updated May 2023

IDM STOCK SCORING CALCULATION

(1) Stock Price $ 6.09   Score *4*
(2) Price 4 Years Ago $ 4.79   Score *3*
(3) Current to Four Year Price Score *9*
(4) Book Value $ 6.53   Score *4*
(5) Price to Book Comparison Score *6*
(6) Analyst Buys # 2   Score *3*

(7) Analysts Strong Buys # 0 Score *0*
(8) Dividend Yield % 9.20   Score *10*
(9) Operating Margin % 4.48   Score *1*
(10) Trading Volume 216,871   Score *4*
(11) Price to Earnings 6.7   Score *9*

Total of All 11 Scores = 53

This stock's total score in 2021 was **49**, in 2020 it was **42**, in 2019 it was **36**.

HISTORICAL STOCK PRICES & DIVIDEND PAYOUTS

Year	Dividend	Stock	Year	Dividend	Stock
2022	$ 6.47	$ 0.14	2010	$ 8.24	$ 0.13
2021	$ 8.67	$ 0.14	2009	$ 4.30	$ 0.12
2020	$ 3.69	$ 0.14	2008	$ 8.80	$0.12
2019	$ 4.70	$ 0.14	2007	$ 7.66	$ 0.12
2018	$ 7.37	$ 0.14	2006	$ 7.72	$ 0.16
2017	$ 5.94	$ 0.14	2005	$ 8.31	$ 0.16
2016	$ 5.52	$ 0.14	2004	$ NA	$ NA
2015	$ 5.46	$ 0.14	2003	$ NA	$ NA
2014	$ 5.75	$ 0.14	2002	$ NA	$ NA
2013	$ 5.17	$ 0.14	2001	$ NA	$ NA
2012	$ 4.85.	$ 0.14	2000	$ NA	$ NA
2011	$ 10.45	$ 0.20	1999	$ NA	$ NA

NOTES: DBM. is a Canada-based integrated distributor in the building materials and related products sector.

DOMINION LENDING CENTRES INC

(DLCG)

Updated May 2023

IDM STOCK SCORING CALCULATION

(1) Stock Price $ 2.42   Score *3*
(2) Price 4 Years Ago $ 7.82   Score *4*
(3) Current to Four Year Price Score *1*
(4) Book Value $ 7.14   Score *4*
(5) Price to Book Comparison Score *10*
(6) Analyst Buys # 0   Score *0*

(7) Analysts Strong Buys # 1 Score *3*
(8) Dividend Yield % 6.61   Score *8*
(9) Operating Margin % 0   Score *0*
(10) Trading Volume 262,380 Score *5*
(11) Price to Earnings -3.6x Score *10*

Total of All 11 Scores = 48

This stock's total score in 2021 was **NA**, in 2020 it was **NA**, in 2019 it was **NA**.

HISTORICAL STOCK PRICES & DIVIDEND PAYOUTS

Year	Stock	Dividend	Year	Stock	Dividend
2022	$ 4.76	$ 0.03	2010	$ NA	$ NA
2021	$ 6.65	$ 0.03	2009	$ NA	$ NA
2020	$ 4.70	$ 0.03	2008	$ NA	$ NA
2019	$ 7.75	$ 0.03	2007	$ NA	$ NA
2018	$ 6.86	$ 0.03	2006	$ NA	$ NA
2017	$ 5.81	$ 0.03	2005	$ NA	$NA
2016	$ 5.99	$ 0.03	2004	$ NA	$ NA
2015	$ 6.30.	$ 0.03	2003	$ NA	$ NA
2014	$ 6.72	$ 0.03	2002	$ NA	$ NA
2013	$ NA	$ NA	2001	$ NA	$ NA
2012	$ NA	$ N A	2000	$ NA	$ NA
2011	$ NA	$ NA	1999	$ NA	$ NA

NOTES: DLCG is a Canada-based mortgage company. The Company operates through two segments: the Core Business Operations segment and the Non-Core Business Asset Management segment.

DREAM RESIDENTIAL REIT

(DRR.U)

Updated May 2023

IDM STOCK SCORING CALCULATION

(1) Stock Price $ 7.85   *Score 4*
(2) Price 4 Years Ago $ 0   *Score 1*
(3) Current to Four Year Price *Score 0*
(4) Book Value $ 18.73   *Score 6*
(5) Price to Book Comparison *Score 10*
(6) Analyst Buys # 0   *Score 0*

(7) Analysts Strong Buys # 0   *Score 0*
(8) Dividend Yield % 5.35   *Score 8*
(9) Operating Margin % 34.18   *Score 6*
(10) Trading Volume 200   *Score 0*
(11) Price to Earnings 0.7x   *Score 0*

Total of All 11 Scores = 35

This stock's total score in 2021 was **NA** , in 2020 it was **NA**, in 2019 it was **NA**.

HISTORICAL STOCK PRICES & DIVIDEND PAYOUTS

Year	Stock	Dividend	Year	Stock	Dividend
2022	$ 9.00	$0.03	2010	$ NA	$ NA
2021	$ NA	$ NA	2009	$ NA	$ NA
2020	$ NA	$ NA	2008	$ NA	$ NA
2019	$ NA	$ NA	2007	$ NS	$ NA
2018	$ NA	$ NA	2006	$ NA	$ NA
2017	$ NA	$ NA	2005	$ NA	$ NA
2016	$ NA	$ NA	2004	$ NA	$ NA
2015	$ NA	$ NA	2003	$ NA	$ NA
2014	$ NA	$ NA	2002	$ NA	$ NA
2013	$ NA	$ NA	2001	$ NA	$ NA
2012	$ NA	$ NA	2000	$ NA	$ NA
2011	$ NA	$ NA	1999	$ NA	$ NA

NOTES: DRR.U is a Canada-based Real Estate Investment Trust (REIT), formed for the purpose of acquiring and owning residential rental real estate properties.

DREAM IMPACT TRUST

(MPCT.UN)

Updated May 2023

IDM STOCK SCORING CALCULATION

(1) Stock Price $ 2.42   Score 3   *(7)* Analysts Strong Buys # 1   Score 3
(2) Price 4 Years Ago $ 7.50   Score 4   *(8)* Dividend Yield % 6.61   Score 8
(3) Current to Four Year Price Score 1   *(9)* Operating Margin % 0   Score 0
(4) Book Value $ 7.14   Score 4   *(10)* Trading Volume 262,380   Score 5
(5) Price to Book Comparison   Score 10   *(11)* Price to Earnings -3.6x   Score 10
(6) Analyst Buys # 0   Score 0

Total of All 11 Scores = 48

This stock's total score in 2021 was **30** , in 2020 it was **NA**, in 2019 it was **NA**.

HISTORICAL STOCK PRICES & DIVIDEND PAYOUTS

Year	Stock	Dividend	Year	Stock	Dividend
2022	$ 4.62	$ 0.03	2010	$ NA	$ NA
2021	$ 6.65	$ 0.03	2009	$ NA	$ NA
2020	$ 4.75	$ 0.03	2008	$ NA	$.NA
2019	$ 7.85	$ 0.03	2007	$ NA	$ NA
2018	$ 6.89	$ 0.03	2006	$ NA	$ NA
2017	$ 6.01	$ 0.03	2005	$ NA	$ NA
2016	$ 5.99	$ 0.03	2004	$ NA	$ NA
2015	$ 5.97	$ 0.03	2003	$ NA	$ NA
2014	$6.92	$ 0.03	2002	$ NA	$ NA
2013	$ NA	$ NA	2001	$ NA	$ NA
2012	$ NA	$ NA	2000	$ NA	$ NA
2011	$ NA	$ NA	1999	$ NA	$ NA

NOTES: **MPCT**.is a Canada-based open-ended trust, which is focused on impact investing. The Company operates through two segments: Development and investment holdings, and recurring income.

DREAM INDUSTRIAL REAL ESTATE INVESTMENT TRUST (DIR.UN)

Updated May 2023

IDM STOCK SCORING CALCULATION

(1) Stock Price $ 13.79 — Score 5
(2) Price 4 Years Ago $ 11.80 — Score 5
(3) Current to Four Year Price — Score 9
(4) Book Value $ 16.82 — Score 6
(5) Price to Book Comparison — Score 8
(6) Analyst Buys # 8 — Score 5
(7) Analysts Strong Buys # 0 — Score 0
(8) Dividend Yield % 5.08 — Score 8
(9) Operating Margin % 64.39 — Score 8
(10) Trading Volume 194,261 — Score 4
(11) Price to Earnings 15.4x 9 — Score 9

Total of All 11 Scores = 67

This stock's total score in 2021 was **61** , in 2020 it was **NA**, in 2019 it was.**57**

HISTORICAL STOCK PRICES & DIVIDEND PAYOUTS

Year	Stock	Dividend	Year	Stock	Dividend
2022	$ 12.08	$ 0.06	2010	$ NA	$ NA
2021	$ 15.28	$ 0.06	2009	$ NA	$ NA
2020	$ 11.00	$ 0.06	2008	$ NA	$ NA
2019	$ 12.13	$ 0.06	2007	$NA	$ NA
2018	$ 10.06	$ 0.06	2006	$ NA	$ NA
2017	$ 9.05	$ 0.06	2005	$ NA	$ NA
2016	$ 8.73	$ 0.06	2004	$ NA	$ NA
2015	$ 8.18	$ 0.06	2003	$ NA	$ NA
2014	$ 9.73	$ 0.06	2002	$ NA	$ NA
2013	$ 9.08	$ 0.06	2001	$ NA	$ NA
2012	$11.39	$ 0.06	2000	$ NA	$ NA
2011	$ NA	$ NA	1999	$ NA	$ NA

NOTES: DIR.UN is an open-ended real estate investment trust

DREAM OFFICE REAL ESTATE INVESTMENT TRUST

(D.UN)

Updated May 2023

IDM STOCK SCORING CALCULATION

(1) Stock Price $ 14.45   Score 5   *(7) Analysts Strong Buys # 0*   Score 0

(2) Price 4 Years Ago $ 24.59 Score 7   *(8) Dividend Yield % 6.92*   Score 8

(3) Current to Four Year Price Score 2   *(9) Operating Margin % 6.71*   Score 2

(4) Book Value $ 33.23   Score 8   *(10) Trading Volume 127,653*   Score 4

(5) Price to Book Comparison Score 10   *(11) Price to Earnings 70.2x*   Score 2

(6) Analyst Buys # 3   Score 3

Total of All 11 Scores = 51

This stock's total score in 2021 was **67** , in 2020 it was **NA,** in 2019 it was **63**.

HISTORICAL STOCK PRICES & DIVIDEND PAYOUTS

Year	Stock	Dividend	Year	Stock	Dividend
2022	$ 18.27	$ 0.08	2010	$ 24.45	$ 0.18
2021	$ 22.96	$ 0.08	2009	$ 16.50	$ 0.18
2020	$ 20.52	$ 0.08	2008	$ 32.70	$ 0.18
2019	$ 24.59	$ 0.08	2007	$ 43.35	$ 0.18
2018	$24.26	$ 0.08	2006	$ 31.75	$ 0.18
2017	$ 19.91	$ 0.13	2005	$ 26.74	$ 0.18
2016	$ 18.92	$ 0.13	2004	$ 23.45	$ 0.18
2015	$ 29.29	$ 0.19	2003	$ 20.51	$ 0.18
2014	$ 29.02	$ 0.19	2002	$ 17.00	$ NA
2013	$ 30.84	$ 0.19	2001	$ 14.40	$ NA
2012	$ 38.24	$ 0.18	2000	$ 9.20	$ NA
2011	$ 32.42	$ 0.18	1999	$ 11.20	$ NA

NOTES: D.UN is a Canada-based open-ended real estate investment trust. The Company is focused on owning, leasing and managing office properties in urban centers across Canada,

DRI HEALTHCARE TRUST

(DHT.U)

Updated May 2023

IDM STOCK SCORING CALCULATION

(1) Stock Price $ 7.15	Score 4		**(7)** Analysts Strong Buys # 0	Score 0
(2) Price 4 Years Ago $ 0	Score 1		**(8)** Dividend Yield % 4.20	Score 6
(3) Current to Four Year Price	Score 0		**(9)** Operating Margin % 0	Score 0
(4) Book Value $ 0	Score 1		**(10)** Trading Volume 6,100	Score 0
(5) Price to Book Comparison	Score 0		**(11)** Price to Earnings 0.0x	Score 0
(6) Analyst Buys # 0	Score 0			

Total of All 11 Scores = 12

This stock's total score in 2021 was **NA** , in 2020 it was **NA**, in 2019 it was. **NA**

HISTORICAL STOCK PRICES & DIVIDEND PAYOUTS

Year	Stock	Dividend	Year	Stock	Dividend
2022	$ 6.50	$ 0.07	2010	$.NA	$ NA
2021	$ 6.74	$ 0.04	2009	$ NA	$ NA
2020	$ NA	$ NA	2008	$ NA	$ NA
2019	$ NA	$ NA	2007	$ NA	$ NA
2018	$ NA	$ NA	2006	$ NA	$ NA
2017	$ NA	$ NA	2005	$ NA	$ NA
2016	$ NA	$ NA	2004	$ NA	$ NA
2015	$ NA	$ NA	2003	$ NA	$ NA
2014	$ NA	$ NA	2002	$NA	$ NA
2013	$ NA	$ NA	2001	$ NA	$ NA
2012	$ NA	$ NA	2000	$ NA	$ NA
2011	$ NA	$ NA	1999	$ NA	$NA

NOTES: DHT.U no information provided.

DYNACOR GROUP INC

(DNG)

Updated May 2023

IDM STOCK SCORING CALCULATION

(1) Stock Price $ 3.00   Score 3   *(7)* Analysts Strong Buys # 0   Score 0

2) Price 4 Years Ago $ 1.79   Score 2   *(8)* Dividend Yield % 4.00   Score 6

(3) Current to Four Year Price   Score 9   *(9)* Operating Margin % 8.86   Score 2

(4) Book Value $ 2.84   Score 3   *(10)* Trading Volume 22,294   Score 1

(5) Price to Book Comparison   Score 2   *(11)* Price to Earnings 7.6x   Score 9

(6) Analyst Buys # 0   Score 0

Total of All 11 Scores = 37

This stock's total score in 2021 was **NA**, in 2020 it was **NA**, in 2019 it was **NA**.

HISTORICAL STOCK PRICES & DIVIDEND PAYOUTS

Year	Stock	Dividend	Year	Stock	Dividend
2022	$ 3.00	$ 0.01	2010	$ NA	$ NA
2021	$ 2.72	$ 0.01	2009	$ NA	$ NA
2020	$ 2.56	$ 0.01	2008	$ NA	$ NA
2019	$ 1.68	$ 0.01	2007	$ NA	$ NA
2018	$ 1.71	$ 0.01	2006	$ NA	$ NA
2017	$ NA	$ NA	2005	$ NA	$ N A
2016	$ NA	$ NA	2004	$ NA	$ NA
2015	$ NA	$ NA	2003	$ NA	$ NA
2014	$ NA	$ NA	2002	$ NA	$ NA
2013	$ NA	$ NA	2001	$ NA	$ NA
2012	$ NA	$ NA	2000	$ NA	$ NA
2011	$ NA	$ NA	1999	$ NA	$ NA

NOTES: DNG is a Canada-based industrial gold ore processor. The Company is primarily engaged in ore processing and exploration in Peru.

E SPLIT CORPORATION

(ENS)

Updated June 2023

IDM STOCK SCORING CALCULATION

(1) Stock Price $ 15.15   *Score 6*
(2) Price 4 Years Ago $ 12.45   *Score 5*
(3) Current to Four Year Price   *Score 9*
(4) Book Value $ 0   *Score 0*
(5) Price to Book Comparison   *Score 0*
(6) Analyst Buys # 0   *Score 0*

(7) Analysts Strong Buys #0   *Score 0*
(8) Dividend Yield % 10.30   *Score 10*
(9) Operating Margin % 0   *Score 0*
(10) Trading Volume 3,782   *Score 0*
(11) Price to Earnings 0.0x   *Score 0*

Total of All 11 Scores = 31

This stock's total score in 2021 was **12,** in 2020 it was **9**, in 2019 it was **NA**.

HISTORICAL STOCK PRICES & DIVIDEND PAYOUTS

Year	Stock	Dividend	Year	Stock	Dividend
2022	$ 14.90	$ 0.13	2010	$ NA	$ NA
2021	$ 14.59	$ 0.13	2009	$ NA	$ NA
2020	$ 12.10	$ 0.13	2008	$ NA	$ NA
2019	$ 12.45	$ 0.13	2007	$ NA	$ NA
2018	$ 13.30	$ 0.13	2006	$ NA	$ NA
2017	$ NA	$ NA	2005	$ NA	$ NA
2016	$ NA	$ NA	2004	$ NA	$ NA
2015	$ NA	$ NA	2003	$ NA	$ NA
2014	$ NA	$ NA	2002	$ NA	$ NA
2013	$ NA	$ NA	2001	$ NA	$ NA
2012	$ NA	$ NA	2000	$ NA	$ NA
2011	$ NA	$ NA	1999	$ NA	$ NA

NOTES: ENS is a Canada-based mutual fund established as a corporation

ECORA RESOURCES PLC

(ECOR)

Updated June 2023

IDM STOCK SCORING CALCULATION

(1) Stock Price $ 2.03   Score *3*
(2) Price 4 Years Ago $ 3.21   Score *3*
(3) Current to Four Year Price Score *2*
(4) Book Value $ 1.57   Score *2*
(5) Price to Book Comparison   Score *1*
(6) Analyst Buys # 2   Score *2*

(7) Analysts Strong Buys # 0   Score *0*
(8) Dividend Yield % 6.05   Score *8*
(9) Operating Margin % 79.88 Score *10*
(10) Trading Volume 10,120   Score *1*
(11) Price to Earnings 3.4x   Score *10*

Total of All 11 Scores= 43

This stock's total score in 2021 was **NA**, in 2020 it was **NA**, in 2019 it was **NA**.

HISTORICAL STOCK PRICES & DIVIDEND PAYOUTS

Year	Stock	Dividend	Year	Stock	Dividend
2022	$ 2.22	$ 0.02	2010	$ 4.34	$ NA
2021	$ 3.21	$ NA	2009	$ NA	$ NA
2020	$ 2.83	$ NA	2008	$ NA	$ NA
2019	$ 3.21	$ NA	2007	$ NA	$ NA
2018	$ 3.35	$ NA	2006	$ NA	$ NA
2017	$ 1.86	$ NA	2005	$ NA	$ NA
2016	$ 1.50	$ NA	2004	$ NA	$ NA
2015	$ 2.05	$ NA	2003	$ NA	$ N A
2014	$ 3.03	$ N A	2002	$ NA	$ NA
2013	$ 3.50	$ NA	2001	$ NA	$ NA
2012	$ 4.50	$ NA	2000	$ NA	$ NA
2011	$ 4.80	$ NA	1999	$ NA	$ NA

NOTES: ECOR is a United Kingdom based natural resource royalty company.

ELYSEE DEVELOPMENT CORPORATION
(ELC)
Updated July 2023

IDM STOCK SCORING CALCULATION

(1) Stock Price $ 0.44   Score *1*   *(7)* Analysts Strong Buys # *0* Score *0*
(2) Price 4 Years Ago $ 0.37   Score *1*   *(8)* Dividend Yield % 4.49   Score *6*
(3) Current to Four Year Price Score *9*   *(9)* Operating Margin % *0*   Score *0*
(4) Book Value $ 0.54   Score *1*   *(10)* Trading Volume 450   Score *0*
(5) Price to Book Comparison Score *8*   *(11)* Price to Earnings -5.1x   Score *0*
(6) Analyst Buys # *0*   Score *0*

Total of All 11 Scores = 26

This stock's total score in 2021 was **36**, in 2020 it was **20**, in 2019 it was **28**.

HISTORICAL STOCK PRICES & DIVIDEND PAYOUTS

Year	Stock	Dividend	Year	Stock	Dividend
2022	$ 0.73	$ 0.02	2010	$ 0.37	$ NAN
2021	$ 0.56	$ 0.03	2009	$ 0.72	$ NA
2020	$ 0.34	$ 0.02	2008	$ 1.45	$ NA
2019	$ 0.37	$ 0.01	2007	$ 6.68	$ NA
2018	$ 0.35	$ 0.01	2006	$ 6.90	$ NA
2017	$ 0.28	$ NA	2005	$ 0.90	$ NA
2016	$ 0.27	$ 0.02	2004	$ 1.11	$ NA
2015	$ 0.20	$ NA	2003	$0.97	$ NA
2014	$ 0.15	$ NA	2002	$ 0.77	$ NA
2013	$ 0.13	$ NA	2001	$ 1.13	$ NA
2012	$ 0.15	$ NA	2000	$ 1.81	$ NA
2011	$ 0.26	$ NA	1999	$ 0.90	$ NA

NOTES: EIC is a Canada-based company. As a diversified investment and venture capital firm it is focused on publicly traded companies in the natural resource sector.

EMERA INC

(EMA)

Updated June 2023

IDM STOCK SCORING CALCULATION

(1) Stock Price $ 56.55   Score 9
(2) Price 4 Years Ago $ 53.51   Score 9
(3) Current to Four Year Price Score 7
(4) Book Value $ 42.33   Score 8
(5) Price to Book Comparison   Score 1
(6) Analyst Buys # 4   Score 4

(7) Analysts Strong Buys # 0   Score 0
(8) Dividend Yield % 4.88   Score 8
(9) Operating Margin % 24.28   Score 5
(10) Trading Volume 1,042,805 Score 9
(11) Price to Earnings 13.4x   Score 9

Total of All 11 Scores =69

This stock's total score in 2021 was **66**, in 2020 it was **62**, in 2019 it was **65**.

HISTORICAL STOCK PRICES & DIVIDEND PAYOUTS

Year	Stock	Dividend	Year	Stock	Dividend
2022	$ 60.71	$ 0.66	2010	$ 23.66	$ 0.28
2021	$ 56.24	$ 0.64	2009	$19.76	$ 0.25
2020	$ 54.74	$ 0.61	2008	$ 21.45	$ 0.24
2019	$ 50.31	$ 0.59	2007	$ 21.51	$ 0.22
2018	$ 39.99	$ 0.56	2006	$ 19.10	$ 0.22
2017	$ 47.25	$ 0.52	2005	$ 17.86	$ 0.22
2016	$ 48.68	$ 0.52	2004	$ 19.30	$ 0.22
2015	$ 40.66	$ 0.0	2003	$ 16.64	$ 0.21
2014	$ 33.90	$ 0.36	2002	$ 17.16	$ 0.21
2013	$ 36.90	$ 0.35	2001	$ 17.00	$ 0.21
2012	$ 33.61	$ 0.34	2000	$ 14.50	$ 0.21
2011	$ 31.50	$ 0.33	1999	$ 17.20	$ 0.21

NOTES: EMA is a Canada-based energy and services company.

ENBRIDGE INC

(ENB)

Updated June 2023

IDM STOCK SCORING CALCULATION

(1) Stock Price $ 50.26   *Score* 9   *(7)* Analysts Strong Buys #   *Score* 0
(2) Price 4 Years Ago $ 47.30   *Score* 8   *(8)* Dividend Yield % 7.06   *Score* 8
(3) Current to Four Year Price *Score* 7   *(9)* Operating Margin % 12.92   *Score* 3
(4) Book Value $ 29.57   *Score* 7   *(10)* Trading Volume 8,955,534 *Score* 10
(5) Price to Book Comparison *Score* 0   *(11)* Price to Earnings 42.6x   *Score* 2
(6) Analyst Buys # 1   *Score* 2

Total of All 11 Scores = 56

This stock's total score in 2021 was **70**, in 2020 it was **70**, in 2019 it was **60**.

HISTORICAL STOCK PRICES & DIVIDEND PAYOUTS

Year	Stock	Dividend	Year	Stock	Dividend
2022	$ 57.51	$ 0.86	2010	$ 25.02	$ 0.21
2021	$ 49.18	$ 0.83	2009	$ 18.42	$ 0.18
2020	$ 42.65	$ 0.81	2008	$ 22.46	$ 0.17
2019	$ 49.49	$ 0.74	2007	$ 18.30	$ 0.15
2018	$ 46.20	$ 0.67	2006	$ 16.57	$ 0.14
2017	$ 52.91	$ 0.61	2005	$ 15.86	$ 0.13
2016	$ 53.71	$ 0.53	2004	$ 13.18	$ 0.11
2015	$ 57.01	$ 0.47	2003	$ 12.57	$ 0.10
2014	$ 53.45	$ 0.35	2002	$ 11.40	$ 0.10
2013	$ 45.57	$ 0.32	2001	$ 10.16	$ 0.09
2012	$ 40.66	$ 0.28	2000	$ 8.45	$ 0.08
2011	$ 31.36	$ 0.24	1999	$ 8.43	$ 0.15

NOTES: **ENB** is an energy infrastructure company with business platforms that include a network of crude oil, liquids and natural gas pipelines, regulated natural gas distribution utilities and renewable power generation

ENERGY INCOME FUND
(ENI.UN)
Updated June 2023

IDM STOCK SCORING CALCULATION

(1) Stock Price $ 1.77   Score 2
(2) Price 4 Years Ago $ 1.62   Score 2
(3) Current to Four Year Price Score 7
(4) Book Value $ 2.01   Score 3
(5) Price to Book Comparison Score 8
(6) Analyst Buys # 0   Score 0

(7) Analysts Strong Buys # 0 Score 0
(8) Dividend Yield % 6.78   Score 8
(9) Operating Margin % 69.72 Score 9
(10) Trading Volume 82   Score 0
(11) Price to Earnings 8.5x   Score 9

Total of All 11 Scores = 48

This stock's total score in 2021 was **34**, in 2020 it was **39**, in 2019 it was **26**.

HISTORICAL STOCK PRICES & DIVIDEND PAYOUTS

Year	Stock	Dividend	Year	Stock	Dividend
2022	$ 1.51	$ 0.01	2010	$ 5.89	$ 0.03
2021	$ 1.51	$ 0.01	2009	$ 4.30	$ 0.03
2020	$ 1.22	$ 0.01	2008	$ 6.67	$ 0.03
2019	$ 1.60	$0.01	2007	$ 6.36	$ 0.07
2018	$ 1.96	$ 0.01	2006	$ 8.65	$ 0.07
2017	$ 1.96	$ 0.01	2005	$ 9.90	$ 0.07
2016	$ 2.08	$ 0.01	2004	$ NA	$ NA
2015	$ 2.52	$ 0.01	2003	$ NA	$ NA
2014	$ 3.57	$ 0.01	2002	$.NA	$ NA
2013	$ 3.78	$ 0.03	2001	$ NA	$ NA
2012	$ 3.88	$ 0.03	2000	$ NA	$ NA
2011	$ 6.25	$ 0.01	1999	$ NA	$ NA

NOTES: ENI.UN is a Canada-based closed-end investment fund.

EUROPEAN RESIDENTIAL REAL ESTATE INVESTMENT TRUST
(ERE.UN)
Updated June 2023

IDM STOCK SCORING CALCULATION

(1) Stock Price $ 2.97   Score 3
(2) Price 4 Years Ago $ 4.36   Score 3
(3) Current to Four Year Price Score 2
(4) Book Value $ 3.40   Score 3
(5) Price to Book Comparison Score 8
(6) Analyst Buys # 4   Score 4

(7) Analysts Strong Buys # 0 Score 0
(8) Dividend Yield % 5.92   Score 8
(9) Operating Margin % 58.07 Score 8
(10) Trading Volume 61,856   Score 3
(11) Price to Earnings 11.4x Score 9

Total of All 11 Scores = 51

This stock's total score in 2021 was **32**, in 2020 it was **34**, in 2019 it was **26**.

HISTORICAL STOCK PRICES & DIVIDEND PAYOUTS

Year	Stock	Dividend	Year	Stock	Dividend
2022	$ 4.65	$ 0.01	2010	$ NA	$ NA
2021	$ 4.34	$ 0.01	2009	$ NA	$ NA
2020	$ 4.12	$ 0.01	2008	$ NA	$ NA
2019	$ 4.24	$ 0.04	2007	$ NA	$ NA
2018	$ 3.75	$ 0.09	2006	$ NA	$ NA
2017	$ 3.87	$ 0.14	2005	$ NA	$ NA
2016	$ NA	$ NA	2004	$ NA	$ NA
2015	$ NA	$ NA	2003	$ NA	$ NA
2014	$ NA	$ NA	2002	$ NA	$ NA
2013	$ NA	$ NA	2001	$ NA	$ NA
2012	$ NA	$ NA	2000	$ NA	$ NA
2011	$ NA	$ NA	1999	$ NA	$ NA

NOTES: ERE.UN formerly European Commercial REIT, is a Canada-based unincorporated, real estate investment trust focused non-prime core commercial real estate assets in Germany, France, and the Benelux region.

EVERTZ TECHNOLOGIES LIMITED
(ET)
Updated June 2023

IDM STOCK SCORING CALCULATION

(1) Stock Price $ 12.50   Score *5*

(2) Price 4 Years Ago $ 16.69 Score *6*

(3) Current to Four Year Price Score *2*

(4) Book Value $ 3.03   Score *3*

(5) Price to Book Comparison Score *0*

(6) Analyst Buys # 3   Score *3*

(7) Analysts Strong Buys # 0 Score *0*

(8) Dividend Yield % 6.08   Score *8*

(9) Operating Margin % 20.83 Score *5*

(10) Trading Volume 12,571   Score *1*

(11) Price to Earnings 14.8   Score *9*

Total of All 11 Scores =42

This stock's total score in 2021 was **41,** in 2020 it was **40**, in 2019 it was **49**.

HISTORICAL STOCK PRICES & DIVIDEND PAYOUTS

Year	Stock	Dividend	Year	Stock	Dividend
2022	$ 12.26	$ 0.18	2010	$ 10.32	$ 0.06
2021	$ 14.35	$ 0.17	2009	$ 12.21	$ 0.06
2020	$ 11.62	$ 0.08	2008	$ 14.90	$ 0.06
2019	$ 15.50	$ 0.16	2007	$ 29.02	$ 0.04
2018	$ 14.06	$ 0.16	2006	$ NA	$ NA
2017	$ 15.71	$ 0.16	2005	$ NA	$ NA
2016	$ 14.66	$ 0.15	2004	$ NA	$ NA
2015	$ 12.99	$0.15	2003	$ NA	$ NA
2014	$ 14.47	$ 0.13	2002	$ NA	$ NA
2013	$ 11.39	$ 0.12	2001	$ NA	$ NA
2012	$ 9.66	$ 0.11	2000	$ NA	$ NA
2011	$ 9.66	$ 0.09	1999	$ NA	$ NA

NOTES: ET is an equipment provider to the television broadcast telecommunications and media industries.

EXCHANGE INCOME CORPORATION

(EIF)
Updated June 2023

IDM STOCK SCORING CALCULATION

(1) Stock Price $ 53.65   Score 9

(2) Price 4 Years Ago $ 38.20   Score 8

(3) Current to Four Year Price Score 9

(4) Book Value $ 23.99   Score 7

(5) Price to Book Comparison   Score 0

(6) Analyst Buys # 7   Score 5

(7) Analysts Strong Buys # 0   Score 0

(8) Dividend Yield % 4.70   Score 8

(9) Operating Margin % 11.21 Score 3

(10) Trading Volume 68,723   Score 3

(11) Price to Earnings 20.7   Score 7

Total of All 11 Scores = 59

This stock's total score in 2021 was **55**, in 2020 it was **54**, in 2019 it was **61**.

HISTORICAL STOCK PRICES & DIVIDEND PAYOUTS

Year	Stock	Dividend	Year	Stock	Dividend
2022	$ 42.14	$ 0.20	2010	$ 14.45	$ 0.13
2021	$ 39.41	$ 0.19	2009	$ 11.55	$ 0.13
2020	$ 26.75	$ 0.19	2008	$ 9.80	$ 0.13
2019	$ 36.24	$ 0.18	2007	$12.70	$ 0.13
2018	$ 32.04	$ 0.18	2006	$ 11.60	$ 0.10
2017	$ 33.06	$ 0.17	2005	$ 12.58	$ 0.27
2016	$ 31.40	$ 0.17	2004	$ 8.11	$ 0.17
2015	$ 22.04	$ 0.14	2003	$ NA	$ NA
2014	$ 22.61	$ 0.14	2002	$ NA	$ NA
2013	$ 26.16	$ 0.14	2001	$ NA	$ NA
2012	$ 24.04	$ 0.14	2000	$ NA	$ NA
2011	$ 23.36	$ 0.14	1999	$ NA	$ NA

NOTES: EX is focused on opportunities in aerospace and aviation services and equipment, and manufacturing.

Exco Technologies Ltd
(XTC)
Updated June 2023

IDM STOCK SCORING CALCULATION

(1) Stock Price $ 7.82   eScore 4
(2) Price 4 Years Ago $ 8.34   Score 4
(3) Current to Four Year Price Score 5
(4) Book Value $ 8.96   Score 4
(5) Price to Book Comparison Score 8
(6) Analyst Buys # 0   Score 0

(7) Analysts Strong Buys # 0 Score 0
(8) Dividend Yield % 5.37   Score 8
(9) Operating Margin % 6.12   Score 2
(10) Trading Volume 4,102   Score 0
(11) Price to Earnings 13.7   Score 9

Total of All 11 Scores = 44

This stock's total score in 2021 was **40**, in 2020 it was **43**, in 2019 it was **42**.

HISTORICAL STOCK PRICES & DIVIDEND PAYOUTS

Year	Stock	Dividend	Year	Stock	Dividend
2022	$ 7.99	$ 0.10	2010	$3.40	$ 0.02
2021	$ 10.42	$ 0.10	2009	$ 1.20	$ 0.02
2020	$ 6.36	$ 0.10	2008	$ 3.20	$ 0.02
2019	$ 7.75	$ 0.09	2007	$ 4.62	$ 0.01
2018	$ 8.89	$ 0.09	2006	$ 3.50	$ 0.01
2017	$ 10.68	$ 0.08	2005	$ 4.15	$ 0.01
2016	$ 12.20	$ 0.07	2004	$ 6.50	$ 0.01
2015	$ 15.31	$ 0.06	2003	$ 6.90	$ 0.01
2014	$ 11.02	$ 0.05	2002	$ 6.37	$ NA
2013	$ 6.39	$ 0.04	2001	$ 3.10	$ NA
2012	$ 4.84	$ 0.04	2000	$ 3.50	$ NA
2011	$ 3.90	$ 0.03	1999	$ 4.50	$ NA

NOTES: XTC is a designer, developer and manufacturer of dies, molds, components and assemblies, and consumable equipment for the diecast, extrusion and automotive industries

EXTENDICARE INC
(EXE)
Updated June 2023

IDM STOCK SCORING CALCULATION

(1) Stock Price $ 7.16   Score 4
(2) Price 4 Years Ago $ 8.39   Score 4
(3) Current to Four Year Price Score 2
(4) Book Value $ 1.19   Score 2
(5) Price to Book Comparison Score 0
(6) Analyst Buys # 0   Score 0

(7) Analysts Strong Buys # 0 Score 0
(8) Dividend Yield % 6.70   Score 8
(9) Operating Margin % 1.66 Score 1
(10) Trading Volume 178,413 Score 4
(11) Price to Earnings 218.6   Score 1

Total of All 11 Scores = 26

This stock's total score in 2021 was **37**, in 2020 it was **35**, in 2019 it was **32**.

HISTORICAL STOCK PRICES & DIVIDEND PAYOUTS

Year	Stock	Dividend	Year	Stock	Dividend
2022	$ 6.80	$ 0.04	2010	$ 8.54	$ 0.07
2021	$ 8.51	$ 0.04	2009	$ 6.25	$ 0.07
2020	$ 5.61	$ 0.04	2008	$ 7.20	$ 0.09
2019	$ 8.39	$ 0.04	2007	$17.34	$ 0.09
2018	$ 7.37	$ 0.04	2006	$ 14.46	$ 0.05
2017	$ 10.35	$ 0.04	2005	$ NA	$0.05
2016	$ 8.61	$ 0.04	2004	$ NA	$ NA
2015	$ 8.63	$ 0.04	2003	$ NA	$ NA
2014	$ 7.36	$ .0.04	2002	$ NA	$ NA
2013	$ 6.56	$ 0.04	2001	$ NA	$ NA
2012	$ 7.28	$ 0.07	2000	$ NA	$ NA
2011	$ 10.42	$ 0.07	1999	$ NA	$ NA

NOTES: EXE. is a Canada-based company that offers senior care across Canada

FIERA CAPITAL CORPORATION

(FSZ)

Updated June 2023

IDM STOCK SCORING CALCULATION

(1) Stock Price $ 6.83   Score *4*
(2) Price 4 Years Ago $ 0.00   Score *1*
(3) Current to Four Year Price Score *0*
(4) Book Value $ 3.32   Score *3*
(5) Price to Book Comparison Score *0*
(6) Analyst Buys # 1   Score *2*

(7) Analysts Strong Buys # *0* Score *0*
(8) Dividend Yield % 12.59   Score *2*
(9) Operating Margin % 10.28 Score *3*
(10) Trading Volume 157,787 Score *4*
(11) Price to Earnings 36.9   Score *48*

Total of All 11 Scores =23

This stock's total score in 2021 was **35**, in 2020 it was **36**, in 2019 it was **36**.

HISTORICAL STOCK PRICES & DIVIDEND PAYOUTS

Year	Stock	Dividend	Year	Stock	Dividend
2022	$ 9.95	$ 0.21	2010	$ 5.75	$ 0.06
2021	$ 10.48	$ 0.21	2009	$ 5.19	$ 0.06
2020	$ 9.50	$ 0.21	2008	$ 7.81	$ 0.12
2019	$ 11.28	$ 0.21	2007	$ 10.60	$ 0.09
2018	$ 11.77	$ 0.19	2006	$ 11.25	$ 0.08
2017	$ 14.24	$ 0.17	2005	$ 6.06	$ 0.06
2016	$ 13.11	$ 0.15	2004	$ 7.00	$ 0.06
2015	$ 12.39	$ 0.13	2003	$ 6.35	$ 0.05
2014	$ 12.75	$ 0.11	2002	$ 7.80	$ 0.20
2013	$ 11.42	$ 0.09	2001	$ 18.10	$ 0.20
2012	$ 8.12	$ 0.08	2000	$ 20.10	$ 0.26
2011	$ 7.25	$ 0.08	1999	$ 20.10	$ 0.26

NOTES: **FSZ** is a Canada-based global asset management company, which offers a wide range of traditional and alternative investment solutions, including asset allocation. The Company provides investment advisory and related services to institutional investors, private wealth clients and retail investors.

FINANCIAL 15 SPLIT CORPORATION
(FTN)
Updated June 2023

IDM STOCK SCORING CALCULATION

(1) Stock Price $ 8.72   Score 4
(2) Price 4 Years Ago $ 19.07 Score 6
(3) Current to Four Year Price Score 1
(4) Book Value $ 8.83   Score 4
(5) Price to Book Comparison Score 6
(6) Analyst Buys # 0   Score 0

(7) Analysts Strong Buys # 0 Score 0
(8) Dividend Yield % 17.30   Score 2
(9) Operating Margin % 0   Score 0
(10) Trading Volume 82,125   Score 3
(11) Price to Earnings -7.86   Score 9

Total of All 11 Scores = 35

This stock's total score in 2021 was **23**, in 2020 it was **NA**, in 2019 it was **NA**.

HISTORICAL STOCK PRICES & DIVIDEND PAYOUTS

Year	Stock	Dividend	Year	Stock	Dividend
2022	$ 11.64	$ 0.13	2010	$ 20.67	$ 0.31
2021	$ 11.67	$ 0.31	2009	$ 17.52	$ 0.31
2020	$ 17.90	$ 0.31	2008	$ 29.63	$ 0.31
2019	$ 17.42	$ 0.31	2007	$ 54.18	$ 0.31
2018	$ 25.45	$ 0.31	2006	$ 50.44	$ 0.31
2017	$ 26.25	$0.31	2005	$ 47.77	$ 0.31
2016	$ 20.77	$ 0.31	2004	$ 46.20	$ 0.31
2015	$ 23.55	$ 0.31	2003	$ NA	$ NA
2014	$ 25.50	$ 0.31	2002	$ NA	$ NA
2013	$ 20.77	$ 0.31	2001	$ NA	$.NA
2012	$ 10.75	$ NA	2000	$ NA	$.NA
2011	$ 14.50	$ 0.31	1999	$ NA	$ NA

NOTES: FTN is a mutual fund company, which invests primarily in over 15 Canadian and the United States financial services companies.

FINDEV INC
(FDI)
Updated June 2023

IDM STOCK SCORING CALCULATION

(1) Stock Price $ 0.41   Score *1*
(2) Price 4 Years Ago $ 0.50   Score *1*
(3) Current to Four Year Price Score *2*
(4) Book Value $ 0.83   Score *1*
(5) Price to Book Comparison Score *10*
(6) Analyst Buys # 0   Score *0*

(7) Analysts Strong Buys # 0 Score *0*
(8) Dividend Yield % 7.23   Score *8*
(9) Operating Margin % 72.30 Score *9*
(10) Trading Volume 0   Score *0*
(11) Price to Earnings 7.9x   Score *9*

Total of All 11 Scores = 41

This stock's total score in 2021 was **43**, in 2020 it was **48**, in 2019 it was **40**.

HISTORICAL STOCK PRICES & DIVIDEND PAYOUTS

Year	Stock	Dividend	Year	Stock	Dividend
2022	$ 0.42	$ 0.01	2010	$ 22.40	$ NA
2021	$ 0.51	$ 0.01	2009	$ 9.80	$ NA
2020	$ 0.42	$ 0.01	2008	$ 11.20	$ NA
2019	$ 0.48	$ 0.01	2007	$ 23.80	$ NA
2018	$ 0.51	$ 0.01	2006	$ 6.30	$ NA
2017	$ 0.50	$ 0.01	2005	$ 7.00	$ NA
2016	$ 0.59	$ 0.01	2004	$ NA	$ NA
2015	$ 2.27	$ NA	2003	$ NA	$ NA
2014	$ 3.85	$ NA	2002	$ NA	$ NA
2013	$ 4.02	$ NA	2001	$ NA	$ NA
2012	$ 12.95	$ NA	2000	$ NA	$ NA
2011	$ 25.55	$ NA	1999	$ NA	$ NA

NOTES: FDI is a Canada-based real estate finance company. The Company is focused on financing real estate developers with shorter-term loans of one to five years during the development or redevelopment process.

FIRM CAPITAL MORTGAGE INVESTMENT CORPORATION

(FC)

Updated June 2023

IDM STOCK SCORING CALCULATION

(1) Stock Price $ 10.70   Score 5
(2) Price 4 Years Ago $ 13.84 Score 5
(3) Current to Four Year Price Score 2
(4) Book Value $ 11.57   Score 5
(5) Price to Book Comparison Score 6
(6) Analyst Buys # 1   Score 2

(7) Analysts Strong Buys # 0 Score 0
(8) Dividend Yield % 8.75   Score 10
(9) Operating Margin % 49.72 Score 8
(10) Trading Volume 29,250   Score 1
(11) Price to Earnings 11.5x   Score 9

Total of All 11 Scores = 53

This stock's total score in 2021 was **53**, in 2020 it was **49**, in 2019 it was **51**.

HISTORICAL STOCK PRICES & DIVIDEND PAYOUTS

Year	Stock	Dividend	Year	Stock	Dividend
2022	$ 11.51	$ 0.08	2010	$ 11.48	$ 0.08
2021	$ 14.89	$ 0.08	2009	$ 8.87	$ 0.08
2020	$ 11.26	$ 0.08	2008	$ 10.45	$ 0.08
2019	$ 13.45	$ 0.08	2007	$ 10.85	$ 0.08
2018	$ 13.47	$ 0.08	2006	$ 10.31	$ 0.07
2017	$ 13.04	$ 0.08	2005	$ 11.50	$ 0.07
2016	$ 12.75	$ 0.08	2004	$ 9.88	$ 0.07
2015	$ 12.55	$ 0.08	2003	$ 10.30	$ 0.07
2014	$ 12.37	$ 0.08	2002	$ 10.24	$0.07
2013	$ 13.70	$ 0.08	2001	$ 8.56	$ 0.07
2012	$ 13.30	$ 0.08	2000	$ 9.25	$ 0.07
2011	$ 12.40	$0.08	1999	$ 9.90	$ 0.22

NOTES: FC is a Canada-based mortgage investment company, a non-bank lender that finances a range of properties, which include residential houses, small multi-family residential properties mixed-use residential apartments and store-front properties, investment properties, land and development and construction projects.

FIRM CAPITAL PROPERTY TRUST
(FCD.UN)
Updated June 2023

IDM STOCK SCORING CALCULATION

(1) Stock Price $ 5.30   Score 4
(2) Price 4 Years Ago $ 6.43   Score 4
(3) Current to Four Year Price Score 2
(4) Book Value $ 7.99   Score 4
(5) Price to Book Comparison Score 8
(6) Analyst Buys # 1   Score 2

(7) Analysts Strong Buys # 0 Score 0
(8) Dividend Yield % 9.81   Score 10
(9) Operating Margin % 68.44 Score 8
(10) Trading Volume 28,287 Score 1
(11) Price to Earnings -283.4 Score 0

Total of All 11 Scores = 43

This stock's total score in 2021 was **55**, in 2020 it was **44**, in 2019 it was **NA**.

HISTORICAL STOCK PRICES & DIVIDEND PAYOUTS

Year	Stock	Dividend	Year	Stock	Dividend
2022	$ 6.44	$ 0.04	2010	$ 2.53	$ NA
2021	$ 7.22	$ 0.04	2009	$ 5.95	$ NA
2020	$ 5.00	$ 0.04	2008	$ 16.37	$ NA
2019	$ 6.27	$ 0.04	2007	$ NA	$ NA
2018	$ 6.60	$ 0.04	2006	$ NA	$ NA
2017	$ 6.25	$ 0.04	2005	$ NA	$ NA
2016	$ 6.05	$ 0.04	2004	$ NA	$ NA
2015	$ 5.50	$ 0.03	2003	$ NA	$ NA
2014	$ 5.05	$ 0.03	2002	$ NA	$ NA
2013	$ 5.00	$ 0.13	2001	$ NA	$ NA
2012	$ 1.78	$ NA	2000	$ NA	$ NA
2011	$ 3.57	$ NA	1999	$ NA	$ NA

NOTES: FCD.UN is a Canada-based open-ended real estate investment trust. The Trust focuses on creating value for unit holders through capital preservation and investing to achieve distributable income.

FIRST NATIONAL FINANCIAL CORPORATION
(FN)
Updated June 2023

IDM STOCK SCORING CALCULATION

(1) Stock Price $ 38.50   Score 8

(2) Price 4 Years Ago $ 31.05   Score 8

(3) Current to Four Year Price   Score 9

(4) Book Value $ 11.66   Score 5

(5) Price to Book Comparison   Score 0

(6) Analyst Buys # 0   Score 0

(7) Analysts Strong Buys # 0   Score 0

(8) Dividend Yield % 6.23   Score 8

(9) Operating Margin % 14.77 Score 4

(10) Trading Volume 10485   Score 1

(11) Price to Earnings 13.1x Score 913

Total of All 11 Scores =46

This stock's total score in 2021 was **53**, in 2020 it was **44,** in 2019 it was **52**.

HISTORICAL STOCK PRICES & DIVIDEND PAYOUTS

Year	Stock	Dividend	Year	Stock	Dividend
2022	$ 33.11	$ 0.20	2010	$ 15.14	$ 0.11
2021	$ 44.80	$ 0.19	2009	$ 11.54	$ 0.10
2020	$ 27.09	$ 0.16	2008	$ 11.01	$ 0.09
2019	$ 30.49	$ 0.15	2007	$ 18.52	$ 0.09
2018	$ 27.12	$ 0.14	2006	$ 10.97	$ 0.10
2017	$ 23.82	$ 0.14	2005	$ NA	$ NA
2016	$ 26.51	$ 0.12	2004	$ NA	$ NA
2015	$ 16.13	$ 0.11	2003	$ NA	$ NA
2014	$ 20.01	$ 0.11	2002	$ NA	$ NA
2013	$ 15.57	$ 0.10	2001	$ NA	$ NA
2012	$ 12.94	$ 0.09	2000	$ NA	$ NA
2011	$ 14.71	$ 0.09	1999	$ NA	$ NA

NOTES: FN is a Canada-based parent company of First National Financial LP (FNFLP), which is an originator, underwriter, and servicer of prime residential (single-family and multi-unit) and commercial mortgages.

FREEHOLD ROYALTIES LIMITED
(FRU)
Updated June 2023

IDM STOCK SCORING CALCULATION

(1) Stock Price $ 13.48   Score 5
(2) Price 4 Years Ago $ 8.47   Score 4
(3) Current to Four Year Price Score 9
(4) Book Value $ 6.37   Score 4
(5) Price to Book Comparison   Score 0
(6) Analyst Buys # 2   Score 3

(7) Analysts Strong Buys # 0 Score 0
(8) Dividend Yield % 8.01   Score 10
(9) Operating Margin % 64.06 Score 8
(10) Trading Volume 328,329 Score 5
(11) Price to Earnings 10.1   Score 9

Total of All 11 Scores = 57

This stock's total score in 2021 was **37**, in 2020 it was **42**, in 2019 it was **43**.

HISTORICAL STOCK PRICES & DIVIDEND PAYOUTS

Year	Stock	Dividend	Year	Stock	Dividend
2022	$ 14.52	$ 0.08	2010	$ 15.84	$ 0.14
2021	$ 9.03	$ 0.04	2009	$ 13.85	$ 0.10
2020	$ 3.73	$ 0.01	2008	$ 20.81	$ 0.18
2019	$ 9.20	$ 0.05	2007	$ 14.53	$ 0.15
2018	$ 12.21	$ 0.05	2006	$ 20.60	$ 0.18
2017	$ 12.92	$ 0.05	2005	$ 15.34	$ 0.12
2016	$ 11.59	$ 0.04	2004	$ 15.00	$ 0.10
2015	$ 12.96	$ 0.09	2003	$ 12.84	$ 0.10
2014	$ 26.14	$ 0.14	2002	$ 10.85	$ 0.10
2013	$ 23.83	$ 0.14	2001	$ 9.59	$ 0.12
2012	$ 17.79	$ 0.14	2000	$ 7.95	$ 0.07
2011	$ 19.64	$ 0.14	1999	$ 4.90	$ 0.05

NOTES: FRU. is a Canada-based company, which is engaged in the development and production of oil and natural gas, predominantly in western Canada. The Company's primary focus is acquiring and managing oil and natural gas royalties.

GAMEHOST INC

(GH)

Updated June 2023

IDM STOCK SCORING CALCULATION

(1) Stock Price $ 9.53   Score 4
(2) Price 4 Years Ago $ 9.67   Score 4
(3) Current to Four Year Price Score 5
(4) Book Value $ 4.66   Score 3
(5) Price to Book Comparison Score 0
(6) Analyst Buys # 0   Score 0

(7) Analysts Strong Buys # 0 Score 0
(8) Dividend Yield % 3.78   Score 6
(9) Operating Margin % 30.02 Score 6
(10) Trading Volume 5,157   Score 0
(11) Price to Earnings 13.9x   Score 9

Total of All 11 Scores = 37

This stock's total score in 2021 was **NA**, in 2020 it was **NA**, in 2019 it was **NA**.

HISTORICAL STOCK PRICES & DIVIDEND PAYOUTS

Year	Stock	Dividend	Year	Stock	Dividend
2022	$ 8.34	$ 0.03	2010	$ 8.46	$ 0.07
2021	$ 7.10	$ NA	2009	$ 7.60	$ 0.70
2020	$ 3.80	$ 0.06	2008	$ 11.45	$ 0.07
2019	$ 8.25	$ 0.06	2007	$ 15.20	$ 0.07
2018	$ 11.86	$ 0.06	2006	$ 12.66	$ 0.05
2017	$ 11.17	$ 0.06	2005	$ 9.73	$ 0.04
2016	$ 9.61	$ 0.07	2004	$ 6.58	$ 0.04
2015	$ 11.23	$ 0.07	2003	$ 4.26	$ 0.04
2014	$ 16.61	$ 0.07	2002	$ NA	$ NA
2013	$ 13.28	$ 0.07	2001	$ NA	$ NA
2012	$ 11.96	$ 0.07	2000	$ NA	$ NA
2011	$ 11.20	$ 0.07	1999	$ NA	$ NA

NOTES GH segments include Gaming, Hotel, and Food, Beverage, three casinos offering slot machines, electronic gaming tables, video lottery terminals (VLT's), lottery ticket kiosks and table games.

GEAR ENERGY LTD

(GXE)

Updated June 2023

IDM STOCK SCORING CALCULATION

(1) Stock Price $ 0.97   Score 1
(2) Price 4 Years Ago $ 0.57   Score 1
(3) Current to Four Year Price Score 9
(4) Book Value $ 0.97   Score 1
(5) Price to Book Comparison Score 4
(6) Analyst Buys # 0   Score 0

(7) Analysts Strong Buys # 0 Score 0
(8) Dividend Yield % 12.37   Score 2
(9) Operating Margin % 39.96 Score 6
(10) Trading Volume 236,372 Score 4
(11) Price to Earnings 3.7x   Score 10

Total of All 11 Scores = 38

This stock's total score in 2021 was **NA**, in 2020 it was **NA**, in 2019 it was **NA**.

HISTORICAL STOCK PRICES & DIVIDEND PAYOUTS

Year	Stock	Dividend	Year	Stock	Dividend
2022	$ 1.24	$ 0.01	2010	$ NA	$ NA
2021	$ 0.81	$ NA	2009	$ NA	$ NA
2020	$ 0.19	$ NA	2008	$ NA	$ NA
2019	$ 0.59	$ NA	2007	$ NA	$ NA
2018	$ 1.12	$ N A	2006	$ NA	$ NA
2017	$ 0.77	$ NA	2005	$ NA	$ NA
2016	$ 0.62	$ NA	2004	$ NA	$ NA
2015	$ 2.11	$ NA	2003	$ NA	$ NA
2014	$ 5.29	$ NA	2002	$ NA	$ NA
2013	$ NA	$ NA	2001	$ NA	$ NA
2012	$ NA	$ NA	2000	$ NA	$ NA
2011	$ NA	$ NA	1999	$ NA	$ NA

NOTES: GXE is an oil-focused exploration and production company.

GIBSON ENERGY INC

(GEI)

Updated June 2023

IDM STOCK SCORING CALCULATION

(1) Stock Price $ 21.90   Score 7
(2) Price 4 Years Ago $ 22.7   Score 7
(3) Current to Four Year Price Score 5
(4) Book Value $ 4.12   Score 3
(5) Price to Book Comparison Score 0
(6) Analyst Buys # 3   Score 3

(7) Analysts Strong Buys # 1 Score 3
(8) Dividend Yield % 7.12   Score 8
(9) Operating Margin % 3.79 Score 1
(10) Trading Volume 581,372 Score 6
(11) Price to Earnings 12.4x   Score 9

Total of All 11 Scores = 52

This stock's total score in 2021 was **47**, in 2020 it was **52**, in 2019 it was **47**.

HISTORICAL STOCK PRICES & DIVIDEND PAYOUTS

Year	Stock	Dividend	Year	Stock	Dividend
2022	$ 24.79	$ 0.37	2010	$ NA	$ NA
2021	$ 23.75	$ 0.35	2009	$ NA	$ NA
2020	$ 22.06	$ 0.34	2008	$ NA	$ NA
2019	$ 23.35	$ 0.33	2007	$ NA	$ NA
2018	$ 18.22	$ 0.33	2006	$ NA	$ NA
2017	$ 17.46	$ 0.33	2005	$ NA	$ NA
2016	$ 17.88	$ 0.33	2004	$ NA	$ NA
2015	$ 22.55	$ 0.32	2003	$ NA	$ NA
2014	$ 36.45	$ 0.30	2002	$ NA	$ NA
2013	$ 25.16	$ 0.28	2001	$ NA	$ NA
2012	$ 20.60	$ 0.25	2000	$ NA	$ NA
2011	$18.90	$ 0.28	1999	$ NA	$ NA

NOTES: GEI is a Canada-based integrated service provider to the oil and gas industry with operations across producing regions throughout North America.

GLOBAL DIVIDEND GROWTH SPLIT CORPORATION

(GDV)

Updated June 2023

IDM STOCK SCORING CALCULATION

(1) Stock Price $ 9.91   *Score 4*
(2) Price 4 Years Ago $ 10.80 Score 5
(3) Current to Four Year Price Score 5
(4) Book Value $ 0   *Score 1*
(5) Price to Book Comparison Score 0
(6) Analyst Buys # 0   *Score 0*

(7) Analysts Strong Buys # 0 Score 0
(8) Dividend Yield % 12.11   *Score 2*
(9) Operating Margin % 0   *Score 0*
(10) Trading Volume 24,662 Score 1
(11) Price to Earnings 0.0x   *Score 0*

Total of All 11 Scores = 18

This stock's total score in 2021 was **17**, in 2020 it was **13**, in 2019 it was **9**.

HISTORICAL STOCK PRICES & DIVIDEND PAYOUTS

Year	Stock	Dividend	Year	Stock	Dividend
2022	$ 10.66	$ 0.10	2010	$ NA	$ NA
2021	$ 11.95	$ 0.10	2009	$ NA	$ NA
2020	$ 9.02	$ 0.10	2008	$ NA	$ NA
2019	$ 10.52	$ 0.10	2007	$ NA	$ NA
2018	$ 11.30	$ 0.05	2006	$ NA	$ NA
2017	$ NA	$ NA	2005	$ NA	$ NA
2016	$ NA	$ NA	2004	$ NA	$ NA
2015	$ NA	$NA	2003	$ NA	$ NA
2014	$ NA	$ NA	2002	$ NA	$ NA
2013	$ NA	$ NA	2001	$ NA	$ NA
2012	$ NA	$ NA	2000	$ NA	$ NA
2011	$ NA	$ NA	1999	$ NA	$ NA

NOTES: GDV is a Canada-based mutual fund corporation. The Company is focused on investments in a diversified portfolio of equity securities of capitalization global dividend growth companies.

GOEASY LTD

(GSY)

Updated June 2023

IDM STOCK SCORING CALCULATION

(1) Stock Price $ 109.12   Score 10
(2) Price 4 Years Ago $ 53.00   Score 9
(3) Current to Four Year Price Score 10
(4) Book Value $ 52.88   Score 9
(5) Price to Book Comparison   Score 0
(6) Analyst Buys # 1   Score 2

(7) Analysts Strong Buys # 4   Score 4
(8) Dividend Yield % 3.52   Score 6
(9) Operating Margin % 32.99   Score 6
(10) Trading Volume 16,771   Score 1
(11) Price to Earnings 11.0   Score 9

Total of All 11 Scores = 66

This stock's total score in 2021 was **NA**, in 2020 it was **NA**, in 2019 it was **NA**.

HISTORICAL STOCK PRICES & DIVIDEND PAYOUTS

Year	Stock	Dividend	Year	Stock	Dividend
2022	$ 119.86	$ 0.91	2010	$ 7.60	$ 0.09
2021	$ 158.63	$ 0.66	2009	$ 9.00	$ 0.09
2020	$ 54.68	$ 0.45	2008	$ 16.50	$ 0.09
2019	$ 53.00	$ 0.31	2007	$ 19.00	$ 0.07
2018	$ 40.26	$ 0.23	2006	$ 16.05	$ 0.06
2017	$ 28.30	$ 0.18	2005	$ 18.50	$ 0.04
2016	$ 17.76	$ 0.13	2004	$ 7.83	$ 0.03
2015	$ 16.56	$ 0.10	2003	$ 4.20	$ NA
2014	$ 24.82	$ 0.09	2002	$ 4.33	$ NA
2013	$ 10.75	$ 0.09	2001	$ 2.26	$ NA
2012	$ 10.40	$ 0.09	2000	$ 4.00	$ NA
2011	$ 7.50	$ 0.09	1999	$14.00	$ NA

NOTES: GSY is a Canada-based company that provides non-prime leasing and lending services through its easyhome, easyfinancial and LendCare brands. The easyfinancial lends out unsecured and real estate secured instalment loans.

GOODFELLOW INC

(GDL)

Updated June 2023

IDM STOCK SCORING CALCULATION

(1) Stock Price $ 12.35   *Score* 5

(2) Price 4 Years Ago $ 5.04   *Score* 4

(3) Current to Four Year Price *Score* 10

(4) Book Value $ 21.83   *Score* 7

(5) Price to Book Comparison *Score* 8

(6) Analyst Buys # 0   *Score* 0

(7) Analysts Strong Buys # 0 Score 0

(8) Dividend Yield % 8.10   *Score* 10

(9) Operating Margin % 6.40   *Score* 2

(10) Trading Volume 2,025   *Score* 0

(11) Price to Earnings 3.9x   *Score* 10

Total of All 11 Scores = 56

This stock's total score in 2021 was **53**, in 2020 it was **45**, in 2019 it was **NA**.

HISTORICAL STOCK PRICES & DIVIDEND PAYOUTS

Year	Stock	Dividend	Year	Stock	Dividend
2022	$ 12.97	$ 0.40	2010	$ 11.04	$ 0.30
2021	$ 10.10	$ 0.30	2009	$ 7.48	$ 0.15
2020	$ 3.56	$ 0.10	2008	$ 9.54	$ 0.15
2019	$ 6.24	$ 0.10	2007	$ 14.02	$ 0.30
2018	$ 7.82	$ NA	2006	$ 13.50	$ 0.35
2017	$ 7.17	$ NA	2005	$ 14.05	$ 0.25
2016	$ 11.45	$ 0.15	2004	$11.00	$0.23
2015	$ 9.20	$ 0.15	2003	$5.27	$ 0.07
2014	$ 8.88	$ 0.20	2002	$ 5.75	$ 0.12
2013	$ 9.06	$ 0.20	2001	$ 4.50	$ 0.06
2012	$ 7.81	$ 0.10	2000	$ 4.97	$ 0.08
2011	$ 9.85	$ 0.10	1999	$ 5.02	$ 0.08

NOTES: GDL is a Canada-based company, which is engaged in the remanufacturing and distributing of lumber and hardwood flooring products.

GRANITE REAL ESTATE INVESTMENT TRUST

(GRT.UN)
Updated June 2023

IDM STOCK SCORING CALCULATION

(1) Stock Price $ 82.87   *Score* 9
(2) Price 4 Years Ago $ 60.29 Score 9
(3) Current to Four Year Price Score 9
(4) Book Value $ 85.94   *Score* 9
(5) Price to Book Comparison Score 6
(6) Analyst Buys # 5   *Score* 4

(7) Analysts Strong Buys # 1 Score 3
(8) Dividend Yield % 3.86   *Score* 6
(9) Operating Margin % 64.14 Score 8
(10) Trading Volume 33,782   *Score* 2
(11) Price to Earnings -16.2x   *Score* 8

Total of All 11 Scores = 73

This stock's total score in 2021 was **68**, in 2020 it was **60**, in 2019 it was **69**.

HISTORICAL STOCK PRICES & DIVIDEND PAYOUTS

Year	Stock	Dividend	Year	Stock	Dividend
2022	$ 78.95	$ NA	2010	$ 12.85	$ NA
2021	$ 82.48	$ NA	2009	$ 8.93	$ NA
2020	$ 70.06	$ NA	2008	$ 22.82	$ NA
2019	$ 60.29	$ NA	2007	$ 38.556	$ NA
2018	$ 53.31	$ NA	2006	$ 37.63	$ NA
2017	$ 51.00	$ NA	2005	$ 38.44	$ NA
2016	$ 38.53	$ NA	2004	$ 36.38	$ NA
2015	$ 42.71	$ NA	2003	$ 30.82	$ NA
2014	$ 39.27	$ NA	2002	$ NA	$ NA
2013	$ 36.03	$ NA	2001	$ NA	$ NA
2012	$ 34.55	$ NA	2000	$ NA	$ NA
2011	$ 29.26	$ NA	1999	$ NA	$ NA

NOTES: GRT is a real estate investment trust. The Company operates through the ownership and rental of industrial real estate segment.

GREAT WEST LIFECO INC
(GWO)

Updated June 2023

IDM STOCK SCORING CALCULATION

(1) Stock Price $ 38.07   Score 8

(2) Price 4 Years Ago $ 30.60 Score 8

(3) Current to Four Year Price Score 9

(4) Book Value $ 30.74   Score 8

(5) Price to Book Comparison Score 1

(6) Analyst Buys # 1   Score 2

(7) Analysts Strong Buys # 0 Score 0

(8) Dividend Yield % 5.46   Score 8

(9) Operating Margin % 8.94   Score 2

(10) Trading Volume 1,376,733 Score 9

(11) Price to Earnings 11.7x   Score 10

Total of All 11 Scores = 65

This stock's total score in 2021 was **61**, in 2020 it was **60**, in 2019 it was **52**.

HISTORICAL STOCK PRICES & DIVIDEND PAYOUTS

Year	Stock	Dividend	Year	Stock	Dividend
2022	$ 31.12	$ 0.49	2010	$ 24.07	$ 0.31
2021	$ 36.82	$ 0.44	2009	$ 22.30	$ 0.31
2020	$ 23.80	$ 0.44	2008	$ 29.16	$ 0.29
2019	$ 28.98	$ 0.41	2007	$ 34.55	$ 0.26
2018	$ 32.91	$ 0.39	2006	$ 28.46	$ 0.22
2017	$ 33.29	$ 0.37	2005	$ 29.99	$ 0.20
2016	$ 35.34	$ 0.35	2004	$ 24.10	$ 0.16
2015	$ 37.04	$ 0.33	2003	$ 19.92	$ 0.14
2014	$ 31.76	$ 0.31	2002	$ 18.87	$ 0.11
2013	$ 28.98	$ 0.31	2001	$ 17.17	$ 0.09
2012	$ 22.07	$ 0.31	2000	$ 13.05	$ 0.08
2011	$ 25.48	$ 0.31	1999	$ 11.00	$ 0.06

NOTES: GWO has interests in the life insurance, health insurance, asset management, investment and retirement savings, and reinsurance businesses

HEADWATER EXPLORATION INC

(HWX)

Updated June 2023

IDM STOCK SCORING CALCULATION

(1) Stock Price $ 6.42   *Score 4*
(2) Price 4 Years Ago $ 0.66   *Score 1*
(3) Current to Four Year Price Score 10
(4) Book Value $ 2.32   *Score 3*
(5) Price to Book Comparison Score 0
(6) Analyst Buys # 3   *Score 3*

(7) Analysts Strong Buys # 0 Score 0
(8) Dividend Yield % 6.23   *Score 8*
(9) Operating Margin % 53.16 Score 8
(10) Trading Volume 788,307 Score 8
(11) Price to Earnings 9.9x   *Score 9*

Total of All 11 Scores = 54

This stock's total score in 2021 was **NA**, in 2020 it was **NA**, in 2019 it was **NA**.

HISTORICAL STOCK PRICES & DIVIDEND PAYOUTS

Year	Stock	Dividend	Year	Stock	Dividend
2022	$ 6.50	$ 0.10	2010	$ 5.20	$ NA
2021	$ 4.36	$ NA	2009	$ 2.66	$ NA
2020	$ 1.23	$ NA	2008	$ 8.72	$ NA
2019	$ 0.66	$ NA	2007	$ 11.40	$ NA
2018	$ 0.63	$ NA	2006	$ 5.10	$ NA
2017	$ 0.49	$ NA	2005	$ 2.95	$ NA
2016	$ 0.49	$ NA	2004	$ 0.85	$ NA
2015	$ 0.45	$ NA	2003	$ 0.16	$ NA
2014	$ 0.68	$ NA	2002	$ 1.30	$ NA
2013	$ 0.84	$ NA	2001	$ 1.68	$ NA
2012	$ 0.53	$ NA	2000	$ 0.39	$ NA
2011	$ 2.96	$ NA	1999	$ 0.75	$ NA

NOTES: **HWX** is a Canada-based resource company engaged in the exploration and development and production of petroleum and natural gas in Canada.

HEMISPHERE ENERGY CORP

(HME)

Updated June 2023

IDM STOCK SCORING CALCULATION

(1) Stock Price $ 1.24   Score 2
(2) Price 4 Years Ago $ 0.12   Score 1
(3) Current to Four Year Price Score 10
(4) Book Value $ 0.52   Score 1
(5) Price to Book Comparison   Score 0
(6) Analyst Buys # 0   Score 0

(7) Analysts Strong Buys # 0 Score 0
(8) Dividend Yield % 8.06   Score 10
(9) Operating Margin % 41.32 Score 6
(10) Trading Volume 17,846   Score 1
(11) Price to Earnings 5.7x   Score 9

Total of All 11 Scores = 40

This stock's total score in 2021 was **NA**, in 2020 it was **NA**, in 2019 it was **NA**.

HISTORICAL STOCK PRICES & DIVIDEND PAYOUTS

Year	Stock	Dividend	Year	Stock	Dividend
2022	$ 1.56	$ 0.03	2010	$ 0.19	$ NA
2021	$ 0.89	$ NA	2009	$ 0.32	$ NA
2020	$ 0.11	$ NA	2008	$ 0.45	$ NA
2019	$ 0.12	$ NA	2007	$ 1.02	$ NA
2018	$ 0.27	$ NA	2006	$ 1.05	$ NA
2017	$ 0.21	$ NA	2005	$ 2.55	$ NA
2016	$ 0.22	$ NA	2004	$ 1.25	$ NA
2015	$ 0.30	$ NA	2003	$ 0.50	$ NA
2014	$ 0.78	$ NA	2002	$ 0.75	$ NA
2013	$ 0.46	$ NA	2001	$ 0.65	$ NA
2012	$ 0.58	$ NA	2000	$ 1.25	$ NA
2011	$ 0.50	$ NA	1999	$ 2.25	$ NA

NOTES: HME is a Canada-based oil company engaged in producing oil and natural gas from its Jenner and Atlee Buffalo properties in southeast Alberta.

H & R REAL ESTATE INVESTMENT TRUST
(HR.UN)

Updated June 2023

IDM STOCK SCORING CALCULATION

(1) Stock Price $ 10.36   Score 5   *(7)* Analysts Strong Buys #0   Score 0
(2) Price 4 Years Ago $ 17.47   Score 6   *(8)* Dividend Yield % 5.79   Score 8
(3) Current to Four Year Price   Score 2   *(9)* Operating Margin % 15.54 Score 4
(4) Book Value $ 20.64   Score 7   *(10)* Trading Volume 3,258,696 Score 10
(5) Price to Book Comparison   Score 8   *(11)* Price to Earnings -82.4x   Score 2
(6) Analyst Buys # 1   Score 2

Total of All 11 Scores = 54

This stock's total score in 2021 was **54**, in 2020 it was **47**, in 2019 it was **61**.

HISTORICAL STOCK PRICES & DIVIDEND PAYOUTS

Year	Stock	Dividend	Year	Stock	Dividend
2022	$ 12.45	$ 0.05	2010	$ 13.09	$ 0.05
2021	$ 12.96	$ 0.04	2009	$ 8.45	$ 0.05
2020	$ 7.51	$ 0.04	2008	$ 13.86	$ 0.09
2019	$ 17.47	$ 0.09	2007	$ 17.67	$ 0.09
2018	$ 15.54	$ 0.09	2006	$ 17.21	$ 0.09
2017	$ 16.96	$ 0.09	2005	$ 15.03	$ 0.08
2016	$ 17.33	$ 0.09	2004	$ 12.63	$ 0.08
2015	$ 17.28	$ 0.09	2003	$ 11.97	$ 0.08
2014	$ 17.81	$ 0.09	2002	$ 11.01	$ 0.08
2013	$ 17.10	$0.09	2001	$ 10.09	$ 0.07
2012	$ 18.87	$ 0.07	2000	$ 8.78	$ 0.07
2011	$ 16.66	$ 0.06	1999	$ 8.51	$ 0.07

NOTES: HR.UN is a Canada-based open-ended real estate investment trust operating and developing residential and commercial properties across Canada and in the United States.

HIGH ARTIC ENERGY SERVICES INC

(HWO)

Updated June 2023

IDM STOCK SCORING CALCULATION

(1) Stock Price $ 1.19   Score 2
(2) Price 4 Years Ago $ 3.19   Score 3
(3) Current to Four Year Price   Score 1
(4) Book Value $ 2.37   Score 3
(5) Price to Book Comparison   Score 8
(6) Analyst Buys # 0   Score 0

(7) Analysts Strong Buys # 0   Score 0
(8) Dividend Yield % 4.92   Score 8
(9) Operating Margin % -41.92 Score 0
(10) Trading Volume 13,210   Score 1
(11) Price to Earnings -1.7x   Score 0

Total of All 11 Scores = 26

This stock's total score in 2021 was **NA**, in 2020 it was **NA**, in 2019 it was **NA**.

HISTORICAL STOCK PRICES & DIVIDEND PAYOUTS

Year	Stock	Dividend	Year	Stock	Dividend
2022	$ 1.56	$ 0.01	2010	$ 1.00	$ NA
2021	$ 1.60	$ NA	2009	$ 0.50	$ NA
2020	$ 0.67	$ NA	2008	$ 4.65	$ NA
2019	$ 3.19	$ 0.02	2007	$ 11.50	$ NA
2018	$ 3.82	$ 0.02	2006	$ 57.00	$ 0.49
2017	$ 3.76	$ 0.02	2005	$ NA	$ NA
2016	$ 3.71	$ 0.02	2004	$ NA	$ NA
2015	$ 3.65	$ 0.02	2003	$ NA	$ NA
2014	$ 4.96	$ 0.01	2002	$ NA	$ NA
2013	$ 2.07	$.0.01	2001	$ NA	$ NA
2012	$ 1.61	$ 0.01	2000	$ NA	$ NA
2011	$ 1.42	$ NA	1999	$ NA	$ NA

NOTES: HWO. is a Canada-based energy services provider. The Company's segments include Drilling Services and Ancillary Services.

IGM FINANCIAL INC

(IGM)

Updated June 2023

IDM STOCK SCORING CALCULATION

(1) Stock Price $ 40.73   Score 8   *(7)* Analysts Strong Buys #0   Score 0
(2) Price 4 Years Ago $ 36.46   Score 8   *(8)* Dividend Yield % 5.52   Score 8
(3) Current to Four Year Price Score 9   *(9)* Operating Margin % 29.95 Score 6
(4) Book Value $ 25.50   Score 7   *(10)* Trading Volume 556,986   Score 6
(5) Price to Book Comparison Score 0   *(11)* Price to Earnings 9.5x   Score 9
(6) Analyst Buys # 3   Score 3

Total of All 11 Scores = 64

This stock's total score in 2021 was **65**, in 2020 it was **56**, in 2019 it was **50**.

HISTORICAL STOCK PRICES & DIVIDEND PAYOUTS

Year	Stock	Dividend	Year	Stock	Dividend
2022	$37.18	$ 0.56	2010	$ 40.44	$ 0.51
2021	$ 44.03	$ 0.56	2009	$ 41.15	$ 0.51
2020	$ 32.93	$ 0.56	2008	$ 42.26	$ 0.49
2019	$ 37.39	$ 0.56	2007	$ 51.77	$ 0.43
2018	$ 36.41	$ 0.56	2006	$ 44.51	$ 0.37
2017	$ 40.22	$ 0.56	2005	$ 39.91	$ 0.32
2016	$ 36.33	$ 0.56	2004	$ 33.65	$ 0.28
2015	$ 38.62	$ 0.56	2003	$ 29.00	$ 0.24
2014	$ 51.08	$ 0.54	2002	$ 27.75	$ 0.20
2013	$ 45.09	$ 0.54	2001	$ 21.40	$ 0.17
2012	$ 40.04	$ 0.54	2000	$ 20.35	$ 0.14
2011	$ 48.10	$ 0.51	1999	$ 20.00	$ 0.12

NOTES: : IGM is a Canada-based wealth and asset management company operating as Investors Group Inc. and Mackenzie Financial Corporation, within the advice segment of the financial services market.

INFORMATION SERVICES CORPORATION

(ISV)

Updated June 2023

IDM STOCK SCORING CALCULATION

(1) Stock Price $ 20.97   Score 7   *(7)* Analysts Strong Buys # 0 Score 0

(2) Price 4 Years Ago $ 16.10 Score 6   *(8)* Dividend Yield % 4.39   Score 6

(3) Current to Four Year Price Score 9   *(9)* Operating Margin % 23.64 Score 5

(4) Book Value $ 8.79   Score 4   *(10)* Trading Volume 600   Score 0

(5) Price to Book Comparison Score 0   *(11)* Price to Earnings 12.4x   Score 9

(6) Analyst Buys #1   Score 2

Total of All 11 Scores = 48

This stock's total score in 2021 was **NA**, in 2020 it was **NA**, in 2019 it was **NA**.

HISTORICAL STOCK PRICES & DIVIDEND PAYOUTS

Year	Stock	Dividend	Year	Stock	Dividend
2022	$ 20.01	$ 0.23	2010	$ NA	$ NA
2021	$ 28.29	$ 0.20	2009	$ NA	$ NA
2020	$ 17.67	$ 0.20	2008	$ NA	$ NA
2019	$ 16.19	$ 0.20	2007	$ NA	$ NA
2018	$ 17.03	$ 0.02	2006	$ NA	$ NA
2017	$ 18.71	$ 0.20	2005	$ NA	$ NA
2016	$ 16.69	$ 0.20	2004	$ NA	$ NA
2015	$ 14.95	$ 0.20	2003	$ NA	$ NA
2014	$ 18.99	$ 0.20	2002	$ NA	$ NA
2013	$ NA	$ NA	2001	$ NA	$ NA
2012	$ NA	$ NA	2000	$ NA	$ NA
2011	$ NA	$ NA	1999	$ NA	$ NA

NOTES: **ISV** is a Canada-based company, which is a provider of registry and information management services for public data and records.

INNERGEX RENEWABLE ENERGY INC

(INE)

Updated June 2023

IDM STOCK SCORING CALCULATION

(1) Stock Price $ 13.39   Score 5
(2) Price 4 Years Ago $ 15.03 Score 6
(3) Current to Four Year Price Score 2
(4) Book Value $ 6.45   Score 4
(5) Price to Book Comparison Score 0
(6) Analyst Buys # 4   Score 4

(7) Analysts Strong Buys #0   Score 0
(8) Dividend Yield % 5.38   Score 8
(9) Operating Margin % 22.34 Score 5
(10) Trading Volume 860,220 Score 8
(11) Price to Earnings -40.5   Score 2

Total of All 11 Scores = 44

This stock's total score in 2021 was **43**, in 2020 it was **NA**, in 2019 it was **NA**.

HISTORICAL STOCK PRICES & DIVIDEND PAYOUTS

Year	Stock	Dividend	Year	Stock	Dividend
2022	$ 17.30	$ 0.18	2010	$ 8.38	$ 0.15
2021	$ 21.75	$ 0.18	2009	$ 3.85	$ NA
2020	$ 22.99	$ 0.18	2008	$ 7.90	$ NA
2019	$ 15.03	$ 0.17	2007	$ NA	$ NA
2018	$ 13.81	$ 0.17	2006	$ NA	$ NA
2017	$ 14.26	$ 0.17	2005	$ NA	$ NA
2016	$ 15.64	$ 0.16	2004	$ NA	$ NA
2015	$ 10.73	$ 0.15	2003	$ NA	$ NA
2014	$ 10.81	$ 0.15	2002	$ NA	$ NA
2013	$ 8.67	$ 0.14	2001	$ NA	$ NA
2012	$ 10.33	$ 0.14	2000	$ NA	$ NA
2011	$ 9.98	$ 0.14	1999	$ NA	$ NA

NOTES: INE. is Canadian-based. It owns and operates independent renewable power-generating facilities with a focus on hydroelectric, wind and solar production as well as energy storage technologies.

INPLAY OIL CORP

(IPO)

Updated June 2023

IDM STOCK SCORING CALCULATION

(1) Stock Price $ 2.45   *Score 3*
(2) Price 4 Years Ago $ 0.58   *Score 1*
(3) Current to Four Year Price Score 10
(4) Book Value $ 3.14   *Score 3*
(5) Price to Book Comparison   *Score 8*
(6) Analyst Buys # 1   *Score 2*

(7) Analysts Strong Buys # 0 Score 0
(8) Dividend Yield % 7.35   *Score 8*
(9) Operating Margin % 42.65 Score 6
(10) Trading Volume 24,455   *Score 1*
(11) Price to Earnings 3.0x   *Score 10*

Total of All 11 Scores = 52

This stock's total score in 2021 was **NA**, in 2020 it was **NA**, in 2019 it was **NA**

HISTORICAL STOCK PRICES & DIVIDEND PAYOUTS

Year	Stock	Dividend	Year	Stock	Dividend
2022	$ 3.01	$ NA	2010	$ 1,180.00	$ NA
2021	$ 1.23	$ NA	2009	$ 830.00	$ NA
2020	$ 0.18	$ NA	2008	$ 5,370.00	$ NA
2019	$ 0.69	$ NA	2007	$ 4,600.00	$ NA
2018	$ 1.85	$ NA	2006	$ 5,100.00	$ NA
2017	$ 1.52	$ NA	2005	$7,419.00	$ NA
2016	$ 2.74	$ NA	2004	$ 7,903.00	$ NA
2015	$ 60.00	$ NA	2003	$ NA	$ NA
2014	$ 235.00	$ NA	2002	$ NA	$ NA
2013	$ 140.00	$ NA	2001	$ NA	$ NA
2012	$ 340.00	$ N A	2000	$ NA	$ NA
2011	$ 800.00	$ NA	1999	$ NA	$ NA

NOTES: IPO. is a Canada-based company engaged in the acquisition, exploration and development of petroleum and natural gas properties, and the production and sale of crude oil, natural gas and natural gas liquids.

INOVALIS REAL ESTATE INVESTMENT TRUST

(INO.UN)
Updated June 2023

IDM STOCK SCORING CALCULATION

(1) Stock Price $ 3.34   Score 3
(2) Price 4 Years Ago $ 9.75   Score 4
(3) Current to Four Year Price   Score 1
(4) Book Value $ 8.76   Score 4
(5) Price to Book Comparison   Score 10
(6) Analyst Buys # 0   Score 0

(7) Analysts Strong Buys #   Score 0
(8) Dividend Yield % 12.35   Score 2
(9) Operating Margin % -136.97 Score 0
(10) Trading Volume 112,768   Score 4
(11) Price to Earnings -2.9   Score 0

Total of All 11 Scores = 28

This stock's total score in 2021 was **43** , in 2020 it was **47**, in 2019 it was **65**.

HISTORICAL STOCK PRICES & DIVIDEND PAYOUTS

Year	Stock	Dividend	Year	Stock	Dividend
2022	$ 7.19	$ 0.07	2010	$ NA	$ NA
2021	$ 9.79	$ 0.07	2009	$ NA	$ NA
2020	$ 7.68	$ 0.07	2008	$ NA	$ NA
2019	$ 9.68	$ 0.07	2007	$ NA	$ NA
2018	$ 9.86	$ 0.07	2006	$ NA	$ NA
2017	$ 9.81	$ 0.07	2005	$ NA	$ NA
2016	$ 9.47	$ 0.07	2004	$ NA	$ NA
2015	$ 8.67	$ 0.07	2003	$ NA	$ NA
2014	$ 9.46	$ 0.07	2002	$ NA	$ NA
2013	$ 9.22	$ 0.07	2001	$ NA	$ NA
2012	$ NA	$ NA	2000	$ NA	$ NA
2011	$ NA	$ NA	1999	$ NA	$ NA

NOTES: INO.UN is a Canada-based open-ended real estate investment trust formed to acquire and own office properties primarily located in France and Germany and also in other European countries.

INTERNATIONAL CLEAN POWER DIVIDEND FUND

(CLP.UN)

Updated June 2023

IDM STOCK SCORING CALCULATION

(1) Stock Price $ 7.01   Score *4*

(2) Price 4 Years Ago $ 0   Score *1*

(3) Current to Four Year Price Score *0*

(4) Book Value $ 7.87   Score *4*

(5) Price to Book Comparison Score *8*

(6) Analyst Buys # 0   Score *0*

(7) Analysts Strong Buys #0   Score *0*

(8) Dividend Yield % 7.13   Score *8*

(9) Operating Margin % 0   Score *0*

(10) Trading Volume 10,900   Score *1*

(11) Price to Earnings -9.2   Score *0*

Total of All 11 Scores = 26

This stock's total score in 2021 was **15** , in 2020 it was **NA**, in 2019 it was **NA**.

HISTORICAL STOCK PRICES & DIVIDEND PAYOUTS

Year	Stock	Dividend	Year	Stock	Dividend
2022	$ 8.07	$ 0.04	2010	$ NA	$ NA
2021	$ 9.10	$ 0.04	2009	$ NA	$ NA
2020	$ NA	$ NA	2008	$ NA	$ NA
2019	$ NA	$ NA	2007	$ NA	$ NA
2018	$ NA	$ NA	2006	$ NA	$ NA
2017	$ NA	$ NA	2005	$ NA	$ NA
2016	$ NA	$ NA	2004	$ NA	$ NA
2015	$ NA	$ NA	2003	$ NA	$ NA
2014	$ NA	$ NA	2002	$ NA	$ NA
2013	$ NA	$ NA	2001	$ NA	$ NA
2012	$ NA	$ NA	2000	$ NA	$ NA
2011	$ NA	$ NA	1999	$ NA	$ NA

NOTES: CLP.UN is a Canada-based investment fund whose objective is to provide investors with a diversified, actively managed portfolio comprised primarily of dividend paying securities of Clean Power Issuers.

K-BRO LINEN INC

(KBL)

Updated June 2023

IDM STOCK SCORING CALCULATION

(1) Stock Price $ 31.15   Score 8
(2) Price 4 Years Ago $ 40.00 Score 8
(3) Current to Four Year Price Score 2
(4) Book Value $ 16.39   Score 6
(5) Price to Book Comparison Score 0
(6) Analyst Buys # 3   Score 3

(7) Analysts Strong Buys # 0 Score 0
(8) Dividend Yield % 3.85   Score 6
(9) Operating Margin % 4.86 Score 2
(10) Trading Volume 279   Score 0
(11) Price to Earnings 52.7x Score 2

Total of All 11 Scores = 37

This stock's total score in 2021 was **NA**, in 2020 it was **NA**, in 2019 it was **NA**.

HISTORICAL STOCK PRICES & DIVIDEND PAYOUTS

Year	Stock	Dividend	Year	Stock	Dividend
2022	$ 32.63	$ 0.10	2010	$ 15.85	$ 0.09
2021	$ 43.39	$ 0.10	2009	$ 12.00	$ 0.09
2020	$ 28.10	$ 0.10	2008	$ 10.53	$ 0.09
2019	$ 39.45	$ 0.10	2007	$ 13.41	$ 0.09
2018	$ 38.29	$ 0.10	2006	$ 15.50	$ 0.09
2017	$ 40.25	$ 0.10	2005	$ 11.65	$ 0.09
2016	$ 44.25	$ 0.10	2004	$ NA	$ NA
2015	$ 50.10	$ 0.10	2003	$ NA	$ NA
2014	$ 38.10	$ 0.10	2002	$ NA	$ NA
2013	$ 36.15	$ 0.10	2001	$ NA	$ N A
2012	$ 25.62	$ 0.10	2000	$ NA	$ NA
2011	$ 21.25	$ 0.09	1999	$ NA	$ NA

NOTES: KBL is a Canada-based owner and operator of laundry and linen processing facilities in Canada, Scotland and the North East of England.

KEYERA CORPORATION

(KEY)

Updated June 2023

IDM STOCK SCORING CALCULATION

(1) Stock Price $ 30.48   Score 8
(2) Price 4 Years Ago $ 33.58 Score 8
(3) Current to Four Year Price Score 5
(4) Book Value $ 12.30   Score 5
(5) Price to Book Comparison Score 0
(6) Analyst Buys # 5   Score 4

(7) Analysts Strong Buys #0 Score 0
(8) Dividend Yield % 6.30   Score 8
(9) Operating Margin % 6.45 Score 2
(10) Trading Volume 147,891 Score 4
(11) Price to Earnings 19.4x   Score 8

Total of All 11 Scores = 52

This stock's total score in 2021 was **43**, in 2020 it was **60** , in 2019 it was **54.**

HISTORICAL STOCK PRICES & DIVIDEND PAYOUTS

Year	Stock	Diviend	Year	Stock	Dividend
2022	$ 33.19	$ 0.16	2010	$ 13.41	$ 0.07
2021	$ 33.31	$ 016	2009	$ 9.84	$ 0.07
2020	$ 20.67	$ 0.16	2008	$ 11.04	$ 0.07
2019	$ 33.58	$ 0.15	2007	$ 9.18	$ 0.06
2018	$ 37.66	$ 0.14	2006	$ 10.27	$ 0.06
2017	$ 40.82	$ 0.14	2005	$ 9.35	$ 0.06
2016	$ 39.52	$ 0.13	2004	$ 6.23	$ 0.05
2015	$ 42.98	$ 0.12	2003	$ 5.52	$ 0.04
2014	$ 40.81	$ 0.11	2002	$ NA	$ NA
2013	$ 28.73	$ 0.09	2001	$ NA	$ NA
2012	$ 22.50	$ 0.09	2000	$ NA	$ NA
2011	$ 21.95	$0.08	1999	$ NA	$ NA

NOTES: **KEY**. operates an integrated Canadian-based midstream business in raw gas gathering pipelines and processing plants, which collect and process raw natural gas, remove waste products and separate the economic components, primarily natural gas liquids (NGLs). The Liquids Business Unit consists of Liquids Infrastructure and Marketing segments.

KILLAM APARTMENT REAL ESTATE INVESTMENT TRUST

(KMP)
Updated June 2023

IDM STOCK SCORING CALCULATION

(1) Stock Price $ 17.50   Score 6

(2) Price 4 Years Ago $ 19.61 Score 6

(3) Current to Four Year Price Score 2

(4) Book Value $ 19.46   Score 6

(5) Price to Book Comparison Score 6

(6) Analyst Buys # 7   Score 5

(7) Analysts Strong Buys # 0 Score 0

(8) Dividend Yield % 4.00   Score 6

(9) Operating Margin % 38.93 Score 6

(10) Trading Volume 97,802 Score 3

(11) Price to Earnings 14.0x Score 9

Total of All 11 Scores = 55

This stock's total score in 2021 was **55**, in 2020 it was **59**, in 2019 it was **56**.

HISTORICAL STOCK PRICES & DIVIDEND PAYOUTS

Year	Stock	Dividend	Year	Stock	Dividend
2022	$ 17.99	$ 0.06	2010	$ 8.41	$ 0.05
2021	$ 20.27	$ 0.06	2009	$ 6.00	$ .05
2020	$ 17.52	$ 0.06	2008	$ 7.10	$ 0.05
2019	$ 18.79	$ 0.06	2007	$ 8.55	$ 0.05
2018	$ 15.26	$ 0.05	2006	$ 10.60	$ NA
2017	$ 12.26	$ 0.05	2005	$ 10.88	$ NA
2016	$ 12.69	$ 0.05	2004	$ 8.28	$ NA
2015	$ 10.00	$ 0.05	2003	$ 2.60	$ NA
2014	$ 10.55	$ 0.05	2002	$ 1.76	$ NA
2013	$ 10.50	$ 0.05	2001	$ 0.80	$ N A
2012	$ 13.13	$ 0.05	2000	$ 0.80	$ NA
2011	$ 10.78	$ 0.05	1999	$ NA	$ NA

NOTES: KMP is a Canada-based real estate investment trust that specializes in the acquisition, management and development of multi-residential apartment buildings, manufactured home communities and commercial properties in Canada.

KP TISSUE INC

(KPT)

Updated June 2023

IDM STOCK SCORING CALCULATION

(1) Stock Price $ 10.48   *Score* 5

(2) Price 4 Years Ago $ 8.11   *Score* 4

(3) Current to Four Year Price   *Score* 9

(4) Book Value $ 7.44   *Score* 4

(5) Price to Book Comparison   *Score* 1

(6) Analyst Buys # 0   *Score* 0

(7) Analysts Strong Buys # 0 Score 0

(8) Dividend Yield % 6.87   *Score 8*

(9) Operating Margin % 0   *Score 0*

(10) Trading Volume 1,160   *Score 0*

(11) Price to Earnings -4.8x   *Score 10*

Total of All 11 Scores = 41

This stock's total score in 2021 was **26**, in 2020 it was **35**, in 2019 it was **35**.

HISTORICAL STOCK PRICES & DIVIDEND PAYOUTS

Year	Stock	Dividend	Year	Stock	Dividend
2022	$ 10.42	$ 0.18	2010	$ NA	$ NA
2021	$ 10.44	$ 0.18	2009	$ NA	$ NA
2020	$ 11.68	$ 0.18	2008	$ NA	$ NA
2019	$ 8.16	$ 0.18	2007	$ NA	$ NA
2018	$ 10.35	$ 0 .18	2006	$ NA	$ NA
2017	$ 14.04	$ 0.18	2005	$ NA	$ NA
2016	$ 11.69	$ 0.18	2004	$ NA	$ NA
2015	$ 14.04	$ 0.18	2003	$ NA	$ NA
2014	$ 15.81	$ 0.18	2002	$ NA	$ NA
2013	$ 17.02	$ 0.18	2001	$ NA	$ NA
2012	$ 17.48	$ NA	2000	$ NA	$ NA
2011	$ NA	$ NA	1999	$ NA	$ NA

NOTES: KPT is a Canada-based company, is limited to holding, a limited partnership interest in Kruger Products L.P producing bathroom and facial tissue, paper towels and napkins.

LABRADOR IRON ORE ROYALY CORPORATION

(LIF)

Updated June 2023

IDM STOCK SCORING CALCULATION

(1) Stock Price $ 30.88   Score8
(2) Price 4 Years Ago $ 32.23   Score 8
(3) Current to Four Year Price Score 5
(4) Book Value $ 9.96   Score 4
(5) Price to Book Comparison   Score 0
(6) Analyst Buys # 1   Score 2

(7) Analysts Strong Buys #0 Score 0
(8) Dividend Yield % 8.44   Score 10
(9) Operating Margin % 75.90 Score 9
(10) Trading Volume 214,409 Score 4
(11) Price to Earnings 8.0x   Score 9

Total of All 11 Scores = 59

This stock's total score in 2021 was **62**, in 2020 it was **58** , in 2019 it was **NA**.

HISTORICAL STOCK PRICES & DIVIDEND PAYOUTS

Year	Stock	Dividend	Year	Stock	Dividend
2022	$ 28.30	$ 0.90	2010	$ 16.04	$ 0.19
2021	$ 49.61	$ 1.75	2009	$ 14.24	$ 0.19
2020	$ 24.08	$ 0.25	2008	$ 19.86	$ 0.19
2019	$ 32.23	$ 0.23	2007	$ 12.38	$ 0.13
2018	$ 21.25	$ 0.21	2006	$ 9.69	$ 0.13
2017	$ 12.77	$ 0.20	2005	$ 8.50	$ 0.13
2016	$ 11.73	$ 0.20	2004	$ 6.57	$ 0.09
2015	$ 11.18	$ 0.20	2003	$ 5.96	$ 0.09
2014	$ 23.67	$ 0.19	2002	$5.54	$ 0.09
2013	$ 22.14	$ 0.19	2001	$ 5.62	$ 0.14
2012	$ 23.97	$ 0.19	2000	$ 4.21	$ 0.09
2011	$ 27.16	$ 0.19	1999	$ 4.04	$ 0.09

NOTES: : **LIF** is a Canada-based company, which owns interests in Iron Ore Company of Canada (IOC) that operates an iron mine near Labrador City, Newfoundland.

LARENTIAN BANK OF CANADA

(LB)

Updated Ju 2023

IDM STOCK SCORING CALCULATION

(1) Stock Price $ 42.88   Score 8   *(7)* Analysts Strong Buys #0 Score 0
(2) Price 4 Years Ago $ 44.9   Score 8   *(8)* Dividend Yield % 4.38   Score 6
(3) Current to Four Year Price   Score 5   *(9)* Operating Margin % 24.22 Score 5
(4) Book Value $ 64.18   Score 9   *(10)* Trading Volume 52,569 Score 3
(5) Price to Book Comparison   Score 8   *(11)* Price to Earnings 9.3x   Score 9
(6) Analyst Buys # 4   Score 4

Total of All 11 Scores = 65

This stock's total score in 2021 was **59**, in 2020 it was **61** , in 2019 it was **63**.

HISTORICAL STOCK PRICES & DIVIDEND PAYOUTS

Year	Stock	Dividend	Year	Stock	Dividend
2022	$ 39.43	$ 0.45	2010	$ 44.87	$ 0.36
2021	$ 42.11	$ 0.40	2009	$ 33.76	$ 0.34
2020	$ 28.98	$ 0.40	2008	$ 40.60	$ 0.32
2019	$ 44.75	$ 0.66	2007	$ 38.90	$ 0.29
2018	$ 53.03	$ 0.62	2006	$ 29.08	$ 0.29
2017	$ 54.03	$ 0.62	2005	$ 27.25	$ 0.29
2016	$ 48.96	$ 0.60	2004	$ 28.20	$ 0.29
2015	$ 47.29	$ 0.56	2003	$ 25.91	$ 0.29
2014	$ 50.36	$ 0.52	2002	$29.75	$ 0.29
2013	$ 45.05	$ 0.50	2001	$ 22.75	$ 0.27
2012	$ 46.28	$ 0.47	2000	$ 21.75	$ 0.23
2011	$ 45.34	$ 0.42	1999	$ 24.25	$ 0.23

NOTES: LB provides financial banking services to its personal, commercial, institutional customers and Capital Markets across Canada and the United States. `

LIFE & BANC SPLIT CORPORATION

(LBS)

Updated June 2023

IDM STOCK SCORING CALCULATION

(1) Stock Price $ 8.58   Score 4
(2) Price 4 Yeas Ago $ 7.68   Score 4
(3) Current to Four Year Price Score 9
(4) Book Value $ 7.03   Score 4
(5) Price to Book Comparison   Score 1
(6) Analyst Buys # 0   Score 0

(7) Analysts Strong Buys # 0 Score 0
(8) Dividend Yield % 13.99   Score 2
(9) Operating Margin % 0   Score 0
(10) Trading Volume 51,486   Score 3
(11) Price to Earnings -4.0x   Score 0

Total of All 11 Scores = 27

This stock's total score in 2021 was **26**, in 2020 it was **NA**, in 2019 it was **NA**.

HISTORICAL STOCK PRICES & DIVIDEND PAYOUTS

Year	Stock	Dividend	Year	Stock	Dividend
2022	$ 9.10	$ 0.10	2010	$ 8.64	$ 0.10
2021	$ 9.38	$ 0.10	2009	$ 8.46	$ 0.10
2020	$ 4.02	$ NA	2008	$ 10.69	$ 0.10
2019	$ 7.68	$ 0.10	2007	$ 3.84	$ 0.10
2018	$ 9.55	$ 0.10	2006	$ 15.00	$ 0.05
2017	$ 9.86	$ 0.10	2005	$ NA	$ NA
2016	$ 7.85	$ 0.10	2004	$ NA	$ NA
2015	$ 9.25	$ 0.10	2003	$ NA	$ NA
2014	$ 10.51	$ 0.10	2002	$ NA	$ NA
2013	$ 7.36	$ 0.10	2001	$ NA	$ NA
2012	$ 6.77	$ 0.10	2000	$ NA	$ NA
2011	$ 7.65	$ 0.10	1999	$ NA	$ NA

NOTES: : **LBS** is a mutual fund company.

LUNDIN MINING CORP

(LUN)

Updated June 2023

IDM STOCK SCORING CALCULATION

(1) *Stock Price $ 10.32*   *Score* 5
(2) *Price 4 Years Ago $ 7.21*   *Score* 4
(3) *Current to Four Year Price Score* 9
(4) *Book Value $8.31*   *Score* 4
(5) *Price to Book Comparison Score* 1
(6) *Analyst Buys # 5*   *Score* 4

(7) *Analysts Strong Buys # 0*   *Score* 0
(8) *Dividend Yield % 3.49*   *Score* 6
(9) *Operating Margin % 15.05 Score* 4
10)Trading Volume 2,285,167 Score 10
(11) Price to Earnings 26.5   *Score* 6

Total of All 11 Scores = 53

This stock's total score in 2021 was **NA** , in 2020 it was **NA** , in 2019 it was **NA**

HISTORICAL STOCK PRICES & DIVIDEND PAYOUTS

Year	Stock	Dividend	Year	Stock	Dividend
2022	$ 11.26	$ 0.09	2010	$ 301	$ NA
2021	$ 11.37	$ 0.06	2009	$ 3.35	$ NA
2020	$ 6.34	$ 0.04	2008	$ 6.22	$ NA
2019	$ 6.04	$ 0.03	2007	$ 12.86	$ NA
2018	$ 7.20	$ 0.03	2006	$ 10.95	$ NA
2017	$ 7.44	$ 0.03	2005	$ 3.43	$ NA
2016	$ 4.36	$ NA	2004	$ 2.58	$ NA
2015	$ 5.13	$ NA	2003	$ 0.68	$ NA
2014	$ 5.69	$ NA	2002	$ 0.66	$ NA
2013	$ 4.00	$ NA	2001	$ 0.48	$ NA
2012	$ 4.22	$ NA	2000	$ 0.76	$ NA
2011	$ 7.44	$ NA	1999	$ 1.00	$ NA

NOTES: **LUN** is a Canada-based metals mining company. Engaged in mining, exploration and development of mineral properties, primarily in Chile, Brazil, Portugal, Sweden and the United States of America, primarily producing copper, zinc, gold and nickel.

MACKENZIE MASTER LP

(MKZ.UN)

Updated June 2023

IDM STOCK SCORING CALCULATION

(1) Stock Price $ 0.45   Score *1*   *(7)* Analysts Strong Buys # 0   Score *0*
(2) Price 4 Years Ago $ 1.0   Score *2*   *(8)* Dividend Yield % 18.60   Score *2*
(3) Current to Four Year Price Score *1*   *(9)* Operating Margin % 85.87% Score *10*
(4) Book Value $ 0   Score *1*   *(10)* Trading Volume 0   Score *0*
(5) Price to Book Comparison Score *0*   *(11)* Price to Earnings 5.3x   Score *10*
(6) Analyst Buys # 0   Score *0*

Total of All 11 Scores = 27

This stock's total score in 2021 was **26** , in 2020 it was **26** , in 2019 it was **31**.

HISTORICAL STOCK PRICES & DIVIDEND PAYOUTS

Year	Stock	Dividend	Year	Stock	Dividend
2022	$ 0.73	$0.10	2010	$ 1.07	$ 0.40
2021	$ 0.86	$ 0.10	2009	$ 1.01	$ 0.43
2020	$ 0.79	$ 0.10	2008	$ 1.30	$ 0.59
2019	$ 1.04	$ 0.12	2007	$ 2.50	$ 0.81
2018	$ 1.03	$ 0.13	2006	$ 2.65	$ 0.91
2017	$ 0.99	$ 0.14	2005	$ 2.50	$ 1.07
2016	$1.00	$ 0.15	2004	$ 4.70	$ 1.26
2015	$ 1.04	$ 0.18	2003	$ 4.57	$ 1.36
2014	$ 0.80	$ 0.20	2002	$ 5.25	$ 1.79
2013	$ 0.81	$ 0.22	2001	$ 7.10	$ 2.40
2012	$ 0.75	$ 0.21	2000	$ 10.00	$ 3.48
2011	$ 1.12	$ 0.24	1999	$ 12.95	$ 4.16

NOTES: **MKZ.UN** is a Canada-based company, which was formed by the consolidation of approximately eight Mackenzie Financial Corporation (Mackenzie) retail limited partnerships.

MANULIFE FINANCIAL CORPORATION

(MFC)

Updated June 2023

IDM STOCK SCORING CALCULATION

(1) Stock Price $ 24.16   Score 7
(2) Price 4 Years Ago $ 21.11 Score 7
(3) Current to Four Year Price Score 9
(4) Book Value $ 25.09   Score 7
(5) Price to Book Comparison Score 6
(6) Analyst Buys #1   Score 2

(7) Analysts Strong Buys #1 Score 3
(8) Dividend Yield % 6.04   Score 8
(9) Operating Margin % 28.44 Score 5
(10) Trading Volume 1,267,564 Score 9
(11) Price to Earnings 8.4x   Score 9

Total of All 11 Scores = 72

This stock's total score in 2021 was **67**, in 2020 it was **69**, in 2019 it was **67**.

HISTORICAL STOCK PRICES & DIVIDEND PAYOUTS

Year	Stock	Dividend	Year	Stock	Dividend
2022	$ 23.43	$ 0.33	2010	$ 15.45	$ 0.13
2021	$ 22.84	$ 0.28	2009	$ 20.30	$0.26
2020	$ 17.95	$ 0.28	2008	$ 38.16	$ 0.24
2019	$ 23.80	$ 0.25	2007	$ 39.84	$ 0.22
2018	$ 23.09	$ 0.22	2006	$ 36.50	$ 0.17
2017	$ 23.33	$ 0.20	2005	$28.83	$ 0.15
2016	$ 17.89	$ 0.18	2004	$ 27.02	$ 0.10
2015	$ 21.38	$ 0.17	2003	$ 20.00	$ 0.13
2014	$ 21.32	$ 0.13	2002	$ 19.09	$ 0.07
2013	$ 16.83	$ 0.13	2001	$ 21.17	$ 0.06
2012	$ 12.34	$ 0.13	2000	$ 19.9	$ 0.07
2011	$13.39	$ 0.13	1999	$ NA	$ NA

NOTES: **MFC** is a holding company of The Manufacturers Life Insurance Company (MLI), a Canadian life insurance company. The Company operates as a financial services company with principal operations in Asia, Canada, and the United States.

MCCAN MORTGAGE CORPORATION

(MKP)

Updated June 2023

IDM STOCK SCORING CALCULATION

(1) Stock Price $ 15.95   Score 6   *(7)* Analysts Strong Buys #1 Score 3
(2) Price 4 Years Ago $ 15.15   Score 6   *(8)* Dividend Yield % 9.03   Score 10
(3) Current to Four Year Price Score 7   *(9)* Operating Margin % 33.37 Score 6
(4) Book Value $ 14.26   Score 5   *(10)* Trading Volume 12,961   Score 1
(5) Price to Book Comparison Score 1   *(11)* Price to Earnings 8.3x   Score 9
(6) Analyst Buys # 0   Score 0

Total of All 11 Scores = 54

This stock's total score in 2021 was **54**, in 2020 it was **42**, in 2019 it was **52**.

HISTORICAL STOCK PRICES & DIVIDEND PAYOUTS

Year	Stock	Dividend	Year	Stock	Dividend
2022	$ 17.72	$ 0.36	2010	$ 12.27	$ 0.25
2021	$ 16.37	$ 0.32	2009	$ 11.84	$ 0.24
2020	$ 14.81	$ 0.32	2008	$ 8.32	$ 0.22
2019	$ 15.01	$ 0.30	2007	$ 9.32	$ 0.22
2018	$ 17.41	$ 0.35	2006	$ 9.54	$ 0.20
2017	$ 16.96	$ 0.30	2005	$ 9.15	$ 0.18
2016	$ 13.90	$ 0.28	2004	$ 8.08	$ 0.16
2015	$ 11.54	$ 0.27	2003	$ 7.53	$ 0.16
2014	$ 14.11	$ 0.27	2002	$ 8.22	$ 0.16
2013	$ 13.23	$ 0.27	2001	$ 7.94	$ 0.16
2012	$ 13.41	$ 0.26	2000	$ 7.13	$ 0.16
2011	$ 13.83	$ 0.26	1999	$ 7.79	$ 0.16

NOTES: **MKP.** is a Canada-based loan company generating a reliable stream of income by investing in a diversified portfolio of mortgages, including residential, residential construction, non-residential construction and commercial loans, securities, loans and real estate investments

MCCHIP RESOURCES INC

(MCS)

Updated June 2023

IDM STOCK SCORING CALCULATION

(1) Stock Price $ 0.89   Score 1

(2) Price 4 Years Ago $ 0.65   Score 1

(3) Current to Four Year Price Score 9

(4) Book Value $ 1.41   Score 2

(5) Price to Book Comparison Score 8

(6) Analyst Buys # 0   Score 0

(7) Analysts Strong Buys # 0 Score 0

(8) Dividend Yield % 6.74   Score 8

(9) Operating Margin % 0   Score 0

(10) Trading Volume 3   Score 0

(11) Price to Earnings -13.2x Score 9

Total of All 11 Scores = 38

This stock's total score in 2021 was **50**, in 2020 it was **26,** in 2019 it was **23**.

HISTORICAL STOCK PRICES & DIVIDEND PAYOUTS

Year	Stock	Dividend	Year	Stock	Dividend
2022	$ 0.76	$ 0.04	2010	$ 0.97	$ NA
2021	$ 0.83	$ 0.04	2009	$ 1.00	$ NA
2020	$ 0.40	$ 0.02	2008	$ 1.00	$ 0.05
2019	$ 0.65	$ 0.03	2007	$ 3.42	$ 0.05
2018	$ 0.52	$ 0.10	2006	$ 3.15	$ NA
2017	$ 0.60	$ NA	2005	$ 2.30	$ NA
2016	$ 0.55	$ NA	2004	$ 1.00	$ 0.07
2015	$ 1.00	$ NA	2003	$ 0.85	$ NA
2014	$ 1.52	$ 0.05	2002	$0.41	$NA
2013	$ 1.80	$ NA	2001	$ 0.35	$ NA
2012	$ 1.82	$ NA	2000	$ 0.15	$ NA
2011	$ 2.25	$ 0.10	1999	$ NA	$ NA

NOTES: MCS is engaged in the natural resource industry. The Company invests in petroleum interests in Western Canada, as well as direct and indirect interests in minerals.

MEDICAL FACILITIES CORPORATION

(DR)

Updated 2023

IDM STOCK SCORING CALCULATION

(1) Stock Price $ 8.05   *Score 4*

(2) Price 4 Years Ago $ 4.71   *Score 3*

(3) Current to Four Year Price Score 9

(4) Book Value $ 4.02   *Score 3*

(5) Price to Book Comparison Score 0

(6) Analyst Buys # 0   *Score 0*

(7) Analysts Strong Buys # 0 Score 0

(8) Dividend Yield % 4.00   *Score 6*

(9) Operating Margin % 7.80   *Score 2*

(10) Trading Volume 51,060   *Score 3*

(11) Price to Earnings 22.6x   *Score 7*

Total of All 11 Scores = 37

This stock's total score in 2021 was **33**, in 2020 it was **NA**, in 2019 it was **NA**.

HISTORICAL STOCK PRICES & DIVIDEND PAYOUTS

Year	Stock	Dividend	Year	Stock	Dividend
2022	$ 9.85	$ 0.08	2010	$ 9.28	$ 0.09
2021	$ 7.01	$ 0.07	2009	$ 7.84	$ 0.09
2020	$ 4.37	$ 0.07	2008	$ 9.76	$ 0.09
2019	$ 12.9	$ 0.09	2007	$ 12.19	$ 0.09
2018	$ 14.35	$ 0.09	2006	$ 9.30	$ 0.09
2017	$ 14.03	$ 0.09	2005	$ 12.89	$ 0.09
2016	$ 21.92	$ 0.09	2004	$ 11.89	$ 0.09
2015	$ 17.05	$ 0.09	2003	$ NA	$ NA
2014	$ 18.10	$ 0.09	2002	$ NA	$ NA
2013	$ 15.71	$ 0.09	2001	$ NA	$ NA
2012	$ 14.20	$ 0.09	2000	$ NA	$ N A
2011	$ 10.41	$ 0.09	1999	$ NA	$ NA

NOTES: :DR is a Canada-based company, which owns interests in over six entities (the Centers), approximately five of which either own a specialty surgical hospital (SSH) or an ambulatory surgery center (ASC).

MELCOR DEVELOPMENTS LTD

(MRD)

Updated June 2023

IDM STOCK SCORING CALCULATION

(1) Stock Price $ 11.13   Score 5

(2) Price 4 Years Ago $ 12.75   Score 5

(3) Current to Four Year Price   Score 2

(4) Book Value $ 37.71   Score 8

(5) Price to Book Comparison Score 10

(6) Analyst Buys # 0   Score 0

(7) Analysts Strong Buys # 0 Score 0

(8) Dividend Yield % 5.75   Score 8

(9) Operating Margin % 57.20 Score 8

(10) Trading Volume 6,019   Score 0

(11) Price to Earnings 4.0x   Score 10

Total of All 11 Scores = 56

This stock's total score in 2021 was **NA**, in 2020 it was **NA**, in 2019 it was **NA**.

HISTORICAL STOCK PRICES & DIVIDEND PAYOUTS

Year	Stock	Dividend	Year	Stock	Dividend
2022	$ 15.43	$ 0.14	2010	$ 13.10	$ 0.15
2021	$ 13.40	$ 0.10	2009	$ 8.25	$ 0.10
2020	$ 7.53	$ 0.08	2008	$ 12.82	$ 0.25
2019	$ 13.30	$ 0.13	2007	$ 27.40	$ 0.20
2018	$ 15.04	$ 0.13	2006	$ 18.50	$ 0.15
2017	$ 15.39	$ 0.13	2005	$ 7.10	$ 0.07
2016	$ 14.49	$ 0.12	2004	$ 4.95	$ 0.06
2015	$ 17.30	$ 0.15	2003	$ 3.87	$ 0.06
2014	$ 26.50	$ 0.28	2002	$ 3.70	$ 0.05
2013	$ 18.80	$ 0.25	2001	$ 2.50	$ 0.04
2012	$ 14.95	$ 0.22	2000	$ 1.92	$ 0.04
2011	$ 15.50	$ 0.20	1999	$ 1.85	$ 0.03

NOTES: MRD is a Canada-based real estate development and asset management company. It, manages, and owns residential communities, business and industrial parks, office buildings, retail commercial centers, and golf courses.

MELCOR REAL ESTATE INVESTMENT TRUST

(MR.UN)
Updated June 2023

IDM STOCK SCORING CALCULATION

(1) Stock Price $ 4.70   *Score 3*   *(7) Analysts Strong Buys # 0*   *Score 0*
(2) Price 4 Years Ago $ 7.70   *Score 4*   *(8) Dividend Yield % 10.21*   *Score 10*
(3) Current to Four Year Price Score 2   *(9) Operating Margin % 53.12*   *Score 8*
(4) Book Value $ 14.59   *Score 5*   *(10) Trading Volume 1,400*   *Score 0*
(5) Price to Book Comparison Score 10   *(11) Price to Earnings 8.4x*   *Score 9*
(6) Analyst Buys # 0   *Score 0*

Total of All 11 Scores = 51

This stock's total score in 2021 was 41, in 2020 it was 44, in 2019 it was 47.

HISTORICAL STOCK PRICES & DIVIDEND PAYOUTS

Year	Stock	Dividend	Year	Stock	Dividend
2022	$ 6.27	$ 0.04	2010	$ NA	$ NA
2021	$ 6.90	$ 0.04	2009	$ NA	$ NA
2020	$ 3.65	$ 0.03	2008	$ NA	$ NA
2019	$ 7.65	$ 0.06	2007	$ N A	$ NA
2018	$ 8.23	$ 0.06	2006	$ NA	$ NA
2017	$ 8.75	$ 0.06	2005	$ NA	$ NA
2016	$ 8.52	$ 0.06	2004	$ NA	$ NA
2015	$ 8.22	$ 0.06	2003	$ NA	$ NA
2014	$ 10.26	$ 0.06	2002	$ NA	$ NA
2013	$ 10.15	$ 0.06	2001	$ NA	$ NA
2012	$ NA	$ NA	2000	$ NA	$ NA
2011	$ NA	$ NA	1999	$ NA	$ NA

NOTES: : **MR.UN** is a Canada-based open-ended real estate investment trust

219

MINT INCOME FUND

(MID.UN)

Updated June 2023

IDM STOCK SCORING CALCULATION

(1) Stock Price $ 6.48   Score 4
(2) Price 4 Years Ago $ 6.22   Score 4
(3) Current to Four Year Price Score 7
(4) Book Value $ 6.92   Score 4
(5) Price to Book Comparison Score 6
(6) Analyst Buys # 0   Score 0

(7) Analysts Strong Buys # 0   Score 0
(8) Dividend Yield % 7.41   Score 8
(9) Operating Margin % 82.75 Score 10
(10) Trading Volume 400   Score 0
(11) Price to Earnings 11.1x   Score 9

Total of All 11 Scores =52

This stock's total score in 2021 was **26** , in 2020 it was **52**, in 2019 it was **28**.

HISTORICAL STOCK PRICES & DIVIDEND PAYOUTS

Year	Stock	Dividend	Year	Stock	Dividend
2022	$ 6.87	$ 0.04	2010	$9.33	$ 0.07
2021	$ 6.27	$ 0.04	2009	$ 7.45	$ 0.07
2020	$5.10	$ 0.04	2008	$ 12.38	$ 0.10
2019	$ 6.13	$ 0.04	2007	$ 12.00	$ 0.10
2018	$ 7.05	$ 0.04	2006	$ 12.89	$ 0.10
2017	$ 6.45	$ 0.04	2005	$ 13.10	$ 0.10
2016	$ 7.03	$ 0.04	2004	$ 9.77	$ 0.20
2015	$ 8.02	$ 0.06	2003	$ 7.80	$ 0.18
2014	$ 10.81	$ 0.06	2002	$ 7.35	$ 0.18
2013	$ 9.64	$ 0.06	2001	$ 6.60	$ 0.17
2012	$ 9.63	$ 0.06	2000	$ 5.60	$ 0.17
2011	$ 10.12	$ 0.06	1999	$ 6.40	$ 0.20

NOTES: MID.UN is a Canada-based closed-end investment trust producing a high level of sustainable income and to minimizing the risk of investing in high income securities on a cost-effective basis.

MORGUARD REAL ESTATE INVESTMENT TRUST

(MRT.UN)
Updated June 2023

IDM STOCK SCORING CALCULATION

(1) Stock Price $ 5.40   Score *4*
(2) Price 4 Years Ago $ 12.26   Score *1*
(3) Current to Four Year Price   Score *0*
(4) Book Value $ 16.36   Score *6*
(5) Price to Book Comparison Score *10*
(6) Analyst Buys # 0   Score *0*

(7) Analysts Strong Buys #0   Score *0*
(8) Dividend Yield % 4.44   Score *6*
(9) Operating Margin % 27.31 Score *5*
(10) Trading Volume 19,000   Score *1*
(11) Price to Earnings -2.5x   Score *10*

Total of All 11 Scores = 43

This stock's total score in 2021 was **60**, in 2020 it was **67**, in 2019 it was **64**.

HISTORICAL STOCK PRICES & DIVIDEND PAYOUTS

Year	Stock	Dividend	Year	Stock	Dividend
2022	$ 5.06	$ 0.02	2010	$ 13.75	$ 0.07
2021	$ 6.40	$ 0.02	2009	$ 11.95	$ 0.07
2020	$ 4.26	$ 0.04	2008	$ 8.49	$ 0.07
2019	$ 11.74	$ 0.08	2007	$ 13.46	$ 0.07
2018	$ 12.47	$ 0.08	2006	$ 11.50	$ 0.07
2017	$ 14.76	$ 0.08	2005	$ 10.95	$ 0.07
2016	$ 15.51	$ 0.08	2004	$ 9.32	$ 0.07
2015	$ 13.67	$ 0.08$	2003	$ 8.75	$ 0.07
2014	$ 19.25	$ 0.08	2002	$ 8.90	$ 0.07
2013	$ 16.43	$ 0.08	2001	$ 8.55	$ 0.23
2012	$ 17.08	$ 0.08	2000	$ 8.35	$ 0.23
2011	$ 14.91	$ 0.07	1999	$ 8.20	$ 0.23

NOTES: MRT.UN is a Canada-based closed-end trust. The Trust's objective is to accumulate a Canadian portfolio of real estate assets and then manage the portfolio to generate steady, dependable returns to unitholders.

MULLEN GROUP LIMITED

(MTL)

Updated June 2023

IDM STOCK SCORING CALCULATION

(1) Stock Price $ 15.29   Score *6*
(2) Price 4 Years Ago $ 10.09   Score *5*
(3) Current to Four Year Price Score *9*
(4) Book Value $ 10.47   Score *5*
(5) Price to Book Comparison Score *1*
(6) Analyst Buys # 2   Score *3*

(7) Analysts Strong Buys # *0* Score *0*
(8) Dividend Yield % 4.71   Score *8*
(9) Operating Margin % 11.29 Score *3*
(10) Trading Volume 192,639   Score *4*
(11) Price to Earnings 8.6x   Score *9*

Total of All 11 Scores = 53

This stock's total score in 2021 was **41**, in 2020 it was **NA** , in 2019 it was **NA**.

HISTORICAL STOCK PRICES & DIVIDEND PAYOUTS

Year	Stock	Dividend	Year	Stock	Dividend
2022	$14.60	$ 0.06	2010	$ 14.37	$ 0.13
2021	$ 12.88	$ 0.04	2009	$ 15.77	$ 0.13
2020	$ 9.79	$ 0.03	2008	$ 19.50	$ 0.15
2019	$ 8.73	$ 0.05	2007	$ 18.71	$ 0.15
2018	$ 16.04	$ 0.05	2006	$ 25.20	$ 0.15
2017	$ 17.05	$ 0.03	2005	$ 23.25	$ 0.14
2016	$ 15.70	$ 0.03	2004	$ 14.00	$ 0.08
2015	$ 19.11	$ 0.10	2003	$ 9.87	$ 0.07
2014	$ 27.32	$ 0.10	2002	$ 10.66	$ 0.07
2013	$ 25.25	$ 0.10	2001	$ 10.50	$ 0 .07
2012	$ 21.81	$ 0.25	2000	$ 8.16	$ 0.07
2011	$ 22.25	$ 0.25	1999	$ 6.81	$ NA

NOTES: MTL is a Canada-based company that supplies trucking and logistics services to the oil and natural gas industry in western Canada. It

NATIONAL BANK OF CANADA

(NA)

Updated June 2023

IDM STOCK SCORING CALCULATION

(1) Stock Price $ 98.71   Score 9
(2) Price 4 Years Ago $ 63.88 Score 9
(3) Current to Four Year Price Score 9
(4) Book Value $ 64.60   Score 9
(5) Price to Book Comparison   Score 0
(6) Analyst Buys # 4   Score 4

(7) Analysts Strong Buys # 0 Score 0
(8) Dividend Yield % 4.13   Score 6
(9) Operating Margin % 41.35 Score 6
(10) Trading Volume 302,429 Score 5
(11) Price to Earnings 10.6x Score 9

Total of All 11 Scores = 66

This stock's total score in 2021 was **NA**, in 2020 it was **NA**, in 2019 it was .**NA**

HISTORICAL STOCK PRICES & DIVIDEND PAYOUTS

Year	Stock	Dividend	Year	Stock	Dividend
2022	$ 84.47	$ 0.92	2010	$ 29.49	$ 0.31
2021	$ 95.49	$ 0.71	2009	$ 26.87	$ 0.31
2020	$ 61.52	$ 0.71	2008	$ 25.00	$ 0.31
2019	$ 63.88	$ 0.68	2007	$ 26.99	$ 0.30
2018	$ 63.12	$ 0.62	2006	$ 28.50	$ 0.25
2017	$ 56.15	$ 0.58	2005	$ 28.69	$ 0.22
2016	$ 44.71	$ 0.55	2004	$ 21.60	$ 0.19
2015	$ 46.92	$ 0.52	2003	$ 20.45	$ 0.14
2014	$ 45.26	$ 0.48	2002	$ 14.72	$ 0.12
2013	$ 39.50	$ 39.50	2001	$ 12.12	$ 0.10
2012	$ 37.34	$ 0.40	2000	$ 11.67	$ 0.10
2011	$ 39.11	$ 0.35	1999	$ 9.05	$ 0.09

NOTES: : **NA** offers financial services to individuals, businesses, institutional clients and government.

NEO PERFORMANCE MATERIALS INC

(NEO)

Updated June 2023

IDM STOCK SCORING CALCULATION

(1) Stock Price $ 8.20   *Score* 4
(2) Price 4 Years Ago $ 12.51 *Score* 5
(3) Current to Four Year Price *Score* 2
(4) Book Value $ 13.91   *Score* 5
(5) Price to Book Comparison *Score* 8
(6) Analyst Buys # 1   *Score* 2

(7) Analysts Strong Buys # 1 Score 3
(8) Dividend Yield % 4.88   Score 8
(9) Operating Margin % 4.25 Score 1
(10) Trading Volume 76,574 Score 3
(11) Price to Earnings -50.9x Score 0

Total of All 11 Scores = 41

This stock's total score in 2021 was **NA** , in 2020 it was **NA**, in 2019 it was **NA**.

HISTORICAL STOCK PRICES & DIVIDEND PAYOUTS

Year	Stock	Dividend	Year	Stock	Dividend
2022	$ 14.55	$ 0.10	2010	$ NA	$ NA
2021	$ 16.49	$ 0.10	2009	$ NA	$ NA
2020	$ 10.65	$ 0.10	2008	$ NA	$ NA
2019	$ 12.51	$ 0.10	2007	$ NA	$ NA
2018	$ 16.28	$ 0.10	2006	$ NA	$ NA
2017	$ 17.90	$ NA	2005	$ NA	$ NA
2016	$` NA	$ NA	2004	$ NA	$ NA
2015	$ NA	$ NA	2003	$ NA	$ NA
2014	$ NA	$ NA	2002	$ NA	$ NA
2013	$ NA	$ NA	2001	$ NA	$ NA
2012	$ NA	$ NA	2000	$ NA	$ NA
2011	$ NA	$ NA	1999	$ NA	$ NA

NOTES: **NEO** is a Canada-based company that manufactures magnetic powders and magnets, specialty chemicals, metals, and alloys.

NERGENRX INC
(NXG)
Updated July 2023

IDM STOCK SCORING CALCULATION

(1) Stock Price $ 0.30   Score *1*   *(7)* Analysts Strong Buys # *0*   Score *0*
(2) Price 4 Years Ago $ 0.24   Score *1*   *(8)* Dividend Yield % 6.67   Score *8*
(3) Current to Four Year Price Score *9*   *(9)* Operating Margin %-0.37   Score *0*
(4) Book Value $ 0.13   Score *1*   *(10)* Trading Volume 0   Score *0*
(5) Price to Book Comparison Score *0*   *(11)* Price to Earnings -101.4x   Score *0*
(6) Analyst Buys # *0*   Score *0*

Total of All 11 Scores = 20

This stock's total score in 2021 was **NA**, in 2020 it was **NA**, in 2019 it was **NA**.

HISTORICAL STOCK PRICES & DIVIDEND PAYOUTS

Year	Stock	Dividend	Year	Stock	Dividend
2022	$ 0.28	$ 0.01	2010	$ 0.26	$ NA
2021	$ 0.34	$ NA	2009	$ 0.17	$ NA
2020	$ 0.17	$ NA	2008	$ 0.25	$ NA
2019	$ 0.24	$ NA	2007	$ 0.22	$ NA
2018	$ 0.23	$ NA	2006	$ 0.35	$ NA
2017	$ 0.24 .	$ NA	2005	$ NA	$ NA
2016	$ 0.16	$ NA	2004	$ NA	$ NA
2015	$ 0.15	$ NA	2003	$ NA	$ NA
2014	$ 0.20	$ NA	2002	$ NA	$ NA
2013	$ 0.17	$ NA	2001	$ NA	$ NA
2012	$ 0.22	$ NA	2000	$ NA	$ NA
2011	$ 0.25	$ NA	1999	$ NA	$ NA

NOTES: **NXG** is a Canada-based third-party administrator focused on building technology platforms. It equips managing and self-managing group benefit plans, group pension plans and patient support programs with a range of software-as-a-service solutions.

NEWPORT EXPLORATION LIMITED

(NWX)

Updated June 2023

IDM STOCK SCORING CALCULATION

(1) Stock Price $ 0.25   Score *1*   *(7)* Analysts Strong Buys #0   Score *0*

(2) Price 4 Years Ago $ 0.26   Score *1*   *(8)* Dividend Yield % 15.69   Score *2*

(3) Current to Four Year Price Score *5*   *(9)* Operating Margin % 0   Score *0*

(4) Book Value $ 0.05   Score *1*   *(10)* Trading Volume 16652   Score *1*

(5) Price to Book Comparison *Score 0*   *(11)* Price to Earnings 7.6x   Score *9*

(6) Analyst Buys # 0   Score *0*

Total of All 11 Scores = 20

This stock's total score in 2021 was **29**, in 2020 it was **27**, in 2019 it was **NA**.

HISTORICAL STOCK PRICES & DIVIDEND PAYOUTS

Year	Stock	Dividend	Year	Stock	Dividend
2022	$ 0.44	$ 0.02	2010	$ 0.04	$ NA
2021	$ 0.39	$ 0.02	2009	$ 0.04	$ NA
2020	$ 0.30	$ 0.01	2008	$ 0.06	$ NA
2019	$ 0.26	$ NA	2007	$ 0.17	$ NA
2018	$ 0.23	$ NA	2006	$ 0.05	$ NA
2017	$ 0.14	$ NA	2005	$ 0.08	$ NA
2016	$ 0.17	$ NA	2004	$ 0.05	$ NA
2015	$ 0.16	$ NA	2003	$ 0.10	$ NA
2014	$ 0.18	$ NA	2002	$ 0.14	$ NA
2013	$ 0.01	$ NA	2001	$ 0.18	$ NA
2012	$ 0.01	$ NA	2000	$ 1.51	$ NA
2011	$ 0.05	$ NA	1999	$ 0.56NXR	$ NA

NOTES: NWX is a Canada-based company engaged in the acquisition and exploration of natural resource properties.

NEXUS INDUSTRIAL REAL ESTAT INVESTMENT TRUST
NXR.UN
Updated July 2023

IDM STOCK SCORING CALCULATION

(1) Stock Price $ 8.42   Score 4   *(7) Analysts Strong Buys # 1*   Score 3
(2) Price 4 Years Ago $ 7.96   Score 4   *(8) Dividend Yield % 7.60*   Score 10
(3) Current to Four Year Price Score 7   *(9) Operating Margin % 105.25* Score 10
(4) Book Value $ 9.96   Score 4   *(10) Trading Volume 28,872*   Score 1
(5) Price to Book Comparison Score 8   *(11) Price to Earnings 6.2x*   Score 9
(6) Analyst Buys # 3   Score 3

Total of All 11 Scores = 63

This stock's total score in 2021 was **49**, in 2020 it was **57**, in 2019 it was **64**.

HISTORICAL STOCK PRICES & DIVIDEND PAYOUTS

Year	Stock	Dividend	Year	Stock	Dividend
2022	$10.25	$0.05	2010	$NA	$NA
2021	$11.03	$0.05	2009	$NA	$NA
2020	$6.60	$0.05	2008	$NA	$NA
2019	$7.26	$0.05	2007	$NA	$NA
2018	$7.96	$0.05	2006	$NA	$NA
2017	$8.12	$0.05	2005	$NA	$NA
2016	$7.60	$0.05	2004	$NA	$NA
2015	$7.20	$0.05	2003	$NA	$NA
2014	$7.80	$0.05	2002	$NA	$NA
2013	$4.80	$NA	2001	$NA	$NA
2012	$8.00	$NA	2000	$NA	$NA
2011	$NA	$NA	1999	$NA	$NA

NOTES: NXR.UN is a Canada-based real estate investment trust focused on increasing unitholder value through the acquisition of industrial properties in Canada and the United States, and the ownership and management of its portfolio of properties.

NORTHLAND POWER INC
(NPI)
Updated July 2023

IDM STOCK SCORING CALCULATION

(1) Stock Price $ 26.72   *Score* 7
(2) Price 4 Years Ago $ 25.48 *Score* 7
(3) Current to Four Year Price *Score* 7
(4) Book Value $ 17.56   *Score* 6
(5) Price to Book Comparison *Score* 0
(6) Analyst Buys # 6   *Score* 5

(7) Analysts Strong Buys # 3 *Score* 4
(8) Dividend Yield % 4.48   *Score* 6
(9) Operating Margin % 40.42 *Score* 6
(10) Trading Volume 193,127 *Score* 4
(11) Price to Earnings 9.8x   *Score* 9

Total of All 11 Scores = 61

This stock's total score in 2021 was **NA**, in 2020 it was **NA**, in 2019 it was **NA**.

HISTORICAL STOCK PRICES & DIVIDEND PAYOUTS

Year	Stock	Dividend	Year	Stock	Dividend
2022	$45.14	$0.10	2010	$14.47	$0.09
2021	$40.05	$0.10	2009	$10.64	$0.09
2020	$36.70	$0.10	2008	$12.28	$0.09
2019	$25.62	$0.1	2007	$13.19	$0.09
2018	$24.66	$0.10	2006	$14.45	$0.09
2017	$24.70	$0.09	2005	$14.40	$0.09
2016	$24.80	$0.09	2004	$11.35	$0.08
2015	$15.32	$0.09	2003	$11.33	$0.08
2014	$17.76	$0.09	2002	$10.80	$0.08
2013	$16.35	$0.09	2001	$10.81	$0.07
2012	$18.68	$0.09	2000	$8.95	$0.07
2011	$15.48	$0.09	1999	$9.95	$0.21

NOTES: **NPI** is a Canada-based global power producer developing, building, owning, and operating iWind, Efficient Natural Gas, Onshore Renewable Utilities in Asia, Europe, Latin America and North America.

NORTHWEST HEALTHCARE PROPERTIES REIT

(NWH.UN)

Updated June 2023

IDM STOCK SCORING CALCULATION

(1) Stock Price $ 6.28 Score *4*
(2) Price 4 Years Ago $ 11.78 Score *5*
(3) Current to Four Year Price Score *2*
(4) Book Value $ 10.21 Score *5*
(5) Price to Book Comparison Score *8*
(6) Analyst Buys # 1 Score *2*

(7) Analysts Strong Buys # Score *0*
(8) Dividend Yield % 12.74 Score *2*
(9) Operating Margin % 26.22 Score *5*
(10) Trading Volume 1,353,266 Score *9*
(11) Price to Earnings -12.3 Score *9*

Total of All 11 Scores = 51

This stock's total score in 2021 was **54**, in 2020 it was **53**, in 2019 it was **47**.

HISTORICAL STOCK PRICES & DIVIDEND PAYOUTS

Year	Stock	Dividend	Year	Stock	Dividend
2022	$ 13.15	$ 0.07	2010	$ NA	$ NA
2021	$ 12.73	$ 0.07	2009	$ NA	$ NA
2020	$ 11.25	$ 0.07	2008	$ NA	$ NA
2019	$ 11.63	$ 0.07	2007	$ NA	$ NA
2018	$ 11.29	$ 0.07	2006	$ NA	$ NA
2017	$ 10.62	$ 0.07	2005	$ NA	$ NA
2016	$ 10.21	$ 0.07	2004	$ NA	$ NA
2015	$ 7.97	$ 0.07	2003	$ NA	$ NA
2014	$ 10.00	$ 0.07	2002	$ N A	$ NA
2013	$ 11.14	$ 0.07	2001	$ NA	$ NA
2012	$ 13.10	$ 0.07	2000	$ NA	$ NA
2011	$ 11.75	$ 0.07	1999	$ NA	$ NA6.28

NOTES: **NWH.UN** is a Canada-based open-ended real estate investment trust operating 149 properties throughout Canada, Brazil, Germany, Australia, and New Zealand.

OLYMPIA FINANCIAL GROUP INC

(OLY)

Updated July 2023

IDM STOCK SCORING CALCULATION

(1) Stock Price $ 71.75   Score 9
(2) Price 4 Years Ago $ 45.49   Score 3
(3) Current to Four Year Price Score 10
(4) Book Value $ 10.52   Score 5
(5) Price to Book Comparison   Score 0
(6) Analyst Buys # 0   Score 0

(7) Analysts Strong Buys # 0   Score 0
(8) Dividend Yield % 7.59   Score 10
(9) Operating Margin % 27.79 Score 5
(10) Trading Volume 56   Score 0
(11) Price to Earnings 10.0x   Score 9

Total of All 11 Scores = 51

This stock's total score in 2021 was **49**, in 2020 it was **54**, in 2019 it was **48**.

HISTORICAL STOCK PRICES & DIVIDEND PAYOUTS

Year	Stock	Dividend	Year	Stock	Dividend
2022	$ 61.50	$ 0.27	2010	$ 25.19	$ 0.39
2021	$ 46.74	$ 0.23	2009	$ 23.69	$ 0.35
2020	$ 39.00	$ 0.23	2008	$ 32.27	$ 0.24
2019	$ 41.00	$ 0.23	2007	$ 18.89	$ 0.16
2018	$ 48.50	$ 0.20	2006	$ 14.95	$ 0.08
2017	$ 37.75	$ 0.17	2005	$ NA	$ NA
2016	$ 22.95	$ 0.50	2004	$ 3.07	$ NA
2015	$ 24.02	$ 0.65	2003	$ 3.03	$ NA
2014	$ 36.00	$ 0.65	2002	$ 1.96	$ NA
2013	$ 31.48	$ 0.55	2001	$ 1.53	$ NA
2012	$ 30.54	$ 0.55	2000	$ 1.43	$ NA
2011	$ 33.21	$ 0.51	1999	$ 0.48	$ NA

NOTES: OLY through its subsidiary Olympia Trust Company operates account administration of registered accounts that invest in arm's length mortgages and syndicated mortgages. Through its Private Health Services Plan division, it markets, sells, and administers health and dental benefits, plus a Foreign Exchange division.

ORCA ENERGY GROUP INC

(ORC.B)

Updated July 2023

IDM STOCK SCORING CALCULATION

(1) Stock Price $ 5.24   *Score* 4
(2) Price 4 Years Ago $ 6.21   *Score* 4
(3) Current to Four Year Price *Score* 2
(4) Book Value $ 5.97   *Score* 4
(5) Price to Book Comparison   *Score* 8
(6) Analyst Buys # 0   *Score* 0

(7) Analysts Strong Buys #0   *Score* 0
(8) Dividend Yield % 10.12   *Score* 10
(9) Operating Margin % 44.90 *Score* 6
(10) Trading Volume 10,334   *Score* 1
(11) Price to Earnings 3.3x   *Score* 10

Total of All 11 Scores = 49

This stock's total score in 2021 was **46**, in 2020 it was **44**, in 2019 it was **NA**.

HISTORICAL STOCK PRICES & DIVIDEND PAYOUTS

Year	Stock	Dividend	Year	Stock	Dividend
2022	$ 5.10	$ NA	2010	$ 3.72	$ NA
2021	$ 5.64	$ NA	2009	$ 3.04	$ NA
2020	$ 5.50	$ NA	2008	$ 7.28	$ NA
2019	$ 6.21	$ NA	2007	$ 12.81	$ NA
2018	$ 5.92	$ NA	2006	$ 4.91	$ NA
2017	$ 3.64	$ NA	2005	$ 3.27	$ NA
2016	$ 3.09	$ NA	2004	$ 0.91	$ NA
2015	$ 2.95	$ NA	2003	$ NA	$ NA
2014	$ 3.00	$ NA	2002	$ NA	$ NA
2013	$ 1.96	$ NA	2001	$ NA	$ NA
2012	$ 2.45	$ NA	2000	$ NA	$ NA
2011	$ 4.55	$ NA	1999	$ NA	$ NA

NOTES: ORC.B is a Canadian company, is engaged in the hydrocarbon exploration, development and supply of gas in Tanzania, and oil appraisal and gas exploration in Italy

PARAMOUNT RESOURCES LTD

(POU)

Updated July 2023

IDM STOCK SCORING CALCULATION

(1) *Stock Price $ 28.80*   *Score 7*

(2) *Price 4 Years Ago $ 7.94*   *Score 7*

(3) *Current to Four Year Price Score 10*

(4) *Book Value $ 23.79*   *Score 7*

(5) *Price to Book Comparison Score 1*

(6) *Analyst Buys # 1*   *Score 2*

(7) *Analysts Strong Buys # 1   Score 3*

(8) *Dividend Yield % 5.21*   *Score 8*

(9) *Operating Margin % 48.39 Score 6*

(10) *Trading Volume 223,589   Score 4*

(11) *Price to Earnings 4.9*   *Score 10*

Total of All 11 Scores = 62

This stock's total score in 2021 was **NA**, in 2020 it was **NA**, in 2019 it was **NA**.

HISTORICAL STOCK PRICES & DIVIDEND PAYOUTS

Year	Stock	Dividend	Year	Stock	Dividend
2022	$ 29.94	$ 0.10	2010	$.NA	$.NA
2021	$ 19.15	$ 0.02	2009	$.NA	$.NA
2020	$.NA	$.NA	2008	$.NA	$.NA
2019	$.NA	$.NA	2007	$.NA	$.NA
2018	$.NA	$.NA	2006	$.NA	$.NA
2017	$.NA	$.NA	2005	$.NA	$.NA
2016	$.NA	$.NA	2004	$.NA	$.NA
2015	$.NA	$.NA	2003	$.NA	$.NA
2014	$.NA	$.NA	2002	$.NA	$.NA
2013	$.NA	$.NA	2001	$.NA	$.NA
2012	$.NA	$.NA	2000	$.NA	$.NA
2011	$.NA	$.NA	1999	$.NA	$.NA

NOTES: POU is a Canada-based energy company that explores and develops both conventional and unconventional petroleum and natural gas.

PAREX RESOURCES INC

(PXT)

Updated July 2023

IDM STOCK SCORING CALCULATION

(1) Stock Price $ 26.56   Score 7
(2) Price 4 Years Ago $ 22.30 Score 7
(3) Current to Four Year Price Score 9
(4) Book Value $ 20.80   Score 7
(5) Price to Book Comparison Score 1
(6) Analyst Buys # 3   Score 3

(7) Analysts Strong Buys # 0 Score 0
(8) Dividend Yield % 5.65   Score 8
(9) Operating Margin % 58.11 Score 8
(10) Trading Volume 468,914 Score 5
(11) Price to Earnings 3.9   Score 10

Total of All 11 Scores = 65

This stock's total score in 2021 was **NA**, in 2020 it was **NA**, in 2019 it was **NA**.

HISTORICAL STOCK PRICES & DIVIDEND PAYOUTS

Year	Stock	Dividend	Year	Stock	Dividend
2022	$ 23.79	$ 0.12	2010	$ 5.63	$ NA
2021	$ 20.48	$ 0.12	2009	$ .4.02	$ NA
2020	$ 16.01	$ NA	2008	$ NA	$ NA
2019	$ 22.30	$ NA	2007	$ NA	$ NA
2018	$ 22.70	$ NA	2006	$ NA	$ NA
2017	$ 15.68	$ NA	2005	$ NA	$ NA
2016	$ 12.51	$ NA	2004	$ NA	$ NA
2015	$ 8.55	$ NA	2003	$ NA	$ NA
2014	$ 14.05	$ NA	2002	$ NA	$ NA
2013	$ 5.13	$ NA	2001	$ NA	$ NA
2012	$ 4.75	$ NA	2000	$ NA	$ NA
2011	$ 7.38	$ NA	1999	$ NA	$ NA

NOTES: PPXT is a Canada-based exploration and production company engaged in the business of the exploration, development, production and marketing of oil and natural gas in Colombia.

PARKLAND CORPORATION

(PKI)

Updated July 2023

IDM STOCK SCORING CALCULATION

(1) Stock Price $ 33.00   Score 8
(2) Price 4 Years Ago $ 43.13 Score 8
(3) Current to Four Year Price Score 2
(4) Book Value $ 17.31   Score 6
(5) Price to Book Comparison Score 0
(6) Analyst Buys # 5   Score 4

(7) Analysts Strong Buys # 0 Score 0
(8) Dividend Yield % 4.12   Score 6
(9) Operating Margin % 2.29 Score 1
(10) Trading Volume 331,516 Score 5
(11) Price to Earnings 16.4x   Score 8

Total of All 11 NAScores = 48

This stock's total score in 2021 was **NA**, in 2020 it was **NA**, in 2019 it was **NA**.

HISTORICAL STOCK PRICES & DIVIDEND PAYOUTS

Year	Stock	Dividend	Year	Stock	Dividend
2022	$ 35.93	$ 0.33	2010	$ 10.57	$ 0.10
2021	$ 37.67	$ 0.10	2009	$ 10.80	$ 0.10
2020	$ 36.97	$ 0.10	2008	$ 9.81	$ 0.10
2019	$ 43.41	$ 0.10	2007	$ 16.27	$ 0.09
2018	$ 40.66	$ 0.10	2006	$ 9.45	$ 0.06
2017	$ 27.02	$ 0.10	2005	$ 5.98	$ 0.05
2016	$ 23.17	$ 0.09	2004	$ 6.86	$ 0.04
2015	$ 23.82	$ 0.09	2003	$ 5.64	$ 0.04
2014	$ 20.59	$ 0.09	2002	$ 3.74	$ 0.04
2013	$ 17.16	$ 0.09	2001	$ 2.88	$ 0.03
2012	$ 14.24	$ 0.09	2000	$ 2.99	$ 0.03
2011	$ 12.21	$ 0.09	1999	$ 4.22	$ 0.02

NOTES: PKI is a Canada-based food and convenience retailer and an independent marketer, distributor, and refiner of fuel and petroleum products. It operates through four segments: Canada, International, USA, and Refining.

PEMBINA PIPELINE CORPORATION

(PPL)

Updated July 2023

IDM STOCK SCORING CALCULATION

(1) Stock Price $ 41.65   Score 8   *(7)* Analysts Strong Buys # 1 Score 3

(2) Price 4 Years Ago $ 44.51 Score 8   *(8)* Dividend Yield % 6.41   Score 8

(3) Current to Four Year Price Score 5   *(9)* Operating Margin % 32.60 Score 6

(4) Book Value $ 28.60   Score 7   *(10)* Trading Volume 3,427,788 Score 10

(5) Price to Book Comparison Score 1   *(11)* Price to Earnings 8.5x   Score 9

(6) Analyst Buys # 4   Score 4

Total of All 11 Scores = 69

This stock's total score in 2021 was **48**, in 2020 it was **65**, in 2019 it was **67**.

HISTORICAL STOCK PRICES & DIVIDEND PAYOUTS

Year	Stock	Dividend	Year	Stock	Dividend
2022	$ 48.89	$ 0.21	2010	$ 18.58	$ 0.13
2021	$ 38.45	$ 0.21	2009	$ 15.10	$ 0.13
2020	$ 32.55	$ 0.21	2008	$ 18.40	$ 0.12
2019	$ 47.89	$ 0.20	2007	$ 17.64	$ 0.11
2018	$ 43.89	$ 0.19	2006	$ 16.95	$ 0.10
2017	$ 42.49	$ 0.17	2005	$ 15.56	$ 0.09
2016	$ 39.46	$ 0.16	2004	$ 11.89	$ 0.09
2015	$ 36.50	$ 0.15	2003	$ 12.17	$ 0.09
2014	$ 45.68	$ 0.14	2002	$ 11.65	$ 0.09
2013	$ 32.68	$ 0.14	2001	$ 9.75	$ 0.09
2012	$ 26.72	$ 0.14	2000	$ 7.70	$ 0.08
2011	$ 25.49	$ 0.13	1999	$ 8.50	$ 0.08

NOTES: **PPL** owns an integrated system of pipelines that transport various hydrocarbon liquids and natural gas products produced primarily in western Canada.

PEYTO EXPLORATION & DEVELOPMENT CORPORATIONS
(PEY)
Updated July 2023

IDM STOCK SCORING CALCULATION

(1) Stock Price $ 10.96   Score 5
(2) Price 4 Years Ago $ 3.20   Score 3
(3) Current to Four Year Price Score 10
(4) Book Value $ 11.88   Score 5
(5) Price to Book Comparison Score 6
(6) Analyst Buys # 2   Score 3

(7) Analysts Strong Buys # 0 Score 0
(8) Dividend Yield % 12.04   Score 2
(9) Operating Margin % 61.37 Score 8
(10) Trading Volume 700,481 Score 6
(11) Price to Earnings 5.0x   Score 10

Total of All 11 Scores = 58

This stock's total score in 2021 was **NA**, in 2020 it was **NA**, in 2019 it was **NA**.

HISTORICAL STOCK PRICES & DIVIDEND PAYOUTS

Year	Stock	Dividend	Year	Stock	Dividend
2022	$ 12.25	$ 0.05	2010	$ 14.09	$ 0.12
2021	$ 7.23	$ 0.01	2009	$ 9.37	$ 0.12
2020	$ 1.79	$ 0.01	2008	$ 20.15	$ 0.15
2019	$ 3.20	$ 0.02	2007	$ 17.16	$ 0.14
2018	$ 10.82	$ 0.06	2006	$ 23.68	$ 0.14
2017	$ 22.16	$ 0.11	2005	$ 33.85	$ 0.12
2016	$ 34.68	$ 0.11	2004	$ 16.77	$ 0.09
2015	$ 28.30	$ 0.11	2003	$ 10.50	$ 0.07
2014	$ 40.31	$ 0.10	2002	$ 3.25	$ NA
2013	$ 29.54	$ 0.08	2001	$ 1.57	$ NA
2012	$ 21.40	$ 0.06	2000	$ 0.80	$ NA
2011	$ 21.50	$ 0.06	1999	$ 0.12	$ NA

NOTES: PEY. is a Canada-based oil and natural gas company that conducts exploration, development, and production activities in Canada.

PHX ENERGY SERVICES CORPORATION
(PHX)
Updated July 2023

IDM STOCK SCORING CALCULATION

(1) Stock Price $ 6.06   Score 4
(2) Price 4 Years Ago $ 2.89   Score 3
(3) Current to Four Year Price Score 10
(4) Book Value $ 3.48   Score 3
(5) Price to Book Comparison   Score 0
(6) Analyst Buys # 0   Score 0

(7) Analysts Strong Buys # 2 Score 4
(8) Dividend Yield % 9.90   Score 10
(9) Operating Margin %13.81 Score 3
(10) Trading Volume 8,399   Score 0
(11) Price to Earnings 4.5x   Score 10

Total of All 11 Scores = 47

This stock's total score in 2021 was **NA**, in 2020 it was **NA**, in 2019 it was **NA**.

HISTORICAL STOCK PRICES & DIVIDEND PAYOUTS

Year	Stock	Dividend	Year	Stock	Dividend
2022	$ 4.84	$ 0.07	2010	$ 9.25	$ 0.04
2021	$ 4.12	$ 0.03	2009	$ 6.95	$ 0.09
2020	$ 2.84	$ 0.03	2008	$ 15.70	$ 0.09
2019	$ 1.04	$ NA	2007	$ 8.90	$ 0.07
2018	$ 2.54	$ NA	2006	$ 8.45	$ 0.07
2017	$ 2.04	$ NA	2005	$ 8.25	$ 0.04
2016	$ 2.06	$ NA	2004	$ 4.15	$ 0.04
2015	$ 4.56	$ 0.02	2003	$ 1.27	$ 0.05
2014	$ 15.34	$ 0.07	2002	$ 1.42	$ NA
2013	$ 10.53	$ 0.06	2001	$ 6.00	$ NA
2012	$ 9.12	$ 0.06	2000	$ 5.20	$ NA
2011	$ 10.39	$ 0.04	1999	$ 0.50	$ NA

NOTES: PHX is a Canada-based oil and natural gas services company. The Company provides horizontal and directional drilling technology and services to oil and natural gas producing companies.

PINE CLIFF ENERGY LTD
(PNE)
Updated July 2023

IDM STOCK SCORING CALCULATION

(1) Stock Price $ 1.43   Score 2
(2) Price 4 Years Ago $ 0.13   Score 1
(3) Current to Four Year Price Score 10
(4) Book Value $ 0.38   Score 1
(5) Price to Book Comparison Score 0
(6) Analyst Buys # 2   Score 3

(7) Analysts Strong Buys # 0 Score 0
(8) Dividend Yield %9.09   Score 10
(9) Operating Margin % 40.69 Score 6
(10) Trading Volume 218,673   Score 4
(11) Price to Earnings 5.3   Score 10

Total of All 11 Scores = 47

This stock's total score in 2021 was **NA**, in 2020 it was **NA**, in 2019 it was **NA**.

HISTORICAL STOCK PRICES & DIVIDEND PAYOUTS

Year	Stock	Dividend	Year	Stock	Dividend
2022	$ 1.89	$ 0.01	2010	$ 0.32	$ NA
2021	$ 0.39	$ NA	2009	$ 0.16	$ NA
2020	$ 0.12	$ NA	2008	$ 0.80	$ NA
2019	$ 0.13	$ NA	2007	$ 1.35	$ NA
2018	$ 0.42	$ NA	2006	$ 0.65	$ NA
2017	$ 0.69	$ NA	2005	$ 0.58	$ NA
2016	$ 0.87	$ NA	2004	$ NA	$ NA
2015	$ 1.13	$ NA	2003	$ NA	$ NA
2014	$ 1.83	$ NA	2002	$ NA	$ NA
2013	$ 1.03	$ NA	2001	$ NA	$ NA
2012	$ 0.64	$ NA	2000	$ NA	$ NA
2011	$ 0.18	$ NA	1999	$ NA	$ NA

NOTES: PNE is a Canadian based natural gas and crude oil company engaged in acquisition, exploration, development and production.

PINE TRAIL REAL ESTATE INVESTMENT TRUST
(PINE.UN)
Updated July 2023

IDM STOCK SCORING CALCULATION

(1) Stock Price $ 0.06   Score *1*
(2) Price 4 Years Ago $ 0.1   Score *1*
(3) Current to Four Year Price Score *1*
(4) Book Value $ 0.09   Score *1*
(5) Price to Book Comparison Score *8*
(6) Analyst Buys # 0   Score *0*

(7) Analysts Strong Buys # 0 Score *0*
(8) Dividend Yield % 6.00   Score *8*
(9) Operating Margin % -34.9 Score *0*
(10) Trading Volume 16,000   Score *1*
(11) Price to Earnings -14.1x   Score *O*

Total of All 11 Scores = 21

This stock's total score in 2021 was **NA,** in 2020 it was **NA**, in 2019 it was **NA**.

HISTORICAL STOCK PRICES & DIVIDEND PAYOUTS

Year	Stock	Dividend	Year	Stock	Dividend
2022	$ 0.06	$ NA	2010	$ NA	$ NA
2021	$ 0.08	$ NA	2009	$ NA	$ NA
2020	$ 0.14	$ NA	2008	$ NA	$ NA
2019	$ 0.15	$ NA	2007	$ NA	$ NA
2018	$ NA	$ NA	2006	$ NA	$ NA
2017	$ NA	$ NA	2005	$ NA	$ NA
2016	$ NA	$ NA	2004	$ NA	$ NA
2015	$ NA	$ NA	2003	$ NA	$ NA
2014	$ NA	$ NA	2002	$ NA	$ NA
2013	$ NA	$ NA	2001	$ NA	$ NA
2012	$ NA	$ NA	2000	$ NA	$ NA
2011	$ NA	$ NA	1999	$ NA	$ NA

NOTES: PINE.UN is a Canada-based trust that acquires commercial properties.

PIPESTONE ENERGY CORPORATION

(PIPE)

Updated July 2023

IDM STOCK SCORING CALCULATION

(1) Stock Price $ 2.27   Score *3*
(2) Price 4 Years Ago $ 1.33   Score *2*
(3) Current to Four Year Price   Score *9*
(4) Book Value $ 2.45   Score *3*
(5) Price to Book Comparison Score *6*
(6) Analyst Buys # 0   Score *0*

(7) Analysts Strong Buys # 1 Score *3*
(8) Dividend Yield % 5.29   Score   *8*
(9) Operating Margin % 48.59 Score *6*
(10) Trading Volume 354,016 Score *5*
(11) Price to Earnings 2.4x   Score *10*

Total of All 11 Scores = 55

This stock's total score in 2021 was **NA**, in 2020 it was **NA**, in 2019 it was **NA**.

HISTORICAL STOCK PRICES & DIVIDEND PAYOUTS

Year	Stock	Dividend	Year	Stock	Dividend
2022	$ 4.29	$ NA	2010	$ 1.35	$ NA
2021	$ 2.11	$ NA	2009	$ 2.80	$ NA
2020	$ 0.51	$ NA	2008	$ NA	$ NA
2019	$ 1.33	$ NA	2007	$ NA	$ NA
2018	$ 3.60	$ NA	2006	$ NA	$ NA
2017	$ 3.55	$ NA	2005	$ NA	$ NA
2016	$ 2.45	$ NA	2004	$ NA	$ NA
2015	$ 1.35	$ NA	2003	$ NA	$ NA
2014	$ 2.15	$ NA	2002	$ NA	$ NA
2013	$ 0.50	$ NA	2001	$ NA	$ NA
2012	$ 1.05	$ NA	2000	$ NA	$ NA
2011	$ 1.35	$ NA	1999	$ NA	$ NA

NOTES: PIPE is a Canadian based natural gas and crude oil company engaged in acquisition, exploration, development, and production.

PIZZA PIZZA ROYALTY CORPORATION

(PZA)

Updated July 2023

IDM STOCK SCORING CALCULATION

(1) Stock Price $ 14.81 Score 5   *(7) Analysts Strong Buys # 0 Score 0*
(2) Price 4 Years Ago $ 9.99 Score 4   *(8) Dividend Yield %6.08* Score 8
(3) Current to Four Year Price Score 9   *(9) Operating Margin % 98.24 Score 10*
(4) Book Value $ 9.09 Score 4   *(10) Trading Volume 14,326* Score 1
(5) Price to Book Comparison Score 0   *(11) Price to Earnings 16.6x* Score 8
(6) Analyst Buys # 0 Score 0

Total of All 11 Scores = 49

This stock's total score in 2021 was **48**, in 2020 it was **52**, in 2019 it was **57**.

HISTORICAL STOCK PRICES & DIVIDEND PAYOUTS

Year	Stock	Dividend	Year	Stock	Dividend
2022	$ 13.16	$ 0.07	2010	$ 6.82	$ 0.08
2021	$ 11.23	$ 0.06	2009	$ 6.56	$ 0.08
2020	$ 8.79	$ 0.05	2008	$ 8.66	$ 0.08
2019	$ 9.53	$ 0.07	2007	$ 9.75	$ 0.07
2018	$ 12.09	$ 0.07	2006	$ 10.02	$ 0.07
2017	$ 16.44	$ 0.07	2005	$ 10.04	$ 0.06
2016	$ 14.72	$ 0.07	2004	$ NA	$ NA
2015	$ 13.61	$ 0.07	2003	$ NA	$ NA
2014	$ 13.65	$ 0.07	2002	$ NA	$ NA
2013	$ 12.44	$ 0.07	2001	$ NA	$ NA
2012	$ 10.06	$ 0.06	2000	$ NA	$ NA
2011	$ 8.93	$ 0.06	1999	$ NA	$ NA

NOTES: PZA operates through receipt of royalty income from the ownership of the Pizza Pizza and Pizza 73 Rights and Marks segment. Pizza Pizza is a franchise-oriented restaurant business operating in the province of Ontario.

PLAZA RETAIL REAL ESTATE INVESTMENT TRUST

(PLZ.UN)
Updated July 2023

IDM STOCK SCORING CALCULATION

(1) Stock Price $ 3.97   Score 3
(2) Price 4 Years Ago $ 4.15   Score 3
(3) Current to Four Year Price Score 5
(4) Book Value $ 5.10   Score 4
(5) Price to Book Comparison Score 8
(6) Analyst Buys # 0   Score 0

(7) Analysts Strong Buys # 0 Score 0
(8) Dividend Yield % 7.05   Score 8
(9) Operating Margin % 59.81 Score 8
(10) Trading Volume 29,270   Score 1
(11) Price to Earnings 11.4x   Score 9

Total of All 11 Scores = 49

This stock's total score in 2021 was **39**, in 2020 it was **49**, in 2019 it was **49**.

HISTORICAL STOCK PRICES & DIVIDEND PAYOUTS

Year	Stock	Dividend	Year	Stock	Dividend
2022	$ 4.15	$ 0.02	2010	$ 3.43	$ 0.05
2021	$ 4.57	$ 0.02	2009	$ 2.43	$ 0.05
2020	$ 3.31	$ 0.02	2008	$ 3.38	$ 0.04
2019	$ 4.15	$ 0.02	2007	$ 4.19	$ 0.04
2018	$ 4.26	$ 0.02	2006	$ 2.83	$ 0.03
2017	$ 4.48	$ 0.02	2005	$ 2.33	$ 0.03
2016	$ 4.86	$ 0.02	2004	$ 1.64	$ 0.02
2015	$ 4.33	$ 0.02	2003	$ 0.89	$ NA
2014	$ 3.96	$ 0.02	2002	$ 0.81	$ NA
2013	$ 4.08	$ 0.06	2001	$ 0.60	$ NA
2012	$ 4.92	$ 0.05	2000	$ 0.69	$ NA
2011	$ 4.62	$ 0.05	1999	$ 1.04	$ NA

NOTES: : PLZ.UN is a Canada-based open-ended real estate investment trust. The Company's objective is to deliver a growing yield to unitholders from a diversified portfolio of retail properties.

POLARIS RENEWABLE ENERGY INC

(PIF)

Updated July 2023

IDM STOCK SCORING CALCULATION

(1) Stock Price $ 14.25   Score 5
(2) Price 4 Years Ago $ 13.77   Score 5
(3) Current to Four Year Price Score 7
(4) Book Value $ 16.98   Score 6
(5) Price to Book Comparison Score 8
(6) Analyst Buys # 0   Score 0

(7) Analysts Strong Buys #0 Score 0
(8) Dividend Yield % 5.71   Score 8
(9) Operating Margin % 24.70 Score 5
(10) Trading Volume 20,546   Score 1
(11) Price to Earnings 50.4   Score 2

Total of All 11 Scores = 47

This stock's total score in 2021 was **56**, in 2020 it was **58**, in 2019 it was **62**.

HISTORICAL STOCK PRICES & DIVIDEND PAYOUTS

Year	Stock	Dividend	Year	Stock	Dividend
2022	$ 19.98	$ NA	2010	$ 4,380.00	P$ NA
2021	$ 14.52	$ NA	2009	$ 5,593.00	$ NA
2020	$ 14.59	$ NA	2008	$ 9,566.27	$ NA
2019	$ 15.05	$ NA	2007	$ 10,052.69	$ NA
2018	$ 13.70	$ NA	2006	$ 8,269.15	$ NA
2017	$ 17.20	$ NA	2005	$ 7,701.66	$ NA
2016	$ 8.10	$ NA	2004	$ 8,512.36	$ NA
2015	$ 12.50	$ NA	2003	$ NA	$ NA
2014	$ 60.00	$ NA	2002	$ NA	$ NA
2013	$ 440.00	$ NA	2001	$ NA	$ NA
2012	$ 480.00	$ NA	2000	$ NA	$ NA
2011	$ 950.00	$ NA	1999	$ NA	$ NA

NOTES: : Polaris Infrastructure Inc. is a Canada-based company, which is engaged in the acquisition, development and operation of renewable energy projects in Latin America

POWER CORPORATION

(POW)

Updated July 2023

IDM STOCK SCORING CALCULATION

(1) Stock Price $35.66   *Score* 8
(2) Price 4 Years Ago $ 28.14   *Score* 7
(3) Current to Four Year Price *Score* 9
(4) Book Value $ 32.79   *Score* 8
(5) Price to Book Comparison   *Score* 2
(6) Analyst Buys # 1   *Score* 2

(7) Analysts Strong Buys #0   *Score* 0
(8) Dividend Yield % 5.89   *Score* 8
(9) Operating Margin % 4.19   *Score* 1
(10) Trading Volume 6,140,062 *Score* 10
(11) Price to Earnings 13.7x   *Score* 9

Total of All 11 Scores = 64

This stock's total score in 2021 was **64**, in 2020 it was **60,** in 2019 it was **62**.

HISTORICAL STOCK PRICES & DIVIDEND PAYOUTS

Year	Stock	Dividend	Year	Stock	Dividend
2022	$ 36.88	$ 0.49	2010	$ 25.51	$ 0.29
2021	$ 38.65	$ 0.45	2009	$ 27.19	$ 0.29
2020	$ 23.97	$ 0.45	2008	$ 29.75	$ 0.29
2019	$ 28.14	$ 0.41	2007	$ 39.85	$ 0.24
2018	$ 29.95	$ 0.38	2006	$ 28.70	$ 0.20
2017	$ 30.94	$ 0.36	2005	$ 31.60	$ 0.17
2016	$ 27.50	$ 0.34	2004	$ 27.00	$ 0.14
2015	$ 32.81	$ 0.31	2003	$ 20.12	$ 0.12
2014	$ 30.60	$ 0.26	2002	$ 20.15	$ 0.10
2013	$ 27.28	$ 0.29	2001	$ 16.80	$ 0.09
2012	$ 23.74	$ 0.29	2000	$ 15.55	$ 0.07
2011	$ 28.80	$ 0.29	1999	$ 12.87	$ 0.06

NOTES: POW's principal asset is Power Financial Corporation Its segments are Great-West Lifeco Inc., IGM Financial Inc and Pargesa Holding SA. Lifeco . It offers life insurance, health insurance, retirement and investment services.

PRECIOUS METAL AND MINING TRUST

(MMP.UN)

Updated July 2023

IDM STOCK SCORING CALCULATION

(1) Stock Price $ 2.04   Score 3
(2) Price 4 Years Ago $ 1.70   Score 2
(3) Current to Four Year Price   Score 9
(4) Book Value $ 1.97   Score 2
(5) Price to Book Comparison   Score 2
(6) Analyst Buys # 0   Score 0

(7) Analysts Strong Buys # 0 Score 0
(8) Dividend Yield % 5.88   Score 8
(9) Operating Margin % 0   Score 0
(10) Trading Volume 10,743 Score 1
(11) Price to Earnings -6.3   Score 9

Total of All 11 Scores = 36

This stock's total score in 2021 was **48**, in 2020 it was **38**, in 2019 it was **19**.

HISTORICAL STOCK PRICES & DIVIDEND PAYOUTS

Year	Stock	Dividend	Year	Stock	Dividend
2022	$ 2.23	$ 0.01	2010	$ 7.98	$ 0.10
2021	$ 2.32	$ 0.01	2009	$ 6.19	$ 0.10
2020	$ 2.04	$ 0.01	2008	$ 10.00	$ 0.10
2019	$ 1.68	$ 0.01	2007	$ 12.75	$ 0.07
2018	$ 1.85	$ 0.02	2006	$ 10.05	$ 0.04
2017	$ 2.19	$ 0.02	2005	$ NA	$ NA
2016	$ 3.23	$ 0.02	2004	$ NA	$ N A
2015	$ 2.14	$ 0.01	2003	$ NA	$ NA
2014	$ 2.71	$ 0.04	2002	$ NA	$ NA
2013	$ 3.48	$ 0.07	2001	$ NA	$ NA
2012	$ 7.53	$ 0.10	2000	$ NA	$ NA
2011	$ 9.90	$ 0.10	1999	$ NA	$ NA

NOTES: MMP.UN is a Canada-based company. The Company is an investment trust.

PREMIUM INCOME CORPORATION

(PIC.A)

Updated July 2023

IDM STOCK SCORING CALCULATION

(1) Stock Price $ 4.95   Score 3   **(7)** Analysts Strong Buys # 0   Score 0.
(2) Price 4 Years Ago $ 6.40   Score 4   **(8)** Dividend Yield % 16.42   Score 2
(3) Current to Four Year Price Score 2   **(9)** Operating Margin % 70.34   Score 9
(4) Book Value $ 19.26   Score 6   **(10)** Trading Volume 17,410   Score 1
(5) Price to Book Comparison   Score 10   **(11)** Price to Earnings -2.0   Score 0
(6) Analyst Buys # 0   Score 0

Total of All 11 Scores = 37

This stock's total score in 2021 was **43**, in 2020 it was **37**, in 2019 it was **41**.

HISTORICAL STOCK PRICES & DIVIDEND PAYOUTS

Year	Stock	Dividend	Year	Stock	Dividend
2022	$ 6.75	$ 0.20	2010	$ 7.42	$ 0.20
2021	$ 6.65	$ 0.20	2009	$ 5.54	$ 0.14
2020	$ 3.54	$ 0.10	2008	$ 4.15	$ 0.27
2019	$ 6.27	$ 0.20	2007	$ 13.27	$ 0.27
2018	$ 7.72	$ 0.20	2006	$ 14.15	$ 0.27
2017	$ 6.82	$ 0.20	2005	$ 16.33	$ 0.27
2016	$ 6.40	$ 0.20	2004	$ 15.09	$ 0.27
2015	$ 5.65	$ 0.20	2003	$ 15.94	$ 0.27
2014	$ 8.61	$ 0.20	2002	$ 15.10	$ 0.27
2013	$ 5.85	$ 0.20	2001	$ 16..93	$ 0.27
2012	$ 6.06	$ 0.20	2000	$ 15.51	$ 0.27
2011	$ 6.15	$ 0.20	1999	$ 16.25	$ 0.27

NOTES: PIC.A is a split share company. The Fund's investment objectives are to provide with cumulative preferential quarterly cash distributions.

PRIME DIVIDEND CORPORATION

(PDV)

Updated July 2023

IDM STOCK SCORING CALCULATION

(1) Stock Price $ 5.60   Score *4*

(2) Price 4 Years Ago $ 6.96   Score *4*

(3) Current to Four Year Price Score *2*

(4) Book Value $ 5.70   Score *4*

(5) Price to Book Comparison Score *6*

(6) Analyst Buys # 0   Score *0*

(7) Analysts Strong Buys # 0 Score *0*

(8) Dividend Yield % 10.24   Score *10*

(9) Operating Margin % 0   Score *0*

(10) Trading Volume 94   Score *0*

(11) Price to Earnings -3.3x   Score *0*

Total of All 11 Scores = 30

This stock's total score in 2021 was **23**, in 2020 it was **NA**, in 2019 it was **NA**.

HISTORICAL STOCK PRICES & DIVIDEND PAYOUTS

Year	Stock	Dividend	Year	Stock	Dividend
2022	$ 8.40	$ 0.07	2010	$ 8.31	$ 0.08
2021	$ 8.27	$ 0.06	2009	$ 8.11	$ 0.08
2020	$ 4.89	$ 0.03	2008	$ 12.53	$ 0.10
2019	$ 7.51	$ 0.06	2007	$ 17.17	$ 0.12
2018	$ 9.26	$ 0.08	2006	$ 17.07	$ 0.12
2017	$ 9.34	$ 0.07	2005	$ 17.64	$ 0.11
2016	$ 7.39	$ 0.06	2004	$ NA	$ NA
2015	$ 7.216	$ 0.08	2003	$ NA	$ NA
2014	$ 10.51	$ 0.08	2002	$ NA	$ NA
2013	$ 7.75	$ 0.08	2001	$ NA	$ NA
2012	$ 6.87	$ 0.08	2000	$ NA	$ NA
2011	$ 7.97	$ 0.08	1999	$ NA	$ NA

NOTES: PDV. is a mutual fund company. The Company's investment objective is to invest primarily in a portfolio of common shares.

PROPEL HOLDINGS INC

(PRL)

Updated July 2023

IDM STOCK SCORING CALCULATION

(1) Stock Price $ 7.50   Score 4

(2) Price 4 Years Ago $ 0   Score 1

(3) Current to Four Year Price   Score 0

(4) Book Value $ 3.15   Score 3

(5) Price to Book Comparison   Score 0

(6) Analyst Buys # 2   Score 3

(7) Analysts Strong Buys # 3   Score 4

(8) Dividend Yield % 5.33   Score 8

(9) Operating Margin % 16.13   Score 4

(10) Trading Volume 10,798   Score 1

(11) Price to Earnings 10.9x   Score 9

Total of All 11 Scores = 37

This stock's total score in 2021 was **NA**, in 2020 it was **NA**, in 2019 it was **NA**.

HISTORICAL STOCK PRICES & DIVIDEND PAYOUTS

Year	Stock	Dividend	Year	Stock	Dividend
2022	$ 8.35	$0.10	2010	$ NA	$ NA
2021	$ 10.61	$ 0.10	2009	$ NA	$ NA
2020	$ NA	$ NA	2008	$ NA	$ NA
2019	$ NA	$ NA	2007	$ NA	$ NA
2018	$ NA	$ NA	2006	$ NA	$ NA
2017	$ NA	$ NA	2005	$ NA	$ NA
2016	$ NA	$ NA	2004	$ NA	$ NA
2015	$ NA	$ NA	2003	$ NA	$ NA
2014	$ NA	$ NA	2002	$ NA	$ NA
2013	$ NA	$ NA	2001	$ NA	$ NA
2012	$ NA	$ NA	2000	$ NA	$ NA
2011	$ NA	$ NA	1999	$ NA	$ NA

NOTES: Propel Holdings, Inc. is a Canada-based online financial technology company that operates through its two brands: MoneyKey and CreditFresh. MoneyKey brand, is a state-licensed direct lender and offers either installment loans or lines of credit to new customers in several states in the United States.

PRO REAL ESTATE INVESTMENT TRUST

(PRV.UN)
Updated July 2023

IDM STOCK SCORING CALCULATION

(1) Stock Price $ 5.32   Score 4
(2) Price 4 Years Ago $ 7.25   Score 5
(3) Current to Four Year Price Score 2
(4) Book Value $ 8.26   Score 4
(5) Price to Book Comparison Score 8
(6) Analyst Buys # 2   Score 3

(7) Analysts Strong Buys # 0 Score   0
(8) Dividend Yield % 8.46   Score 10
(9) Operating Margin % 51.98 Score 8
(10) Trading Volume 36,890   Score 2
(11) Price to Earnings 6.4x   Score 9

Total of All 11 Scores = 54

This stock's total score in 2021 was **35** , in 2020 it was **52**, in 2019 it was **62**.

HISTORICAL STOCK PRICES & DIVIDEND PAYOUTS

Year	Stock	Dividend	Year	Stock	Dividend
2022	$ 6.55	$ 0.04	2010	$ NA	$ NA
2021	$ 6.97	$ 0.04	2009	$ NA	$ NA
2020	$ 4.56	$ 0.04	2008	$ NA	$ NA
2019	$ 7.14	$ 0.05	2007	$ NA	$ NA
2018	$ 6.84	$ 0.05	2006	$ NA	$ NA
2017	$ 6.60	$ 0.05	2005	$ NA	$ NA
2016	$ 6.18	$ 0.05	2004	$ NA	$ NA
2015	$ 6.63	$ 0.05	2003	$ NA	$ NA
2014	$ 6.60	$ 0.05	2002	$ NA	$ NA
2013	$ 8.25	$ 0.06	2001	$ NA	$ NA
2012	$ 6.00	$ NA	2000	$ NA	$ NA

NOTES: PRO Real Estate Investment Trust is a Canada-based open-ended real estate investment trust.

REAL ESTATE SPLIT CORP

(RS)

Updated July 2023

IDM STOCK SCORING CALCULATION

(1) Stock Price $ 13.90   nn Score 5
(2) Price 4 Years Ago $ 0   Score 1
(3) Current to Four Year Price Score 0
(4) Book Value $ 0   Score 0
(5) Price to Book Comparison Score 0
(6) Analyst Buys # 0   Score 0

(7) Analysts Strong Buys # 0 Score 0
(8) Dividend Yield % 11.22   Score 2
(9) Operating Margin % 0   Score 0
(10) Trading Volume 15633   Score 1
(11) Price to Earnings 0.0x   Score 0

Total of All 11 Scores = 10

This stock's total score in 2021 was **16**, in 2020 it was **NA**, in 2019 it was **NA**.

HISTORICAL STOCK PRICES & DIVIDEND PAYOUTS

Year	Stock	Dividend	Year	Stock	Dividend
2022	$ 17.04	$ 0.13	2010	$ NA	$ NA
2021	$ 17.85	$ 0.10	2009	$ NA	$ NA
2020	$ 14.50	$ 0.10	2008	$ NA	$ NA
2019	$ NA	$ NA	2007	$ NA	$ NA
2018	$ NA	$ NA	2006	$ NA	$ NA
2017	$ NA	$ NA	2005	$ NA	$ NA
2016	$ NA	$ NA	2004	$ NA	$ NA
2015	$ NA	$ NA	2003	$ NA	$ NA
2014	$ NA	$ NA	2002	$ NA	$ NA
2013	$ NA	$ NA	2001	$ NA	$ NA
2012	$ NA	$ NA	2000	$ NA	$ NA
2011	$ NA	$ NA	1999	$ NA	$ NA

NOTES: RS is a Canadian based mutual fund company managed by Middlefield Limited.

RE ROYALTIES LTD

(RE)

Updated July 2023

IDM STOCK SCORING CALCULATION

(1) Stock Price $ 0.72   Score *1*

(2) Price 4 Years Ago $ 0.84   Score *1*

(3) Current to Four Year Price Score *2*

(4) Book Value $ 0.48   Score *1*

(5) Price to Book Comparison Score *0*

(6) Analyst Buys # 0   Score *0*

(7) Analysts Strong Buys # 0   Score *0*

(8) Dividend Yield % 5.56   Score *8*

(9) Operating Margin % 35.06 Score *6*

(10) Trading Volume 0   Score *0*

(11) Price to Earnings 712.9x Score *1*

Total of All 11 Scores = 20

This stock's total score in 2021 was **17**, in 2020 it was **10**, in 2019 it was **9**.

HISTORICAL STOCK PRICES & DIVIDEND PAYOUTS

Year	Stock	Dividend	Year	Stock	Dividend
2022	$ 0.73	$ 0.01	2010	$ NA	$ NA
2021	$ 1.20	$ 0.01	2009	$ NA	$ NA
2020	$ 1.02	$ 0.01	2008	$ NA	$ NA
2019	$ 0.84	$ 0.01	2007	$ NA	$ NA
2018	$ NA	$ NA	2006	$ NA	$ NA
2017	$ NA	$ NA	2005	$ NA	$ NA
2016	$ NA	$ NA	2004	$ NA	$ NA
2015	$ NA	$ NA	2003	$ NA	$ NA
2014	$ NA	$ NA	2002	$ NA	$ NA
2013	$ NA	$ NA	2001	$ NA	$ NA
2012	$ NA	$ NA	2000	$ NA	$ NA
2011	$ NA	$ NA	1999	$ NA	$ NA

NOTES: RE is a Canada based company engaged in the acquisition of royalties from renewable energy technologies.

RIOCAN REAL ESTATE INVESTMENT TRUST

(REI.UN)

Updated July 2023

IDM STOCK SCORING CALCULATION

(1) Stock Price $ 19.20   Score 6
(2) Price 4 Years Ago $ 26.46 Score 7
(3) Current to Four Year Price Score 2
(4) Book Value $ 25.73   Score 7
(5) Price to Book Comparison Score 8
(6) Analyst Buys # 5   Score 4

(7) Analysts Strong Buys # 0 Score 0
(8) Dividend Yield % 5.63   Score 8
(9) Operating Margin % 15.21 Score 4
(10) Trading Volume 428,232   Score 5
(11) Price to Earnings 29.9x Score 6

Total of All 11 Scores = 57

This stock's total score in 2021 was **48**, in 2020 it was **69**, in 2019 it was **64**.

HISTORICAL STOCK PRICES & DIVIDEND PAYOUTS

Year	Stock	Dividend	Year	Stock	Dividend
2022	$ 20.29	$ 0.09	2010	$ 19.90	$ 0.12
2021	$ 22.18	$ 0.08	2009	$ 14.18	$ 0.12
2020	$ 15.79	$ 0.12	2008	$ 19.50	$ 0.11
2019	$ 26.72	$ 0.10	2007	$ 21.97	$ 0.11
2018	$ 24.61	$ 0.12	2006	$ 20.93	$ 0.10
2017	$ 24.45	$ 0.12	2005	$ 21.40	$ 0.10
2016	$ 27.58	$ 0.12	2004	$ 16.18	$ 0.10
2015	$ 25.63	$ 0.12	2003	$ 14.25	$ 0.10
2014	$ 26.75	$ 0.12	2002	$ 12.72	$ 0.09
2013	$ 28.45	$ 0.12	2001	$ 10.45	$ 0.09
2012	$ 28.58	$ 0.12	2000	$ 9.00	$ 0.09
2011	$ 25.96	$ 0.12	1999	$ 9.45	$ 0.09

NOTES: REI.UN is a Canada-based closed-end real estate investment trust that owns and manages shopping centers with ownership interests in a portfolio of 230 properties including residential rental and 13 development properties.

ROGERS SUGAR INC

(RSI)

Updated July 2023

IDM STOCK SCORING CALCULATION

(1) Stock Price $ 5.77   Score 4
(2) Price 4 Years Ago $ 5.76   Score 4
(3) Current to Four Year Price Score 6
(4) Book Value $ 2.79   Score 3
(5) Price to Book Comparison Score 0
(6) Analyst Buys # 0   Score 0

(7) Analysts Strong Buys # 0 Score 0
(8) Dividend Yield % 6.24   Score 8
(9) Operating Margin % 1.76   Score 1
(10) Trading Volume 89,393   Score 3
(11) Price to Earnings -33.1   Score 5

Total of All 11 Scores = 34

This stock's total score in 2021 was **39**, in 2020 it was **26**, in 2019 it was **40**.

HISTORICAL STOCK PRICES & DIVIDEND PAYOUTS

Year	Stock	Dividend	Year	Stock	Dividend
2022	$ 6.42	$ 0.09	2010	$ 4.89	$ 0.04
2021	$ 5.86	$ 0.09	2009	$ 4.28	$ 0.04
2020	$ 4.66	$ 0.09	2008	$ 4.30	$ 0.04
2019	$ 5.83	$ 0.09	2007	$ 4.33	$ 0.04
2018	$ 5.34	$ 0.09	2006	$ 4.18	$ 0.03
2017	$ 6.31	$ 0.09	2005	$ 4.17	$ 0.03
2016	$ 5.77	$ 0.09	2004	$ 3.90	$ 0.12
2015	$ 4.55	$ 0.09	2003	$ 4.00	$ 0.12
2014	$ 4.89	$ 0.09	2002	$ 4.71	$ 0.12
2013	$ 6.17	$ 0.09	2001	$ 4.00	$ 0.10
2012	$ 6.18	$ 0.09	2000	$ 6.40	$ 0.20
2011	$ 5.18	$ 0.09	1999	$ 6.95	$ 0.19

NOTES: : RSI holds all of the common shares of Lantic Inc (Lantic) which operates as a refiner, processor, distributor, and marketer of sugar products in Canada.

ROYAL BANK OF CANADA

(RY)

Updated July 2023

IDM STOCK SCORING CALCULATION

(1) Stock Price $ 125.52   Score 10
(2) Price 4 Years Ago $ 108.73 Score 10
(3) Current to Four Year Price   Score 9
(4) Book Value $ 78.14   Score 9
(5) Price to Book Comparison   Score 0
(6) Analyst Buys # 5   Score 4

(7) Analysts Strong Buys # 0   Score 0
(8) Dividend Yield % 4.30   Score 6
(9) Operating Margin % 35.97   Score 6
(10) Trading Volume 4,305,251 Score 5
(11) Price to Earnings 12.4   Score 9

Total of All 11 Scores = 68

This stock's total score in 2021 was **73**, in 2020 it was **76**, in 2019 it was **76**.

HISTORICAL STOCK PRICES & DIVIDEND PAYOUTS

Year	Stock	Dividend	Year	Stock	Dividend
2022	$ 123.04	$ 1.28	2010	$ 54.37	$ 0.50
2021	$ 127.90	$ 1.08	2009	$ 56.40	$ 0.50
2020	$ 96.91	$ 1.08	2008	$ 46.25	$ 0.50
2019	$ 99.58	$ 1.02	2007	$ 53.32	$ 0.46
2018	$ 94.56	$ 0.94	2006	$ 48.44	$ 0.36
2017	$ 101.23	$ 0.87	2005	$ 40.30	$ 0.30
2016	$ 79.60	$ 0.81	2004	$ 30.12	$ 0.26
2015	$ 73.70	$ 0.77	2003	$ 32.50	$ 0.21
2014	$ 78.34	$ 0.71	2002	$ 24.86	$ 0.19
2013	$ 66.56	$ 0.63	2001	$ 24.32	$ 0.18
2012	$ 55.17	$ 0.57	2000	$ 23.00	$ 0.05
2011	$ 54.34	$ 0.54	1999	$ 15.50	$ 0.12

NOTES: RY provides personal and commercial banking, wealth management services, insurance, investor services and capital markets products and services on a global basis.

RUSSEL METALS INC

(RUS)

Updated July 2023

IDM STOCK SCORING CALCULATION

(1) Stock Price $ 36.13   Score 8   *(7)* Analysts Strong Buys # 0 Score 0
(2) Price 4 Years Ago $ 22.16 Score 7   *(8)* Dividend Yield % 4.43   Score 6
(3) Current to Four Year Price Score 9   *(9)* Operating Margin % 9.67 Score 3
(4) Book Value $ 25.10   Score 7   *(10)* Trading Volume 135,291 Score 4
(5) Price to Book Comparison Score 1   *(11)* Price to Earnings 6.5x   Score 9
(6) Analyst Buys # 1   Score 2

Total of All 11 Scores = 56

This stock's total score in 2021 was **55**, in 2020 it was **49**, in 2019 it was **49**.

HISTORICAL STOCK PRICES & DIVIDEND PAYOUTS

Year	Stock	Dividend	Year	Stock	Dividend
2022	$ 32.90	$ 0.38	2010	$ 19.75	$ 0.25
2021	$ 34.61	$ 0.38	2009	$ 14.4	$ 0.25
2020	$ 14.84	$ 0.38	2008	$ 30.80	$ 0.45
2019	$ 21.24	$ 0.38	2007	$ 33.61	$ 0.45
2018	$ 29.28	$ 0.38	2006	$ 25.49	$ 0.35
2017	$ 24.00	$ 0.38	2005	$ 15.67	$ 0.20
2016	$ 22.99	$ 0.38	2004	$ 9.70	$ 0.10
2015	$ 24.49	$ 0.38	2003	$ 5.49	$ 0.07
2014	$ 32.99	$ 0.35	2002	$ 4.75	$ 0.05
2013	$ 25.40	$ 0.35	2001	$ 3.45	$ 0.05
2012	$ 26.26	$ 0.35	2000	$ 4.10	$ 0.05
2011	$ 24.56	$ 0.28	1999	$ 4.00	$ NA

NOTES: RUS. is a metals distribution and processing company that distributes steel products. It operates through three segments: metals service centers, energy products and steel distributors.

SAGICOR FINANCIAL COMPANY LIMITED

(SFC)

Updated July 2023

IDM STOCK SCORING CALCULATION

(1) Stock Price $ 4.40   Score 3
(2) Price 4 Years Ago $ 8.40   Score 4
(3) Current to Four Year Price Score 2
(4) Book Value $ 4.00   Score 3
(5) Price to Book Comparison Score 1
(6) Analyst Buys # 1   Score 2

(7) Analysts Strong Buys #1 Score 3
(8) Dividend Yield % 6.91   Score 8
(9) Operating Margin % -9.26 Score 0
(10) Trading Volume 700   Score 0
(11) Price to Earnings 6.4x   Score 9

Total of All 11 Scores = 35

This stock's total score in 2021 was **36**, in 2020 it was **33**, in 2019 it was **NA**.

HISTORICAL STOCK PRICES & DIVIDEND PAYOUTS

Year	Stock	Dividend	Year	Stock	Dividend
2022	$ 6.25	$ NA	2010	$ NA	$ NA
2021	$ 6.07	$ NA	2009	$ NA	$ NA
2020	$ 6.70	$ NA	2008	$ NA	$ NA
2019	$ 8.40	$ NA	2007	$ NA	$ NA
2018	$ 9.73	$ NA	2006	$ NA	$ NA
2017	$ 9.75	$ NA	2005	$ NA	$ NA
2016	$ NA	$ NA	2004	$ NA	$ NA
2015	$ NA	$ NA	2003	$ NA	$ NA
2014	$ NA	$ NA	2002	$ NA	$ NA
2013	$ NA	$ NA	2001	$ NA	$ NA
2012	$ NA	$ NA	2000	$ NA	$ NA
2011	$ NA	$ NA	1999	$ NA	$ NA

NOTES: SFC is a Canada-based financial services providing life insurance products in the United States.

SAILFISH ROYALTY CORP

(FISH)

Updated July 2023

IDM STOCK SCORING CALCULATION

(1) Stock Price $ 0.81   Score 1   *(7)* Analysts Strong Buys # 0 Score 0
(2) Price 4 Years Ago $ 1.30   Score 2   *(8)* Dividend Yield % 8.18   Score 10
(3) Current to Four Year Price Score 1   *(9)* Operating Margin % -77.10 Score 0
(4) Book Value $ 0.77   Score 1   *(10)* Trading Volume 6,105   Score 0
(5) Price to Book Comparison Score 10   *(11)* Price to Earnings -21.7x   Score 0
(6) Analyst Buys # 0   Score 0

Total of All 11 Scores = 25

This stock's total score in 2021 was **NA**, in 2020 it was **NA**, in 2019 it was **NA**.

HISTORICAL STOCK PRICES & DIVIDEND PAYOUTS

Year	Stock	Dividend	Year	Stock	Dividend
2022	$ 1.21	$ NA	2010	$ NA	$ NA
2021	$ 1.34	$ NA	2009	$ NA	$ NA
2020	$ 1.12	$ NA	2008	$ NA	$ NA
2019	$ 1.30	$ NA	2007	$ NA	$ NA
2018	$ 1.35	$ NA	2006	$ NA	$ NA
2017	$ NA	$ NA	2005	$ NA	$ NA
2016	$ NA	$ NA	2003	$ NA	$ NA
2014	$ NA	$ NA	2002	$ NA	$ NA
2013	$ NA	$ NA	2001	$ NA	$ NA
2012	$ NA	$ NA	2000	$ NA	$ NA
2011	$.NA	$ NA	1999	$ NA	$ NA

NOTES: FISH is a precious metals royalty and streaming company with assets in the Americas.

SECURE ENERGY SERVICES INC

(SES)

Updated July 2023

IDM STOCK SCORING CALCULATION

(1) Stock Price $ 6.49   *Score 4*
(2) Price 4 Years Ago $ 7.20   *Score 4*
(3) Current to Four Year Price Score 4
(4) Book Value $ 4.09   *Score 3*
(5) Price to Book Comparison Score 0
(6) Analyst Buys # 3   *Score 3*

(7) Analysts Strong Buys # 0 Score 0
(8) Dividend Yield % 6.16   *Score 8*
(9) Operating Margin % 4.3 Score 1
(10) Trading Volume 295,851 Score 5
(11) Price to Earnings 10.1x   Score 9

Total of All 11 Scores = 42

This stock's total score in 2021 was **NA**, in 2020 it was **NA**, in 2019 it was **NA**.

HISTORICAL STOCK PRICES & DIVIDEND PAYOUTS

Year	Stock	Dividend	Year	Stock	Dividend
2022	$ 5.89	$ 0.01	2010	$ 3.50	$ NA
2021	$ 4.22	$ 0.01	2009	$ NA	$ NA
2020	$ 1.66	$ NA	2008	$ NA	$ NA
2019	$ 6.57	$ 0.02	2007	$ NA	$ NA
2018	$ 7.85	$ 0.02	2006	$ NA	$ NA
2017	$ 8.56	$ 0.02	2005	$ NA	$ NA
2016	$ 8.47	$ 0.02	2004	$ NA	$ NA
2015	$ 10.49	$ 0.02	2003	$ NA	$ NA
2014	$ 26.63	$ 0.02	2002	$ NA	$ NA
2013	$ 14.77	$ 0.01	2001	$ NA	$ NA
2012	$ 7.86	$ NA	2000	$ NA	$ NA
2011	$ 9.87	$ NA	1999	$ NA	$ NA

NOTES: SES is a Canada based environmental and infrastructure company.

SIENNA SENIOR LIVING INC

(SIA)

Updated July 2023

IDM STOCK SCORING CALCULATION

(1) Stock Price $ 11.20   Score 5
(2) Price 4 Years Ago $ 19.45 Score 6
(3) Current to Four Year Price Score 2
(4) Book Value $ 5.96   Score 4
(5) Price to Book Comparison Score 0
(6) Analyst Buys # 1   Score 2

(7) Analysts Strong Buys # 0 Score 0
(8) Dividend Yield % 8.36   Score 10
(9) Operating Margin % 1.73   Score 1
(10) Trading Volume 146,284 Score 4
(11) Price to Earnings -52.0x   Score 2

Total of All 11 Scores = 36

This stock's total score in 2021 was **34** , in 2020 it was **30**, in 2019 it was **47**.

HISTORICAL STOCK PRICES & DIVIDEND PAYOUTS

Year	Stock	Dividend	Year	Stock	Dividend
2022	$ 13.81	$ 0.08	2010	$ 9.33	$ 0.07
2021	$ 15.99	$ 0.08	2009	$ 13.56	$ NA
2020	$ 9.08	$ 0.08	2008	$ 17.49	$ NA
2019	$ 19.45	$ 0.08	2007	$ 14.30	$ NA
2018	$ 16.69	$ 0.07	2006	$ NA	$ NA
2017	$ 17.71	$ 0.07	2005	$ NA	$ NA
2016	$ 17.14	$ 0.07	2004	$ NA	$ NA
2015	$ 15.28	$ 0.07	2003	$ NA	$ NA
2014	$ 12.91	$ 0.07	2002	$ NA	$ NA
2013	$ 12.79	$ 0.07	2001	$ NA	$ NA
2012	$ 11.77	$ 0.07	2000	$ NA	$ NA
2011	$ 10.55	$ 0.07	1999	$ NA	$ NA

NOTES: SIA is a Canada-based seniors' living providers.

SLATE GROCERY REAL ESTATE INVESTMENT TRUST

(SGR.UN)

Updated July 2023

IDM STOCK SCORING CALCULATION

(1) Stock Price $ 13.15   Score 5   *(7)* Analysts Strong Buys # 0   Score 0
(2) Price 4 Years Ago $ 12.72   Score 5   *(8)* Dividend Yield % 8.71   Score 10
(3) Current to Four Year Price Score 7   *(9)* Operating Margin % 0   Score 0
(4) Book Value $ 0   Score 1   *(10)* Trading Volume 32,468   Score 2
(5) Price to Book Comparison   Score 0   *(11)* Price to Earnings 0.0x   Score 0
(6) Analyst Buys # 0   Score 0

Total of All 11 Scores = 30

This stock's total score in 2021 was **36.**, in 2020 it was **NA**, in 2019 it was NA.

HISTORICAL STOCK PRICES & DIVIDEND PAYOUTS

Year	Stock	Dividend	Year	Stock	Dividend
2022	$ 14.04	$ NA	2010	$ NA	$ NA
2021	$ 13.28	$ NA	2009	$ NA	$ NA
2020	$ 9.21	$ NA	2008	$ NA	$ NA
2019	$ 12.72	$ NA	2007	$ NA	$ NA
2018	$ 12.78	$ NA	2006	$ NA	$ NA
2017	$ 13.53	$ NA	2005	$ NA	$ NA
2016	$ 13.61	$ NA	2004	$ NA	$ NA
2015	$ 14.12	$ NA	2003	$ NA	$ NA
2014	$ 12.70	$ NA	2002	$ NA	$ NA
2013	$ NA	$NA	2001	$ NA	$ NA
2012	$ NA	$ NA	2000	$ NA	$ NA
2011	$ NA	$ NA	1999	$ NA	$ NA

NOTES: SGR.UN is a Canada-based real estate investment trust that owns and operates United States grocery-anchored real estate.

SLATE OFFICE REAL ESTATE INVESTMENT TRUST

(SOT.UN)

Updated July 2023

IDM STOCK SCORING CALCULATION

(1) Stock Price $ 1.97   Score 2
(2) Price 4 Years Ago $ 5.86   Score 4
(3) Current to Four Year Price   Score 1
(4) Book Value $ 8.05   Score 4
(5) Price to Book Comparison Score 10
(6) Analyst Buys # 0   Score 0

(7) Analysts Strong Buys # 0   Score 0
(8) Dividend Yield % 6.09   Score 8
(9) Operating Margin % 36.63 Score 6
(10) Trading Volume 3,571   Score 0
(11) Price to Earnings -3.06x Score 0

Total of All 11 Scores = 35

This stock's total score in 2021 was **51**, in 2020 it was **49** in 2019 it was **57**.

HISTORICAL STOCK PRICES & DIVIDEND PAYOUTS

Year	Stock	Dividend	Year	Stock	Dividend
2022	$ 4.96	$ 0.03	2010	$ NA	$ NA
2021	$ 5.34	$ 0.03	2009	$ NA	$ NA
2020	$ 3.67	$ 0.03	2008	$ NA	$ NA
2019	$ 6.01	$ 0.03	2007	$ NA	$ NA
2018	$ 7.56	$ 0.03	2006	$ NA	$ NA
2017	$ 7.96	$ 0.06	2005	$ NA	$ NA
2016	$ 8.12	$ 0.06	2004	$ NA	$ NA
2015	$ 6.77	$ 0.06	2003	$ NA	$ NA
2014	$ 8.82	$ 0.06	2002	$ NA	$ NA
2013	$ 9.55	$ 0.06	2001	$ NA	$ NA
2012	$ NA	$ NA	2000	$ NA	$ NA

NOTES: SOT.UN is a Canada-based open-ended investment trust focused on acquiring, owning, and leasing a portfolio of diversified revenue-producing commercial real estate properties in Canada with an emphasis on office properties.

SMART CENTRES REAL ESTATE INVESTMENT TRUST

(SRU.UN)

Updated July 2023

IDM STOCK SCORING CALCULATION

(1) Stock Price $ 23.71   *Score* 7
(2) Price 4 Years Ago $ 33.50   *Score* 8
(3) Current to Four Year Price *Score* 2
(4) Book Value $ 30.11   *Score* 8
(5) Price to Book Comparison *Score* 8
(6) Analyst Buys # 1   *Score* 2

(7) Analysts Strong Buys # 0 *Score* 0
(8) Dividend Yield % 7.80   *Score* 10
(9) Operating Margin % 46.60 *Score* 6
(10) Trading Volume 7,042   *Score* 0
(11) Price to Earnings 13.9x *Score* 9

Total of All 11 Scores = 60

This stock's total score in 2021 was **49**, in 2020 it was **67**, in 2019 it was **59**.

HISTORICAL STOCK PRICES & DIVIDEND PAYOUTS

Year	Stock	Dividend	Year	Stock	Dividend
2022	$ 27.36	$ 0.15	2010	$ 21.64	$ 0.13
2021	$ 29.22	$ 0.15	2009	$ 15.03	$ 0.13
2020	$ 21.13	$ 0.15	2008	$ 20.75	$ 0.13
2019	$ 32.23	$ 0.15	2007	$ 26.12	$ 0.13
2018	$ 30.53	$ 0.15	2006	$ 24.30	$ 0.12
2017	$ 31.75	$ 0.14	2005	$ 23.00	$ 0.11
2016	$ 38.20	$ 0.14	2004	$ 14.69	$ 0.10
2015	$ 29.41	$ 0.13	2003	$ 9.95	$ 0.10
2014	$ 26.34	$ 0.13	2002	$ 3.93	$ NA
2013	$ 24.99	$ 0.13	2001	$ NA	$ NA
2012	$ 29.90	$ 0.13	2000	$ NA	$ NA
2011	$ 24.24	$ 0.13	1999	$ NA	$ NA

NOTES: SRU.UN is a Canada-based real estate investment trust that develops, leases, constructs, owns and manages shopping centers, office buildings, high-rise and low-rise condominium and rental residences, seniors' housing, town house units, and self-storage rental facilities in Canada.

SOURCE ROCK ROYALTIES LIMITED
(SRR)
Updated July 2023

IDM STOCK SCORING CALCULATION

(1) Stock Price $ 0.78 — Score 1   *(7)* Analysts Strong Buys # 0 Score 0
(2) Price 4 Years Ago $ 0 — Score 1   *(8)* Dividend Yield % 8.46 — Score 10
(3) Current to Four Year Price — Score 0   *(9)* Operating Margin % 41.31 Score 6
(4) Book Value $ 0.61 — Score 1   *(10)* Trading Volume 38,000 — Score 2
(5) Price to Book Comparison — Score 1   *(11)* Price to Earnings 16.8x — Score 8
(6) Analyst Buys # 0 — Score 0

Total of All 11 Scores =30

This stock's total score in 2021 was **NA**, in 2020 it was **NA**, in 2019 it was **NA**.

HISTORICAL STOCK PRICES & DIVIDEND PAYOUTS

Year	Stock	Dividend	Year	Stock	Dividend
2022	$ 0.77	$ 0.01	2010	$ NA	$ NA
2021	$ NA	$ NA	2009	$ NA	$ NA
2020	$ NA	$ NA	2008	$ NA	$ NA
2019	$ NA	$ NA	2007	$ NA	$ NA
2018	$ NA	$ NA	2006	$ NA	$ NA
2017	$ NA	$ NA	2005	$ NA	$ NA
2016	$ NA	$ NA	2004	$ NA	$ NA
2015	$ NA	$ NA	2003	$ NA	$ NA
2014	$ NA	$ NA	2002	$ NA	$ NA
2013	$ NA	$ NA	2001	$ NA	$ NA
2012	$ NA	$ NA	2000	$ NA	$ NA
2011	$ NA	$ NA	1999	$ NA	$ NA

NOTES: SSR is a Canada-based pure-play oil and gas royalty company whose primary business is to receive royalty revenue from oil and natural gas properties.

SSC SECURITY SERVICES CORP
(SECU)
Updated July 2023

IDM STOCK SCORING CALCULATION

(1) Stock Price $ 2.79   Score 3
(2) Price 4 Years Ago $ 3.45   Score 3
(3) Current to Four Year Price Score 2
(4) Book Value $ 3.60   Score 3
(5) Price to Book Comparison Score 8
(6) Analyst Buys # 0   Score 0

(7) Analysts Strong Buys # 0   Score 0
(8) Dividend Yield % 4.30   Score 6
(9) Operating Margin % 0.09   Score 0
(10) Trading Volume 1,234   Score 0
(11) Price to Earnings 2834.6x Score 1

Total of All 11 Scores =26

This stock's total score in 2021 was **NA,** in 2020 it was **NA**, in 2019 it was **NA**.

HISTORICAL STOCK PRICES & DIVIDEND PAYOUTS

Year	Stock	Dividend	Year	Stock	Dividend
2022	$ 2.60	$ 0.03	2010	$ NA	$ NA
2021	$ 2.52	$ 0.03	2009	$ NA	$ NA
2020	$ 2.40	$ 0.03	2008	$NA	$ NA
2019	$ 2.37	$ 0.03	2007	$NA	$ NA
2018	$3.00	$ 0.03	2006	$ NA	$ NA
2017	$6.18	$ NA	2005	$ NA	$ NA
2016	$7.47	$ NA	2004	$ NA	$ NA
2015	$7.08	$ NA	2003	$ NA	$ NA
2014	$7.92	$ NA	2002	$ NA	$ NA
2013	$5.79	$ NA	2001	$ NA	$ NA
2012	$4.80	$ NA	2000	$ NA	$ NA
2011	$ NA	$ NA	1999	$ NA	$ NA

NOTES: SECU. is a Canada company. Through its subsidiary, Security Resource Group Inc. (SRG), provides cyber security and physical security services to commercial, industrial, and public sector clients.

STINGRAY GROUP INC

(RAY.B)

Updated July 2023

IDM STOCK SCORING CALCULATION

(1) Stock Price $ 5.36   Score 4
(2) Price 4 Years Ago $ 6.49   Score 4
(3) Current to Four Year Price Score 2
(4) Book Value $ 4.13   Score 3
(5) Price to Book Comparison Score 1
(6) Analyst Buys # 0   Score 0

(7) Analysts Strong Buys # 0 Score 0
(8) Dividend Yield % 5.60   Score 8
(9) Operating Margin % 20.34 Score 5
(10) Trading Volume 0   Score 0
(11) Price to Earnings 0.0x   Score 0

Total of All 11 Scores = 27

This stock's total score in 2021 was **27**, in 2020 it was **32**, in 2019 it was **19**.

HISTORICAL STOCK PRICES & DIVIDEND PAYOUTS

Year	Stock	Dividend	Year	Stock	Dividend
2022	$ 6.40	$ 0.07	2010	$ NA	$ NA
2021	$ 7.26	$ 0.07	2009	$ NA	$ NA
2020	$ 5.35	$ 0.07	2008	$ NA	$ NA
2019	$ 6.70	$ 0.07	2007	$ NA	$ NA
2018	$ 8.85	$ 0.06	2006	$ NA	$ NA
2017	$ 7.73	$ 0.04	2005	$ NA	$ NA
2016	$ 7.00	$ 0.04	2004	$ NA	$ NA
2015	$ 6.78	$ 0.03	2003	$ NA	$ NA
2014	$ NA	$ NA	2002	$ NA	$ NA
2013	$ NA	$ NA	2001	$ NA	$ NA
2012	$ NA	$ NA	2000	$ NA	$ NA
2011	$ NA	$ NA	1999	$ NA	$ NA

NOTES: RAY.B. is a business-to-business (B2B) music, media and technology company via audio television channels, radio stations, subscription video-on-demand (SVOD) content, karaoke products, digital signage, in-store music, and music applications.

SUNCOR ENERGY INC

(SU)

Updated July 2023

IDM STOCK SCORING CALCULATION

(1) Stock Price $ 39.09   Score 8

(2) Price 4 Years Ago $ 40.69 Score 8

(3) Current to Four Year Price Score 5

(4) Book Value $ 29.43   Score 7

(5) Price to Book Comparison Score 1

(6) Analyst Buys #2   Score 3

(7) Analysts Strong Buys # 4   Score 4

(8) Dividend Yield % 5.33   Score 8

(9) Operating Margin % 21.60 Score 5

(10) Trading Volume 222,618 Score 4

(11) Price to Earnings6.5x   Score 9

Total of All 11 Scores = 62

This stock's total score in 2021 was **NA**, in 2020 it was **NA**, in 2019 it was **NA**.

HISTORICAL STOCK PRICES & DIVIDEND PAYOUTS

Year	Stock	Dividend	Year	Stock	Dividend
2022	$ 44.552	$ 0.47	2010	$ 34.40	$ 0.10
2021	$ 29.10	$ 0.21	2009	$ 39.05	$ 0.05
2020	$ 23.67	$ 0.21	2008	$ 65.53	$ 0.05
2019	$ 41.59	$ 0.42	2007	$ 47.86	$ 0.05
2018	$ 53.94	$ 0.36	2006	$ 45.17	$ 0.04
2017	$ 43.30	$ 0.32	2005	$ 23.06	$ 0.03
2016	$ 34.07	$ 0.29	2004	$ 17.13	$ 0.03
2015	$ 34.37	$ 0.28	2003	$ 12.44	$ 0.03
2014	$ 41.37	$ 0.23	2002	$ 13.30	$ 0.02
2013	$ 32.04	$ 0.20	2001	$ 9.65	$ 0.02
2012	$ 28.26	$ 0.13	2000	$ 8.87	$ 0.02
2011	$ 37.01	$ 0.11	1999	$ 7.00	$ 0.02

NOTES: SU. is a Canada-based integrated energy company. Segments include Oil Sands, Exploration and Production (E&P), and Refining and Marketing.

SUN LIFE FINANCIAL INC

(SLF)

Updated July 2023

IDM STOCK SCORING CALCULATION

(1) Stock Price $ 67.40   Score 9

(2) Price 4 Years Ago $ 54.57   Score 9

(3) Current to Four Year Price   Score 9

(4) Book Value $ 38.88   Score 8

(5) Price to Book Comparison   Score 0

(6) Analyst Buys # 3   Score 3

(7) Analysts Strong Buys # 0   Score 0

(8) Dividend Yield % 4.45   Score 6

(9) Operating Margin % 34.16   Score 6

(10) Trading Volume 84,096   Score 3

(11) Price to Earnings 13.6x   Score 9

Total of All 11 Scores = 62

This stock's total score in 2021 was **65**, in 2020 it was **64**, in 2019 it was **68**.

HISTORICAL STOCK PRICES & DIVIDEND PAYOUTS

Year	Stock	Dividend	Year	Stock	Dividend
2022	$ 63.68	$ 0.69	2010	$ 29.96	$ 0.36
2021	$ 64.96	$ 0.55	2009	$ 29.50	$ 0.36
2020	$ 48.30	$ 0.55	2008	$ 38.73	$ 0.36
2019	$ 54.14	$ 0.52	2007	$ 51.23	$ 0.34
2018	$ 54.95	$ 0.47	2006	$ 42.27	$ 0.30
2017	$ 44.81	$ 0.43	2005	$ 52.75	$ 0.23
2016	$ 43.41	$ 0.40	2004	$ 37.19	$ 0.22
2015	$ 38.99	$ 0.38	2003	$ 29.70	$ 0.17
2014	$ 37.53	$ 0.36	2002	$ 29.15	$ 0.14
2013	$ 30.19	$ 0.36	2001	$ 38.43	$ 0.12
2012	$ 22.69	$ 0.36	2000	$ 33.94	$ 0.12
2011	$ 28.04	$ 0.36	1999	$ NA	$ NA

NOTES: SLF is the holding company of Sun Life Assurance Company of Canada, an international financial services organization providing insurance, wealth, and asset management solutions to individual and corporate clients.

SUPERIOR PLUS CORPORATION

(SPB)

Updated July 2023

IDM STOCK SCORING CALCULATION

(1) Stock Price $ 9.35   Score 4

(2) Price 4 Years Ago $ 13.27 Score 5

(3) Current to Four Year Price Score 2

(4) Book Value $ 6.32   Score 4

(5) Price to Book Comparison Score 1

(6) Analyst Buys # 3   Score 3

(7) Analysts Strong Buys # 2 Score 4

(8) Dividend Yield % 7.70 10   Score 10

(9) Operating Margin % -2.98   Score 0

(10) Trading Volume 53,490   Score 3

(11) Price to Earnings -15.1x   Score 0

Total of All 11 Scores = 36

This stock's total score in 2021 was **50**, in 2020 it was **37**, in 2019 it was **49**.

HISTORICAL STOCK PRICES & DIVIDEND PAYOUTS

Year	Stock	Dividend	Year	Stock	Dividend
2022	$ 11.57	$ 0.06	2010	$ 13.54	$ 0.14
2021	$ 15.56	$ 0.06	2009	$ 10.79	$ 0.14
2020	$ 11.24	$ 0.06	2008	$ 12.60	$ 0.14
2019	$ 13.64	$ 0.06	2007	$ 15.10	$ 0.13
2018	$ 12.59	$ 0.06	2006	$ 11.00	$ 0.13
2017	$ 11.41	$ 0.06	2005	$ 32.20	$ 0.20
2016	$ 11.40	$ 0.06	2004	$ 25.60	$ 0.18
2015	$ 11.29	$ 0.06	2003	$ 21.64	$ 0.17
2014	$ 13.88	$ 0.05	2002	$ 19.52	$ 0.43
2013	$ 12.31	$ 0.05	2001	$ 16.00	$ 0.33
2012	$ 7.48	$ 0.05	2000	$ 12.65	$ 0.33
2011	$ 11.21	$ 0.10	1999	$ 15.70	$ 0.25

NOTES: SPB is a Canada-based corporation. The Company operates provides distribution, wholesale procurement, and related services in relation to propane, heating oil and other refined fuels.

SURGE ENERGY INC

(SGY)

Updated July 2023

IDM STOCK SCORING CALCULATION

(1) Stock Price $ 7.99   Score 4
(2) Price 4 Years Ago $ 9.09   Score 4
(3) Current to Four Year Price Score 2
(4) Book Value $ 8.69   Score 4..
(5) Price to Book Comparison Score 6
(6) Analyst Buys # 3   Score 3

(7) Analysts Strong Buys # 0 Score 0
(8) Dividend Yield % 6.01   Score 8
(9) Operating Margin % 32.62 Score 6
(10) Trading Volume 278,666   Score 5
(11) Price to Earnings 2.6   Score 10

Total of All 11 Scores = 52

This stock's total score in 2021 was ,**NA** in 2020 it was **NA**, in 2019 it was **NA**.

HISTORICAL STOCK PRICES & DIVIDEND PAYOUTS

Year	Stock	Dividend	Year	Stock	Dividend
2022	$ 9.69	$ 0.04	2010	$ 43.77	$ NA
2021	$ 4.59	$ NA	2009	$ 18.70	$ NA
2020	$ 2.72	$ NA	2008	$ 32.30	$ NA
2019	$ 9.09	$ 0.07	2007	$ 31.87	$ NA
2018	$ 20.82	$ 0.07	2006	$ 60.35	$ NA
2017	$ 17.59	$ 0.07	2005	$ 53.12	$ NA
2016	$ 20.14	$ 0.05	2004	$ 45.47	$ NA
2015	$ 19.46	$ 0.21	2003	$ 23.37	$ NA
2014	$ 72.93	$ 0.42	2002	$ 8.71	$ NA
2013	$ 52.02	$ 0.30	2001	$ 15.72	$ NA
2012	$ 62.22	$ NA	2000	$ 4.88	$ NA
2011	$ 82.02	$ NA	1999	$ 1.91	$ NA

NOTES: SGY is an oil and gas exploration and production company.

SUSTAINABLE POWER & INFASTRUCTURE SPLIT CORP (PWI)

Updated July 2023

IDM STOCK SCORING CALCULATION

(1) Stock Price $ 6.50   Score 4
(2) Price 4 Years Ago $ 0   Score 1
(3) Current to Four Year Price Score 0
(4) Book Value $ 16.28   Score 6
(5) Price to Book Comparison Score 10
(6) Analyst Buys # 0   Score 0

(7) Analysts Strong Buys # 0   Score 0
(8) Dividend Yield % 12.31   Score 2
(9) Operating Margin % 0   Score 0
(10) Trading Volume 190   Score 0
(11) Price to Earnings -2.0x   Score 0

Total of All 11 Scores = 23

This stock's total score in 2021 was **NA**, in 2020 it was **NA**, in 2019 it was **NA**.

HISTORICAL STOCK PRICES & DIVIDEND PAYOUTS

Year	Stock	Dividend	Year	Stock	Dividend
2022	$ 8.84	$ 0.07	2010	$ NA	$ NA
2021	$ 9.95	$ 0.07	2009	$ NA	$ NA
2020	$ NA	$ NA	2008	$ NA	$ NA
2019	$ NA	$ NA	2007	$ NA	$ NA
2018	$ NA	$ NA	2006	$ NA	$ NA
2017	$ NNA	$ NA	2005	$ NA	$ NA
2016	$ NA	$ NA	2004	$ NA	$ NA
2015	$NA	$ NA	2003	$ NA	$ NA
2014	$ NA	$ NA	2002	$ NA	$ NA
2013	$ NA	$ NA	2001	$ NA	$ NA
2012	$ NA	$ NA	2000	$ NA	$ NA
2011	$ NA	$ NA	1999	$ NA	$ NA

NOTES: PWI is a Canada-based mutual fund consisting primarily of dividend-paying securities of power and infrastructure companies, facilitating the multi-decade transition toward decarbonization and environmental sustainability.

TC ENERGY CORPORATION
(TRP)
Updated July 2023

IDM STOCK SCORING CALCULATION

(1) Stock Price $ 51.67   Score 9   *(7)* Analysts Strong Buys # 1   Score 3

(2) Price 4 Years Ago $ 65.66   Score 9   *(8)* Dividend Yield % 7.20   Score 8

(3) Current to Four Year Price   Score 2   *(9)* Operating Margin % 22.61   Score 5

(4) Book Value $ 33.39   Score 8   *(10)* Trading Volume 5,819,053 Score 10

(5) Price to Book Comparison   Score 0   *(11)* Price to Earnings 32.2x   Score 5

(6) Analyst Buys # 2   Score 3

Total of All 11 Scores = 62

This stock's total score in 2021 was **63,** in 2020 it was **72**, in 2019 it was **NA**.

HISTORICAL STOCK PRICES & DIVIDEND PAYOUTS

Year	Stock	Dividend	Year	Stock	Dividend
2022	$ 66.37	$ 0.90	2010	$ 36.71	$ 0.40
2021	$ 61.64	$ 0.87	2009	$ 31.14	$ 0.38
2020	$ 56.83	$ 0.81	2008	$ 40.00	$ 0.36
2019	$ 66.00	$ 0.75	2007	$ 37.41	$ 0.34
2018	$ 56.88	$ 0.69	2006	$ 32.13	$ 0.32
2017	$ 62.11	$ 0.63	2005	$ 32.59	$ 0.30
2016	$ 61.19	$ 0.56	2004	$ 25.55	$ 0.29
2015	$ 49.96	$ 0.52	2003	$ 24.85	$ 0.27
2014	$ 50.89	$ 0.48	2002	$ 22.90	$ 0.25
2013	$ 47.14	$ 0.46	2001	$ 18.99	$ 0.23
2012	$ 42.50	$ 0.44	2000	$ 11.30	$ 0.20
2011	$ 40.43	$ 0.42	1999	$ 20.25	$ 0.28

NOTES: TRP is an energy infrastructure company engaged in natural gas and liquids pipelines, power generation and natural gas. storage facilities.

TDB SPLIT CORP

(XTD)

Updated July 2023

IDM STOCK SCORING CALCULATION

(1) *Stock Price $ 4.03*   *Score 3*

(2) *Price 4 Years Ago $ 6.35*   *Score 4*

(3) *Current to Four Year Price*   *Score 2*

(4) *Book Value $ 0*   *Score 1*

(5) *Price to Book Comparison*   *Score 0*

(6) *Analyst Buys # 0*   *Score 0*

(7) *Analysts Strong Buys # 0* *Score 0*

(8) *Dividend Yield % 14.89*   *Score 2*

(9) *Operating Margin % 0*   *Score 0*

(10) *Trading Volume 6,192*   *Score 0*

(11) *Price to Earnings 0.0x*   *Score 0*

Total of All 11 Scores = 12

This stock's total score in 2021 was **13**, in 2020 it was **NA**, in 2019 it was **NA**.

HISTORICAL STOCK PRICES & DIVIDEND PAYOUTS

Year	Stock	Dividend	Year	Stock	Dividend
2022	$ 4.87	$ 0.05	2010	$ 4.00	$ 0.05
2021	$ 5.03	$ 0.05	2009	$ 4.58	$ 0.05
2020	$ 2.34	$ NA	2008	$ 8.41	$ 0.05
2019	$ 6.48	$ 0.05	2007	$ 9.75	$ 0.05
2018	$ 6.77	$ 0.05	2006	$ NA	$ NA
2017	$ 6.39	$ 0.05	2005	$ NA	$ NA
2016	$ 5.02	$ 0.05	2004	$ NA	$ NA
2015	$ 4.82	$ 0.05	2003	$ NA	$ NA
2014	$ 5.95	$ 0.05	2002	$ NA	$ NA
2013	$ 3.20	$ 0.05	2001	$ NA	$ NA
2012	$ 4.05	$ 0.05	2000	$ NA	$ NA
2011	$ 4.85	$ 0.05	1999	$ NA	$ NAT

Notes: XTD is a mutual fund Company that invests primarily in common shares of the Toronto-Dominion Bank.

TELUS CORPORATION

(T)

Updated July 2023

IDM STOCK SCORING CALCULATION

(1) Stock Price $ 24.32   Score *7*
(2) Price 4 Years Ago $ 24.13 Score *7*
(3) Current to Four Year Price Score *6*
(4) Book Value $ 11.58   Score *5*
(5) Price to Book Comparison Score *0*
(6) Analyst Buys # 8   Score *5*

(7) Analysts Strong Buys # 0 Score *0*
(8) Dividend Yield % 5.98   Score *8*
(9) Operating Margin % 14.90 Score *4*
(10) Trading Volume 6,432,809 Score *10*
(11) Price to Earnings 23.7x   Score *7*

Total of All 11 Scores = 59

This stock's total score in 2021 was **60**, in 2020 it was **57,** in 2019 it was **68**.

HISTORICAL STOCK PRICES & DIVIDEND PAYOUTS

Year	Stock	Dividend	Year	Stock	Dividend
2022	$ 28.89	$ 0.34	2010	$ 10.11	$ 0.13
2021	$ 27.86	$ 0.32	2009	$ 7.71	$ 0.12
2020	$ 22.61	$ 0.29	2008	$ 11.15	$ 0.11
2019	$ 25.14	$ 0.28	2007	$ 15.92	$ 0.09
2018	$ 22.84	$ 0.26	2006	$ 11.38	$ 0.07
2017	$ 22.97	$ 0.25	2005	$ 10.45	$ 0.05
2016	$ 20.80	$ 0.23	2004	$ 5.50	$ 0.04
2015	$ 21.17	$ 0.21	2003	$ 5.85	$ 0.04
2014	$ 20.82	$ 0.19	2002	$ 2.70	$ 0.04
2013	$ 18.59	$ 0.17	2001	$ 8.18	$ 0.09
2012	$ 14.66	$ 0.15	2000	$ 10.41	$ 0.09
2011	$ 13.16	$ 0.14	1999	$ 7.45	$ 0.09

NOTES: T provides a range of telecommunications products and services. The Company operates through two segments: wireless and wireline.

THE NORTH WEST COMPANY INC

(NWC)

Updated July 2023

IDM STOCK SCORING CALCULATION

(1) Stock Price $ 31.90   Score 8
(2) Price 4 Years Ago $ 29.70 Score 7
(3) Current to Four Year Price Score 7
(4) Book Value $ 13.20   Score 5
(5) Price to Book Comparison Score 0
(6) Analyst Buys # 0   Score 0

(7) Analysts Strong Buys # 0 Score 0
(8) Dividend Yield % 4.76   Score 8
(9) Operating Margin % 7.21   Score 2
(10) Trading Volume 145,908 Score 4
(11) Price to Earnings 13.4x   Score 9

Total of All 11 Scores = 50

This stock's total score in 2021 was **50**, in 2020 it was **45**, in 2019 it was **50**.

HISTORICAL STOCK PRICES & DIVIDEND PAYOUT

Year	Stock	Dividend	Year	Stock	Dividend
2022	$ 33.57	$ 0.37	2010	$ 19.94	$ 0.34
2021	$ 35.83	$ 0.36	2009	$ 15.92	$ 0.32
2020	$ 27.91	$ 0.33	2008	$ 17.04	$ 0.32
2019	$ 30.16	$ 0.33	2007	$ 20.69	$ 0.27
2018	$ 30.29	$ 0.32	2006	$ 14.66	$ 0.18
2017	$ 30.45	$ 0.32	2005	$ 10.58	$ 0.16
2016	$ 30.81	$ 0.31	2004	$ 8.21	$ 0.15
2015	$ 24.94	$ 0.29	2003	$ 8.03	$ 0.13
2014	$ 24.51	$ 0.29	2002	$ 6.16	$ 0.13
2013	$ 23.68	$ 0.28	2001	$ 4.98	$ 0.12
2012	$ 21.80	$ 0.26	2000	$ 3.76	$ 0.10
2011	$ 20.22	$ 0.24	1999	$ 5.13	$ 0.10

NOTES: NWC is a Canada-based retailer of food and everyday products and services to underserved rural communities and urban neighborhood markets in Northern Canada, Western Canada, rural Alaska, the South Pacific islands, and the Caribbean.

THE TORONTO-DOMINION BANK

(TD)

Updated July 2023

IDM STOCK SCORING CALCULATION

(1) Stock Price $ 83.88   Score 9   *(7)* Analysts Strong Buys # 0   Score 0

(2) Price 4 Years Ago $ 77.60 Score 9   *(8)* Dividend Yield % 4.58   Score 8

(3) Current to Four Year Price Score 7   *(9)* Operating Margin % 34.35   Score 6

(4) Book Value $ 61.14   Score 9   *(10)* Trading Volume 5,286,449 Score 10

(5) Price to Book Comparison Score 1   *(11)* Price to Earnings 10.6x   Score 9

(6) Analyst Buys # 7   Score 5

Total of All 11 Scores = 73

This stock's total score in 2021 was **69**, in 2020 it was **72**, in 2019 it was **74**.

HISTORICAL STOCK PRICES & DIVIDEND PAYOUTS

Year	Stock	Dividend	Year	Stock	Dividend
2022	$ 83.18	$ 0.89	2010	$ 35.84	$ 0.30
2021	$ 87.09	$ 0.79	2009	$ 29.10	$ 0.30
2020	$ 61.68	$ 0.79	2008	$ 32.03	$ 0.29
2019	$ 76.52	$ 0.74	2007	$ 36.27	$ 0.27
2018	$ 75.63	$ 0.67	2006	$ 28.50	$ 0.22
2017	$ 65.17	$ 0.60	2005	$ 27.59	$ 0.20
2016	$ 56.65	$ 0.55	2004	$ 21.82	$ 0.17
2015	$ 52.36	$ 0.51	2003	$ 18.97	$ 0.14
2014	$ 55.59	$ 0.47	2002	$ 18.55	$ 0.14
2013	$ 43.68	$ 0.41	2001	$ 20.17	$ 0.14
2012	$ 39.75	$ 0.36	2000	$ 19.45	$ 0.13
2011	$ 38.24	$ 0.33	1999	$ 18.06	$ 0.19

NOTES: TD operates as a bank in North America. The Company's segments include Canadian Retail, U.S. Retail, Wholesale Banking and corporate.

TIDEWATER MIDSTREAM AND INFASTRUCTURE LTD

(TWM)

Updated July 2023

IDM STOCK SCORING CALCULATION

(1) Stock Price $ 0.96   Score   1   *(7)* Analysts Strong Buys # 1   Score 3

(2) Price 4 Years Ago $ 1.40   Score 2   *(8)* Dividend Yield % 4.17   Score 6

(3) Current to Four Year Price   Score 2   *(9)* Operating Margin % 1.00   Score 0

(4) Book Value $ 1.66   Score 2   *(10)* Trading Volume 94,773   Score 3

(5) Price to Book Comparison   Score 8   *(11)* Price to Earnings -7.0   Score 0

(6) Analyst Buys # 2   Score 3

Total of All 11 Scores =30

This stock's total score in 2021 was **35**, in 2020 it was **27**, in 2019 it was **NA**.

HISTORICAL STOCK PRICES & DIVIDEND PAYOUTS

Year	Stock	Dividend	Year	Stock	Dividend
2022	$ 1.28	$ 0.01	2010	$ NA	$ NA
2021	$ 1.43	$ 0.01	2009	$ NA	$ NA
2020	$ 0.82	$ 0.01	2008	$ NA	$ NA
2019	$ 1.40	$ 0.01	2007	$ NA	$ NA
2018	$ 1.24	$ 0.01	2006	$ NA	$ NA
2017	$ 1.30	$ 0.01	2005	$ NA	$ NA
2016	$ 1.24	$ 0.01	2004	$ NA	$ NA
2015	$ 1.39	$ 0.01	2003	$ NA	$ NA
2014	$ NA	$ NA	2002	$ NA	$ NA
2013	$ NA	$ NA	2001	$ NA	$ NA
2012	$ NA	$ NA	2000	$ NA	$ NA
2011	$ NA	$ NAN	1999	$ NA	$ NA

NOTES: TWM is a Canada-based company engaged in the natural gas processing, fractionation, liquids upgrading, storage and transportation, and marketing.

TIER ONE CAPITAL LP

(TLP.UN)

Updated July 2023

IDM STOCK SCORING CALCULATION

(1) Stock Price $ 3.00   Score *3*

(2) Price 4 Years Ago $ 5.05   Score *4*

(3) Current to Four Year Price   Score *2*

(4) Book Value $ 5.15   Score *4*

(5) Price to Book Comparison   Score *8*

(6) Analyst Buys # 0   0   Score *0*

(7) Analysts Strong Buys # 0   Score *0*

(8) Dividend Yield % 16.67   Score *2*

(9) Operating Margin %0   Score.*0*

(10) Trading Volume 0   Score *0*

(11) Price to Earnings -4.7x   Score *0*

Total of All 11 Scores = 23

This stock's total score in 2021 was **NA**, in 2020 it was **NA**, in 2019 it was **NA**.

HISTORICAL STOCK PRICES & DIVIDEND PAYOUTS

Year	Stock	Dividend	Year	Stock	Dividend
2022	$ 3.70	$ 0.13	2010	$ 1.87	$ NA
2021	$ 3.30	$ 0.13	2009	$ 1.75	$ NA
2020	$ 3.90	$ 0.13	2008	$ NA	$ NA
2019	$ 4.74	$ NA	2007	$ NA	$ NA
2018	$ 5.04	$ NA	2006	$ NA	$ NA
2017	$ 5.35	$ 0.13	2005	$ NA	$ NA
2016	$ 6.80	$ 0.13	2004	$ NA	$ NA
2015	$ 6.00	$ 0.13	2003	$ NA	$ NA
2014	$ 6.20	$ NA	2002	$ NA	$ NA
2013	$ 2.35	$ NA	2001	$ NA	$ NA
2012	$ 3.18	$ NA	2000	$ NA	$ NA
2011	$ 2.13	$ NA	1999	$ NA	$ NA

NOTES: TLP.UN is a Canada-based limited partnership focused on providing growing Canadian companies with the working capital needed to execute their growth strategies and acquisition plans. It invests primarily in the debt securities of businesses, which have the potential for long-term growth.

TIMBERCREEK FINANCIAL CORPORATION

(TF)

Updated July 2023

IDM STOCK SCORING CALCULATION

(1) Stock Price $ 7.51   Score 4
(2) Price 4 Years Ago $ 9.60   Score 4
(3) Current to Four Year Price Score 2
(4) Book Value $8.33   Score 4
(5) Price to Book Comparison   Score 6
(6) Analyst Buys #0   Score 0

(7) Analysts Strong Buys # 0   Score 0
(8) Dividend Yield % 9.19   Score 10
(9) Operating Margin % 59.21   Score 8
(10) Trading Volume 10,399   Score 1
(11) Price to Earnings 11.0x   Score 9

Total of All 11 Scores = 48

This stock's total score in 2021 was **50**, in 2020 it was **56**, in 2019 it was **44**.

HISTORICAL STOCK PRICES & DIVIDEND PAYOUTS

Year	Stock	Dividend	Year	Stock	Dividend
2022	$ 8.23	$ 0.06	2010	$ NA	$ NA
2021	$ 9.02	$ 0.06	2009	$ NA	$ NA
2020	$ 8.29	$ 0.06	2008	$ NA	$ NA
2019	$ 9.66	$ 0.06	2007	$ NA	$ NA
2018	$ 9.35	$ 0.06	2006	$ NA	$ NA
2017	$ 9.36	$ 0.06	2005	$ NA	$ NA
2016	$ 8.32	$ 0.06	2004	$ NA	$ NA
2015	$ NA	$ NA	2003	$ NA	$ NA
2014	$ NA	$ NA	2002	$ NA	$ NA
2013	$ NA	$ NA	2001	$ NA	$ NA
2012	$ NA	$ NA	2000	$ NA	$ NA
2011	$ NA	$ NAN	1999	$ NA	$ NA

NOTES: TF is a Canada-based non-banking commercial real estate lender providing shorter-duration, customized financing solutions to professional real estate investors.

TITAN MINING CORPORATION
(TI)
Updated July 2023

IDM STOCK SCORING CALCULATION

(1) Stock Price $ 0.43   Score *1*
(2) Price 4 Years Ago $ 0.45   Score *1*
(3) Current to Four Year Price Score *5*
(4) Book Value $ 0.10   Score *1*
(5) Price to Book Comparison Score *0*
(6) Analyst Buys # 0   Score *0*

(7) Analysts Strong Buys # 0 Score *0*
(8) Dividend Yield % 9.30   Score *10*
(9) Operating Margin % -7.09   Score *0*
(10) Trading Volume 223   Score *0*
(11) Price to Earnings 16.2x   Score *8*

Total of All 11 Scores = 26

This stock's total score in 2021 was **NA,** in 2020 it was **NA**, in 2019 it was **NA**.

HISTORICAL STOCK PRICES & DIVIDEND PAYOUTS

Year	Stock	Dividend	Year	Stock	Dividend
2022	$ 0.50	$ 0.01	2010	$ NA	$ NA
2021	$ 0.24	$ NA	2009	$ NA	$ NA
2020	$ 0.25	$ NA	2008	$ NA	$ NA
2019	$ 0.45	$ NA	2007	$ NA	$ NA
2018	$ 1.28	$ NA	2006	$ NA	$ NA
2017	$ NA	$ NA	2005	$ NA	$ NA
2016	$ NA	$ NA	2004	$ NA	$ NA
2015	$ NA	$ NA	2003	$ NA	$ NA
2014	$ NA	$ NA	2002	$ NA	$ NA
2013	$ NA	$ NA	2001	$ NA	$ NA
2012	$ NA	$ NA	2000	$ NA	$ NA
2011	$ NA	$ NA	1999	$ NA	$ NA

NOTES: TI is engaged in the acquisition, exploration, development, and production of mineral properties.

TOP 10 SPLIT TRUST

(TXT.UN)

Updated July 2023

IDM STOCK SCORING CALCULATION

(1) Stock Price $ 2.09   *Score 3*
(2) Price 4 Years Ago $ 2.90   *Score 3*
(3) Current to Four Year Price Score 2
(4) Book Value $ 1.40   *Score 2*
(5) Price to Book Comparison Score 1
(6) Analyst Buys # 0   *Score 0*

(7) Analysts Strong Buys # 0 Score 0
(8) Dividend Yield % 6.76   *Score 8*
(9) Operating Margin % 0   *Score 0*
(10) Trading Volume 0   *Score 0*
(11) Price to Earnings -0.8x   *Score 0*

Total of All 11 Scores =19

This stock's total score in 2021 was **19**, in 2020 it was **32**, in 2019 it was **20**.

HISTORICAL STOCK PRICES & DIVIDEND PAYOUTS

Year	Stock	Dividend	Year	Stock	Dividend
2022	$ 3.15	$ 0.06	2010	$ 4.25	$ 0.08
2021	$ 3.35	$ 0.08	2009	$ 2.65	$ 0.05
2020	$ 1.68	$ 0.01	2008	$ 6.91	$ 0.15
2019	$ 2.99	$ 0.05	2007	$ 10.04	$ 0.22
2018	$ 4.00	$ 0.08	2006	$ 9.75	$ 0.20
2017	$ 3.64	$ 0.07	2005	$ 11.04	$ 0.40
2016	$ 3.30	$ 0.06	2004	$ 12.90	$ 0.40
2015	$ 4.50	$ 0.09	2003	$ 13.32	$ 0.30
2014	$ 4.26	$ 0.09	2002	$ 13.20	$ 0.50
2013	$ 2.34	$ 0.06	2001	$ 23.00	$ 0.50
2012	$ 1.35	$ 0.02	2000	$ 26.50	$ 0.50
2011	$ 4.16	$ 0.08	1999	$ 25.25	$ 0.50

NOTES: TXT.UN is a Canada-based closed-end investment trust designed to provide unitholders with exposure to over six Canadian banks and approximately four Canadian life insurance companies

TOPAZ ENERGY CORPORATION

(TPZ)

Updated July 2023

IDM STOCK SCORING CALCULATION

(1) Stock Price $ 20.92   *Score 7*   *(7) Analysts Strong Buys # 3 Score 4*
(2) Price 4 Years Ago $ 0   *Score 1*   *(8) Dividend Yield % 5.74   Score 8*
(3) Current to Four Year Price Score 0   *(9) Operating Margin % 35.60 Score 6*
(4) Book Value $ 9.45   *Score 4*   *(10) Trading Volume 117,877 Score 54*
(5) Price to Book Comparison Score 0   *(11) Price to Earnings 31.4x   Score 5*
(6) Analyst Buys # 1   *Score 2*

Total of All 11 Scores =41

This stock's total score in 2021 was **32**, in 2020 it was **NA**, in 2019 it was **NA**.

HISTORICAL STOCK PRICES & DIVIDEND PAYOUTS

Year	Stock	Dividend	Year	Stock	Dividend
2022	$ 23.41	$ 0.26	2010	$ NA	$ NA
2021	$ 14.73	$ 0.20	2009	$ NA	$ NA
2020	$ 13.69	$ 0.20	2008	$ NA	$ NA
2019	$ NA	$ NA	2007	$ NA	$ NA
2018	$ NA	$ NA	2006	$ NA	$ NA
2017	$ NA	$ NA	2005	$ NA	$ NA
2016	$ NA	$ NA	2004	$ NA	$ NA
2015	$ NA	$ NA	2003	$ NA	$ NA
2014	$ NA	$ NA	2002	$ NA	$ NA
2013	$ NA	$ NA	2001	$ NA	$ NA
2012	$ NA	$ NA	2000	$ NA	$ NA
2011	$ NA	$ NA	1999	$ NA	$ NA

NOTES: TPZ is a Canada-based royalty and energy infrastructure company. The Company owns interest in various gas producing plants,

TRANSALTA RENEWABLE INC

(RNW)

IDM STOCK SCORING CALCULATION

(1) Stock Price $ 13.24   Score 5   *(7)* Analysts Strong Buys # 0 Score 0
(2) Price 4 Years Ago $ 13.80   Score 5   *(8)* Dividend Yield % 7.10   Score 8
(3) Current to Four Year Price   Score 5   *(9)* Operating Margin % 16.98 Score 4
(4) Book Value $ 6.58   Score 4   *(10)* Trading Volume 1,159,573 Score 9
(5) Price to Book Comparison   Score 0   *(11)* Price to Earnings 45.3x   Score 2
(6) Analyst Buys # 0   Score 0

Total of All 11 Scores =42

This stock's total score in 2021 was **46**, in 2020 it was **45**, in 2019 it was **52**.

HISTORICAL STOCK PRICES & DIVIDEND PAYOUTS

Year	Stock	Dividend	Year	Stock	Dividend
2022	$17.47	$ 0.08	2010	$ NA	$ NA
2021	$ 22.55	$ 0.08	2009	$ NA	$ NA
2020	$ 14.96	$ 0.08	2008	$ NA	$ NA
2019	$ 13.30	$ 0.08	2007	$ NA	$ NA
2018	$ 12.21	$ 0.08	2006	$ NA	$ NA
2017	$ 14.31	$ 0.07	2005	$ NA	$ NA
2016	$ 14.46	$ 0.07	2004	$ NA	$ NA
2015	$ 11.11	$ 0.07	2003	$ NA	$ NA
2014	$ 11.44	$ 0.06	2002	$ NA	$ NA
2013	$ 10.00	$ 0.05	2001	$ NA	$ NA
2012	$ NA	$ NA	2000	$ NA	$ NA
2011	$ NA	$ NA	1999	$ NA	$ NA

NOTES: RNW. is a Canada-based company that owns a portfolio of renewable and natural gas power generation facilities and other infrastructure assets.

TRANSCONTINENTAL INC

(TCL.A)

Updated July 2023

IDM STOCK SCORING CALCULATION

(1) Stock Price $ 13.45   Score 5
(2) Price 4 Yeas Ago $ 15.95   Score 6
(3) Current to Four Year Price Score 2
(4) Book Value $ 21.67   Score 7
(5) Price to Book Comparison   Score 8
(6) Analyst Buys # 2   Score 3

(7) Analysts Strong Buys # 0   Score 0
(8) Dividend Yield % 6.69   Score 8
(9) Operating Margin % 6.53   Score 2
(10) Trading Volume # 10,037   Score 1
(11) Price to Earnings 9.9x   Score 9

Total of All 11 Scores = 51

This stock's total score in 2021 was **50**, in 2020 it was **54**, in 2019 it was **46**.

HISTORICAL STOCK PRICES & DIVIDEND PAYOUTS

Year	Stock	Dividend	Year	Stock	Dividend
2022	$ 15.84	$ 0.23	2010	$ 13.74	$ 0.09
2021	$ 23.89	$ 0.23	2009	$ 8.06	$ 0.08
2020	$ 14.50	$ 0.23	2008	$ 14.45	$ 0.08
2019	$ 14.12	$ 0.22	2007	$ 21.28	$ 0.07
2018	$ 30.79	$ 0.21	2006	$ 18.69	$ 0.07
2017	$ 25.97	$ 0.20	2005	$ 25.97	$ 0.06
2016	$ 18.81	$ 0.18	2004	$ 26.69	$ 0.04
2015	$ 15.69	$ 0.17	2003	$ 19.75	$ 0.04
2014	$ 15.66	$ 0.16	2002	$ 8.82	$ 0.02
2013	$ 12.45	$ 0.14	2001	$ 5.86	$ 0.01
2012	$ 9.69	$ 0.14	2000	$ 4.48	$ 0.01
2011	$ 14.59	$ 0.14	1999	$ 4.18	$ 0.01

NOTES: TCL.A is a printing company. It has operations in print, flexible packaging, publishing, and digital media, both in Canada and the United States

TRANSCONTINENTAL INC

(TCL.B)

Updated July 2023

IDM STOCK SCORING CALCULATION

(1) Stock Price $ 13.58   Score 5
(2) Price 4 Years Ago $ 14.88 Score 5
(3) Current to Four Year Price Score 5
(4) Book Value $ 21.67   Score 7
(5) Price to Book Comparison Score 8
(6) Analyst Buys # 0   Score 0

(7) Analysts Strong Buys # 0 Score 0
(8) Dividend Yield % 6.63   Score 8
(9) Operating Margin % 6.53 Score 2
(10) Trading Volume 0   Score 0
(11) Price to Earnings 10.0x Score 9

Total of All 11 Scores = 49

This stock's total score in 2021 was **21**, in 2020 it was **39**, in 2019 it was **47**.

HISTORICAL STOCK PRICES & DIVIDEND PAYOUTS

Year	Stock	Dividend	Year	Stock	Dividend
2022	$ 16.01	$ 0.23	2010	$ 13.80	$ 0.09
2021	$ 23.69	$ 0.23	2009	$ 8.25	$0.08
2020	$ 15.02	$ 0.23	2008	$ 17.16	$ 0.08
2019	$ 15.10	$ 0.22	2007	$ 20.37	$ 0.07
2018	$ 31.79	$ 0.21	2006	$ 18.80	$ 0.07
2017	$ 25.15	$ 0.20	2005	$ 26.69	$ 0.06
2016	$ 19.23	$ 0.18	2004	$ 23.65	$ 0.04
2015	$ 14.42	$ 0.17	2003	$ 19.00	$ 0.04
2014	$ 14.45	$0.16	2002	$ 9.43	$ 0.02
2013	$ 11.77	$ 0.14	2001	$ 5.60	$ 0.01
2012	$ 9.78	$ 0.14	2000	$ 4.62	$ 0.01
2011	$ 14.60	$ 0.14	1999	$ 4.30	$ 0.01

NOTES: TCL.A is a printing company. It has operations in print, flexible packaging, publishing, and digital media, both in Canada and the United States

TRICAN WELL SERVICE LTD

(TCW)

Updated July 2023

IDM STOCK SCORING CALCULATION

(1) Stock Price $ 3.67   Score 3
(2) Price 4 Years Ago $ 1.01   Score 2
(3) Current to Four Year Price Score 10
(4) Book Value $ 2.20   Score 3
(5) Price to Book Comparison Score 0
(6) Analyst Buys # 2   Score 3

(7) Analysts Strong Buys # 1 Score 3
(8) Dividend Yield % 4.36   Score 6
(9) Operating Margin % 16.26 Score 4
(10) Trading Volume 305,41   Score 5
(11) Price to Earnings   7.8x   Score 9

Total of All 11 Scores = 48

This stock's total score in 2021 was **NA**, in 2020 it was **NA**, in 2019 it was **NA**.

HISTORICAL STOCK PRICES & DIVIDEND PAYOUTS

Year	Stock	Dividend	Year	Stock	Dividend
2022	$ 3.27	$ NA	2010	$ 14.50	$ 0.05
2021	$ 2.51	$ NA	2009	$ 10.91	$ 0.05
2020	$ 0.93	$ NA	2008	$ 24.40	$ 0.05
2019	$ 1.01	$ NA	2007	$ 23.47	$ 0.05
2018	$ 2.95	$ NA	2006	$ 20.88	$ 0.05
2017	$ 3.40	$ NA	2005	$ 15.90	$ NA
2016	$ 2.15	$ NA	2004	$ 7.12	$ NA
2015	$ 2.89	$ NA	2003	$ 3.12	$ NA
2014	$ 17.92	$ 0.15	2002	$ 2.91	$ NA
2013	$ 14.27	$ 0.15	2001	$ 2.83	$ NA
2012	$ 12.18	$ 0.15	2000	$ 1.98	$ NAN
2011	$ 21.27	$ 0.05	1999	$ 108	$ NA

NOTES: TCW is a Canada-based oilfield services company providing specialized products, equipment, services, and technology for use in the drilling, completion, stimulation and reworking of oil and gas wells.

TRUE NORTH COMMERCIAL REAL ESTATE INVESTMENT TRUST

(TNT.UN)

Updated July 2023

IDM STOCK SCORING CALCULATION

(1) Stock Price $ 2.52   Score 3
(2) Price 4 Years Ago $ 6.68   Score 4
(3) Current to Four Year Price Score 1
(4) Book Value $ 5.69   Score 4
(5) Price to Book Comparison Score 10
(6) Analyst Buys # 0   Score 0

(7) Analysts Strong Buys # 0   Score 0
(8) Dividend Yield % 11.79   Score 2
(9) Operating Margin % 6.11   Score 2
(10) Trading Volume 238,442   Score 4
(11) Price to Earnings 25.1x   Score 7

Total of All 11 Scores = 37

This stock's total score in 2021 was **51**, in 2020 it was **53**, in 2019 it was .**56**

HISTORICAL STOCK PRICES & DIVIDEND PAYOUTS

Year	Stock	Dividend	Year	Stock	Dividend
2022	$ 6.55	$ 0.05	2010	$ NA	$ NA
2021	$ 7.51	$ 0.05	2009	$ NA	$ NA
2020	$ 5.83	$ 0.05	2008	$ NA	$ NA
2019	$ 6.71	$ 0.05	2007	$ NA	$ NA
2018	$ 6.53	$ 0.05	2006	$ NA	$ NA
2017	$ 6.18	$ 0.05	2005	$ NA	$ NA
2016	$ 5.99	$ 0.05	2004	$ NA	$ NA
2015	$ 5.67	$ 0.05	2003	$ NA	$ NA
2014	$ 6.48	$ 0.05	2002	$ NA	$ NA
2013	$ 6.29	$ 0.05	2001	$ NA	$ NA
2012	$ 8.00	$ NA	2000	$ NA	$ NA
2011	$ NA	$ NA	1999	$ NA	$ NA

NOTES: TNT.UN is a Canada-based unincorporated, open-ended real estate investment trust owning 49 commercial properties in Alberta, British Columbia, Ontario, Nova Scotia and New Brunswick.

URBANFUND CORP
(UFC)
Updated July 2023

IDM STOCK SCORING CALCULATION

(1) Stock Price $ 1.03   Score 2   *(7)* Analysts Strong Buys # 0 Score 0
(2) Price 4 Years Ago $ 0.70   Score 1   *(8)* Dividend Yield % 4.85   Score 8
(3) Current to Four Year Price Score 9   *(9)* Operating Margin % 42.48 Score 6
(4) Book Value $ 1.38   Score 2   *(10)* Trading Volume 500   Score 0
(5) Price to Book Comparison   Score 8   *(11)* Price to Earnings 7.9x   Score 9
(6) Analyst Buys # 0   Score 0

Total of All 11 Scores =45

This stock's total score in 2021 was **NA**, in 2020 it was **NA**, in 2019 it was **NA**.

HISTORICAL STOCK PRICES & DIVIDEND PAYOUTS

Year	Stock	Dividend	Year	Stock	Dividend
2022	$ 0.90	$ 0.01	2010	$ 0.26	$ NA
2021	$ 1.10	$ 0.01	2009	$ 0.20	$ NA
2020	$ 0.63	$ 0.01	2008	$ 0.30	$ NA
2019	$ 0.70	$ 0.01	2007	$ 0.35	$ NA
2018	$ 0.70	$ 0.01	2006	$ 0.12	$ NA
2017	$ 0.74	$ 0.01	2005	$ 0.10	$ NA
2016	$ 0.35	$ NA	2004	$ 0.07	$ NA
2015	$ 0.30	$ NA	2003	$ 0.08	$ NA
2014	$ 0.25	$ NA	2002	$ 0.11	$ NA
2013	$ 0.21	$ NA	2001	$ 0.04	$ NA
2012	$ 0.14	$ NA	2000	$ 0.10	$ NA
2011	$ 0.30	$ NA	1999	$0.12	$ NA

NOTES: UFC. is a Canada-based company that owns, develops, and operates a real estate portfolio focused on both residential and commercial properties.

WAJAX CORPORATION

(WJX)

Updated July 2023

IDM STOCK SCORING CALCULATION

(1) Stock Price $ 27.28   Score 7
(2) Price 4 Years Ago $ 15.73   Score 6
(3) Current to Four Year Price   Score 9
(4) Book Value $ 20.95   Score 7
(5) Price to Book Comparison   Score 1
(6) Analyst Buys #2   Score 3

(7) Analysts Strong Buys # 0   Score 0
(8) Dividend Yield % 4.84   Score 8
(9) Operating Margin % 5.69   Score 2
(10) Trading Volume 53,598   Score 3
(11) Price to Earnings 8.2x   Score 9

Total of All 11 Scores = 55

This stock's total score in 2021 was **48**, in 2020 it was **49**, in 2019 it was **46**.

HISTORICAL STOCK PRICES & DIVIDEND PAYOUTS

Year	Stock	Dividend	Year	Stock	Dividend
2022	$ 22.76	$ 0.25	2010	$ 24.97	$ 0.15
2021	$ 22.85	$ 0.25	2009	$ 16.29	$ 0.20
2020	$ 8.37	$ 0.25	2008	$ 32.25	$ 0.34
2019	$ 15.14	$ 0.25	2007	$ 36.35	$ 0.32
2018	$ 25.35	$ 0.25	2006	$ 43.99	$ 0.27
2017	$ 23.74	$ 0.25	2005	$ 20.50	$ 0.28
2016	$ 14.93	$ 0.25	2004	$ 9.25	$ 0.04
2015	$ 21.47	$ 0.25	2003	$ 5.25	$ NA
2014	$ 36.98	$ 0.20	2002	$ 5.20	$ NA
2013	$ 34.58	$ 0.20	2001	$ 5.25	$ NA
2012	$ 49.04	$ 0.27	2000	$ 4.60	$ NA
2011	$ 37.20	$ 0.18	1999	$ 8.60	$ NA

NOTES: WJX provides sales, parts, and services to a broad range of customers in diverse sectors of the Canadian economy, including construction, mining, industrial and commercial, transportation, metal processing, government and utilities, and oil and gas.

WALL FINANCIAL CORPORATION

(WFC)

Updated July 2023

IDM STOCK SCORING CALCULATION

(1) Stock Price $ 19.35   Score 6
(2) Price 4 Years Ago $ 22.20   Score 7
(3) Current to Four Year Price Score 2
(4) Book Value $ 7.27   Score 4
(5) Price to Book Comparison Score 0
(6) Analyst Buys # 0   Score 0

(7) Analysts Strong Buys # 0   Score 0
(8) Dividend Yield % 15.50   Score 2
(9) Operating Margin % 31.72 Score 6
(10) Trading Volume 212   Score 0
(11) Price to Earnings 30.0x   Score 6

Total of All 11 Scores = 33

This stock's total score in 2021 was **NA**, in 2020 it was **NA**, in 2019 it was **NA**.

HISTORICAL STOCK PRICES & DIVIDEND PAYOUTS

Year	Stock	Dividend	Year	Stock	Dividend
2022	$ 11.4	$ NA	2010	$ 9.50	$ NA
2021	$ 18.60	$ NA	2009	$ 7.15	$ NA
2020	$ 18.75	$ NA	2008	$ 8.00	$ NA
2019	$ 22.20	$ NA	2007	$ 8.50	$ NA
2018	$ 26.42	$ NA	2006	$ 5.90	$ NA
2017	$ 20.29	$ NA	2005	$ 5.75	$ NA
2016	$ 14.50	$ NA	2004	$ 4.01	$ NA
2015	$ 13.05	$ NA	2003	$ 3.75	$ NA
2014	$ 11.91	$ NA	2002	$ 3.00	$ NA
2013	$ 10.72	$ NA	2001	$ 2.86	$ NA
2012	$ 11.00	$ NA	2000	$ 2.75	$ NA
2011	$ 17.58	$ NA	1999	$ 3.00	$ NA

NOTES: WFC is a Canada-based real estate company focused on the development, management and construction of residential and commercial rental units, residential housing units for sale, and development and hotel management of hotels.

WESTERN FOREST PRODUCTS INC

(WEF)

Updated July 2023

IDM STOCK SCORING CALCULATION

(1) Stock Price $ 1.05   Score 2

(2) Price 4 Years Ago $ 1.20   Score 2

(3) Current to Four Year Price Score 2

(4) Book Value $ 2.04   Score 3

(5) Price to Book Comparison   Score 8

(6) Analyst Buys # 1   Score 2

(7) Analysts Strong Buys # 0   Score 0

(8) Dividend Yield % 4.76   Score 8

(9) Operating Margin % 0.70   Score 0

(10) Trading Volume 278,149   Score 5

(11) Price to Earnings 61.5x   Score 2

Total of All 11 Scores = 34

This stock's total score in 2021 was **NA**, in 2020 it was **NA**, in 2019 it was **NA**.

HISTORICAL STOCK PRICES & DIVIDEND PAYOUTS

Year	Stock	Dividend	Year	Stock	Dividend
2022	$ 1.26	$ 0.01	2010	$ 0.33	$ NA
2021	$ 2.12	$ 0.01	2009	$ 0.22	$ NA
2020	$ 2.20	$ 0.01	2008	$ 0.76	$ NA
2019	$ 0.69	$ 0.02	2007	$ 2.30	$ NA
2018	$ 2.37	$ 0.02	2006	$ 1.80	$ NA
2017	$ 2.80	$ 0.02	2005	$ 4.15	$ NA
2016	$ 2.12	$ 0.02	2004	$ 11.25	$ NA
2015	$ 1.76	$ 0.02	2003	$ NA	$ NA
2014	$ 2.45	$ 0.02	2002	$ NA	$ NA
2013	$ 1.53	$ 0.02	2001	$ NA	$ NA
2012	$ 0.98	$ NA	2000	$ NA	$ NA
2011	$ 0.77	$ NA	1999	$ NA	$ NA

NOTES: WEF. is an integrated forest products company building a margin-focused log and lumber business.

WESTSHORE TERMINALS

(WTE)

Updated July 2023

IDM STOCK SCORING CALCULATION

(1) Stock Price $ 32.05   Score 8

(2) Price 4 Years Ago $ 22.20   Score 7

(3) Current to Four Year Price Score 9

(4) Book Value $ 11.34   Score 5

(5) Price to Book Comparison   Score 0

(6) Analyst Buys # 1   Score 2

(7) Analysts Strong Buys # 0   Score 0

(8) Dividend Yield % 4.37   Score 6

(9) Operating Margin % 36.44 Score 6

(10) Trading Volume 32,012   Score 3

(11) Price to Earnings 27.3x   Score 6

Total of All 11 Scores = 52

This stock's total score in 2021 was **48**, in 2020 it was **51**, in 2019 it was **NA**.

HISTORICAL STOCK PRICES & DIVIDEND PAYOUTS

Year	Stock	Dividend	Year	Stock	Dividend
2022	$ 31.55	$ 0.30	2010	$ 18.87	$ 0.41
2021	$ 17.32	$ 0.20	2009	$ 11.45	$ 0.28
2020	$ 17.41	$ 0.16	2008	$ 18.67	$ 0.47
2019	$ 21.47	$ 0.16	2007	$ 13.15	$ 0.25
2018	$ 24.58	$ 0.16	2006	$ 10.57	$ 0.27
2017	$ 20.91	$ 0.16	2005	$ 12.00	$ 0.20
2016	$ 19.05	$ 0.16	2004	$ 7.45	$ 0.14
2015	$ 30.96	$ 0.33	2003	$ 5.70	$ 0.17
2014	$ 32.50	$ 0.33	2002	$ 6.21	$ 0.16
2013	$ 28.99	$ 0.33	2001	$ 5.30	$ 0.17
2012	$ 24.65	$ 0.32	2000	$ 3.17	$ 0.15
2011	$ 23.86	$ 0.24	1999	$ 6.00	$ 0.19

NOTES: WTE is a Canada- limited partnership units-based company, which owns all of the of Westshore Terminals Limited Partnership (Westshore), which is a limited partnership. Westshore operates a coal storage and loading terminal in British Columbia.

WHITECAP RESOURCES INC

(WCP)

Updated July 2023

IDM STOCK SCORING CALCULATION

(1) Stock Price $ 9.59   Score 4
(2) Price 4 Years Ago $ 3.67   Score 3
(3) Current to Four Year Price Score 10
(4) Book Value $ 8.30   Score 4
(5) Price to Book Comparison Score 1
(6) Analyst Buys # 3   Score 3

(7) Analysts Strong Buys # 2 Score 4
(8) Dividend Yield % 6.04   Score 8
(9) Operating Margin % 42.89 Score 6
(10) Trading Volume 1,375,216 Score 9
(11) Price to Earnings 4.6x   Score 10

Total of All 11 Scores = 62

This stock's total score in 2021 was **NA**, in 2020 it was **NA**, in 2019 it was **NA**.

HISTORICAL STOCK PRICES & DIVIDEND PAYOUTS

Year	Stock	Dividend	Year	Stock	Dividend
2022	$ 9.26	$ 0.04	2010	$ 4.50	$ NS
2021	$ 5.29	$ 0.02	2009	$ 1.95	$ NA
2020	$ 2.58	$ 0.01	2008	$ 4.00	$ NA
2019	$ 4.84	$ 0.03	2007	$ 5.20	$ NA
2018	$ 8.57	$ 0.03	2006	$ 10.00	$ NA
2017	$ 9.65	$ 0.02	2005	$ 3.20	$ NA
2016	$ 9.96	$ 0.02	2004	$ 2.50	$ NA
2015	$ 9.93	$ 0.06	2003	$ 2.20	$ NA
2014	$ 16.46	$ 0.06	2002	$ 3.00	$ NA
2013	$ 12.09	$ 0.05	2001	$ NA	$ NA
2012	$ 7.11	$ NA	2000	$ NA	$ NA
2011	$ 7.55	$ NA	1999	$ NA	$ NA

NOTES: WCP is a Canada-based oil and gas company engaged in acquiring, developing, and holding interests in petroleum and natural gas properties and assets.

YELLOW PAGES LIMITED

(Y)

Updated July 2023

IDM STOCK SCORING CALCULATION

(1) Stock Price $ 12.30   Score 5
(2) Price 4 Years Ago $7.95   Score 4
(3) Current to Four Year Price Score 9
(4) Book Value $ 3.53   Score 3
(5) Price to Book Comparison Score 0
(6) Analyst Buys # 0   Score 0

(7) Analysts Strong Buys # 0 Score 0
(8) Dividend Yield % 6.50   Score 8
(9) Operating Margin % 28.34 Score 5
(10) Trading Volume 17,205   Score 1
(11) Price to Earnings 3.6x   Score 10

Total of All 11 Scores =45

This stock's total score in 2021 was **40**, in 2020 it was **29**, in 2019 it was **NA**.

HISTORICAL STOCK PRICES & DIVIDEND PAYOUTS

Year	Stock	Dividend	Year	Stock	Dividend
2022	$ 12.86	$ 0.15	2010	$ NA	$ NA
2021	$ 14.29	$ 0.15	2009	$ NA	$ NA
2020	$ 11.70	$ 0.11	2008	$ NA	$ NA
2019	$ 7.74	$ NA	2007	$ NA	$ NA
2018	$ 10.12	$ NA	2006	$ NA	$ NA
2017	$ 6.83	$ NA	2005	$ NA	$ NA
2016	$ 19.11	$ NA	2004	$ NA	$ NA
2015	$ 17.61	$ NA	2003	$ NA	$ NA
2014	$ 17.90	$ NA	2002	$ NA	$ NA
2013	$ 11.99	$ NA	2001	$ NA	$ NA
2012	$ 6.36	$ NA	2000	$ NA	$ NA
2011	$	$ NA	1999	$ NA	$ NA

NOTES: YPL is a digital media and marketing solutions company providing local businesses, national brands, and consumers with the tools to interact and transact within digital economy.

ZOOMERMEDIA LTD
(ZUM)
Updated July 2023

IDM STOCK SCORING CALCULATION

(1) Stock Price $ 0.04   *Score 1*

(2) Price 4 Years Ago $ 0.04   *Score 1*

(3) Current to Four Year Price   *Score 6*

(4) Book Value $ 0.20   *Score 1*

(5) Price to Book Comparison   *Score 10*

(6) Analyst Buys # 0   *Score 0*

(7) Analysts Strong Buys # 0 Score 0

(8) Dividend Yield % 6.67   *Score 8*

(9) Operating Margin % 4.07 Score 1

(10) Trading Volume 33,000   *Score 2*

(11) Price to Earnings 300.0x Score 1

Total of All 11 Scores =31

This stock's total score in 2021 was **NA**, in 2020 it was **NA**, in 2019 it was **NA**.

HISTORICAL STOCK PRICES & DIVIDEND PAYOUTS

Year	Stock	Dividend	Year	Stock	Dividend
2022	$ 0.11	$ NA	2010	$ 0.18	$
2021	$ 0.11	$ NA	2009	$ 0.12	$ NA
2020	$ 0.04	$ NA	2008	$ 0.26	$ NA
2019	$ 0.03	$ NA	2007	$ 0.09	$ NA
2018	$ 0.03	$ NA	2006	$ 0.05	$ NA
2017	$ 0.04	$ NA	2005	$ 0.03	$ NA
2016	$ 0.05	$ NA	2004	$ 0.04	$ NA
2015	$ 0.05	$ NA	2003	$ 0.06	$ NA
2014	$ 0.09	$ NA	2002	$ 0.05	$ NA
2013	$ 0.10	$ NA	2001	$ 0.07	$ NA
2012	$ 0.10	$ NA	2000	$ 0.02	$ NA
2011	$ 0.19	$ NA	1999	$ 1.02	$ NA

NOTES: ZUM is a Canada-based multimedia company operating television stations, radio stations, a print segment, the activities of the Canadian Association of Retired Persons (CARP), digital companies and produces various trade shows and live events.

CHAPTER 11

CAREFUL MONEY MANAGEMENT (1ch11)

"You can't have your cake and eat it too", my mother used to say.

If you are going broke trying to "look rich", then you need to accept the reality that your attitude towards money is a problem. The objective of investing is to obtain financial independence. You want to eventually realize enough of a reliable income from your investments that you can live well without the need for employment or the worry of outliving your savings.

To reach this objective you need to start accumulating enough cash as early in life as possible to invest in financially strong, high dividend-paying stocks. Such stocks will pay ever increasing dividends in tandem with ever increasing share prices. Before you need that dividend income to live on, you keep steadily reinvesting your dividends. You will be surprised how rapidly your portfolio will double again and again over your lifetime.

However, before you can even think of investing in stocks you need to pay off all debts (2ch11) with intolerably high interest rates. It makes no sense to be paying credit card interest of 20% when you are only receiving 6% to 8% in dividend income. However, if you are still enjoying a 2.5% for a mortgage rate, it then makes little sense to selling your stocks to minimize you mortgage payment (3ch11), when you are receiving a 6% to 8% dividend return. While mortgage rates are now climbing close to your dividend return percentage, they will eventually return to a rate closer to the hundred-year average of 3.5%.

Being mindful of interest rates, includes your spouse's debts. (4ch11) Married couples are usually responsible for one another's debts. Financial compatibility and agreement on how to handle debt is important. Surveys have shown that 90% of respondents view financial responsibility by a prospective spouse as an appealing trait. 53 % of respondents said they would avoid a relationship with someone who was debt burdened. 60 percent had been in relationships with partners who were reckless with money, and they now avoid relationships with the financially irresponsible. While infidelity may be the number one reason for divorce, the number two reason is money.

Important financial decisions require joint consideration and agreement. Most likely you will be sharing at least one bank account, and no one likes surprises. Your "partner" needs to be able to carryon with your investment plans if you become incapacitated.

Couples in Alberta, British Columbia, New Brunswick, Ontario, Saskatchewan, the Northwest Territories, Nunavut, and Yukon can take advantage of Canada's special dividend income tax benefits. $110,000 worth of annual dividends can be realized tax free in a joint income tax return (5ch11) (the other provinces are not as generous). This tax-free status gets diluted if you have employment income, pension income or income from rental property which all get taxed at normal income tax rates. This dividend income would have to be realized from your trading account, not your Registered Retirement accounts. Also note the "dividend income" from Real Estate Investment Trusts can be classified as "returns" and not dividends unless the REIT stipulates, they are returning the capital you originally invested.

My portfolio is 100% dividend stocks and even with paying income tax on my Canada Pension Plan payments I have far more disposable cash than I ever had when I was working and paying taxes that used to eat up about 50% of my income. Since tax rules change constantly, it is wise for an experienced certified professional accountant to do your income tax. It may cost you a few hundred dollars, but it could save you tens of thousands of dollars plus minimize any problems with Revenue Canada.

Until you are free of high interest obligations, you would be wise to question every dollar spent. The people, I know, who have worked hard to accumulate millions of dollars in assets, don't drive overly expensive show cars, wear expensive designer clothes, live in 10,000 square foot mansions, or engage in an overly extravagant lifestyle (6ch11). Before they spend a dollar, they think about the realizable cost benefit of that dollar. These are not impulsive people.

 In the legendary1996 book, **"The Millionaire Next Door"**(7ch11) *(Authors: Professors Thomas J. Stanley, Ph.D. and William D. Dank, Ph.D./ Publisher: Longstreet Press Inc., Marietta, Georgia, USA,)* the authors describe how 50 years ago they began studying the wealthy. They started their research in what they thought was the most logical place, the well-to-do areas across the USA. They soon discovered that people in the impressive upscale homes who drove expensive cars rarely had a net worth in the millions of dollars. The learned that the foundation of the lifestyle of these seemingly wealthy people was not a high net worth, it was high debt.

The cost of creating this illusion of wealth diminishes any chance of ever achieving real wealth. One that would allow you to stop working and still maintain your lifestyle.

 Our society conditions us to expect to be working for forty years of our lives. It does not attempt to show us how to achieve financial independence as early in our lives as possible. Investing is not a topic taught in secondary schools or even those approaching retirement, but it should be.

What expenses would I cut if I were one of those high-income, low wealth individuals maxed out on my credit cards and struggling to keep from going deeper into debt?

1. **Automobile expense** (8ch11)- Each vehicle you own could be costing you $8,000 or more a year (insurance, fuel, parking, repairs, car payments, licensing, and maintenance). The interest on car loans is now averaging about 7% per annum or more.

   Can you cut back to one car? Could you use Uber? Walk? A bicycle? Take public transportation? These alternative modes of transportation could save you thousands of dollars annually. Savings that could pay down debt or be invested.

   A new car loses between 20% and 30% of its purchase price as soon as you drive it it off the dealer's lot. The average new car is reported to now be more than $60,000, the immediate loss to your wealth with a new car is not insignificant. Let someone else take the depreciation loss. Buying a used car with low mileage that is a few years old is a cost-effective purchase.

   If a second car is a necessity, look for a "grandma car" that you can buy for a few thousand dollars. This could be an 8-year-old car with fewer than 50,000 miles on it, small, well maintained, and fuel-efficient. Ideally you would want to buy it direct from the "grandma". Pay a mechanic to check this used car to make sure you are not purchasing one that will soon require expensive repairs. Avoid cars over 12 years as seals and metal parts do corrode and disintegrate in time.

   To get the ultimate return on your investment in a car, plan on keeping it until it accumulates 200,000 kilometres. With the money you have saved in buying a used car, you will be able to keep the car in good repair.

   Pamper your car. If possible, keep it in a garage to protect it from the sun and the weather. Avoid unnecessary use of it. Plan your trips to do all your errands at once.

2. **Accommodation expense** (9ch11)- If you are spending over 40% of your income on accommodation, then you could be classified as "house poor". If you are a homeowner in such a situation, consider selling our existing home and buying a more affordable residence.

   Apply the equity gained in the sale of your unaffordable house to paying off debts and building an investment portfolio. The sooner you become debt free, and have a portfolio that is generating investment income, the quicker you will achieve the goal of financial independence.

   With a smaller house, your monthly expenses will shrink e.g., lower taxes, heating, cooling, maintenance, services, and insurance costs. To minimize commuting cost, live close to your work or close to a major public transportation corridor.

   If you are no longer working or have a job that allows you to work remotely, consider relocating. Living in a large city is expensive. The average price of a small home can easily exceed $1,000,000 in a city like Toronto. To rent a modest apartment can exceed $3,000 per month. Moving to a smaller town can be a viable option.

There are towns where you can buy a nice home for less than $100,000. An example would be Elliot Lake (10ch11), a town of 11,000 people, in Northern Ontario, where you can buy a well-maintained condominium apartment for less than $50,000. Elliott Lake did not exist until 1957 when its uranium mines were first developed.

While moving away from family and friends, can be unappealing, living with a mountain of debt is stressful and unhealthy. The cost of maintaining social contact with distant family and friends through the internet has become very affordable.

3. **Electronic communication expense** (11ch11)- Cable television, satellite television, telephone and internet access can cost thousands of dollars annually. If you must have cable or satellite television, negotiate with your suppliers. Play one supplier against the other. Never accept the first price they offer for their services. Tell them their competitors are offering almost the identical service for a third less. This is often enough for them to find a way to handle your price objection.

Electronic communications are one of the few expenses that seem to get better and cost less each year. Check with suppliers every six months to see if better prices are available. Technology is transforming and reducing costs. Do not assume the price you are now paying is the one with which you should be satisfied. For example, it is possible to get cell phone service for less than $20 a month if you own a phone that has been paid for. Most suppliers will want to charge you closer to $50 for cell phone service.

Most suppliers, to stay ahead of inflation, sneak in a small price increase every year. Read your monthly statements carefully. They know that most customers will neither notice nor challenge an increase. They expect a customer's inertia will stop them from shopping for competitive rates. Do not expect them to notify you of any price decreases. You must ask for them. We live in a capitalist society, and this is the way capitalism works.

 If you have internet service, it is debatable whether you still require cable television service. Online streaming services, like Netflix and Amazon Prime, are good entertainment alternatives. Hundreds of internet news services can keep you fully informed and even customize the news to your specific interests.

Online telephone services can reduce telephone costs. Consider buying a phone service like MagicJack. I purchased this service for my business line. I receive 5 years of service for a flat charge of $165. Not only can I phone anyone in North America without an additional charge from anywhere in the world, I can communicate without charge with anyone in the world who also has the MagicJack service (12ch11). When I travel abroad, the phone service travels with me. It is immediately activated as soon as I plug it into any internet modem or my laptop. Many of those I am in contact with are never quite sure where I am physically located.

4. **Books** - Buying printed books (13ch11), newspapers and magazines can be expensive. Buy electronic publications that can be read on tablets, e-readers, and computers. A mountain of e-books is available for free or for less than five dollars (e.g. *"100 Great Novels You Should Read Before You Die"* - for 99 cents). Many public libraries provide free access to e-books (however their restrictions on accessing their e-books may make them a less attractive reading source than KOBO or Kindle). To me it is not just the cost but also the convenience each morning of being able to read the newspaper on my iPad in bed without having to go downstairs and retrieve a printed paper at the front door on a cold winter's day.

5. **Tobacco, Coffee and Alcohol** (14ch11)- Tobacco, coffee and alcohol consumption can be pleasurable social, habits. However, they are not a necessity. If you can reduce their consumption, you may not only be saving thousands of dollars annually but banishing habits that may not be contributing to good health. Dropping a lifetime habit is never easily done but it is possible.

6. **Vacations** (15ch11)- If you must go deeply into debt to go on a vacation, then you should question whether you can really afford such a vacation. Everyone needs a break from their normal routine. Can you plan a vacation that will minimize your debt, not increase it? Trading houses with someone in another country for a few weeks is a possibility. Travelling by car to explore cities you have never previously explored, can save the thousands of dollars in flight expenses while providing an escape from your routine.

Once financial independence is achieved, your whole life can become one extended vacation. You will then have the freedom to travel to a foreign country for several months instead of for only a week or two. The travel costs for three months of vacation in a foreign county can be equivalent to what you may have been used to spending on a two-week vacation. Comfortable, furnished condominiums in tropical locations can be rented monthly for $2,000 or less.

Thanks to the internet, you can access your bank account from almost anywhere in the world. All your foreign expenses can be charged to a credit card which you can easily pay off credit card charges each month via your internet bank connection.

Non-Residency (16ch11)- Abandoning your citizenship is probably one of the most difficult life decisions anyone would ever have to make. For a few hundred thousand dollars, citizenship in several countries without income tax laws can be established within a few months.

If you did live abroad for over six months, as a non-Canadian resident you can avoid paying Canadian income tax. It does have some complications, such as losing your provincial medical coverage. It would take a few months to be reinstated on your return to Canada. Another complication would be proving to Revenue Canada that you really had severed your Canadian residency. This would require closing bank accounts and all your other registered connections.

8. **Food** (16ch11) - Eating fabulous meals, paired with exquisite wines, in renowned restaurants is an expensive form of entertainment. The bragging rights may make you feel good for a few days. In a week it may be difficult to remember exactly what had been so incredible about the experience. Frequent gourmet dining will delay reaching your objective of financial independence.

   Once financial independence is achieved, you can wine and dine to the extent of your dividend income. No longer are you saving to reach it. However, having carefully invested your money and made many sacrifices to achieve financial independence you may never feel the same about lavish spending. Frugality is a hard habit to break once it is internalized.

9. **Gifts** (17ch11)- Until you get out of debt, limit social situations where expensive gifts are expected. Accept that you can no longer afford to accept invitations to every wedding, baby shower, birthday party, etc. This may be the hardest sacrifice you will have to make to achieve your goal. Celebrations are not only important in maintaining relationships, but fun.

   Charitable donations (18ch11) fall under gifts. Moderate your charitable donations so you can financially secure your own future? Be generous when you can finally afford to be generous.

10. **Accounting** (19ch11)- Pay your bills electronically. This not only saves time and postage but creates a historical record of expenses that can be instantly referred to at tax time. Charge everything you can to a credit card, so you have a detailed record of exactly what you have been spending money on. It is too easy when using cash to lose sight of where your money went. As well, cards that return a percentage of your expenditures can reduce your costs.

    Companies do make billing mistakes. If you think that a monthly invoice is larger than normal, compare previous statements over the last 18 months. Are there any unexplained increases? If there are, ask the vendor for an explanation. Use this call as an opportunity to also ask how you could lower your monthly billing. They may offer discounts if they feel a customer relationship is in jeopardy.

    Thousands of companies distribute discount coupons. Some are instantly available online from services such as canadiancoupons.net. They can save you money.

Before making any significant purchase do a Google search to see how competitive prices are. Often you can find better prices online than you can by visiting a store. If you can wait a day or two you for delivery you can order online and forego the expense and time in traveling to a store.

11. Credit Cards (20ch11) - Never pay for the use of a credit card and never incur a past due charge. The banks count on half of their card holders not paying off their card balance by the due date. They want to charge interest of almost 2% per month on unpaid balances. In addition, the banks are also receiving up to 2.5% from the stores who accept your credit card. Despite this 2.5% charge, retailers still love credit cards because they know that customers with credit cards do not pay as much attention to price as those who pay cash. They especially love those who see shopping as a form of entertainment.

Some retailers complain how unfair it is for banks to take a percentage of every sale charged to a credit card. They ignore the reality that if they established their own in-house credit card service, they would not only incur administrative costs, but on average, they would lose 5% of their sales to bad debt. This is what retailers traditionally lost before credit cards were introduced. Therefore, the 2.5% the retailer may be paying a bank is a bargain.

Credit consultants will often recommend that those addicted to credit card spending should destroy their credit cards and revert to a debit card which will not allow them to spend money that is not in their bank account.

While credit cards are a convenience, they have almost become a necessity. It is important that you recognize that you are being manipulated to spend more money than you need to spend. Good times or bad, the banks always make billions of profitable dollars from their "small" charges. This may sound cynical, but most Canadian bank stocks give any investment portfolio a good dependable base of rising share prices and rising dividend payouts.

An emergency cash fund (21ch11) should be set aside. It could be equivalent to what you would normally spend in 3 months. Once your investment account is established, in an emergency, you can immediately sell enough shares to cover a sudden demand for cash. To sell the stocks would cost you, as a self-directed investor, less than $10 dollars, no matter how much money was involved. Hopefully the emergency occurs when your share prices are higher than what you paid for them.

If you wanted to get emergency cash out of bonds or mutual funds you could be required to pay hundreds or thousands of dollars in fees or commissions.

I have heard investment advisors tell those planning their retirement that they should target a retirement income from passive investments equivalent to 70% to 80% of their current income (without government subsidies)". From my experience after being retired for almost two decades I believe most retired people can live well on less than half (22ch11) of the income they enjoyed from full employment. This is due to senior tax breaks, fewer clothing expenses, no commuting costs and many other living expenses that disappear.

Much of your income was being lost to income tax. A reliable tax-free dividend income takes away much of the insecurity of no longer having employment income. Interestingly dividend income keeps growing as your portfolio grows, even as you subtract your living expenses from the portfolio. Your biggest concern may become trying to decide whether to invest your surplus cash or to spend it on affordable luxuries.

After reading this chapter one reader told me she thought a frugal lifestyle would take all the joy out of living. However, unless you are focused on your financial objective, an occasional exception can quickly become the norm and you will never establish a large enough financial cushion to protect yourself from unforeseen setbacks. Frugal living and investing do require discipline.

This raises the question of how much money is too much money to save? There are cynics who suggest that the financial service industry scares investors into saving-too-much, so that the advisor can receive an ongoing commission income from your portfolio for decades. While this cynicism may be justified, I have not met any retirees who complain about having too much money invested. Many of the retirees I know have health issues of a minor or major nature. They spend significant amounts on health and pain reduction products. A large, ever growing stock portfolio is "living-a-comfortable-life" insurance for them.

CHAPTER 12
FINAL WORDS

If you have reached this far in the book, it means you have a real interest in investing. Now, where do you go from here?

If you are already a self-directed investor, this book may have given you some ideas, tips, shortcuts, and insights that you had not previously considered. If you are a full-service investor, I hope it has opened your eyes to the fact that successful self-investing is not the complicated scary beast that financial advisors want you to believe it is. You should now be able to see how you can successfully manage your own investments and perhaps save yourself hundreds of thousands of dollars in portfolio management charges over your lifetime.

The readers I am most concerned about are those who have never invested in anything more than a savings account. What was it that made them read this book? What were they looking for? Do they now delay investing (1ch12) and say that they will get around to it "later" when they are older and closer to retirement or maybe when they receive money from an inheritance or from winning the lottery?

The compounding benefits of reinvested dividends speed up the achievement of financial independence. This goal, once achieved, can enhance a family's life experiences, their health, and their self-confidence. The future is uncertain. Counting on future circumstances occurring before you start to build a strong portfolio may be something, twenty years from now, that you will regret not having done.

So how does one break out of the bonds of inertia and start investing? To get started I think you need to start saving for an initial investment of $5,000 (2ch12). This reasonable goal should be enough to commit you to building a portfolio. As you patiently save this initial $5,000, you can use all the tools in this book to help you identify the 20 stocks that will be the best choice for YOUR portfolio when you are ready to invest that $5,000.

Only you can choose the 20 stocks. If someone selected YOUR stocks for you, you would never be certain that their 20 were the best. At the first sign of a recession, you might panic and sell your shares. This sale of stocks would be at the worst possible time to sell. Have no doubt that within the next ten years you will go through a recession or a market crash. They occur frequently and you invest so they will have a minimum impact on your wealth.

You need to personally confirm that YOUR 20 stocks paid their dividends through all the previous recessions and that their share prices always returned to new record heights after the recession. It is critical that your faith in your stocks is based on you personally scoring each stock.

Scoring will help you sort out 20 good stocks. Pick the one you think is the "best". This is the one in which you invest your first $5,000. One down, nineteen to go. Continue to put aside a portion of your monthly income and add to it the small amount of dividend income you will start to receive from your first stock purchase. When you have saved the next $5,000 invest it in the second stock on your priority list. You keep doing this until you have purchased all 20 stocks. $5,000 in 20 stocks gives you a significant portfolio of $100,000. This may take you several years, but it gives you a strong portfolio and brings you closer to financial independence.

With an average dividend yield of about 6%, your $100,000 portfolio is going to be generating $6,000 in tax free money. That is a substantial amount. YOUR 20 stocks have safely spread your risk. The one or two stocks that may temporarily divert from their historical good behavior patterns would have a negligible impact upon YOUR strong portfolio. From periodic scoring of YOUR 20 stocks, you will confirm they are maintaining a score over 50 and still paying a good dividend.

As you continue contributing to your 20 stocks. You will find that some will grow in value faster than others. Your objective is to have no more than 5% or your wealth in any one stock. With your additional dividend cash, you can buy more shares in those of the 20 whose percentage of your portfolio is now below 5%. Investing this way, you can expect your portfolio to double within 5 years.

Eventually your monthly dividend income will exceed your monthly living expenses. You have now achieved financial independence. You are free to walk away from your job (if that is what you choose to do) and live off your dividend income knowing your share prices and dividend income will continue to grow.

Looking for a short cut, one of my readers asked me, "Why not borrow money (3ch12) at a 2 to 3 percent annual interest rate and invest it in your portfolio since it is going to grow at 8 to 10 percent per year."

My response was that for the last 100 years inflation (4ch12) has averaged 3.5%. For most of my life interest rates were usually more than 6%. In the seventies interest rates climbed into the high teens. The odds are that you may have to be generating far more than a 9% gain in your portfolio just to remain on the plus side. Interest rates are always for a set period. You do not want to be faced with an unaffordable interest rate when your loan comes up for renewal.

You are building a portfolio to last your lifetime. Banks rarely lose money. They are quick to adjust their lending rates to make sure they never lose. It is important that you are in control of your finances and never have to liquidate your stock portfolio to pay loan obligations. Opportunities may arise where you may be able to make more money by safely lending at a higher interest rate then you can earn investing it. This is doubtful because with stocks you are also realizing appreciation of share prices. However, flexibility is important.

There are situations where borrowing money for an investment does make sense. For example, if you own a second property on which we have a 2.25% mortgage. It covers perhaps 20% of the property's total equity. You may have received a good 5-year fixed rate not only for the security of the real estate you already owned but also on the value of your stock portfolio investments. It would make little sense to liquidate investment accounts now earning more than 6% just to have the property mortgage free. Furthermore, the value of that property is growing at a rate much greater than 10% a year. When the mortgage comes up for renewal in a few years, it might then make sense to liquidate stocks at that time to remove debt if interest rates are still high. This would remove the monthly mortgage expense from your dividend-based cash flow that you are now paying. This second property helps to safely diversify your wealth.

Another reader asked was there any reason why he couldn't" just put money in a dividend fund (5ch12) (instead of investing it in individual stocks? Presumably the fund manager tracks the best dividend companies."

I assured him that he had far more faith in fund managers than I did. Once he gives the investment company his cash, he loses control over this money. He would have only a vague idea of what the money was invested in. The fund manager can change stocks in the fund on a whim. You would be paying a charge every year you owned that fund. The charge could be as high as 2% of your investment for something you could do better yourself for free. Over many years this 2% could represent tens of thousands of dollars that could have been invested by you to enhance your wealth instead of the investment company managing the fund. Also, if you ever needed to liquidate the fund you can run into all kinds of complications, expenses and delays that are deliberately built into these contractual agreements by fund companies.

 Fund managers, to keep their jobs are expected to at least match the indices that their "boss" is using to judge their fund's performance. Thus, the fund managers concentrate on matching the stocks to indices. Like all indices, the indices include some mediocre and poor stocks that you would have scored and eliminated if you were building a dividend portfolio. It is not the fund manager's money. If the fund performs poorly, he will shrug his shoulders and advise you that he did as well as the index.

 A fund is a sales vehicle created by the investment company for their sales representatives (the financial advisors) (6ch12) to sell. It doesn't have to be the best fund in the world to be sold. Most investors will invest in it because the sales representative made it sound like the best investment vehicle ever created. Selling funds is what they are paid to do. Most investment advisors know little about dividend stocks because they don't need to know much about dividend stocks to sell funds. There is little money to be made by them in selling dividend stocks to investors. The investors who know little about investing naively accept whatever they are being sold by investment advisors about a fund. They do not read the fund prospectuses which legally bind them to the fund and its obligations.

A reader, who I suspect is an investment advisor, promoted a "cash value whole life insurance that gives a dividend (7ch12) of 6% year over year, TAX FREE. That seems far less volatile than playing the markets unless you are looking for a minimum of 10% - 12% capital gain. It has the added death benefit which means your family inherits all that benefit tax free because life insurance cannot be taxed. Other benefits include access to the cash value at any time, through indirect recognition."

What he neglected to mention was how much it would cost to buy such life insurance which would, for example, give you an annual income of $100,000? How would your income payments grow with inflation? How much would be paid to your heirs on your death? If you needed several hundred thousand dollars quickly for an emergency, how do you liquidate such a life insurance policy and what penalty would you pay to liquidate it?

Selling Life Insurance is a very profitable business. They are not a charity giving away a free benefit. I understand selling a policy like this could give the sales rep a commission of 10% or more. Like any investment you do not buy into it unless you totally understand what you have bought and what it is going to cost you over the many years.

Another reader wrote that he could hardly wait before he too could live off his dividends. While his stocks were only paying him pennies per day now, someday his 150 different dividend-paying stocks (8ch12) would be paying him hundreds of dollars per day. I have scored thousands of stocks. There are not 150 stocks out there strong enough to create a safe generous dividend portfolio. Just trying to properly score or analyze 150 stocks would take days. Quality is what is important in a portfolio, not quantity.

It is interesting how many readers are concerned about hiding their money from the tax man. For example, on wrote, "I live off my rental income, which is more reliable, more predictable and allows me to hide more cash. It's not how much money you make, it is how much money you can hide. If you want to hide money buy rentals".

Another, in a European country, wrote," I'm searching for some credible and reliable fintech that I can add to my portfolio to avoid local taxes."

Such notes make me realize how beneficial it is for Canadians to be able to earn dividend income of $55,000 tax free. Of course, why you should be paying any taxes on dividend income is a big question. The company who is paying you dividends from their profits has already paid an income tax on this money. As a shareholder, you are an "owner" of that business, no matter how many or how few shares you own. You are being double taxed.

When this double taxation question was raised with one investment advisor he scoffed and said that the number of people earning $55,000 in dividends each year is a small fraction of one percent of investors. He is probably right as most investors are speculators intent on getting rich by buying stocks at a low price and selling them at a high price. The idea that you can prosper from dividend stocks without the assistance of an investment advisor is not something that an investment advisor wants you to consider.

The question of dividend income lead to a reader asking, "in order to generate a 6-figure dividend income, how much money would I need to invest?"

To realize an income of $100,000 solely from dividends (9ch12) equates back to the dividend yield percent of your stocks. It excludes any capital gains and increases in dividend payments in a twelve-month period. If your stocks are paying on average a 6% dividend you are going to need about $1,500,000 invested. However, normally the Canada Pension Plan, the Old Age Security payments, and any other income you might be receiving need to be considered in calculating your expected retirement income.

Do not be surprised when one day you receive a letter from Service Canada that informs you that, *"Under Canada's public pension system, Old Age Security pension recipients with an expected net income of more than $79,845 in the 2021 tax year must pay back all of their OAS pension through an automated monthly recovery. Your recovery tax amount is based on the income you reported on your last tax return"*. To avoid such a letter, keep as much of your money if you can, growing in a Registered Retirement Savings Plan or Registered Income Fund for as long as possible. Your RRSP can be like an emergency insurance policy to be liquidated only if necessary. The dividend from a second trading account separate from your RRSP is the one whose dividend income you can live on. However, a point is reached as you reach your late seventies where you will want to start removing large amount from your RRSP. The 30% income tax you are charged beats the 50% income tax your estate may have to pay.

One reader recommended a different road to wealth and income. He wrote, "I am making more money year over year since I became a hard money lender (10ch12), I make 12% return over 12 months which goes up to 18% if a project goes over."

Since I come from a long background in commercial credit and collections several warning bells rang when I read this note. How do you find those who wish to borrow money from you? Do you advertise? Is that expensive? If you are getting a 12% to 18% return, these must be borrowers who are not able to borrow from banks at rates closer to 5%? Would they be high credit risks? What do you do when they don't or can't pay you? What percentage of your loan portfolio would default on their payments? How do you check their credit worthiness? Do you have to be licensed to lend money like this? Somehow, owning financially strong companies paying high dividends seems easier and safer than high risk lending.

Throughout all my books I try to open the reader's eyes to investment opportunities and to the dangers lurking within the investment industry. (11ch12). If you wish to be a successful investor

YOU do have to spend time carefully selecting YOUR stocks. While some may think that it is too much work and that they can delegate their investments to a financial advisor, I suggest before doing it that they subscribe for a few weeks to the free daily financial industry news releases that I receive. The following are just a few of the daily extracts from those I have received:

"RBC Dominion Securities Inc. (RBC DS) has been fined $350,000 by the Investment Industry Regulatory Organization of Canada (IIROC) for supervisory failings…. SC whose elderly client — referred to as SK …Following SK's death in October 2014, SC began transferring money from SKL to his and his spouse's margin accounts, beginning in December 2014. RBC DS approved three transfers totaling more than $3 million."

A former fund rep has been fined and suspended for locking a client into a deferred sales charge (DSC) fund redemption schedule when she could have purchased cheaper, no-load funds that would have served her better.

A Mutual Fund Dealers Association of Canada (MFDA) hearing panel approved a settlement agreement with a former Investors Group Financial Services Inc. rep in Medicine Hat, Alta., who admitted to violating MFDA rules by recommending a trade that needlessly subjected his client to a seven-year Deferred Service Charge schedule and generated commissions for himself…. she was sold more than $400,000 worth of a DSC mutual fund that generated approximately $15,346 in commissions for the rep…Four days later, he switched her to a portfolio of new mutual funds in the I-Profile program. However, the new funds retained the DSC schedule from the original fund, so the client paid $17,200 in DSC fees when she redeemed some of those funds.

A former investment advisor has been fined and suspended for violating securities rules….,he engaged in excessive, unsuitable trading for two sets of clients — both retired couples — and that he borrowed $95,000 from a client in 2017 who died two years later without being repaid. "It appears that he has only one 'tactical' trade strategy that is being applied across a number of client accounts, and that the client accounts do not appear to be benefiting, while [he] appears to be earning a commission."

A Toronto trader working at a Canadian asset management company has been charged in the U.S. for insider trading and running a multimillion-dollar front-running scheme….The U.S. Department of Justice claims…he made $3.6 million between January 2015 and April 2021 using five accounts in the names of three of his relatives to hide his identity… those accounts would buy high quantities of stocks and then sell them for a profit later that day when his employer executed an order to buy, increasing the value of the shares.

A regulatory hearing panel has fined and permanently banned a former mutual fund representative accused of inappropriate personal financial dealings with a couple of clients…she took money from clients and deposited it into her personal bank accounts.

"Fewer than one in four Canadians understands the costs of investing based on standard fee summaries, "...., we found that only 23% of investors correctly identified their total cost of investing when they were given a status quo fee summary with an additional disclosure that some fees were not included," .... most investors struggle to understand their investing costs, with more than four in five failing to identify the types of costs included in their fee summaries." ....Even experienced investors struggle to understand key terms and how their choices influence the type and amount of fees they pay,"....The report blamed the low level of comprehension on "the inherent complexity of investment fees and how they relate to investor choices"

And finally, "The <u>Investment Industry Regulatory Organization of Canada</u> (IIROC) has deemed a former Toronto investment advisor liable for failing to know his client and for excessive trading outside the bounds of good business practice.

According to an IIROC document dated July 6, he was a registered investment advisor when he took on a 66-year-old former lawyer, as a client in February 2014. A little more than a year earlier, the Law Society of Upper Canada, known today as the Law Society of Ontario, had determined that the client did not have the capacity to practice law as he was suffering from cognitive decline due to Alzheimer's Disease.

In early February 2014, the advisor met with a person opened an account for GA. In the days leading up to the meeting, he emailed several account opening documents to person opening the account including blank NCAF, a blank Irrevocable Power of Attorney – Securities form, and a blank Trading Authority Authorization form, among others.

In his testimony provided to IIROC, the witness reportedly said that the meeting to open the account lasted "five minutes tops," which the regulator said was too short for a prospective client that representative had no prior relationship with. The account opening forms were already filled when they had collected them, IIROC said, and he did not discuss the content of the forms with GA before opening an account for him.

According to IIROC, the NCAF indicated client's investment objective as 100% speculative, his risk tolerance as 100% high, and his investment knowledge as Good.

IIROC said that over the following seventeen months, the advisor engaged in excessive trading within the *GA account, which represented approximately 73% of his assets under administration over the time that it was open. During that time, he executed 168 high-risk, speculative, and short-term trades, compared to seven trades he did in all his other clients' accounts combined.*

This trading was not profitable and resulted in losses to the client in excess of $1.3 million," IIROC said. *"In comparison, the total gross commissions on the account exceeded $232,000, resulting in a commission to equity ratio of 39.09 (annualized), which, in our view, constitutes further evidence of the excessive trading in the account."*

The above examples emphasize the "swimming in the tank with ravenous sharks" aspect of investing.

The industry trumpets their rules and regulations in the following two extracts which obviously by their very wording seem to suggest these rules will only be paid lip service to by full-service investment advisors servicing naïve clients. It is not an oversight on the industry's part that their contracts are difficult to understand, and clients do not understand what they are being charged for. Stealing money from passive, trusting clients is just too easy and too much of a temptation.

"Assess the potential and actual impact of costs on the client's overall return. As costs can have a significant impact on a client's return over time, you must assess the relative costs (both initial and ongoing) and consider their impact on the client when making a suitability determination. The regulators call out that this must include all compensation paid, directly or indirectly, to the dealer or advisor. It is not necessary to recommend the lowest-cost product; just to be sure to consider the impact of costs... However, where most elements of several comparable products are equal, it will be more difficult to justify recommending a higher-cost product without a good rationale.

Consider account-type suitability...A suitability assessment must include the type of account recommended, the dealer/ advisor compensation option, and the nature of the services offered to a client. They must be suitable and put the client's interest first. The CFRs require that the advisor explain the features and associated costs of different types of accounts available to the client and recommend the type of account that puts the client's interest first.

I have tried to make it as easy as possible for you, with the charts and information on each Canadian high dividend stock, to build a safe, generous dividend portfolio. I even provide the stock scoring software I used to score the stocks, so you could take the most up to date information on a stock and re-score it just before buying. I went into detail as to how and why the 9 information elements that make up the score were selected and weighed. Nothing is hidden. The best 20 stocks for your portfolio can be found in a few hours, not days or weeks.

In the next twenty years you will go through at least two stock market crashes. Unless YOU have complete faith in the quality of the 20 stocks that YOU chose for YOUR portfolio you will not stick with your strong stocks through the inevitable market crashes. A recession is the worst possible time to sell a stock. The share prices of financially strong companies do come back, and they do reach new record highs.

THE END

INDEX

Through out the book, the following extracts have been high lighted and sequentially numbered. For example, in the first item, "**100,000 solely from dividends**....9ch12 "is the 9th item highlighted extracted for the index from Chapter 12. The index system was created this way to accommodate those who purchased the book in electronic formats that do not have page numbers.

The varying print sizes, bolding and italic formats conform to the way these extractions appear in book to help to help you quickly find them.

(1) Phrase From the Book (2) Sequence number # (3) Within Chapter

C

D

E

F

G

H

I

L

M

N

O

P

R

S

T

W

EIGHT OTHER BOOKS

by

Ian Duncan MacDonald

IAN'S OTHER INVESTMENT BOOKS

NEW YORK STOCK EXCHANGES 106 BEST HIGH DIVIDEND STOCKS

CANADIAN HIGH DIVIDEND HANDBOOK

AMERICAN HIGH DIVIDEND HANDBOOK

SAFER BETTER DIVIDEND INVESTING

INCOME AND WEALTH FROM SELF-DIRECTED INVESTING

In easy-to-understand language Ian MacDonald explains in all his six investment books (including this one) why self-investing is the safest, least expensive way to invest. Step-by-step he shows you how you can realize a safe annual 6% income while your portfolio continues to grow year-after-year. He reveals the concerns you should have when entrusting your money to investment advisors.

In his books you will learn:
-How to open an online stock trading account.
-How to find the best 20 dividend paying stocks for your financially strong portfolio.
-How the book's scoring tables help you to identify the best growth and dividend stocks.
-How the FREE PC scoring software makes it fast and easy to sort out the best stocks.
-How to buy your verified stocks.
-How to easily and quickly monitor your purchased stocks on a regular basis.

A LOGICAL, EASY TO UNDERSTAND INVESTMENT SYSTEM

Created for those seeking safe financial independence without fearing the loss of their life savings. Ian 's formula for investment success is, **"Build your safe portfolio by** investing equally in 20 stocks of financially strong companies paying a dividend of 6% or greater". Not only can such a portfolio deliver a safe annual dividend income of 6% or more but the growing share prices of such stocks and reinvesting your dividends can double the value of your portfolio in 5 years.

Each of Ian's books has been an evolution in making it easier for investors unfamiliar with investing to achieve safe financial independence and for experienced investors to find strong dividend stocks more quickly for their existing portfolios.

NEW YORK STOCK EXCHANGE'S 106 BEST HIGH DIVIDEND STOCKS

. The book identifies, scores and analyzes the best 106 dividend stocks out of the 2,788 stocks traded on the New York Stock Exchange. It was released in December of 2022.

In a 2-page analysis of each stock, you can compare each of the 106 high dividend stock's strengths based on average volumes traded, operating margins, book values, dividend yield percent, price-to-earnings and of course their composite scores. Share prices and dividend payouts are supplied for each year back to 1999. You can easily see how these strong companies were minimally impacted by the stock market crashes of 2000, 2008 and 2020. Many continued to increase their dividend payouts through these crashes.

Fluctuating share prices are a result of competitive bidding between positive speculators and negative speculators reacting to media hype, rumors, and investment promotions. While it is impossible to accurately predict future share prices, it is far easier to predict future dividend payouts. Dividends are derived from profits. Profits are the result of the wise revenue and expense decisions made by company executives. While profits can influence speculators. Speculators do not control profits.

The book shows you how to choose the best 20 stocks on the New York Stock Exchange whose dividends can average a return of 6% and, in most years, grow the portfolio's capital value by 12% or more. If you invest your annual dividend income you can expect to double the value of your portfolio within five years.

COMMENTS ON NEW YORK STOCK EXCHANGE'S 106 BEST DIVIDEND STOCKS

Very insightful book! Great information about high dividend stocks…. **Lawrence**

4.0 out of 5 stars <u>A simple foundation to get started and grow confidence along the way</u>
I purchased Ian's "Income and Wealth from Self-Directed Investing" along with this book. The first book is a little more personal, conversational and introductory - you see where MacDonald is coming from in terms of helping friends out who have been burned as well as he himself, even after working and saving and entrusting so much.

This book gets to the technical method more quickly and lays out enough information that you can calculate and begin to understand otherwise potentially foreign things yourself. I decided to reverse engineer his methods in Google Sheets and after reading some Reddit threads and searching some YouTube videos I did some very novice site scrapes and was able to apply his 11 categories on the fly.

I'm only getting started on his method so I can't say what returns have been yet, but this book equipped me to feel confident that I at least understand the method I'm applying. My hope is that I will continue to learn along the way and as I understand it better and get older, I will be able to be more and more serious and can share the same 'aha's with my children and others around me.

As mentioned in the book, don't just copy down the symbols or the scores - they will have already changed. You will be MUCH more confident if you take some extra time to try to construct it yourself. Think about it - you've taken the time to commandeer your own investing and your own money. You owe it to yourself to know the basics of what you're doing - and MacDonald gives you a method where you can get started and begin to learn just that.....**Alan**

"I have been following Ian and his investment strategy for 6 months and even as rough as the market has been my dividends keep coming in and I reinvest them, allowing me to purchase more stock shares at a reduced rate thus adding to the next dividend amount. I cannot wait to get this so I can see what additional information I can gain. I love the podcasts too! Reinforcement on the principles and great Q&A!"......**Romine**

"I read this one cover to cover in a few hours. Ian does an excellent job covering the material and his examples allowed me to verify I was on the right track evaluating stocks. I hope he has another book or two coming in the near future."

5.0 out of 5 stars <u>Ian is the "real thing"</u>
Thanks for your great weekly podcast and another great read.

5.0 out of 5 stars **Good read, useful insight**
Good book, adjust for current year and keep using!....Dennis

CANADIAN HIGH DIVIDEND HANDBOOK

In this, the third of Ian Duncan MacDonald's investment books he provides you with charts on all Canadian companies traded on the Toronto Stock Exchange paying dividends of 3.5% or more. For each company listed in the easy-to-read charts, he shows the three-year trend of each stock's score, prices, and dividend yield percentage. The book was released in 2021.

The objective of the charts s to help you quickly build a strong dividend portfolio of twenty stocks.

You scan through the charts looking for what you think are the twenty strongest stocks paying the best dividends. When you have compiled a list of the best 20 stocks, you then go to the unique page for each of the stocks to weigh the strength and weakness of the stock. This includes checking their share prices and dividend payments over the last twenty years. You are looking for price and dividend payouts that have increased steadily year-after-year even during recessions and pandemics.

Once you have settled on YOUR twenty stocks you rescore them to verify that no significant risk changes have occurred since the stocks were scored for the book. **You score them with the free software you request to be e-mailed to you after you bought the book**. You now purchase the stocks as a self-directed investor.

No longer will you be buying stocks because of market hype, rumors or just because some advisor has recommended them. You will know exactly what you have bought and why you bought it.

It is important that you have faith in your stocks because in the next market downturn you will not panic and sell at the worst possible time, the financially strong, high dividend, stocks that you so carefully selected. You will know that despite the share price dropping that the dividends of these stocks have always been paid steadily through all the market crashes. You also know these share prices always bounced back and reached new record highs. Furthermore, if one stock did deviate from traditional behavior you know that your other nineteen financially strong stocks will more than make up any shortfalls.

In the next market crash, you relax, live off your dividend income and wait for the speculators to come their senses and invest in the financially strong stocks that you already own, and which always recover. The typical market downturn occurs about every four years and takes about a year to recover.

If you are saving for your retirement or for financial independence, you will want to continuously reinvest your dividends. Within five years this could result in you doubling the value of your portfolio. How is this possible. The stocks in your portfolio, as verified by their historical records, are providing you with three revenue flows:

(1) The monthly or quarterly dividend payouts
(2) The ever-increasing amounts being paid out by financially strong companies.
(3) The ever-increasing share prices of these financially strong companies

The other factor that allows you to build your portfolio quickly is that none of its value is being taken away by investment advisor fees every year. You pay a negligible amount to acquire the stocks and that is the only expense you face. If you are married and make a joint income tax return, you would have to jointly exceed $110,000 in dividend income before you would pay income tax on your dividend income.

The book is a straightforward, honest guide, not based on textbook theory, but on someone's successful hands-on experience.in increasing his portfolio by more than 300% while extracting a very generous six-digit dividend income over the last 16 years. You too can do it.

4.0 out of 5 stars - **Good information even for an old investor like me**

I like the information contained in the book and the logic supporting it. A good and useful buy…Alomone

5.0 out of 5 stars **Chapter one - as expected.** And a freebee! …. Stacey
Report

AMERICAN HIGH DIVIDEND HANDBOOK

You are shown a safe, uncomplicated way to achieve financial independence. In this, the fourth of Ian Duncan MacDonald's investment books, he provides you with useful charts covering all **286 common stocks traded on the New York Stock Exchange and the NASDAQ paying dividends of 3.5% or more.** The easy-to-read charts are sorted by score, share price, dividend yield percent and alphabetically. They make it easy to find the strongest high dividend candidates for your portfolio. The book was released in 2021.

You next go to the unique page for each of your choices and further assess their strengths and weaknesses. Here, you also view a summary of the stock's share prices and dividend payments over the last twenty years. What you want to confirm is that their share prices and dividend payouts have increased steadily year-after-year even during recessions and pandemics.

Finally, just prior to buying the stocks you rescore them with the **Free stock scoring software that is emailed, on request, to those who have bought the book.** This last step confirms there have been no significant risk change since the stocks were scored in September of 2021.

Now, when you purchase shares, you are not buying them because of market hype or rumors. You are buying them because you have carefully assessed their strength and their long-established profitable behavior.

In the next stock market crash you will not panic because you know that despite all share prices dropping that the dividends of your stocks have always been paid through market crashes and their share prices have always recovered and achieved new record highs. You will live on your dividend income and wait for the inevitable recovery.

Unlike speculative stocks, a portfolio of financially strong companies paying high dividends never stops growing because it provides you with three easily verifiable revenue flows:
(1) The regular monthly or quarterly dividend payouts
(2) The ever-increasing dividend amounts being paid out by financially strong companies.
(3) The ever-increasing share prices of financially strong companies.

No one can accurately predict future share prices.
97% of speculators are said to lose money in the stock market, trying to buy low and sell high.
Speculators only control share prices, they do not control a company's profits from which dividends are paid. The managers of the company control profits and profits are predictable.
Invest in financially strong dividend paying companies.

READERS COMMENTS

SAFER BETTER DIVIDEND INVESTING

In his second investment book **"Safer Better Dividend Investing"** Ian not only shows investors how to find 20 stocks for their portfolios but he makes it easy by listing and scoring all 628 U.S. common stocks traded on the New York Stock Exchange and the NASDAQ that were paying a dividend of 6% or more in August of 2020. He also includes 199 Canadian stocks traded on the Toronto Stock Exchange paying a dividend of 3.5% or more. The strength and potential of each stock is established in the score applied to each stock. They are listed alphabetically, by descending score, by descending share price and by descending dividend percentage. The book was released in 2020.

To ensure that you have the most up-to-date score before purchasing your stock, everyone who buys this book can request a **FREE copy of Ian's STOCK SCORING SOFTWARE.**

Over the last year, Ian has answered hundreds of interesting questions from investors. He now shares 128 questions and his answers in the new book. Questions like:

How does the Great Depression 1929 compare to the 2020 recession?

Why do so many investors not trust investment advisors?

Do you see Tesla as an overpriced stock?

Is it too late to start investing at 35?

What are some lies stockbrokers tell themselves?

Many investors hesitate to buy stocks because they do not understand how to identify a financially strong company. The first chapters of the book explain in easy, to understand language the importance of the eight key information items Ian used to build his stock scoring system. The eight critical items are:*(1) A stock's current price. (2) A stock's historical prices. (3) A stock's current "book" value.(4) How analysts rate the stock.(5) A stock's dividend yield percent.(6) A stock's operating margin.(7) A stock's average daily volume of shares traded.(8) A stock's price-too-earnings ratio.* The detailed stock scoring matrix is provided so that the scores can be easily understood.

In **"Safer Better Dividend Investing"** Ian not only shows investors how to find 20 stocks for their portfolios but he makes it easy by listing and scoring all 628 U.S. common stocks traded on the New York Stock Exchange and the NASDAQ that were paying a dividend of 6% or more in August of

2020. He also includes 199 Canadian stocks traded on the Toronto Stock Exchange paying a dividend of 3.5% or more. The strength and potential of each stock is established in the score applied to each stock. They are listed alphabetically, by descending score, by descending share price and by descending dividend percentage.

READERS COMMENTS

5.0 out of 5 stars - **Great way to buy stocks with confidence!** -. I have been following Ian and his investment strategy for 6 months and even as rough as the market has been my dividends keep coming in and I reinvest them, allowing me to purchase more stock shares at a reduced rate thus adding to the next dividend amount. Well worth the time to read!...**Romine**

Practical Advice - When I first entered the workforce, I avoided the stock market because everyone in my hometown who lost their business took a three-month correspondence course and became stockbrokers. Relying on financial advice from any of these people would be the equivalent of taking weight loss advice from a five-hundred-pound person.
A few years later I realized that stockbrokers are salesmen who are provided information from research departments on a routine basis and seldom, if ever, do their own research or even have an investment philosophy. I have used a full-service broker as well as several no load mutual funds and have been pleased with the results. However, the dividends yields are low in comparison to the value of the accounts.
McDonald's book discusses numerous investment alternatives and their pros and cons. For example, he explains why real estate can be such a time consuming and expensive investment. He also discussed the pitfalls of purchasing collectibles as investments. McDonald is highly suspicious of investment professionals and their motivation to manage people's money. He has developed a system of evaluating and purchasing high quality dividend paying stock that will continue to pay dividends in a bear market. McDonald explains why CEO's consider protecting dividends such a high priority. Purchasers of the book are provided free software to evaluate and select individual shares of stock for their portfolio. The system is user friendly and logical. This book is recommended for anyone interested in setting up a self-direct brokerage account. .... **John**

4.0 out of 5 stars – **Enlightening.** The book is worth every penny, enlightening and is a must for novices like me. It reads like it's from the heart. Many of my questions have been answered in your book"....J

3.0 out of 5 stars - **Long book**. It's a well written book, longer than a weekend read. It may be better in audio. It's impactful information as I have glanced through several chapters.

INCOME AND WEALTH FROM SELF-DIRECTED INVESTING

Released in 2018, this was Ian's first investment book. It was written in response to an 80-year-old widow's plea for help. In three years, her financial advisor had lost $300,000 of her life savings. She correctly feared outliving her saving. After reviewing her portfolio and monthly investment statements Ian was appalled. Although she was intelligent and had been a successful businesswoman, she recognized that when it came to investing, she was financially illiterate. Over a few months, Ian taught her how to invest the way he did.

The widow went on to pick her own stocks and within a year had recovered what she had lost. Knowing that Ian was a writer, she pushed him to write an investment book that would teach others like her how to invest safely and successfully.

The book is written in easy-to-understand language, with no financial industry jargon. It reveals the concerns investors should have about entrusting their money to investment advisors. Step-by-step he not only explains why self-directed investing the safest, least expensive way is to invest but walks the reader through the entire process of finding and purchasing 20 stocks for their unique portfolio. He shows you how any investor can realize an annual 6% income while watching their portfolio grow year-after-year. He The basics are explained in detail:

The following comments by the book's readers show how they benefited from the book: **"Income and Wealth from Self-Directed Investing"**

"This book provides an education in investing, for those who want to take control of their own money. learn how to choose stocks for your own self-directed portfolio. A software program is also available, free, with the purchase of this book.... Ian MacDonald will show you how to choose 20 stocks for your portfolio, each yielding at least 6% in annual income. The income from your chosen stocks will provide a comfortable retirement. This is more than just another self-help book. It can be a lifesaver."...ALLAN

" Some great advice and very easy to follow. The school system should make it a mandatory read by at the least grade ten or twelve. Chapter 11 is worth the price many times over as a life lesson for young folks. I wish I had seen chapter 4 many years ago...You must be a very patient man to have researched and written chapters 13 to 16....". WAYNE

"This book is great.... Thank you for the great insight!"......GENE
"My son has bought your book on my recommendation as I am helping him get his savings and investing in better order. "...WAYNE
***

"I find your approach to investing pragmatic and easy to follow"....GENE

..."I have not put your book down I since started reading it"...ANDREW
***

"...I am already a DIY investor ... and will use your scoring system to double check against my current stock picks.... I'm interested to apply the scoring to my US stocks."...GORDON
***

..." Finally, I have found the way to reorganize my investments... It fits my investing style and goals perfectly. I have been a self-directed dividend/growth/value investor for the last 5 years after bailing out of advised management provided by various firms since about 1998...."..ROBERT
***

"... I was trying to find an adviser who could review my portfolio and provide self-guidance. I found that most advisers are either Asset Under Management, Brokers, Insurance or Annuity salesmen. They either charge a big fee to manage or an upfront fee to purchase an insurance or annuity policy. I found a few people online who really want to educate people. Here are a few I follow: Paul Merriman, Chris Pedersen, Michael Kitces, Roger Whitney and now Ian MacDonald!"...RON
***

3 NOVELS

Now for something different. You may enjoy an Ian MacDonald novel,

BEWARE THE ABANDONED.

A New Mexico based capitalist sect recruits clever, abandoned children off the world's streets. They turn thieves and pickpockets into successful capitalists. The sect is then rewarded with a percentage of their graduates' income and wealth for the rest of their graduates' lives.

The story takes place in Paris, Las Vegas, Philadelphia, New Mexico, and Delaware. Both the mob and the FBI are seeking John Cross, the sect's graduate. He killed a guard when forcefully retrieved the millions the mob stole from him. Who will find him first and how many more will die. You may have a hard time putting this novel down.

BEWARE THE ABANDONED can be purchased from Amazon. Go to:

https://www.amazon.ca/BEWARE-ABANDONED-IAN-DUNCAN-MACDONALD/dp/0991931793

***

USING DROUGHT USA,

Rob Lyons, a Secretary of State employee, is sent undercover to Canada. His assignment is to offer independent nationhood to two Canadian provinces, Quebec and Alberta. They in return will not interfere in the US invasion of the province of Ontario.

It is an election year; the president has two objectives. First, to solve the Southwest USA's drought problem by diverting water from Lake Superior to the headwaters of the Colorado River. Second, and to win votes in California, Arizona, New Mexico, and Nevada for his water solving plan.

The People's Republic of China solved their drought problem with a 2,600-mile water diversion project. The 800-mile water diversion the President proposes in the US seems minor by comparison.

Can Rob Lyon's evade those out to stop his journey across the frozen Canadian landscape. Would Canada be able to repel this US invasion?

A greedy Washington lobbyist, a native chief thirsting for revenge and a love interest make this a page turner.

USING DROUGHT USA can be purchased from Amazon. Go to:

https://www.amazon.ca/USING-DROUGHT-USA-DUNCAN-MACDONALD/dp/0991931769

***

Ian's first novel,

DUEL,

Rob Lyons, a Secretary of State employee, is sent to the Caribbean Island of St Matts, to convince the island to not lease a long abandoned British Naval Base to the People's Republic of Chinese. A Chines naval base so close to America's would be as great a threat to the USA as the Cuban missile crisis was. It would confirm China's dominance of the region. With the withering away of communism, America has neglected the many island nations and Central America countries bordering Caribbean. China has poured hundreds of millions of dollars in aid into this vacuum left by the United States

The assassination of the island's greedy Prime Minister, the threat of nuclear war, an evacuation of the island's entire population by the US, a wedding and 80,000 monkeys will keep you turning pages.

DUEL can be purchased from Amazon. Go to:

https://www.amazon.ca/DUEL-Threatening-Massive-Nuclear.../dp/0991931750

Made in the USA
Monee, IL
25 November 2023

47078658R00181